The Politics of Irish

Reimagining Ireland

Volume 108

Edited by Dr Eamon Maher,
Technological University Dublin – Tallaght Campus

PETER LANG

Oxford • Bern • Berlin • Bruxelles • New York • Wien

'The latest battlefield in the ongoing debate over secularism in Ireland is education. The role of the Catholic Church in education has come under increasing scrutiny in recent years as Ireland has liberalised. Yet that role is frequently misunderstood and is shrouded in myth. Now in their ground-breaking work, *The Politics of Irish Primary Education: Reform in an Era of Secularisation*, Seán McGraw and Jonathan Tiernan have given us a book that is both timely and important in addressing the evolving role of religion and of the Catholic Church in a rapidly changing Irish society.

In the aftermath of landmark referenda on marriage equality and abortion there have been loud calls to reduce, or eliminate altogether, the Catholic Church's involvement and control over primary education. Such control has long been seen as a bastion of the Church's influence in shaping Irish young people, families, communities and indeed the nation itself. This book combines a rich historical study of Irish primary education with an astute analysis of how policy reforms have unfolded in contemporary Ireland in areas such as divestment, school admissions and curriculum development. It also offers unique insights into how such reforms are likely to shape Irish society into the future.

McGraw and Tiernan weave an impressively wide ranging and diverse set of data into engaging policy case studies in a way that covers emotionally charged issues, often featuring passionate polar opposites, in objective, measured, and thoughtful ways. This is an urgent and important book that will shape critical debates in both Irish education and indeed across Irish society in the years ahead. Anyone with an interest in Ireland's future should read it.'

— *Gary Murphy, Professor of Politics, Dublin City University*

The Politics of Irish Primary Education

Reform in an Era of Secularisation

Sean McGraw and Jonathan Tiernan

PETER LANG

Oxford • Bern • Berlin • Bruxelles • New York • Wien

Bibliographic information published by Die Deutsche Nationalbibliothek. Die Deutsche Nationalbibliothek lists this publication in the Deutsche Nationalbibliografie; detailed bibliographic data is available on the Internet at http://dnb.d-nb.de.

A catalogue record for this book is available from the British Library.

Library of Congress Cataloging-in-Publication Data
Names: McGraw, Sean D., author. | Tiernan, Jonathan, 1981- author.
Title: The politics of Irish primary education : reform in an era of secularisation / Sean McGraw and Jonathan Tiernan.
Description: New York : Peter Lang, [2022] | Series: Reimagining Ireland ; volume number 108 | Includes bibliographical references and index. |
Identifiers: LCCN 2021056322 (print) | LCCN 2021056323 (ebook) | ISBN 9781800797093 (Paperback) | ISBN 9781800797109 (eBook) | ISBN 9781800797116 (ePub)
Subjects: LCSH: Education, Primary--Ireland. | Educational change--Ireland. | Secularism--Ireland. | Catholic Church--Education--Ireland--History. Classification: LCC LA669.62 .M34 2022 (print) | LCC LA669.62 (ebook) | DDC 372.24/109417--dc23/eng/20220207
LC record available at https://lccn.loc.gov/2021056322
LC ebook record available at https://lccn.loc.gov/2021056323

Cover image by Maggie Klaers.
Cover design by Peter Lang Ltd.

ISSN 1662-9094
ISBN 978-1-80079-709-3 (print)
ISBN 978-1-80079-710-9 (ePDF)
ISBN 978-1-80079-711-6 (ePub)

© Peter Lang Group AG 2022

Published by Peter Lang Ltd, International Academic Publishers, Oxford, United Kingdom
oxford@peterlang.com, www.peterlang.com

Sean McGraw and Jonathan Tiernan have asserted their right under the Copyright, Designs and Patents Act, 1988, to be identified as Authors of this Work.

This publication has been peer reviewed.

For Kris and Sinéad
For all that has been, thank you.
For all that will be, yes!!!

Contents

Figures

Tables

Acknowledgements

We are grateful for several decades of experience in Irish education. We have been privileged to work and learn with and to interview thousands of students, teachers, parents, school leaders, members of boards of management and patrons over those years. We have also been fortunate to interact with educational experts, academics, civil society advocates, politicians and religious leaders, all of whom have shared their passions, perspectives and insights on the importance of education for themselves personally, as well as for Irish students, families and Irish society more broadly. This book has been a work of love and gratitude for all those who teach and inspire young people to become the best versions of themselves. The gift that is an Irish education remains quite remarkable and it has been captivating to observe how primary schools have evolved as Irish society has been transformed over the past several decades. We appreciate the magnitude and complexity of these changes and have attempted to shed light on what explains the nature of these reforms and adaptations.

There are many people, communities and institutions that we want to acknowledge and thank. First, we want to thank several intellectual communities that have been formative for us. In particular, we have both spent several years working with the University of Notre Dame in Ireland and are grateful to Kevin Whelan, Lisa Caulfield and Angela Mitchell (and their families) for their unwavering friendship, hospitality and support.

Second, we have interacted with scholars from many of Ireland's leading third level institutions, including DCU, TCD, UCD, UCC, UCG, Mary Immaculate College, Marino Institute, St Patrick's College Maynooth, NUI Maynooth and Queen's University Belfast, and we are indebted to them for their probing questions, comments and insights. Special thanks to Daire Keogh, Gary Murphy and Eoin O'Malley (and their families) at DCU for their incredible companionship and mentorship.

Next, we would like to thank Boston College, and in particular their students, who have assisted us in our research. Catherine Levine and David

O'Neill provided diligent qualitative and quantitative research. Larissa Foy was one of the strongest researchers we have ever worked with and are especially indebted to her for her work on the media study and the divestment case studies. Her meticulous investigative skills and thoughtful assessment were crucial to our overall analysis.

We also want to thank Harvard University's Minda de Gunzburg Center for European Studies for providing a home base for Sean during the research and writing of this book. Grzegorz Ekiert, Peter Hall, Robert Putnam and Sebastian Royo provided excellent support, guidance and encouragement.

In addition to the many intellectual communities, there are countless individuals who through their friendship and insights have supported us and enhanced the final product. We are grateful for the blessing of great teachers and mentors who have had a formative impact, including Frank Tivnan, Paddy Nangle, Estelle Pilon, Cathy Lucero, Fr John-Paul Sheridan, Sean Campbell, Bishop Tom Deenihan, Dr Rachel Moreno and Prof. Pat Dolan. Several academic and politician friends have graciously supported our work, including Ken Carty, David Farrell, Muiris MacCarthaigh, Niamh Hardiman, Meg Rithmire, Jason Lakin, Paul Bodnar, Fr Rodrigo Zarazaga, SJ, TJ D'Agostino, Tom Doyle, Senator Mark Daly and Mary McAleese. Dr Barbara Searle, Dr Matt Robinson and Fr Ken Hughes, SJ, have been invaluable personal and spiritual guides for Sean over the past several years.

Our ultimate editorial genius and behind the scenes collaborator has been Patrick McGraw! His perceptive and penetrating questions, comments and suggestions at every stage of research and writing pushed us to articulate a clearer argument and produce a better overall book. We are indebted to him for his patience and diligence, as well as his humour and wisdom.

We were able to interview hundreds of people over the course of several years. A special thanks to each of these leaders for their candour and for their willingness to share their passionate perspectives on why Irish primary education is so important to them. To all those who graciously took the time to review and comment on previous drafts we say, míle buíochas!

We would not have been able to complete this project during a global pandemic if it were not for our friends and family. There are too many friends to name, but some have been particularly loyal and supportive these past several years, including the McGraw, Trustey, Tiernan, Klaers, Kouatli, Anderson, Bannish, Fitzgerald, Hoyt, Kaneb, McVeigh, Surapaneni, Kalbas, Silk, Zurcher, Raleigh, Shannon, Keegan, Mattison, Ryan, Rosato, Zavignin-McMahon, Celio-Mazzone, Sims-Kingston, Evans, Buras-Carmosino, Ledingham, Coash, Krawczyk-Appelman, Kagan, Wyttenbach, Fennell, Smith, McLean, Wright, Reinhart, Murphy, Toner, Kolettis, King, Kollman, Manley, Novak, O'Malley-Mahon, Fillenwarth, Lee, Fitzsimons, Manning, Mullen, Stevens-O'Callaghan, Ward, McCreanor and Hannan families. The fellowship received over the years from the St Pat's, ACE, PH, One Foundation, Foróige and Irish Jesuit communities is treasured. A special thanks to Fr Nate Wills, CSC, for his joy, persistence, creativity, fidelity and for sharing his amazing Wills and Mulrooney families.

Our own parents and siblings, as well as our new families have been especially patient and understanding. The strong, humorous, determined and resilient love of Kris, Caroline and Claire have fortified Sean and freed him to embrace this project with freedom and joy. Sinéad's constant encouragement, selfless love and loyal support were gifts that unlocked Jonathan's ability to contribute fully and freely to this project.

Finally, we would like to thank Tony Mason and Eamon Maher and their team at Peter Lang! They believed in us and our project and helped us produce an even better book with their wise counsel and encouraging support.

We hope you enjoy this labour of love! Despite the countless people who have helped and inspired us during this project, please know that any errors or misunderstandings are ours alone.

PART I

Primary Education Reform: Background and Context

What's Next? A Campaign to Limit the Catholic Church's Role in Primary Education

I. Introduction

On 26 May 2018, thousands of people flooded into the courtyard of Dublin Castle, the former seat of British power in Ireland, to celebrate the victory of the 'Repeal the 8th' campaign that legalised abortion in Ireland. Similar scenes occurred in the same location three years earlier when the right to same-sex marriage was achieved in Ireland. The legalisation of abortion so soon after victory in the same-sex marriage referendum was, for many present in Dublin Castle and around the world, a defining moment in dismantling the control of the Catholic Church, which had dominated much of Ireland's recent history. Unlike the independence from British rule that was marked by a violent struggle, freedom from the perceived undue influence of the Church was a focused, yet gradual and sustained campaign that was waged over decades to change the minds and hearts of Irish citizens and eventually to pass new laws.

The campaign for the liberalisation of Ireland's laws, and wider society, had its first significant victory in 1979 with the legalisation of contraception, followed in 1993 with the decriminalisation of homosexuality, and the 1995 vote to legalise divorce. The two more recent victories on same-sex marriage (2015) and abortion (2018) cemented the nation's liberal shift from the conservatism that marked early decades of the State. In the words of then Taoiseach Leo Varadkar, this was 'the culmination of a quiet revolution that's taken place in Ireland for the past 10 or 20 years. This has been a great exercise in democracy, and the people have spoken.'[1] *The*

[1] 'Abortion Referendum: Yes Secures Landslide Victory', *The Irish Times*, 26 May 2018.

New York Times was more pointed, calling the vote to legalise abortion a 'rebuke to Catholic conservatism … the latest, and harshest, in a string of rejections of the church's authority in recent years'.[2] In Ireland, known as a bastion of Catholicism for so long, it may incorrectly be seen as having been fuelled simply by a singular desire to throw off the last vestiges of a Catholic sexual morality viewed by many as outdated and repressive. The growing liberalisation that has taken hold in Ireland over recent decades is a result of both a corps of dedicated and focused campaigners, many of whom committed large parts of their lives to such issues, and the slow and unrelenting march of secularisation that has been witnessed across Europe over the same period.

The irony of the victories of recent years is that most of the millions who voted yes, and those who filled the cobbled square of Dublin Castle to celebrate both referenda victories, were themselves the products of Catholic schools. They had been the recipients of years of religious education on the teachings of the Church, and yet attitudes towards social and moral issues had significantly evolved for many Catholic school graduates. In the days that followed the abortion vote, many of those who had contributed to the success of the Repeal campaign, including civil society leaders, academics, individual citizens and even politicians, began pondering a similar question, 'What's next?'

For many, the answer centred on the monopolistic control of the Catholic Church in education, specifically primary education where the Church controlled almost 90 % of all schools. Michael Barron, a key civil society activist in the marriage equality campaign, tweeted in support of the Labour Party's demand for a Citizens' Assembly to debate Church control of education.[3] University College Dublin political scientist, Aidan Regan, tweeted: 'Irish public opinion is clearly pro-choice. The next policy challenge is to translate this into education policy. @FineGael must legislate to force the Catholic Church to divest from taxpayer funded schools. It's

---

2   De Freytas-Tamura, 'Ireland Votes to End Abortion Ban, in Rebuke to Catholic Conservatism', *The New York Times,* 26 May 2018.

3   Michael Barron, 29 May 2018. Available at: <https://twitter.com/michaelnbarron> (Accessed: 12 March 2021).

time to secularise education.'[4] Countless individuals tweeted similar calls for education as the next policy to be reformed: 'Repeal the 8th Right [,] next on the to do list, let's get the Catholic Church out of our school system.'[5] Politicians weighed in as well. The Social Democrats echoed Labour's calls for reform, claiming that 'it is time to take religion out of the school day entirely' as they proposed establishing a fully secular education system.[6]

These demands for reform were spirited and widespread. There was a palpable feeling at the time that if individuals, civil society activists, the media and academics maintained the intensity and frequency of their demands for change, then politicians would support reform. Perhaps there would be another day of celebration mirroring those days in May 2015 and 2018 in Dublin Castle. Reducing or eliminating the role of the Catholic Church in education seemed achievable during those days of 'What's next?' conversations. Less than eight weeks after the abortion referendum, the Dáil (Irish parliament) passed the Education (Admissions to School) Act in mid-July 2018. This act barred Catholic schools from admitting students to their schools based on their religious beliefs or practices. No student from then on could ever be denied admittance to a Catholic school based on their religion. This was a tangible victory for educational reformers seeking to weaken the Church's role in Irish primary schools.

That this reform victory came on the heels of the abortion referendum encouraged those seeking even further reduction of the Catholic Church's role in primary schools. Immediately, attention turned to moving religious education and sacramental preparation outside the school day altogether and moving one step closer to a secular educational system. This would be a dramatic change from the current state funded educational system run by private denominational and non-denominational patrons, where nearly 90 % of Irish primary schools are Catholic (Table 1.1).

---

4   Aidan Regan, 27 May 2018. Available at: <https://twitter.com/Aidan_Regan> (Accessed: 12 March 2021).

5   Wheltonio Anderas, 26 May 2018. Available at: <https://twitter.com/Anneanswe rs> (Accessed: 12 March 2021).

6   Róisín Shortall, 29 May 2018. Available at: <https://twitter.com/SocDems> (Accessed: 18 February 2021).

Table 1.1. Overview of patronage at primary level 2020/21[a]

Patron	Number of Schools	% of Schools
Catholic	2,757	89 %
Protestant (Church of Ireland)	172	6 %
Educate Together	95	3 %
An Foras Pátrúnachta	36	1 %
Community National Schools	25	1 %
Other	23	1 %
	3,108	

[a]A school 'patron' is a private entity tasked by the Department of Education to manage a primary school, employ staff and take responsibility, through a local Board of Management and school principal, for the day-to-day operations of the school, and the delivery of the national curriculum. The patron also has responsibility for the 'characteristic spirit'(ethos) of the school and the provision of a patron's programme, Religious Education, in the case of faith schools. On behalf of the state, the Department of Education provides funding to operate the school including for staff salaries and running costs.

It was unclear what a changed educational system would look like. This is reminiscent of a well-known Irish joke about a tourist asking a farmer for directions to another town, to which the farmer replies, 'Well, if I were you, I wouldn't start from here.' Nobody would start from where the system currently stands if they were designing a new primary education system now. The contemporary Irish primary system, which is privately run and publicly funded, has its roots in the establishment of a national school system in 1831 that had as its aim to 'unite in one system children of different creeds'.[7] The aspirational model of Catholic and Protestant joint patrons that would fulfil this aim failed to materialise, due in part to

---

7   *The Stanley Letter* 1831, *Irish National Schools Trust*. Available at: <http://irishnationalschoolstrust.org/wp-content/uploads/2015/04/Stanley-letter-1831-Boards-Of-Management.pdf> (Accessed: 21 February 2021).

the significant network of Catholic primary schools already in existence.[8]
Instead, a system of denominational schooling funded by the State developed, which was fundamentally different to what emerged elsewhere,
both in the wider British Empire and across Europe, where 'parallel systems evolved with denominational schools existing side by side with local
authority controlled schools'.[9]

The pivotal role of the Catholic Church in education was formalised
with the birth of the Irish Free State in 1922. Ireland's educational system
became a de facto semi-state endeavour with responsibility for education
primarily shared by the fledgling State and the Catholic Church. This sym-
biotic relationship and denominational structure of education was later
enshrined in the Irish Constitution in 1937, where the State consolidated
its commitment to 'provide for' education, rather than taking responsibility
for providing it itself. Under this arrangement, the State became the finan-
cier on an increasing scale throughout the 1900s and the Catholic Church
was the lead provider of primary schools. This dynamic was not unique to
education and was mirrored in social services and healthcare as well. The
Catholic Church took the lead in the delivery of these key public services
on behalf of the new Irish State, which was quite limited financially. These
arrangements, forged in the embers of a War of Independence and a Civil
War, continue to cast a shadow on public debate to the present day.[10] As
Irish society has become more diverse and Catholic beliefs, behaviours
and overall sense of belonging have dramatically changed, demands for
educational reforms have grown.

The tectonic plates have been shifting in Ireland, but institutional
change often lags decades behind attitudinal and behavioural change. The
declining influence of the institutional Catholic Church in shaping Irish
political, social and cultural life in the face of recent transformations in
Irish society has created a window of opportunity for key policy changes to
occur. The Catholic Church had once dominated virtually every aspect of
Irish society. Beginning with the 'Devotional Revolution' in the post-famine

---

8   Jonathan Tiernan, 'Contextualising Catholic Education in Ireland', *Educatio
     Catholica Journal,* Vol. 1–2, February 2020.
9   Mary Sturt, *The Education of the People*. London: Routledge and Kegan Paul, 1967.
10   Tiernan, 2020.

period in the second half of the nineteenth century, the Catholic Church was the key social institution in Ireland. All aspects of Irish life became rooted in the life of parishes, and the Catholic hierarchy and priests and religious were integral to all aspects of Irish society. In the period since Irish independence in 1922, the Catholic Church became embedded even further into the institutional life of the Irish State. The Irish Constitution (1937) was essentially a Catholic document, and Irish political, social and economic institutions and policies were steeped in Catholic ethos and open to influence by Church leaders and personnel. A slow period of modernisation and secularisation began in the 1960s. The process was blown open by the combined effects of Ireland's rapid economic growth in the 1990s and a devastating clerical sex abuse crisis and subsequent cover-up by religious, political and civil authorities. As a result, the institutional Church has gone from bedrock of Irish politics and society to an almost entirely marginalised moral voice and source of local organisation around the country.

Previous scholarship has described this marginalisation of the Church within the educational sector. For example, O'Sullivan argues that since the 1950s, there has been a cultural evolution within Irish education whereby the once dominant theocentric and religious system has slowly morphed into a capitalist culture. This new market-focused culture has increasingly emphasised such values as equality of opportunity, employability, gender inclusion and egalitarianism over and above a child's faith development. Therefore, O'Sullivan suggests that Irish education during this cultural shift has become more focused on preparing students at all levels to be successful members of a modern and global economy. As a result, religious leaders such as bishops, priests and religious women and men have gradually been losing their ability to shape educational institutions and policy. In their place, those with secular knowledge and professional expertise in pedagogy, curriculum, assessment, evaluation and management are assuming leadership roles and dictating educational policy and practice.[11] These developments within Irish education are reflective of broader changes within Irish society, but they also underscore the importance of

11   Denis O'Sullivan, *Cultural Politics and Irish Education Since the 1950s: Policy Paradigms and Power*. Dublin: Institute for Public Administration, 2005.

schools as key social institutions that evolve slowly due the multiple sets of relationships and layers of authority and decision-making.

As a result of these breath-taking changes, Ireland represents a striking case study of what happens in a society when the country's key social institution experiences such dramatic decline. The Irish Constitution remains deeply imbued with Catholic ideals, but society has changed, and much debate has emerged about what it means to be Irish. As the Church becomes one institution among many in a context of growing pluralism, what fills the void once dominated by the Church? The Church no longer speaks for Ireland. The ways in which moral debates were conducted during the constitutional referendum campaigns that voted in favour of permitting same-sex marriage (2015) and abortion (2018) provide crucial material to understand what secularisation in Ireland is and how it has evolved and how it in turn has affected education reform. The powerful role of media and other civil society groups in shaping civic discourse, altering public opinion and pressuring political parties to act on such controversial issues is key. The side-lining of the institutional Church during these debates signals a noticeable shift in how policy is enacted in Ireland.

The steps taken to secularise Ireland's largely denominational primary school system have been slow and incremental. Although there have been several attempts since 2011 to diversify the patronage of primary schools so parents and children have increasing numbers of non-Catholic school alternatives, this 'divestment' process has been unsuccessful and the numbers of new schools in areas of growing population has been negligible. Since new legislation was passed in 2018, Catholic schools can no longer use religious affiliation (and a baptismal requirement) as a criterion for accepting students when there are limited places. More recent campaigns to constrain religion within education are focusing on limiting or removing religious education courses from the required curriculum and forcing religion to be taught outside the normal school day. How successful these campaigns will be in dramatically altering the role of religion in primary schools remains an open question.

This book provides a comprehensive study of educational policy reform in Ireland with several distinct audiences in mind. First, this book will appeal to anyone interested in the breath-taking social, economic

and cultural changes occurring within Ireland in recent decades and the
impact this is having on Irish politics, especially in the twenty-first century. In particular, Ireland's changing society poses many challenges to the
Irish Constitution and the ways Church and State are linked within the
educational sphere.

Second, the book addresses key lessons from the same-sex marriage
and abortion referenda to better understand the evolving nature of Church
and State relationships in Ireland. Anyone interested in the politics of religion and morality, as well as how secularisation affects policy-making,
will benefit from the breadth and depth of analysis provided in this book.
Educational policy is different and more complex than morality politics.
However, an examination of how various civil society groups, policy entrepreneurs, media, bureaucrats, politicians and political parties have interacted within Ireland and its State institutions over the last fifty years in
each of these policy areas provides a useful lens to compare policy reform
in an era of secularisation.

Third, this study provides several rich case studies of how policy issues
are defined as problems and proposed as alternative solutions. The choices
associated with issue framing and their potential solutions affect whether
policies increase in salience and are eventually passed into legislation.
Rather than focusing narrowly on civil servants and government officials
to understand the policy-making process, we underscore how the interplay
of civil society activists and organisations, the media, public opinion and
political parties and elites determines the parameters within which public
officials can engage policy and ultimately how policy reforms live or die.
Scholars and those interested in how political parties engage controversial issues during times of social change will also be particularly interested
in this analysis.

Next, educational professionals, specialists, scholars, bureaucrats,
teachers, leaders and parents will learn and could potentially benefit from
the detailed description of critical contemporary educational issues, as
well as the explanations and predictions offered about how future reforms
will likely unfold. The pace and degree of social, economic, cultural and
political change experienced in Ireland in recent decades make it a telling
case for those interested in how policy changes occur in changing societies.

This book also offers a rich and novel set of data, including original sources, that shed light on the various dynamics at work within the primary education sector. The inclusion of multiple sources of empirical evidence supports the overall argument and shares new insights. First, we, the authors, interviewed leaders and elites from virtually all the major actors and institutions. These interviews allowed us to interact with and learn from senior leaders from the Church, Educate Together, Community National Schools, civil society groups advocating reform and a citizens' assembly, the National Council for Curriculum and Assessment, the Department of Education and Skills and political parties.[12] Second, the book shares previously unreleased data from the Church and Department of Education to underscore the changing numbers of school types across Ireland. This contextualises how both State and Church leaders are seeking to respond to changing demographics and plan for the future. Third, we include data from political party manifestoes and parliamentary surveys to trace how parties and individual candidates and elected officials have positioned themselves on key educational issues. We share evidence from McGraw's 2011 and 2016 originally designed and implemented parliamentary surveys that draws on results from face-to-face interviews of two-thirds of TDs (Teachta Dála, or member of the lower house of the Irish parliament, hereinafter TD) on several issues, including their positions on Church involvement in Irish primary education. Fourth, we provide original analysis of media coverage of educational issues and actors involved in the main educational reform debates. An examination over time of how Ireland's two leading newspapers, the *Irish Independent* and *The Irish Times*, engaged educational reform sheds light on the nature of the reform process. Finally, there are detailed case studies of the three main reform issues of divestment, admissions and curriculum. One particularly novel aspect of this part of the book is a close investigation into how the Church has

---

12   The Department of Education was established in 1924. It has undergone several name changes including becoming the Department of Education and Science in 1997 and the Department of Education and Skills in 2010. As of October 2020, it is returned to its original name of the Department of Education. We use Department of Education and Skills and Department of Education interchangeably throughout the text.

responded differently to the issue of divestment in urban, commuter and rural areas due to the strong, but varied contexts that each type of locale exhibits. With the multiple sources of data and thorough description of the actors, institutions, issues and outcomes associated with educational reform in Ireland, our goal is to contribute to a greater understanding of this complex policy area.

II. The Politics of Reform: Issue Definition, Proposed Policy Solutions and the Window of Opportunity for Policy Change

To better understand how educational reform unfolds in Ireland, it is first helpful to review key factors that influence and shape the contours of how policy is made. One of the most noteworthy studies of policy-making identifies several key dimensions to clarify why some issues become more salient and eventually become legislation. Kingdon's *Agenda, Alternatives and Public Policies* brilliantly describes and explains how policy is conducted in the United States and illustrates how issues become part of the political agenda and what influences what legislation is eventually passed.[13] He suggests that there are three streams or processes, each with its own impact and set of dynamics that shapes policy salience and passage.

First, there is the problem stream, which entails how officials become aware of the problem and how an issue is defined. How issues are framed, defined and redefined over time determines the set of potential solutions. If an issue is framed in one way, there may be only one solution. But if the issue is framed in another way, additional solutions become possible. Problem definition is influenced by changing events or indicators that make policy elites and elected officials more aware of an issue, often because there are

---

13   John W. Kingdon, *Agendas, Alternatives, and Public Policies*. Boston: Little, Brown, 1984.

shifting demographics and 'focusing events' that convince the media, the broader public and politicians that there is a problem.

Second, there is the political stream. Here, the combination of the national mood, elections and new administrations greatly influence issue salience and legislative potential. Organised interest groups are very often influential in both promoting and blocking policy progress, but if the national mood and elected politicians are united in support of an agenda, it is likely to gain momentum.

The third stream is the policy stream, which includes the visible and invisible participants who place a policy issue on the agenda, define it and then propose and decide on alternative solutions. Visible participants are those who receive a lot of press and public attention and include prominent government officials, high-level appointees, parliamentarians, the media, political parties and civil society campaigners. The hidden cluster of actors includes academic specialists, bureaucrats and parliamentary staffers. For Kingdon, visible participants set the agenda and invisible participants often shape the alternative policy solutions. An issue will not get on the agenda if the visible participants are not supportive, but the invisible participants have discretion to influence final outcomes in terms of how they shape the detailed alternatives.

In the end, problems, politics and policies each have their own dynamic and path, and real change is more likely to occur when these three streams join. This linkage of the three streams creates a more likely environment for real policy change, bringing together problems, solutions and actors willing to engage and support policy change. This window of opportunity for policy change does not last forever. The window for enacting real change depends on changing social dynamics, rising awareness of a problem or new reality, changes in administration and shifts in the national mood to occur simultaneously. This same policy window can close quickly. Some factors that can close a policy window include when a problem is fixed; when little progress is achieved, and the problem does not appear to be going anywhere; when the crisis that precipitated the elevated issue passes; or even when there is no single or easy solution and the difficulty to deal with an issue leads to inaction. A later chapter on divestment underscores how local opposition and overlapping responsibilities have stalled the potential for greater change. Thus, policy change requires a lot of moving parts to work together simultaneously. There are numerous obstacles and challenges that can easily disrupt and undermine the process, thereby closing the window of opportunity.

The final factor is the presence, persistence and effectiveness of policy entrepreneurs. These entrepreneurs invest their time, energy and resources to mobilise support for their desired policy positions. Such policy entrepreneurs can be elected officials, bureaucrats, civil society advocates and activists, lobbyists, journalists and even academics. Irrespective of their motives, whether self-serving pursuit of power, ideological conviction, or personal experience, these entrepreneurs can greatly influence the policy process. Policy entrepreneurs are often the ones who force the window of policy opportunity open, help keep it open and determine whether change happens before the window is closed. For this reason, we devote several chapters to describing the key actors involved in educational reform, some are policy entrepreneurs seeking change, and others represent long-term vested interests and individuals disinclined to support any change to the status quo for various reasons. The confluence of problems, politics and policies in Irish education reform will be easier to grasp as we increase our understanding of these key actors' interests and actions.

Kingdon's classic study offers a useful lens to view how policy change occurs in the Irish context. These reform campaigns illustrate how issues have been redefined, Kingdon's problem stream, in the light of changing demographics and several triggering events in the 2000s that attracted considerable attention. The 2007 incident where non-White immigrants in Dublin could not gain access to the school of their choice due to their religious background focused Irish society on an emerging problem. In Chapter 8, there is an overview of the marriage equality and abortion campaigns. These campaigns illustrate how issues have been redefined in the light of the significant social, economic and political changes in Ireland over the last several decades. As society shifted and the problems were redefined in terms of equality and inclusion, the political scene was evolving too, which is consistent with Kingdon's political stream. The declining levels of party attachment among Irish voters and the increased competition and volatility of Irish elections created new windows of opportunity and new coalitions of support for emerging issues within Ireland. After the collapse of the Irish economy in 2008–10, there was a palpable demand among citizens and political parties for reforms of all types. This national mood for change was another key aspect of the shifting political stream described by Kingdon. In the policy stream, Kingdon's third stream within the overall policy process, the long-term activism of key civil society actors, members of the media and political parties capitalised on an opening policy window to pass landmark legislation. It appears that there may exist a 'tipping point' at which otherwise risk-averse politicians become willing to alter legislation and, in some cases, amend the Constitution. The combination of these factors made new values and different technical solutions more acceptable to Irish society and politicians alike, paving the way for real policy change as the Kingdon model suggests. The lessons from the marriage equality and abortion campaigns that resulted in major policy shifts are instructive for understanding how educational reform issues are being addressed and resolved in varied ways.

Although similar secularising trends exist within the educational sphere that helped make these earlier policy shifts possible, the overall process of change in education is quite different. Activist civil society groups have consistently sought to alter public opinion on educational issues since the 1970s, and the media has responded in varied ways depending on how the issues were framed and what political processes were associated with them. Additionally, the nature of the questions is somewhat different. The issues of same-sex marriage and abortion both required a change in the Constitution, but both changes focused on rights that affected individuals not schools and communities. Furthermore, both issues were framed largely in secular tones that highlighted the importance of human rights. One could be personally opposed to same-sex marriage and/or abortion, but simultaneously not want to limit another person's ability to choose something that will affect the other person's life but not necessarily infringe on one's own choices and lifestyle.

In the case of all three reform issues: same-sex marriage; abortion; and greater diversity and pluralism within education; the roots of reform campaigns date back nearly fifty years. Early reforms were attempted in the 1970s and subsequently advanced by committed advocates with increasing efficacy in recent years. The same-sex marriage and abortion campaigns achieved success in proximity decades later, which points to a confluence of conditions, including growing secularisation, a much-weakened Catholic Church, and increasing public support leading to the political will to finally address the issues legislatively. Education reform is growing from similar conditions but with additional contexts that we outline below.

The secularisation process appears different in the educational sphere even though the importance of civil and social rights remains at the heart of the debate. First, as we will discuss in more detail in later chapters, the constitutional questions relating to education are more complex. The Constitution underscores the responsibility of the State to 'provide for' primary education for all citizens. The Constitution also clearly protects religious freedom, parents' right to educate their children as they deem appropriate, patrons' right to own property, and patrons' (religious or secular) rights to form students in their own ethos or characteristic spirit (Articles 42 and 44). These various rights often conflict with one another and must, therefore, be addressed and resolved during the policy process.

Second, unlike the previous campaigns where the Church was perceived as 'telling' people what the Catholic position was, with many people reacting negatively to the Church's pleas, there exists widespread agreement in Irish society that the State should provide sufficient educational alternatives for all citizens. Virtually everyone in Ireland supports religious freedom and wants parents to freely choose what type of school their children attend – denominational, multi-denominational or non-denominational schools – so they are not discriminated against. Nevertheless, there is no clear path to achieve this at the primary level. The combination of limited resources to build new schools and the challenge of how Catholic patrons might divest some of their schools when the demand is uncertain means that not everyone gets what they want. As State officials, politicians and Church leaders alike have discovered, there can be serious backlash from parents and local communities when someone seeks to change the patronage of their school. Ironically, the ideological human rights argument may not be universally appealing because it potentially dictates to certain parents and local communities that only secular forms of education are acceptable.

The multitude of constitutional issues and the complexity of attitudes in a rapidly changing society highlight the more nuanced nature of secularisation in Ireland. It is not simply about declining religious beliefs and practices, although these are important. Nor is it merely about the loss of moral authority of the Church to influence how its followers believe and act and educate their children, because there is often much more support for Church at the local level and among specific church leaders and communities. As a result, civil society activists and certain media personalities with clear ideological motivations may not be able to employ the same playbook as they previously did in the same-sex marriage and abortion referenda campaigns. Therefore, the problem, political and policy strands are more varied and complex within education and warrant deeper analysis.

III. Chapter Outline and Overview of the Argument

This book is divided into three primary sections. In the first section, there are two additional chapters that provide critical background information that help set the context within which policy change in the Irish primary education sector is unfolding. In Chapter 2, we examine the sources of control and power in the primary education sector. It is helpful to break down those areas where the Catholic Church has and continues to have authority within primary education, so we can better understand how reformers are seeking to reduce or eliminate the role of the Church in schools. Additionally, it is also instructive to appreciate the increasing role the State and the Department of Education have in controlling and shaping primary education within Ireland. The balance of power and evolving layers of responsibility within the educational sphere are crucial to understand before examining specific educational reform issues. Chapter 3 highlights the demand for change within Irish society, exploring what the real appetite is for increasing the number and diversity of primary school patrons and the diversity and inclusion within all Irish primary schools.

The second section of the book examines the most important actors within the primary education sector to recognise their preferences, organisations, leaders and the strategies they have employed to advance their interests in a rapidly changing Irish society. In Chapter 4, we explore the structures and evolution of the Catholic Church in Irish education. In outlining the multi-layered and multivocal nature of the Church overall, as well as in the education sector more specifically, we underscore the challenges facing the Church as its near monopoly in education unravels. What may surprise readers is the Church's lack of unity in organisation and purpose, which combines with their declining personnel and financial resources to undermine their ability to provide a coordinated response, as they deal with key education reforms. Next, Chapter 5 describes and explains the development and expansion of Educate Together as the leading multi-denominational educational provider in Ireland. Educate Together, which started as a group of activist parents trying to give their children a multi-denominational educational experience, has grown into a network of schools and powerful lobbyist that is at the heart of every key educational issue within Ireland. Chapter 6 explores the more recent creation and development of the Community National Schools model of multi-denominational schools. For the first time, the State is the patron of primary schools, and this chapter underscores the various reasons why this model emerged and its unfolding impact on the sector as it develops. Chapter 7, the final chapter in this section, focuses on the Irish media's coverage of educational reform. Political analysts often credit the media in Ireland with challenging the authority of the Church and the State, as well as promoting or elevating progressive concerns about equality and inclusion in Irish society. This chapter provides original analysis of media coverage of key educational issues, actors and institutions over the past several decades to show precisely how the media engages educational reform. We test to what extent the media independently helps define how educational problems are framed and what possible solutions are available. We also explore whether the media serves as the venue in which these other key actors and institutions engage educational reform. Given the media's important role in the marriage equality and abortion campaigns, it is informative to observe how it is involved in the politics of educational reform.

The third section of the book conducts detailed analyses of three critical areas of reform within the primary sector to better observe and assess
how the issues have been defined, what solutions have been explored and
what outcomes have occurred. This section begins in Chapter 8 with a
review of the marriage equality and abortion referendum campaigns. This
analysis sheds light on key actors, processes and outcomes that led to these
policy changes, and it also provides useful template for examining the ways
in which educational reforms are likely to unfold. Chapter 9 builds on the
previous chapter and focuses on how Ireland's political parties have engaged educational reform issues. In summarising party positions in election
manifestos, programmes for government and other surveys, the chapter
highlights how parties engage each other, civil society actors, the media
and the public to develop their educational policies. This chapter sets the
stage for the policy case studies in the next three chapters on divestment,
admissions and curriculum. In each of the three case studies, the identified problem is that Ireland's primary sector does not adequately provide
for students and parents of minority religions or no religion, or anyone
who desires a more secular education free from religion, since nearly 90 %
of Irish primary schools are Catholic. The three case studies examine different solutions that seek to overcome this problem by either increasing
the number of non-Catholic primary schools or by enhancing the diversity
and inclusion of all schools. This latter goal is meant to encourage or force
Catholic schools to better engage the realities of an Irish society that is less
religious or not religious at all.

Despite framing every aspect of reform within the context of the
desire to create, foster and sustain an Ireland that is more equal, diverse
and inclusive, the educational reform campaign has experienced varying
degrees of success. There are some similarities across the different issues
in terms of actors, as the Church, civil society, and some party elites are
consistently engaging these issues. However, the different issues affect individuals, schools, local communities and educational activists in distinct
ways, which alters those who support and oppose the respective policy
proposals. Ultimately, political parties are typically the last to weigh in,
waiting for sufficient support and clarity of outcomes before offering their
support. The case studies shed light on how the ways in which issues are

defined and the alternative solutions are proposed influences the varied
outcomes we observe.

In Chapter 10, we discuss divestment, the process whereby Catholic
schools transfer their patronage of primary schools to non- or multi-
denominational patrons. There has been widespread support for divestment in principle as one of the best means to increase the number of multi-
denominational schools among virtually all stakeholders, including the
Church. However, little has been achieved as only eleven schools have
been divested in the decade since 2011. The failure of this policy solution
is due largely to the fact that divestment requires change for too many
people, which leads to competing interests, local opposition and varied
reasons for saving schools that are not about increasing diversity. Unlike
same-sex marriage and abortion that altered the choices that individuals
could make for themselves with indiscernible impact on others, divestment
changes the choices of school type, which in turn alters the choices available to students, parents, teachers and other local individuals and groups
with vested interests. The widespread opposition to divestment at the local
level illustrates that issue definition and solutions matter, and when they
do not align, policy change is unlikely. This chapter also provides a closer
analysis of how the Church engaged divestment in urban, commuter and
urban counties to further underscore how local dynamics undermined
divestment occurring on any large scale.

In the next chapter, Chapter 11, we examine how school admissions
policies were swiftly changed in the 2018 Admissions Bill. Of the three main
educational reforms in Ireland's primary sector examined in detail in this
book, the process leading up to the passing of the Admissions Bill is the
most like what occurred in the marriage equality and abortion campaigns.
Civil society activists and academics took advantage of Ireland's social and
demographic changes to redefine the problem as one of discrimination
against non-religious, secular and minority religious students who had
their rights to an education free of religion denied to them. Like earlier
campaigns, civil society activists and educational reformers highlighted
international standards from the United Nations and European Union to
build support for an equality movement that framed salient issues in terms
of human rights and anti-discrimination. In addition to bolstering legal,

rights-based arguments, reformers appealed to the hearts of Irish citizens through personal stories of hardship and discrimination of non-religious and minority religious students and families. Once sufficient public support and media attention was generated, civil society leaders motivated politicians to support narrow legislative change that could be passed without much public opposition. Reformers largely outmanoeuvred their opponents by framing issues in pithy ways such that irrespective of how real the 'baptismal barrier' really was, the nature of the debate cascaded towards support for change. The near unanimous support among politicians reflected the lack of any concerted opposition and is a testimony to how issue definition and solution identification won the day. The narrow focus limited those who opposed the measure and generated widespread support for this significant educational reform.

Finally, Chapter 12 examines how curriculum changes are being addressed. The combination of the dramatic changes in religious beliefs and practices among Catholics and the growing numbers of non-religious or minority religious students and teachers has led reformers to demand changes to what Irish students learn. Divestment addressed the problem of the lack of an adequate number of non-Catholic schools. Admissions reform addressed how to increase diversity within schools so the demographic background of the student body in all schools, even Catholic schools, was more diverse. Demands for curriculum reform seek to make the educational experience more diverse, equitable and inclusive once students are in school. The primary thrust of reformers is to reduce or eliminate the role of religion in the curriculum and school experience. Therefore, issues such as religious education, sacramental preparation, sex education and ethics are intensely debated. Advocates of reform argue that since Irish primary schools are state-funded schools, no child should be subjected to indoctrination in any of these subjects. This chapter describes the nature of these debates and demonstrates how subtle, small and gradual changes are altering the role of religion within schools. Educational experts and practitioners have dominated these debates while politicians have largely remained silent, allowing the specialists and professionals to figure it out. Although there are similar appeals to secularism, equality, diversity and inclusion, the more bureaucratic character of these policy changes means that whatever changes may occur will likely unfold without much fanfare, but could potentially have a much more far-reaching impact, including the exclusion of religion from any aspect of the normal school day. Again, the issue definition and subsequent policy solutions being proposed greatly alters the politics of reform and leads to widely different outcomes.

The concluding chapter, Chapter 13, summarises the key developments described in the book, outlines the prospects for further reforms in the coming years, offers insights that could benefit other policy studies and proposes additional research that could flow from this study. In terms of future policy reforms, civil society groups will likely remain central actors, committed to advocating for more equal provision at primary level from a rights-based perspective. Experience from the successful marriage equality and abortion campaigns suggests that reformers need to reach the tipping point of 60 % support within Irish society before the major parties offer their backing, thereby opening the path to policy change. Any policy solutions they champion must be able to take account of the practical implications on communities that a changed system will entail. Although there continues to be broad support for many reforms in principle, parents and other affected individuals have forcefully rejected proposals that adversely and directly impact their child's educational experience and choices. The degree to which reforms thread the needle between generating support for rights-based arguments but not impinging on sufficient numbers in local communities and nationally, the more likely further policy change will occur.

The Church no longer holds a monopoly within education and must adapt to the ascendancy of the Department of Education and the growing pluralism of patrons and interests within the education sector. This new reality has eroded the Church's ability to promote and protect its vision, let alone control what happens in its own schools. It is unclear whether the Church can adapt to this new environment and establish authentically Catholic schools that attract students, parents and teachers who genuinely support the Catholic ethos while also supporting enough non-Catholic schools so there is a real choice for those preferring a different experience. If a more coordinated and proactive set of strategies is not employed in the coming years by Church leaders and Catholic school leaders, Catholic schools may gradually become irrelevant in a changing society and a de facto state system will emerge with the Church simply fulfilling the role of landlord.

For the political elites, there is little to be gained from proactively engaging further reforms given the potential for local opposition and lack of consensus on policy alternatives. The education of one's children and the role of faith in the life of a family are both deeply personal and not given to political over-reaching. Irish political parties have proven adept at assigning such salient issues to citizens' assemblies rather than jeopardising internal division and alienation of sections of the electorate. That said, the complexity and number of issues associated with further educational reforms and limits to the Church's involvement in primary schools do not easily translate into issues citizens' assemblies can engage and solve.

For those campaigning for reform at primary level, there is unlikely to be a cathartic moment like was experienced in Dublin Castle in the wake of the same-sex marriage and abortion victories. Given the scale of the Catholic Church's institutional, property and personnel resources in Irish primary schools, the Church will remain, to some degree, involved in Irish primary schools into the future. However, the window of opportunity for the Church to shape outcomes in any meaningful ways may be closing. Until now, politicians think in electoral cycles, campaigners think in terms of generations, but the Church thinks in terms of centuries. Children, however, get one childhood, and the education system and all the key stakeholders must be responsive to that reality, and ensure the system allows for the needs and wishes of all students and their families. That is the task that remains for all involved in shaping the future of Irish primary schools.

CHAPTER 2

Control in Irish Primary Education:
Who Controls What and When

I. Introduction

To better understand the debates on educational reform and the attempts to reduce or eliminate the role of the Catholic Church in Irish primary education, it is instructive to first review the institutional and legal framework of the primary school sector. In this chapter, we pay particular attention to the notion of who controls the various aspects of Irish primary schools. This overview will help contextualise the set of actors seeking reform, whom we discuss in Part II of the book, and the most salient reform issues of divestment, admissions and curriculum, which are examined in detail in Part III of the book.

This introductory overview is important because who has control has been much discussed during reform debates, but it is often misunderstood. These differing understandings of control have influenced how the various actors engaged in these reform debates adopted their respective political and policy choices. Those who advocate for a greater plurality of choice in Irish education often argue that the Catholic Church in Ireland controls primary education and that this control must be wrested away from the Church. How this control is defined is less well understood. Certainly, by force of numbers the Catholic Church is the dominant actor, with 89 % of all primary schools in the State operating under the patronage of local bishops. However, equating the number of schools under the patronage of the Catholic Church with control of the schools does not provide the full picture of true authority in the primary sector. In this chapter, we examine the different characteristics of the Irish education system that affect who has control when and to what extent especially within the primary sector.

The Irish education system is a product of the often-mentioned provision in the Constitution (Art. 42.4) for the State to 'provide for' education rather than to be involved in provision directly. This has led to a dynamic that is unique in the European context whereby the Irish State delegates provision to private patrons but maintains a large degree of oversight across a broad range of domains. The balance between public and private responsibilities has been evolving. Therefore, even though the Church has largely retained control over school property, religious education and governance in Catholic schools, the State has gained considerable authority in recent decades. For example, the State, through the Department of Education, has assumed far-reaching power in areas that we will cover in the following pages, like admissions, curriculum, operational management and inspection, while holding little to no stake in the ownership of school property within the system (see Figure 2.1).

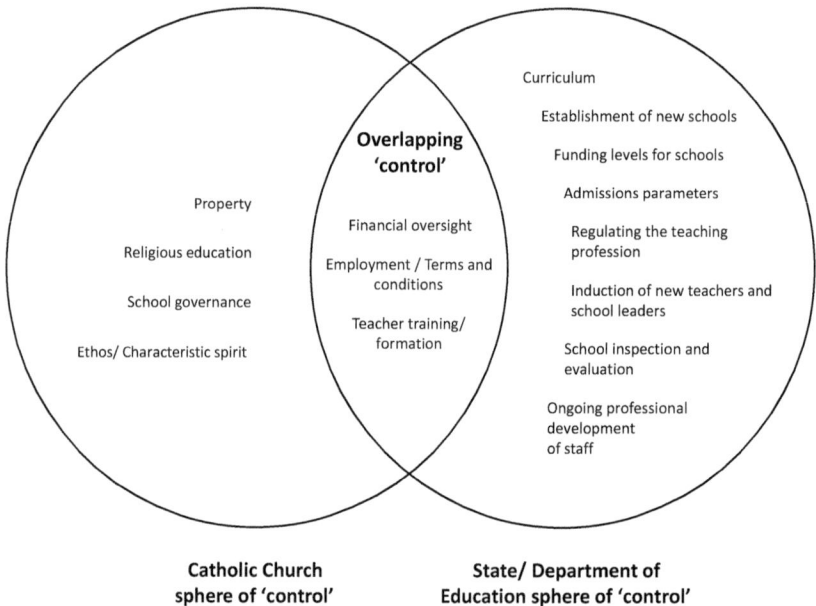

Figure 2.1. Areas of control in Irish primary education.

As support for less Church control in education has gained momentum within Irish society, the tension between the Church and the State over who has control has grown. The ongoing confusion over oversight, authority and ownership has contributed to the limited pace and scope of reconfiguration within the primary system, despite overwhelming agreement on the need for change.

II. Historical Development

Before discussing the different areas of the primary education system where control is exercised, it is important to first understand the legislative and policy landscape that established and continues to shape the system. The roots of the current system can be traced back to the often-cited *Stanley Letter* from 1831 with a number of notable developments since then, the most recent being the Education (Admissions to School) Act in 2018 (see Table 2.1).

The initial vision set out in the *Stanley Letter* (1831) was of a free primary school system that would be non-denominational in nature with students of different faiths having shared secular instruction, with only religious education delivered separately. Lord Stanley favoured schools that would be controlled by Catholic and Protestant joint patrons, with patrons providing land on which the schools would be built with State grants.[1] While the system that ultimately emerged was a denominational one, the model of a private patrons managing a school which was funded publicly was retained and formalised by the new Irish State in its constitution *Bunreacht na hÉireann* in 1937.

The Irish Constitution enshrines legal rights with respect to education to children and parents, educational patrons and the State, most notably in Articles 42 and 44. In the first instance, Article 42 acknowledges that

---

1　　The Stanley Letter 1831, *Irish National Schools Trust*. Available at: <http://irishnationalschoolstrust.org/wp-content/uploads/2015/04/Stanley-letter-1831-Boards-Of-Management.pdf> (Accessed: 21 February 2021).

Table 2.1. Notable legislative and policy developments related to primary education

Year	Legislative and Policy Developments	Relevance
1831	The *Stanley Letter*	Established a national system of primary education in Ireland from which the current system evolved.
1937	*Bunreacht na hÉireann* (Irish Constitution)	Articulated the role of the State as 'providing for' education rather than being responsible for provision directly.
1995	Government White Paper – *Charting Our Education Future*	Outlined how societal and educational development would be achieved through an agreed set of educational aims.
1998	Education Act	Set out for the first time the objectives and principles that underpin the education system and clarified the roles and responsibilities of school staff, patrons, boards of management and the minister.
2011	Forum on Patronage and Pluralism in the Primary Sector	Tasked by the Minister for Education with developing recommendations on the issue of divestment and diversifying primary school provision.
2018	Education (Admissions to School) Act	Removed the ability of Catholic schools to prefer students of the Catholic faith in their admissions policies, while maintaining this provision for schools under the patronage of a minority faith to preference students of the same faith.

Table 2.1. Continued

Year	Legislative and Policy Developments	Relevance
2020	Draft Primary Curriculum Framework	The new framework sets out the proposed purpose, structure and content of the next curriculum for primary schools. It is envisaged that the new curriculum will be finalised by summer 2024 for approval by the Minister for Education.

parents are the 'primary and natural educator of the child' and guarantees that 'parents shall be free to provide this education in their homes or in private schools or in schools recognised or established by the State'. Article 42 outlines the State must 'provide *for* free primary education' and 'shall endeavour to supplement and give reasonable aid to private and corporate educational initiative'. Article 44 addresses further this 'aid' to these private schools and mandates that 'State aid shall not discriminate between schools under the management of different religious denominations'.[2]

These rights, thus enshrined in the Constitution, are not always equal or aligned. In fact, as Irish society rapidly transformed in the period since the 1990s, there have been increasing tensions among those with differing conceptions and values of individual rights and the common good. The issue of competing rights will likely be central to the unfolding primary education landscape, and the role of the State in shaping it. Catholic and other faith-based schools 'are undoubtedly entitled to protect their capability to deliver the type of religious and moral education which forms part of their raison d' être'. However, the State also has a responsibility to balance the competing rights of children of other faiths or none.[3] Battles over what the ultimate goals of education are and who gets to adjudicate

2   *Bunreacht na hÉireann*, Government of the Republic of Ireland, 1937.
3   Dympna Glendenning, *Education and the Law* (2nd edn). Bloomsbury Professional, 2010.

how associated rights in pursuit of such goals are implemented serve as the
backdrop to escalating educational reform debates discussed in this book.

The publishing of the White Paper, *Charting Our Education Future,*
in 1995 set out the philosophical principles that would begin a reshaping of
the Irish education system that had been cast in the 1937 Constitution.[4] The
White Paper outlined, from the perspective of the State, the importance
of promoting quality, equality, pluralism, partnership and accountability
and pointed to its responsibility to 'protect and promote fundamental
human and civil rights in accordance with the Irish Constitution, national
law, [and] relevant international Conventions'.[5] The White Paper set the
stage for the enactment of the Education Act 1998 under then Minister for
Education (and later Taoiseach 2020–22), Micheál Martin TD. This piece
of legislation enunciated, for the first time, 'the objectives and principles
underpinning the education system, while providing for the rights of children and others to education'.[6] The Act 'put on a statutory basis the essential
elements of the education system as they had developed over a period of
160 years and as they were reflected in the Constitution of 1937', including
the private nature of the provision.[7] Furthermore, and with respect to the
key stakeholders including the private patrons, the Act commits to the
ongoing work of education being 'conducted in a spirit of partnership between schools, patrons, students, parents, teachers and other school staff,
the community served by the school and the State', while establishing the
right of the Minister for Education to 'set education policy', at any given
time.[8] If politics occurs when two or more are gathered, it is not difficult
to see that the politics of educational reform have broadened as Irish society has evolved significantly in recent decades. The growing number of
actors and stakeholders, each with their own perspective and set of legal
rights and normative demands, has increased the complexity and salience
of the politics of educational reform.

4   Marie Céline Clegg, 'Policy and Partnership', *Studies an Irish Quarterly Review*,
     Spring 2019, Vol. 108, No. 429.
5   *Charting Our Education Future,* Dept. of Education, 1995, 247.
6   Clegg, Spring 2019.
7   Feichín McDonagh, 'What Constitutes a Catholic School in 2019? A Legal
     Perspective', *Studies An Irish Quarterly Review*, Spring 2019, Vol. 108, No. 429.
8   Education Act, 1998.

In many ways, the explicit highlighting of the principles of 'equality' and 'pluralism' in the 1995 White Paper, coupled with the introduction of rights-based language in line with international conventions, laid the early policy foundations for the *Forum on Patronage and Pluralism in the Primary Sector* that emerged in 2011. Following growing unease amongst various stakeholders over the lack of diversity in school patronage, the Forum on Patronage under the chairmanship of respected educationalist Professor John Coolahan was tasked with the role of advising the Minister for Education. The task was to explore 'how it can best be ensured that the education system can provide a sufficiently diverse number and range of primary schools catering for all religions and none', as well as the practicalities related to divestment.[9] The Forum, which we discuss in greater detail in Chapter 10, was the first significant policy response that emerged to address Ireland's privately controlled denominational primary education system within a context of a rapidly changing Irish society.

The momentum created by the Forum feeds in to the three policy areas explored in this book – divestment, admissions and curriculum. The passing of the Education (Admissions to School) Act in 2018 was a direct legislative response to one of the key recommendations to emerge from the Forum, namely legislation that would require all schools to publish their admissions policies and to eliminate the ability of Catholic schools to make student selections based on their religious background. The relative speed at which this legislation was passed, just six years after the Forum presented its original recommendations to the Minister for Education, highlights the capacity of policy-makers and civil servants to enact significant change to long-standing spheres of control within the primary education system when their political sponsors provide them the political cover and support to act.[10]

9   28 March 2011 – Minister Quinn announces the establishment of a Forum on Patronage and Pluralism in the Primary Sector, <https://www.education.ie/en/Press-Events/Press-Releases/2011-Press-Releases/PR11-3-28.html>.

10   The first draft of the Education (Admissions to Schools) Act was published in 2013, just one year after the Forum's recommendations were presented to the Minister for Education.

A careful reading of the history of Irish education, the Constitution and the Education Act (1998) makes clear that despite the private provision of primary education within Ireland the State controls the system, and increasingly so in recent decades. A lot has changed since Mr Justice John Kenny stated in a well-known 1980 Supreme Court decision that the role of the State in education was simply 'to provide the buildings, to pay the teachers who are under no contractual duty to it but to the manager or trustees [patron], … and to provide minimum standards'. Mr Justice Kenny went on to address directly the issue of control in a historical context and highlighted the State's subordinated position at the outset of the primary school system, 'thus the enormous power which control of education gives was denied to the State: there was interposed between the State and the child the manager or the committee or the board of management.'[11] The ability of the patron of a primary school through a board of management, in this case the Catholic Church through local bishop, to exercise operative control in its schools and by default almost 90 % of the primary system is what we turn to discussing in the next section of this chapter.

A persistent theme throughout the book is that there are multiple and competing constitutional rights within the Irish educational system. As Irish society continues to change, so too do the conceptions of how these rights and overall sense of the common good evolve. The varied ways in which the growing number of key stakeholders interact with politicians and government officials to pursue their interests and rights make the study of educational reform in Ireland that much more exciting and compelling. Each chapter in the second and third parts of this book underscores certain aspects of the constitutional battles associated with Irish education. In Part II of the book, we discuss the various actors that are shaping the educational reform debates, including the Catholic Church, multi-denominational patrons, civil society actors and the media. In Part III, we bring political parties into the analysis and examine the interactions of the key actors, stakeholders and institutions with the policy-making process. As part of this section of the book, we conduct three policy case studies on the critical educational reform issues of divestment, admissions and curriculum change.

---

11   *Crowley and Others vs Ireland and Others,* Decision of the Supreme Court, 1980.

For those interested in more detail pertaining to specific domains of authority and control within the Irish educational system, what follows is a thorough examination of where control rests at primary level. Many domains are clearly attributable to either the patron, in this instance the Catholic Church through individual bishops, or the State. There are also areas of overlap where both central actors have some control, among them is the complex issue of property ownership, viewed by many as a bulwark of the Church against any attempt by the State to remove them completely from the education sector.

III. Control in the Leadership and Management Domain

A. Property and Ownership

In most cases, the Catholic Church owns the property on which its schools operate. Many of these buildings were built with funds donated by the community and the Church, predating the establishment of the Irish State in 1922. The Church's ownership of property has come to the fore in recent years as the divestment debate has developed. There has been an expectation among some that the Church should simply hand over school property that it is divesting to the State, which is contrary to how any other property owner might be expected to behave in such a scenario.[12] Proponents of this argument contend that the operation and maintenance of these buildings, along with teachers' salaries, have been paid in large part by the State for decades and the properties should therefore be considered de facto State property. The reality lies somewhere in the middle. Teachers' salaries are indeed paid by the State; however, the annual operational costs of primary schools are split almost 50/50

---

12   David Tuohy, SJ, *Denominational Education and Politics: Ireland in a European Context*. Dublin: Veritas, 2013.

between the State and local school communities who must raise €46 million annually through parental contributions and other fundraising efforts.[13]

As the new Irish Free State developed, funding for the establishment of new schools or the refurbishment of old ones came from the Department of Education with the land largely donated by the local parish. Therefore, ownership of the properties was generally ceded to the patron, which is the local bishop in the case of Catholic primary schools. Since the early 2000s, the practice has changed. The State, through the Department of Education, now retains ownership of any new school buildings, with a long lease granted to the patron to continue operating the school. The ownership of such schools has added complexity, as very often the land these schools are built on, as before, is donated by the Church and remains Church property. Defenders of Church interests highlight that in addition to providing land and financial support to establish and sustain schools for over a century, the institutional Church also provided priests, brothers and nuns to teach in schools, often for little or no compensation. These contributions of time, talent and financial resources to the educational history of the State are often overlooked or viewed as irrelevant by those advocating the idea of a cost-neutral divestment where property is gifted to the State without compensation. For those within the Church, one can imagine that such a dismissal of this rich contribution seems neither legally permissible nor wholly fair.

In the case of a school closure, the ownership of the building and the land would, historically, revert to the Church since it had provided the land and held the deeds of the property. Therefore, if the land and property were sold, the proceeds of the sale would return to the Church. Since the Department of Education implemented the practice of retaining ownership of the physical buildings, and where the parish donated the land, it is not entirely clear how any proceeds would be allocated if a school under this scenario were to close and the property sold. Thus, the question of who

13   *Restoration of Capitation Grant Campaign Report*, Catholic Primary School Management Association. <https://www.cpsma.ie/restoration-of-capitation-grant-campaign-report/> (Accessed February 10, 2021).

controls the physical school buildings is a complex one to answer. The land that Catholic schools are built on is almost exclusively the property of the Church; however, as the stock of school buildings has been and continues to be upgraded or rebuilt over the coming years the share of actual school buildings owned by the Church will decrease.

B. *Annual Funding*

Beyond the issue of property ownership, one key indicator of control is the ability to set funding levels, i.e. the school budget. In the Irish publicly funded education system, resource levels are determined by the State, through the Department of Education and Skills (DES), by means of an annual capitation payment to schools for every student enrolled. This funding (€183 per student per school year) is subject to fluctuation and is the focus of significant lobbying from management bodies (representing patrons), teachers' unions, politicians and civil society actors.[14] Schools have had to become creative over the years to address funding shortfalls, seeking contributions from parents to cover the cost of photocopying and arts and crafts supplies. Fundraising initiatives have been adopted by cash-strapped schools including sponsored walks, Church-gate collections and bag packing in supermarkets to cover necessities such as light and heat.

Schools serving the most disadvantaged communities are part of the State's Delivering Equality of Opportunity in Schools (DEIS schools) pro-gramme, which was launched by the Department of Education and Skills in 2005. Schools receiving funding from the DEIS programme number nearly one quarter (22 %) of all primary schools, with an over-representation of schools with DEIS status among schools under Catholic patronage.[15] These schools qualify for grants that provide meals and books to disadvantaged students. Additional resources are also provided to help students complete

---

14   The rate quoted is for the 2020/21 school year as outlined in *Circular Letter 0038/ 2020* from the Dept. of Education.

15   *New Report on Diversity in Primary Schools in Ireland*, Economic and Social Research Institute, 23 October 2012. Available at: <https://www.esri.ie/news/ new-report-on-diversity-in-primary-schools-in-ireland>

school and advance their literacy and numeracy proficiency. DEIS schools generally have smaller class sizes of twenty to twenty-four students compared to non-DEIS schools that have upwards of twenty-four students per class, and where class sizes of up to forty-two have occurred.[16] The Department of Education also provides a range of additional resources to DEIS schools to fund initiatives including Home School Liaison coordinator to support children and families suffering from high levels of absenteeism. There were also resources for breakfast clubs to provide a meal for children who may not receive one at home, after school homework clubs to support children whose home life may not be conducive to homework getting done, and summer camps for children who are at risk of regressing academically over the summer months. The multitude of supports represent a targeted response by the State to the needs of the most socially and economically disadvantaged children in the Irish education system. The criteria for schools to meet the threshold for such services is set centrally by the Department and the ability of the patron to tailor responses or expand services to meet specific local needs, or to shape such responses towards a particular aspect of their ethos, is limited in this context.

C. Opening New Schools

The ability to open new schools and meet parental demand, perceived or otherwise, for a particular educational approach or ethos varies from country to country. In the Irish context, the ability of stakeholders to access public funding for the establishment of new private schools does not exist and, it could be argued, is a limiting factor in providing greater choice to parents who feel the denominational nature of the current system is unsuitable for their families. In the United States, for example, the birth of the Charter School movement has enabled a variety of education actors to open schools with a distinctive focus or characteristics. These are publicly funded schools that operate independently

---

16   Sean McCárthaigh, 'One in Five Primary School Students in Classes of at least 30', *The Irish Times,* 2 August 2019.

of the established state system and often serve students from disadvantaged backgrounds who may not be receiving the support and attention they require in their local public school. In England, a similar pathway is available through the 'Free Schools' programme that 'provides teachers, parents, charities, and community groups with the opportunity to set up new, independent, state-funded schools'.[17] In both contexts, the State facilitates the opening of new schools by a wide variety of stakeholders to provide a plurality of choice to meet parental demands and to raise educational outcomes for students. Some criticise this approach as the State adopting a capitalist approach to the provision of education through its outsourcing to private bodies. Interestingly, while this move to private provision has developed elsewhere in recent decades, it is the basis on which the Irish primary system was founded over a hundred years ago.

In Ireland, the responsibility and authority for opening new schools that receive State funding rests with the Department of Education. In 2011, then Minister Ruairí Quinn, TD, established a new set of guidelines that dictate how new schools are established, with an explicit focus on meeting changing demographic need. Within the Planning and Building Unit of the Department of Education, a Forward Planning Unit is tasked with identifying emerging areas where schools will be needed in the future. Once an area is identified, recognised patron bodies (e.g. local Catholic diocese, Educate Together, local ETB, etc.) are invited to signal if they wish to serve as patron for the new school. A list of patrons that indicate a desire to serve as the patron for a planned new school is then circulated, by way of an online survey, to parents in the designated area who have children in preschool and will be seeking school places in the near future. The result of the survey is used to determine the new school's patronage. In principle, the most popular patron selected by the community would be selected to operate the school. Such a process is an attempt to respond democratically to the parental demands at a local level. Despite the best intentions, the process has been greatly influenced by the ability of individual patrons to establish a ground game and 'get out the vote' for their offering. The survey

17   *Set Up a New School*, UK Government. Available at: <https://www.gov.uk/government/get-involved/take-part/set-up-a-new-school>

represents a snapshot in time of a specific subsection of parents who have preschool aged children. Therefore, the survey results may not reflect the desire of a given community as a whole. With just sixty-four new primary schools opened between 2011 and 2019, this is not a viable pathway to rebalancing the overall patronage profile of the Irish primary sector and meeting the demands of parents who are seeking a non-denominational or multi-denominational education for their children. Furthermore, there are no indications from the Department of Education that the barrier to entry for stakeholders wishing to open new schools to meet this need will be removed any time soon.

D. *Student Admissions*

Another marker of control for school patrons is selecting who is admitted to their schools, which we will discuss in greater detail in Chapter 11, but we provide a quick review here. Most Irish primary schools are undersubscribed with only a small percentage (6 % in the case of Catholic schools), and mainly in urban areas, being oversubscribed.[18] Where schools are oversubscribed, their admissions policy sets out criteria for the order in which students are given preference for admission. Such criteria include a sibling attending the school, proximity to the school, and in faith-based schools, until 2018, whether the child applying was of the same faith as the school's ethos. Although this criterion was used infrequently, its existence provided the potential for schools to admit students based on religious affiliation.[19] A campaign to remove this requirement from admission policies, creatively cast as a 'Baptism Barrier' by opponents, grew in recent years. At the forefront of the call for reform was a civil liberties organisation, Equate, who along with other stakeholders campaigned for its removal. This campaign came to fruition with the passing of the Admissions to

---

18   *CPSMA Responds to Minister Bruton's Decision to Remove Religious Criteria from Catholic School Admissions*, Catholic Primary Schools' Management Association, 29 July 2017. Available at: <https://www.cpsma.ie/cpsma-responds-to-minister-brutons-decision-to-remove-religious-criteria-from-catholic-school-admissions/>

19   Niall Murray, 'Schools say baptism barrier is rare', *Irish Examiner*, 23 January 2017.

School Act 2018, which outlawed the use of a child's faith as a criterion for school admission in a Catholic school. The right was retained for schools of minority faiths such as Protestant and Muslim schools. This legislative change was framed by reform advocates as an issue of discrimination. For critics of this change, the shortage of school places in urban areas was due partly to the State's inability to keep pace with changing demographics, rather than an issue of religious discrimination. Data from a 2017 survey conducted by the Catholic Primary Schools Management Association (CPSMA) indicated that when there were waiting lists in oversubscribed schools, religion was almost never the deciding factor in admissions. There were only ninety-seven cases, or 1.2 % of the total of unsuccessful applicants to Catholic primary schools, where a student did not gain admission because they lacked a baptismal certificate. For those highlighting the lack of school placements as the real issue, not religious discrimination, there was a feeling of vindication soon after the passing of the 2018 Bill when the Department of Education announced plans for building sixteen new primary schools in the greater Dublin area to meet demand driven by a shortage of school places.[20] Irrespective of the arguments, the legislation was passed and the Church was perceived to be on the wrong side of an argument that had negligible impact on enrolment in its schools. The Church's failure to recognise concerns about religious discrimination, even if only one child was affected, further undermined its position among large sections of Irish society.

E. Boards of Management

The concept of subsidiarity is a feature of the governance of Irish education system whereby individual patrons delegate the management and governance of their schools to a local voluntary board of management, who in turn appoints a principal to oversee the day-to-day operations and management of the school. With respect to the ethos or characteristic spirit

---

20 Marie Griffin, 'Catholic Schools in Ireland Today – a Changing Sector in a Time of Change', *Studies an Irish Quarterly Review*, Spring 2019, Vol. 108, No. 429.

of an individual school it is the board that has primary responsibility, on behalf of the patron, for promoting and protecting the school's ethos. The Education Act 1998 stated that the board is 'accountable to the patron for so upholding, the characteristic spirit of the school as determined by the cultural, educational, moral, religious, social, linguistic and spiritual values and traditions which inform and are characteristic of the objectives and conduct of the school'.[21] The board also has ultimate responsibility for oversight of the financial accounts of the school, although it has reporting responsibilities in this area to the Department of Education. When constituting the board of management, of which there must be eight members under the Education Act 1998, a patron may directly appoint two members as patron nominees. Historically, one of the patron nominees in Catholic schools would have been the local parish priest, who would have usually served as the chairperson of the board. However, with the declining numbers of clergy and the increased demands on those that remain, this practice is becoming less common. Research conducted by the Irish Primary Principals Network (IPPN) in 2010 reported that less than half (47 %) of chairpersons of primary school boards were religious (priests/rector/sister), and in the intervening decade this number has likely dropped further.[22] Additionally, two members are drawn from the parents of the school, along with the principal and one member of the teaching staff. At the first meeting of the new board, the first six members, with consideration to any additional skills required by the board, collectively propose two additional members to be appointed from the local community. Therefore, the patron, Catholic or otherwise, delegates management to the board, but they directly appoint just two of the eight members. It is increasingly difficult to attract willing community representatives in parishes with several schools all seeking to form their own boards. Also, schools in lower socio-economic areas (of which the largest proportion are Catholic) indicate challenges in recruiting volunteers to the board with the required expertise. The ability of Catholic patrons to

---

21   <http://www.irishstatutebook.ie/eli/1998/act/51/enacted/en/pdf>, 19.
22   *Primary School Governance, Challenges and Opportunities* (2010), Irish Primary Principals Network.

appoint competent and committed board members entrusted with overseeing governance, protecting the ethos of their schools, and hiring the
next generation of Catholic school leaders will likely be a critical factor in
the future of the Catholic schools in Ireland.

F. Teacher Employment

To further understand control in the education system, we must also
understand the employment status of the teachers in Irish primary schools,
which is an issue that is both clear and complex. Technically, the board of
management of each school employs its teachers and principal. It is also
the board of management who initiate dismissal proceedings against a
teacher, a situation that is extremely rare in the Irish context.[23] Along with
a relevant teaching qualification, teachers in a Catholic primary school
are required to hold a Certificate in Religious Education. For most pre-
service teachers, this Certificate is a 'check the box' on the way to meeting
the criteria for employment in a Catholic school. To not complete the
Certificate in Religious Education would limit themselves in relation to
their employment prospects as 89 % of the schools employing teachers
are Catholic. Therefore, it is effectively a requirement for students of all
faiths and none to undertake this course as part of their teacher training
to give themselves the best chance of employment post-graduation.[24]

Once an applicant fulfils these two criteria and is appointed by the
board of management, the extent to which the board exercises control over
the teacher is arguable. Teacher salaries are set nationally by the Government
as part of the broader Irish approach to collective wage agreements with
civil and public servants. The sole teacher's trade union at primary level,
the Irish National Teachers Organisation (INTO), represents teachers'
interests at these negotiations, rather than school patrons or the relevant
management body of the schools. In both the public consciousness as

23 Since schools are not required to report the dismissal of teachers, accurate figures
are not available.
24 Dr Anne Looney, Executive Dean of the Institute of Education at Dublin City
University, Personal Interview, October 2019.

well as in their own minds, teachers are public servants under the employ of the Department of Education. To illustrate this point, one need only look at teachers' social media accounts. A common feature of social media platforms like Facebook and LinkedIn is that users list their place of employment. In the case of Irish primary school teachers, a cursory review of accounts shows that instead of listing the name of the school they teach in (and by whom they are technically employed), teachers will often list the Department of Education as their employer. This ambiguity over their actual employer is unsurprising given that a majority of significant issues relating to pay and conditions are directed out of the Department, and teachers' pension are paid out of the public purse. Once employed, a school's board of management, irrespective of the patronage of the school, has little ongoing input into the particulars of employment of its teachers.

IV. Control in the Teaching and Learning Domain

A. Curriculum

The design, implementation and regulation of the curriculum within Irish primary schools (the focus of Chapter 12), the central activity of schools, is another essential area where control is mixed. All primary schools in Ireland follow the State-mandated curriculum, with the current one dating to 1999. The curriculum covers all subjects within primary schools. The National Council for Curriculum and Assessment (NCCA) is tasked with the development and ongoing review of curriculum by the Minister for Education. As a State curriculum, it is blind to the ethos of particular patrons. This is not unsurprising as the curriculum must be implemented in schools whose ethos encompasses a variety of faith backgrounds and none. It is then up to individual schools to imbue the curriculum with their own distinctive characteristic spirit. Historically, Religious Education is a subject within the curriculum framework and was a key means by which this spirit was fostered. The NCCA has proposed as part of the *Draft Primary Curriculum Framework* the concept of a patron's programme wherein Religious Education would be replaced by 'Religious/ Ethical/ Multi-belief Education – Patron's programme'. Under this framework, a Catholic school in the future would teach Religious Education as part of its patron's programme.[25]

The new primary curriculum is currently under development, with the draft curriculum framework published in 2020. This framework, the foundation on which a newly revised curriculum will be developed, is the product of ongoing consultation with stakeholders including patrons, teachers' unions, schools and parents. The NCCA envisages that the new curriculum for primary schools will be published in the summer of 2024, with implementation of the curriculum to be phased in gradually in subsequent years. As mentioned, while patrons, including the Catholic Church, are consulted as part of the development process, it is the NCCA that ultimately proposes the curriculum to the Minister for adoption and implementation. One proposed change of note in the draft curriculum framework is a reduction in the time allocated for the teaching of the patrons' programme, in schools from two hours and thirty minutes currently down to two hours under the new curriculum. In Catholic schools, Religious Education (RE) is taught in this time, along with preparation for the sacraments at the relevant class levels. The RE programme is the one area of the curriculum over which the Catholic Church as the patron has control. However, the Church's ability to properly fulfil the RE curriculum, as it is currently constituted, is likely to be reduced under the proposed new NCCA curriculum framework. The place and prominence of RE within Catholic schools will be, in no small part, determined by the outcome of this process.

B Initial Teacher Training and Preparation

The training of teachers is also relevant for understanding the wider picture of who has control in Irish education. At the start of the twenty-first

---

25   The term 'Patron's Programme' does not appear in the 1999 Primary Curriculum, instead the subject 'Religious Education' forms a part of the prescribed curriculum.

century, most Irish primary teachers were prepared in colleges of education under the patronage of the Catholic Church. This landscape has
changed dramatically over the past decade and a half. In 2004, primary
teacher preparation was delivered in five faith-based higher education institutions, four of them Catholic. Today, a minority of new teachers taking
up positions in primary schools are formed in colleges under Catholic
patronage. Indeed, the largest provider of teachers for the Irish system is
now an online for-profit enterprise, Hibernia College, that offers a part-
time Professional Master's in Education. One of the two largest Catholic
colleges of education, St Patrick's College in Dublin, was incorporated
into Dublin City University in 2018, a large secular institution. The two
colleges still under Catholic patronage, Mary Immaculate College in
Limerick and Marino Institute of Education in Dublin, are under pressure to merge into larger university structures.[26] It is possible that at least
one of these Catholic institutions will also be incorporated into a larger
secular university in the coming years.

With new teachers being formed, in the main, in a secular context, one
would perhaps expect that the various patrons, including Catholic patrons,
would have a programme of induction focused on forming teachers in the
particular characteristic spirit at the heart of their schools. No such induction programme exists for teachers entering Catholic schools although the
Certificate in Religious Education that students can opt to take as part of
their studies, and is required for teachers in Catholic schools, contributes in
part to addressing this deficit. It is the Department of Education and Skills
through the National Induction Programme for Teachers (NIPT) that
oversees the induction of new teachers. The NIPT's induction programme
Droichead focuses the induction into the profession through a mentorship
approach. The programme is ethos blind, which means that everyone receives the same induction irrespective of whether the new teacher's school
is denominational or multi-denominational. The extent to which patrons
address inducting teachers into their own particular characteristic spirit

26   Siobhan Harkin and Ellen Hazelkorn, 'Restructuring Irish Higher Education
     Through Collaboration and Merger', in Curaj, A. et al. eds, *Mergers and alliances in
     higher education: International practice and emerging opportunities*, Springer, 2015,
     105–21.

or ethos is not clear, but anecdotally it would seem that this is done informally and, to a degree, by osmosis for Catholic patrons. Unlike the trust
bodies who manage Catholic secondary schools, for example, diocese do
not gather new primary teachers for an annual induction day to nurture
and strengthen school ethos amongst new recruits.

C. Oversight and Professional Development of Teachers and Principals

Another domain for understanding control is regulation of the teaching
profession. Responsibility for regulating the teaching profession in Ireland
rests with the Teaching Council, a statutory body established under the
Teaching Council Act 2015 to promote and regulate professional standards in teaching. The Council also advises the Minister for Education
and Skills on the entry criteria for admission onto a programme of Initial
Teaching Education (ITE), i.e. a Bachelor of Education or a Professional
Masters of Education. The Teaching Council maintains the register of
90,000 qualified primary and secondary teachers, the largest such professional register in Ireland. The Council also has responsibility for vetting
all teachers coming into and within the system, a vital element in the safeguarding of children in schools. The Fitness to Teach process, through
which people, including parents, can make complaints of a serious nature
against teachers related to their professional practice and behaviour, also
sits within the Teaching Council.

The authority to select and appoint school principals, like the appointment of teachers, rests with local boards of management. Although
they are the employer, as with teachers, all issues relating to terms and
conditions flow from the Department of Education and Skills. However,
the induction and ongoing formation of principals is under the guidance
of the Professional Development Service for Teachers (PDST) and the
Centre for School Leaders (CSL). Both institutions were established by the
Department of Education and Skills. The *Misneach* programme is a two-year
induction programme for new principals offered by the PDST, and this is
complemented by the mentoring service for new principals offered by the
CSL. The *Misneach* programme has as its focus six core areas and appears

from review not to include programming in the area of ethos promotion or leading a school particular to one patron over another. The PDST is also responsible for the *Tanaiste* programme, a formation programme for new deputy principals. This too is not related to any particular ethos or faith denomination.

Another layer of Department oversight involves examining the quality of teaching and learning in schools, which happens through the process of Whole School Evaluations (WSE). This process is overseen by the Inspectorate, a division with the Department of Education and Skills. The WSE process is typically undertaken in schools every four to eight years and is a comprehensive examination of all aspects of teaching and learning within the school. The characteristic spirit of schools and their patrons is noted as part of the review but is not a central focus. Teaching and learning in all subjects are examined except for Religious Education, Responsibility for oversight of the Religious Education programme lies with patrons themselves. In Catholic primary schools, this task falls to Diocesan Advisors (DAs) in each diocese. In some dioceses where there are a team of DAs, an annual visit to a school would be the norm; however, many dioceses have only a part-time DA and a visit every two to three years is more common. These visits do not take on the formal approach of the WSE, where consultations, reports and follow-up reviews are the standard practice. The visit of a DA is a shorter, more informal process, limited to support for the curricular area of Religious Education, which itself is periodic due to under resourcing.[27] The DA has no formal role in supporting schools around ethos or providing external validation on how the school is tending to this critical responsibility. Although there is evidence that school leaders would welcome support from their diocese on this in tandem with the school self-evaluation process, it has not been forthcoming yet.[28] The impending introduction of the new curriculum

27   The Archdiocese of Dublin, for example, has just three Diocesan Advisors to support its 350 schools in Dublin.
28   Elaine Mahon, 2017. *Investigating the Perceptions of Primary School Communities in the Republic of Ireland Regarding Their Catholic Identity*, Dublin City University [EdD thesis].

may force Catholic patrons to take more ownership of this area according to Dr Anne Looney of Dublin City University's Institute of Education.[29]

Tending to the ongoing professional development of teachers in primary schools is perhaps one of the most important drivers of student attainment.[30] Along with a role in the induction and formation of school leaders, the PDST also holds responsibility for this aspect of school life. While the NCCA is the body tasked with developing curriculum, it is the PDST who must ensure its implementation. Through a national team of curriculum advisors, the PDST provides an annual programme of professional development for staff in schools across all subjects, except for Religious Education. Coordinated professional development across schools in RE is usually confined to the period directly after any new RE curriculum is introduced by the Irish Episcopal Conference (through the Council for Catechetics). Any such professional development is at the discretion of individual principals and is the responsibility of the patron, not the NCCA. Professional development related to the wider primary curriculum is standardised and is 'ethos-neutral', meaning that it is the responsibility of individual schools, principals and teachers to integrate their own characteristic spirit or ethos into the various curriculum areas. There is no designated professional development service specific to such approaches in Catholic schools. However, some dioceses, 3rd Level institutions, and for-profit providers offer one-week professional development courses in the summer specific to Catholic primary teachers. These include the Diocese of Kildare and Leighlin's *ConnetEd* focusing on RE across the school, DCU's Institute of Education's *Growing in Love: Religious Education in Catholic Primary Schools'*, and fluirse.com's *Catholic Education: What's the Point?* Such courses often tend to focus either explicitly on RE or on the broad theme of Catholic Education. Professional development offerings focused on integrating faith across the curriculum are harder to find if

29   Dr Anne Looney, Executive Dean of DCU's Institute of Education. Personal interview, October 2019.

30   *Breaking the Habit of Ineffective Professional Development for Teachers*, McKinsey & Company, 1 January 2012. Available at: <https://www.mckinsey.com/industries/public-and-social-sector/our-insights/breaking-the-habit-of-ineffective-professional-development-for-teachers>

they exist at all. Additionally, Mary Immaculate College and the Marino Institute of Education offer academic programmes in Christian Leadership in Education.

V. Conclusion

The Irish education system, like many internationally, is complex. Making easy characterisations in respect to where control, power, or management lies is challenging. The popular troupe in Ireland is that the control that the Catholic Church exerts over the primary school system has been and remains a problem. Fintan O'Toole, a well-known journalist from *The Irish Times*, suggests that 'the overwhelming church control of the system of primary education results not from charity but from the exercise of power'.[31] Despite such claims, the reality of Church 'control' is overstated. The dominant place of the Church in the primary sector has in fact been in decline for some time, hastened by many of the changes highlighted in this chapter. A comment from as far back as 1987 from the then bishop of Cork and Ross is worthy of reflection in this regard: 'The boards of management in the country's national schools have little or no power over policy, curriculum or staff arrangements and the extent to which they actually manage the schools is highly questionable.'[32] Whatever the merits of the Bishop's statement at the time undoubtedly the intervening decades have seen the State through the Department of Education and its many delegated statutory agencies and bodies assume a large degree of control over virtually every aspect of primary sector education. Later chapters will explore in more detail many of the issues outlined here, underscoring some of the implications for the Catholic Church, the State, and the system more broadly. This chapter has highlighted the tension between the Church and the State in relation to the evolving primary education

31   Fintan O'Toole, 'Lessons in the Power of the Church', *The Irish Times*, 6 June 2009.
32   As reported by John Walshe in the Irish Independent, 5 August 1987 in Michael Farry, *Education and the Constitution*, Round Hall Sweet & Maxwell, 1996, 97.

landscape. The next and final chapter of this introductory section of the book examines the level of demand that exists within Irish society and among parents for changes within the Irish primary school system. Part II of the book then turns to examining the wider cast of important actors who are seeking to influence the future of Irish primary schools. We examine the Church, Educate Together, Community National Schools and mainstream media to better understand how each actor is promoting and defending their interests in the key educational reform debates.

CHAPTER 3

Demand for Change in the Irish Primary Sector

I. Introduction

The dominant national narrative in relation to the primary school system in Ireland is that change is needed and that the current situation of largely denominational provision is not suited to the contemporary context.[1]

Such views are not new, with one commentator advocating for change as far back as 1970, but the calls for change have been growing. The 1970 reformer argued that for the good of denominational education as well as for those who desired an alternative 'it would seem to be a necessary condition for the proper functioning of a committed [Christian] school in a modern society, that parents have a real choice of an alternative. Put bluntly: the present situation is an artificial one, where the nominal Christian or the frankly unbelieving one must willy-nilly send his child to the local confessional [denominational] school.'[2] Over the past decade, a broad spectrum of political, religious and civil society leaders have been calling for increasing pluralism of patronage through the provision of more non-denominational and multi-denominational schools. An important voice in the contemporary debate on the issue of increased pluralism was the then Archbishop of Dublin, Diarmuid Martin: 'From the moment of my appointment as archbishop [2004], I advocated a process of divestment of a substantial number of Catholic schools to foster a more pluralist presence

---

1   Jonathan Tiernan, 'Catholic Schools Must Remain True to Their Foundations –
    Status Quo Will not Achieve This', *The Irish Times,* 30 July 2018.
2   Joseph Veale SJ, 'The Christian School', *Studies, an Irish Quarterly,* Winter 1970,
    Vol. 59, No. 236.

which would reflect changing demographics.'[3] The Archbishop, who happened to be the patron with the largest number of primary schools (452) in the State at the time, has been joined by many others in calls for change. For example, Labour TD and former Government Junior Minister Áodhan O'Riordain has gone a step further, suggesting in 2018 that 'a question should be put to the people, should we take religions and religious influences out of education?'[4]

Later chapters will explore how various actors have sought to increase diversity within the Irish primary sector via policy reforms. Before turning to that analysis, it is instructive to ascertain the nature of demand for change to the current primary school landscape whereby the Catholic Church acts as patron to 89 % of Irish primary schools. Many surveys conducted over the past decade provide insights into the level of demand for change. The surveys and research considered below are drawn from a range of organisations, including the State, the Catholic Church, teacher unions and academics. As such, these surveys represent a comprehensive analysis of the various views that shape the public and political discourse on educational reform of the primary sector. All the stakeholders agree that parental demand should be a key driver of future change, but determining what parents want is disputed depending on who asks and who reports their responses! This battle to represent the 'true' sentiments of parents is ongoing and contentious. Most of the data considered here engages the voice of parents, the very cohort that will be central to any reshaping of the primary sector and for whose children these changes will affect the most.

Although there is significant and growing support for increasing diversity of patronage within the Irish primary sector, there are several factors that militate against changes to patronage that achieve this goal. First, it is unclear what sufficient demand for change is needed in a local area for politicians and State officials to be willing to overcome organised and vocal local opposition. Support for greater primary school patronage options is

3   Patsy McGarry, 'Archbishop Martin Proved Right about School Patronage', *The Irish Times*, 12 July 2017.
4   Harry Manning, '"IRELAND IS DIFFERENT" Labour Senator Aodhan O'Riordain Launches Petition to Remove Role of Religions in Irish Schools and Says Referendum Should Be Held', *The Irish Sun*, 9 July 2018.

often over 30 %, but if these views are not concentrated within a particular area, there may be inadequate demand to warrant divestment or opening a new school. Second, it is not the case that the levels of parents' religiosity perfectly correlate with demand to have their children in a Catholic or non-Catholic school. Not all parents who are less religious prefer a non-Catholic primary school and not all religiously active Catholics choose Catholic schools for religious reasons. Finally, the overall strength of all Irish primary schools leads to high levels of satisfaction among parents. As a result, calls for reforms to the primary sector such as divestment or curriculum reform do not resonate with many parents and local communities. This chapter reviews data that illustrate these three important patterns – overall demand, relationship between religious background and school patronage preferences and levels of satisfaction with existing schools.

These data set the stage for the remainder of the book because they reveal that how a problem is defined influences the various policy alternatives that are proposed to address it. Given the complexity and often contradictory nature of public opinion and parental support for change, with differences between local and personal views and national and institutional ones, we will see why divestment has been a policy failure and admissions and curriculum reforms have experienced different outcomes.

II. The Level of Demand for Diversifying Primary School Patronage

There is widespread agreement that change in the primary sector is necessary to achieve increased diversity of patrons. However, there is no consensus on how to measure accurate levels of demand for multi- and non-denominational schools, let alone how to respond to the changing demand that exists. The existing studies that have sought to measure Irish society's demand for alternative patrons in their local communities have produced conflicting and often contradictory results.

The call for greater diversity in the Irish primary sector was catalysed by the Forum on Patronage and Pluralism, which was established in 2011 by a reform-minded Government (see more details on the Forum in Chapter 10). On the foot of one of the Forum's recommendations to increase the diversity of patrons and the diversity within existing schools, a national survey of parents in thirty-eight Education and Training Board (ETB) areas was conducted in 2013 with a response from 10,715 parents, representing the preferences of 20,400 children. The stated aim of the surveys was 'to establish the level of parental demand for a wider choice in the patronage of primary schools within these areas'.[5] Reports based on the surveys argued that there was 'sufficient parental demand supporting immediate changes in school patronage in 23 of the 38 areas'.[6] The reports did not define what the bar was for identifying an area with sufficient demand. Elsewhere officials suggested that when roughly 35 % to 50 % of parents within an area stated a desire for change that this indicates sufficient demand for change to occur.[7] Of the thirty-eight areas surveyed, thirty areas had populations where at least 30 % of respondents were in favour of wider choice of patronage. However, not all of those in favour of change wished to avail themselves of the options that this wider choice of patronage might bestow on an area. In other words, respondents support more change in principle, but may not want to avail of that option for their children or want that greater choice to alter the local context. Only thirteen of the thirty-eight areas surveyed had a population where 30 % or more of the preferences registered indicated a wish to avail themselves of such choice (see Table 3.1).

These surveys suggest broad support for parents having access to schools offering different patronage, but a reluctance among parents for this wider choice to impact their children directly – perhaps a case of

5   *Report on the Surveys Regarding Parental Preferences on Primary School Patronage*, Dept. of Education and Skills, 2013. [Available at: <https://www.education. ie/en/publications/policy-reports/report-on-the-surveys-regarding-parental-preferences-on-primary-school-patronage.pdf>]
6   *Report on the Surveys Regarding Parental Preferences*, 2013.
7   John Walshe, former Education Journalist/Aide to Minister Ruairí Quinn, Personal Interview, October 2019.

Table 3.1. Areas surveyed with 30 % or more of preferences indicating desire to avail of greater choice of patronage

	Total Preferences	% of responses in support of a wider choice of patronage in the area	% of responses that would avail of a wider choice of patronage in the area
Dublin 6 (Harolds Cross/ Rathmines)	892	66 %	55 %
Wicklow	619	57 %	48 %
Kells	284	52 %	43 %
Westport	359	50 %	41 %
Nenagh	313	44 %	34 %
Youghal	173	45 %	32 %
New Ross	367	40 %	32 %
Fermoy	298	47 %	31 %
Dungarvan	429	46 %	31 %
Cobh	504	38 %	31 %
Leixlip	428	46 %	30 %
Passage West	391	43 %	30 %
Tuam	377	40 %	30 %

nimbyism or, at the least, a lack of desire by many parents to change their children's schools.[8]

As we discuss in greater detail in Chapter 10, which focuses on the issue of divestment, some disquiet was raised by Catholic education advocates in relation to the methodology used and the data generated by

8   Nimbyism or 'Not in My Back Yard' is the phenomenon of someone who does not want something done near where they live, although it does need to be done somewhere.

these surveys, including calling into question whether the surveys contained a representative sample. Additionally, there was some concern that the various Vocational Education Committees (VEC)/ Education and Training Boards (ETB) that conducted the surveys were also a potential new patron, raising conflict of interest concerns.[9] Participation in the surveys was voluntary and some critics posited that parents who had strong feelings in relation to a change agenda may have been more likely to participate, thereby skewing the results. The local advocacy efforts on behalf of Educate Together, whose strength in grassroots organising is generally acknowledged and has been central to the growth of their network, influenced the survey results as well. Educate Together has developed an impressive network of campaign groups, which are 'made up of parents/ carers who want an Educate Together school for their children. In recent years, the Educate Together network has grown substantially, and parental support has been critical to the successful establishment of new schools.'[10]

The 'Code of Conduct' introduced the following year (2014) by the Department of Education in relation to the *Patronage Process for New Schools* was largely a reaction to this experience. These new guidelines detailed the type and thrust of communications patrons could use to attract potential families.[11] New guidelines also set limits on expenditure in relation to local advocacy in areas where a new school is to be established. The report analysing the survey results proposed that the 'main patron [Catholic bishop] in the identified areas should be asked to consider reconfiguration options that would free up accommodation for at least one full stream for provision by the first-choice alternative patron.'[12] As of 2021,

9   Michael Sheils McNamee, 'Here Is How Ireland's Bishops Responded to Being Asked to Hand over Their Schools', *TheJournal.ie*, 1 August 2016. <https://www.thejournal.ie/catholic-schools-divestment-ireland-religion-2876185-Aug2016/> (Accessed: 21 March 2021).
10   *Find a Campaign Group*, Educate Together. <https://www.educatetogether.ie/schools/campaign-groups/> (Accessed: 22 March 2021).
11   *Primary Patronage New Schools 2014, Code of Conduct*, Dept. of Education and Skills, 2014. Available at: <https://www.education.ie/en/Schools-Colleges/Information/Establishing-a-New-School/New-Primary-Schools/Primary-Patronage-New-Schools-2014-Code-of-Conduct.pdf>
12   *Report on the Surveys Regarding Parental Preferences*, 2013.

little progress has been made in respect to this request. One challenge has been that parents often oppose any change that may impact their local school as seen in the case of Malahide/Portmarnock. In this case, outlined further in Chapter 10, a local outcry against the Archdiocese of Dublin's attempt to identify one of the local Catholic schools for divestment made national news. Opposition from staff and parents across many local schools against such a move resulted in the Archdiocese suspending the process.

III. Religious Background and School Patronage

Irish society has become more religiously diverse. The combination of growing numbers of non-religious and minority religious citizens and the evolving beliefs and practices of the majority Catholic population has transformed Irish society. As a result, there have been growing demands to change Ireland's education system to more accurately reflect the diversity of beliefs and practices represented within society. For some, Ireland's education system should become completely secular. For others, more choice should be offered, but existing denominational schools should be retained because religious education is important to them. Countless others fall somewhere on the continuum, and many do not even think about schools primarily in religious or non-religious terms. These complexities underscore the challenge when trying to determine how religious beliefs, practices and identities inform school choice in Ireland. Unfortunately, there is no clear correlation between religious background and school choice preferences.

To better understand some of these dynamics, three national bodies representing Catholic schools undertook a project in 2019 to get an up-to-date and comprehensive picture of public perception of the Catholic school 'brand' and factors determining choice of Catholic schools. The three organisations, the Catholic Primary Schools Management Association (CPSMA), the Catholic Schools Partnership (CSP) and the Association of Management of Catholic Secondary Schools (AMCSS), contracted an external consulting firm, Genesis, to conduct market research on their behalf.

The findings provide a valuable snapshot of the views towards Catholic schools of the parents of school-going children at that time. The report's title, *Articulating a New Positioning of Catholic Education in Ireland*, speaks to a possible awareness among the contracting organisations that there was a need among key Catholic school stakeholders to take control of and be more intentional about telling the story of Catholic schools. The project sought to identify what 'Catholic' might mean in a modern and pluralist Irish education system.[13]

A key element of the project was a national representative survey of 500 parents of school-going children, both primary and secondary.[14] In keeping with broader national trends, the overall numbers attending religious services in Ireland have declined; however, there is still a significant portion of Irish adults (36 %) attending religious services on a weekly basis.[15] Among parents surveyed the percentage attending weekly religious services was slightly lower (22 %) than this national average. A further 20 % of parents indicated that they attend mass at least once a month. When asked if they would have chosen a multi- or non-denominational school had one been available, parents who attended mass at least once a month indicated a lower level of desire for such an option. Of parents who attend religious services weekly, 31 % indicated they would have chosen a multi- or non-denominational school for their child had it been available. This rose to 59 % of parents who indicated they never attended religious services. This dramatic increase among non-religious service attenders implies that

---

13   Genesis, *Articulating a new positioning for Catholic education in Ireland*, September 2021.

14   A sample size of 500 respondents is a fairly common in survey research. Although larger studies often include 1,000 respondents, this only marginally increases the accuracy of the findings. For example, the margin of error for a 500-person study is approximately 4.5 % compared to 3.2 % for 1,000-person survey. <https://www.sciencebuddies.org/science-fair-projects/references/sample-size-surveys>. Given that we rely on these data for more descriptive purposes rather than statistical significance also justifies their use. Additionally, this study represents the most recent data that focuses on critical questions examined in this study and offers suggestive indications of contemporary Irish parents' attitudes.

15   Patsy McGarry, 'The Faith of Ireland's Catholics Continues, Despite All', *The Irish Times*, 11 August 2018.

there may be a relationship, albeit limited and undetermined, between levels of religiosity and school choice. A further 36 % of respondents said they attend mass occasionally, thus maintaining some level of active practice of their faith. Of this cohort of parents, 44 % indicated a preference for multi- or non-denominational education if it had been available. Although most parents who regularly attend religious services stated a preference for retaining a Catholic school option for their children, it is also noteworthy that among parents who identify as non-mass-goers, a significant minority (41 %) would not have opted for a multi- or non-denominational school for their children, indicating a degree of satisfaction with their current choice. It is not fair to say then that there is a strong correlation between religiosity and preference for a particular primary school patron.

Despite the contradictory nature of the data there is a general assumption that as Irish society becomes less religious, there will be fewer people demanding a religious/faith-based education for their children. This is consistent with broader liberalisation of Irish society that has coincided with a decline in religiosity over the past decades, culminating in the passing of the same-sex marriage and abortion referenda in 2015 and 2018, respectively. In both instances, there was at least 60 % support among active voters for changing the Constitution. This change of sentiment took decades to reach a tipping point and both issues were held at arm's length politically until it was clear the public mood was in the 'change' camp. As Chapter 8 will describe in greater detail, marriage equality and abortion referenda were framed around one, clear-cut and binary yes-no decision. With education, there are multiple issues, including preferences for type of school patronage, the quality of education, historic ties to a school and even location. Not only are there more issues involved in these educational debates, but the role of religion in shaping individual preferences on educational issues is varied and complex. A more nuanced picture emerges that points to conflicting experiences of the Church at a local versus a national, institutional level.

The Genesis research split parents into four categories in relation to belief and practice to better contextualise the different types of Catholics there are within Ireland. The report indicated that 22 % were identified as regular mass attenders who are more likely to adhere to the Church's

teachings in all areas; 20 % were categorised as believers with regular practice who believe in the power of the sacraments and have some parish involvement; 46 % were considered believers but with minimal or occasional
practice who might be described as Catholic with a small 'c'; and 13 % were
described as having no belief or practice and dislike Church involvement
in public institutions like health and education.[16] The two groups in the
middle, consisting of 66 % of parents, share a belief in the importance of
Christian values in the moral formation of their children, but they also
have a scepticism of what they perceive as negative institutional instruction from the Church. The degree to which Catholic schools retain the
confidence and support of this majority will be a key determinant in their
future. The success of the same-sex marriage and abortion referenda were
seen by supporters as a step forward towards a more inclusive and modern
Ireland. As of 2021, most parents generally do not consider the Church's
continued involvement in schools as a block to such progress. What might
be protective factors sustaining the current level of support for Catholic
schools are worthy of some reflection.

The Genesis research conducted focus groups that revealed a picture
of what it feels like to be Catholic in a modern Ireland from parents with
school-going children. Respondents indicated that they felt a lack of confidence or even embarrassment or shame in admitting to being practicing
Catholics. Many reported being wary of mentioning their faith in social,
work or even school settings to avoid difficult conversations. At the root of
this reality is a perception that the Church represented all that was wrong
with Irish society in the past and perhaps in the present also – male dominated, lesser role for women, controlling, conservative, abusive, etc. This
institutional face of the Church, often the one most prominently portrayed
in the media and civil society debates, stood in contrast with respondent's
personal experience of the Church at a local level (see Figure 3.1).

This personal experience of Church represented the best of Catholic
values; caring, charity, supportive, etc. Many of the parents mourned the
fact that it is typically the institutional face of the Church that most often

---

16   This figure is slightly above, but in keeping with, the 9.6 % of people who identified
      as not having a faith in the 2016 Census.

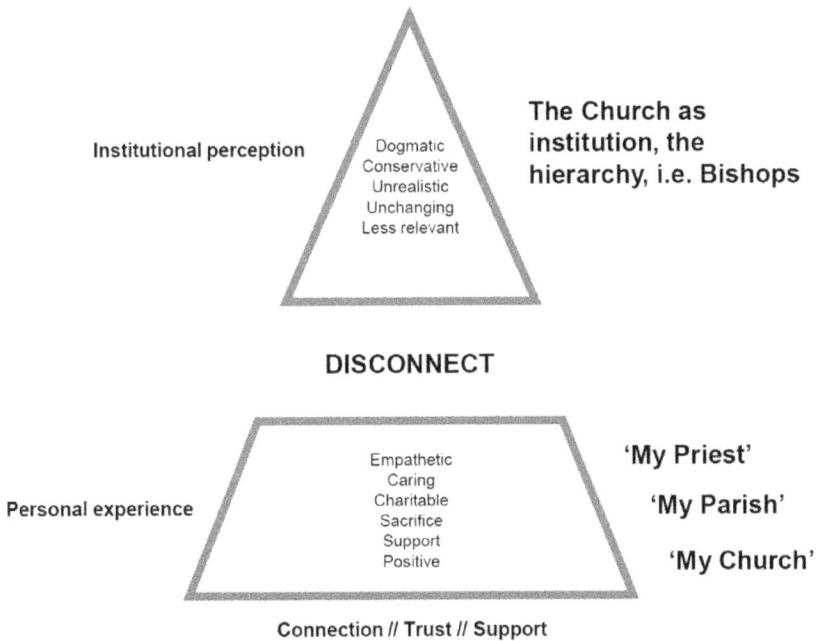

Figure 3.1. Institutional and personal perceptions of the Catholic Church.

Genesis, *Articulating New Positioning of Catholic Education in Ireland*, September 2021.

is represented in public discourse rather than the more personal and positive aspects of Church that they experience at the local level. For parents, the heart of this disconnect is between the national and ideological face of the Catholic Church, which is more distant to their lives and the lives of their children, and the local and personal Church, which they experience through their parish and school. It is this local and personal Church that parents see as 'the Church on its best day' and which they entrust their children to daily at the gates of their local Catholic school.

The focus groups underscored a feeling of an uncomfortableness and/ or sense of conflict with Church teachings and language. Contrast this with some of the more socially progressive norms that parents support such as sexuality, sex education, gender identity and female equality. Parents felt that the institutional Church was out of step with Irish attitudes, but many also experienced a more progressive Church at the local level where schools, principals and some parish priests were more aligned with contemporary attitudes than official Church teaching. Parents recognise that principals often must toe the party line formally on issues such as sex education and sexuality, but they provide more nuanced treatment of such issues in their schools to meet students and families where they are in their own beliefs. This tailoring or tempering of official Church teaching by principals might enable parents to be comfortable with the faith-based nature of their schools as they observe a flexibility at a local level not perceived at the national level. This may help explain why there is less support for divestment in local communities where the experience of Church is often more favourable.

Despite this conflict between personal values to emerging social norms and traditional Church teachings, parents reported a strong desire to pass on the Catholic faith tradition to their children, especially as the world was changing so quickly. The Church's ability to mark and celebrate the important moments in the life of a family (e.g. birth, marriage, death, Christmas, etc.) through the sacraments and religious worship is highly prized, but not necessarily the deciding factor in what parents value in a school with a Catholic ethos. Parents identified a list of benefits they felt emanated from Catholicism and religious practice, including moral values, stability/grounding, social connection, charity/empathy and values and ideals. There was a clear emphasis on values and morality as attractive features of Catholicism. There appears to be more interest in Catholic social teaching and its emphasis on social justice than there is on having strong Catholic religious practices. 86 % of parents rated 'teaching right from wrong' as either valuable or very valuable, making it the highest rated practice of a primary school with a Catholic ethos. Next, 66 % of parents rated 'social inclusion initiatives' and 'discussions/ awareness raising of social issues' as valuable or very valuable.[17] There is a clear preference among parents for practices and activities rooted in the development of a moral compass, an ethical foundation and a social conscience. Although sacramental preparation was important to parents (57 % identified it as valuable or very valuable), they placed less emphasis on practice and faith formation rituals.

---

17   *Articulating New Positioning of Catholic Education in Ireland*, 2021.

There is, it would appear, a disconnect among how parents perceive the role of Religious Education in the teaching of right from wrong and moral formation in Catholic schools. There was a large disparity between the value parents placed on teaching right from wrong (86 %) versus the value placed on religious instruction (46 %). For many parents it would appear there is a belief that the two happen independently of one another. This disconnect could undermine the Catholic school ethos as fewer parents consider the Catholic way of teaching right and wrong any different from more secular ways of understanding such choices. Some Catholic school advocates fear that in time Catholic schools may be seen by parents as no different from Educate Together and Community National Schools in terms of how they teach morals. The other education providers also teach right from wrong, albeit not out of one specific faith tradition. If it is this moral grounding that parents want coupled with sacramental preparation, the other two patrons can offer both as well. These schools teach right from wrong through their own distinct patron's programmes. Additionally, they also offer sacramental preparation after the school day through parishes or by teachers who are paid to provide the instruction independently. It is unclear how Catholic schools will respond to evolving parental preferences that are shifting more towards greater interest in moral and social formation rather than explicitly religious or spiritual formation. The previous example of principals nuancing certain approaches to Church teaching to meet families where they are at may point to Catholic schools moderating views or emphasis to meet local market demands. This could undermine the distinctiveness of the Catholic school ethos over time, leading parents to turn to other patrons for their children's education. In the contemporary context, the changing and varied experiences of Catholicism underscores the diversity even within the Catholic Church in Ireland. Furthermore, the results do not reveal a clear pattern between levels of religiosity and attitudes towards education reforms. In many cases, religiosity may not even be the most relevant factor driving individual preferences about school choice as the next section describes.

IV. School Choice and Understanding Levels of Satisfaction

Overall, there is a high level of satisfaction among parents of primary school-going children with the quality of education being delivered. As a result, there may not be a groundswell of support for divestment of schools to radically diversify Ireland's primary sector given that individual schools are satisfying many of the expressed needs of its students and parents. The Genesis data found that 79 % of parents reported being either 'satisfied' or 'very satisfied' with the school their child was attending. Only 17 % of parents felt 'dissatisfied' or 'very dissatisfied' with no major difference in satisfaction across regional or socio-economic lines. This high level of satisfaction with schools is in keeping with historical trends, where, as far back as 1974, there was a high regard for the job schools were doing.[18] Data from 1974 highlights broad public support with 72 % of respondents stating that schools were either 'excellent' or 'pretty good' when asked, 'How do you rate schools in Ireland today?' However, a significant minority of the public (28 %) felt the performance of schools was 'poor' or 'only fair'. The figures improved notably in the years that followed. A 2004 survey conducted by the Educational Research Centre (Dublin) found that the number of respondents indicating that schools were 'excellent' or 'pretty good' had risen to 82 %, with those rating schools as 'poor' or 'only fair' having fallen to 17 %.[19] This high regard among the public for the job schools are doing may well serve as an important ballast against moves to disrupt the status quo when it comes to the denominational nature of the primary system. However, school patronage has not been identified as a leading factor in driving this high degree of satisfaction within the Irish primary education. Ireland benefits from a highly trained teaching corps. 'Teachers retain the confidence of the public, entry to teacher education is still highly competitive

---

18   George F. Madaus, Patricia J. Fontes, Thomas Kellaghan and Peter W. Airasian, 'Opinions of the Irish Public on Goals and Adequacy of Education', *Irish Journal of Education*, 13 (1979), 87–125.

19   Thomas Kellaghan, Páid McGee, David Millar, and Rachel Perkins, *Views of the Irish Public on Education: A Survey*. Dublin Educational Research Centre, 2004.

from well-qualified candidates, [and] teacher education, both pre-service and in-service, is well regarded.'[20] In Ireland, there is no clear educational advantage between primary schools under different patrons. If high levels of student achievement continue, it appears that most parents will demonstrate little active interest in major educational reform, on the basis of religious grounds or otherwise. The most vocal calls for change are therefore likely to continue to emanate from those who desire fundamental change to the patronage system for ideological reasons. For now, the data points to them being in the minority.

Although there is overwhelming support reported among parents (78 %) in the 2021 Genesis survey for the Catholic Church to have a role in continuing to shape and influence the ethos of primary schools, there is less agreement on the extent to which this role should be exercised. 43 % of parents reported that the Church should have either a 'much more active role' or 'some role' in the ethos of their local school. These respondents believe that the Church should have a role 'equal to that of other community members, such as parents, principals and teachers'. A further 35 % stated that while the Church should continue to have some influence, it should be limited, but what is meant by limited is not articulated. Just 22 % of parents indicated that the Church should have no role in the ethos of their local school, with these parents more likely to be in the younger age group (25–34 years) and identify as having 'no religion'. National trends indicate that this group within the population that identifies as having 'no religion' is likely to continue to rise, having increased from 3.5 % in 2002 to 9.8 % in 2016, making it the largest grouping outside of those identifying as Catholic (78.3 %).[21] As this group expands, one could see increased calls for limiting or eliminating the role of the Catholic Church in education. The extent to which their advocacy can influence or activate those parents for whom it would seem to be a moot point currently will be critical to any future changes to the primary school landscape.

20   John Coolahan, *Attracting, Developing and Retaining Effective Teachers: Country Background report for Ireland.* Project Report. OECD Publishing, 2003.

21   Central Statistics Office, 2016. Available at: <https://www.cso.ie/en/releasesandpublications/ep/p-cp8iter/p8iter/p8rrc/>

To further understand the complex set of beliefs regarding the education context, it is instructive to consider 'easy' and 'hard' questions. Scholars of public opinion data highlight the distinction between the easy and hard facets of questions as a way of explaining how individuals may have complex beliefs on any one topic. Easy questions generally deal with a principle or an overall view, whereas hard questions focus on the implementation of such policies, forcing respondents to choose between solutions or policies.[22] In this sense, asking parents if they support broader choice is an easy question. The hard question is the extent to which parents want something different for their own children who, on the whole, they feel are being served well by their school of choice. Questions framed around the easy question of ethos that seek to identify a desire of change among parents are unlikely to prove instructive as most parent's school choice is not driven primarily by ethos. Once the school meets their criteria on several important 'choice' factors, ethos is less of an issue.

The easy/hard distinction is certainly part of the reason why there are sometimes contradictory results in the data. For example, 51 % of respondents in the Genesis survey indicated that they would choose a multi- or non-denominational school had the choice been available. This is an easy question because it does not affect their real choices. Those in the higher socio-economic groups, and in Dublin, were least likely to indicate a preference for a multi- or non-denominational school. Of primary school parents, 38 % indicated that they would have chosen a multi- or non-denominational school had one been available for their child or children, with lower socio-economic groups somewhat more in favour of this option. Despite these results, when asked in a different question, 72 % of parents revealed that they had a choice of school and sent their child to their preferred option. This represents a hard question because it relates to the actual choices they made for their children. In this case, the numbers suggest higher levels of satisfaction with their current choices than the easy question results imply.

The Genesis research provides a valuable insight into the current factors determining school choice for parents at primary level. The top three factors

22   Pat Lyons, *Public Opinion, Politics and Society in Contemporary Ireland*. Dublin, Ireland and Portland, Oregon: Irish Academic Press, 2008.

indicated by parents were location, academic reputation and reputation for discipline. The Catholic ethos or denominational character of the school was of much lower and even of contradictory importance (Figure 3.2).

For example, only 44 % of parents rated being a 'Catholic school/had a Catholic ethos' as being 'important' or 'very important', but 57 % of parents indicated the ability for their child to 'make their sacraments' was key factor influencing their choice. There seems to be a disconnect in the minds of parents of the role of the sacraments in the faith life of their children. Only 42 % of parents rated 'some element of religious practice/faith formation' as being an important factor in school choice, which might point to a disentangling of communion and confirmation from the ongoing process of faith formation that Catholic schools offer. Tellingly perhaps, parents rated the ability of their children to receive their sacraments at the same level of importance as 'a focus on extra-curricular areas'. This may point to where these milestone moments sit in the minds of parents in the context of the broader faith formation offering of a Catholic school.

The contrast between what influences the choice of a school for parents and what they value once their child is attending the school is also telling. There is a practicality and utility around how parents approach school choice with a focus on convenience, academics and discipline. This gives way to a more values-driven appreciation of the formation that their children enjoy once in school. It may be the case that once a child is in school a deeper reflection occurs on the 'softer' qualities of education, beyond the academic formation that guides making the initial choice. If that is the case, then Catholic schools will have to think deeply about the balance they strike in advocating for their continued relevance.

Among the practices and activities highlighted by parents as being of most value to them and their children was an emphasis on developing a moral compass and fostering an ethical foundation and social conscience. The more Catholic or faith-centred practices like prayer and religious instruction were values at the lower end of the 'top ten' (Figure 3.3).

This preferential option for less explicitly Catholic elements undermines the unique value of Catholic schools, especially since the other leading patrons argue that this ethical rather than religious focus is central to their school models as well (see Chapter 5 on Educate Together

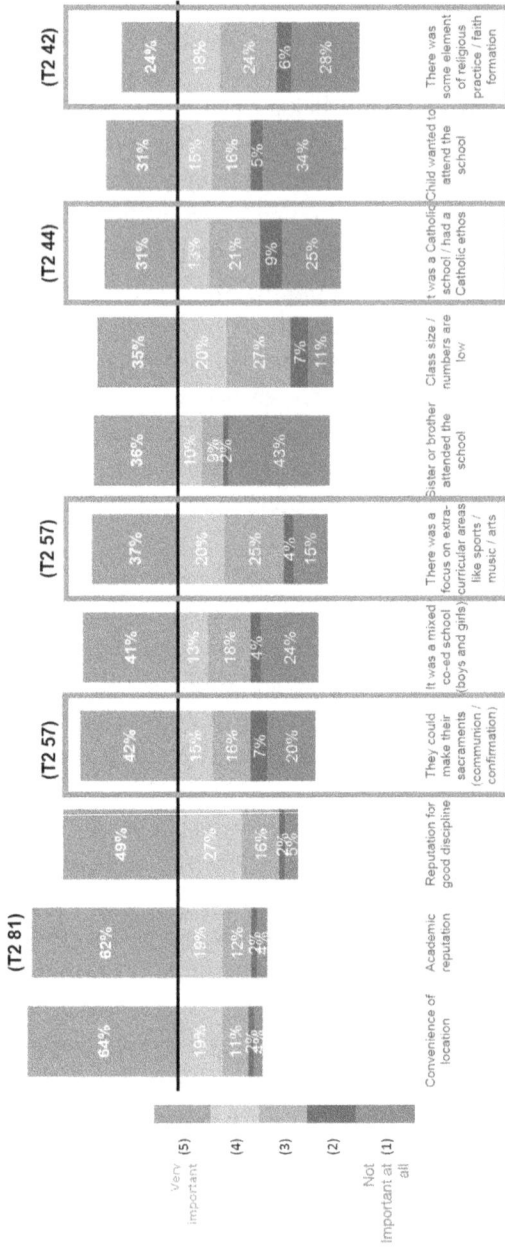

Figure 3.2. Factors influencing school choice for parents.

Genesis Report, 2021.

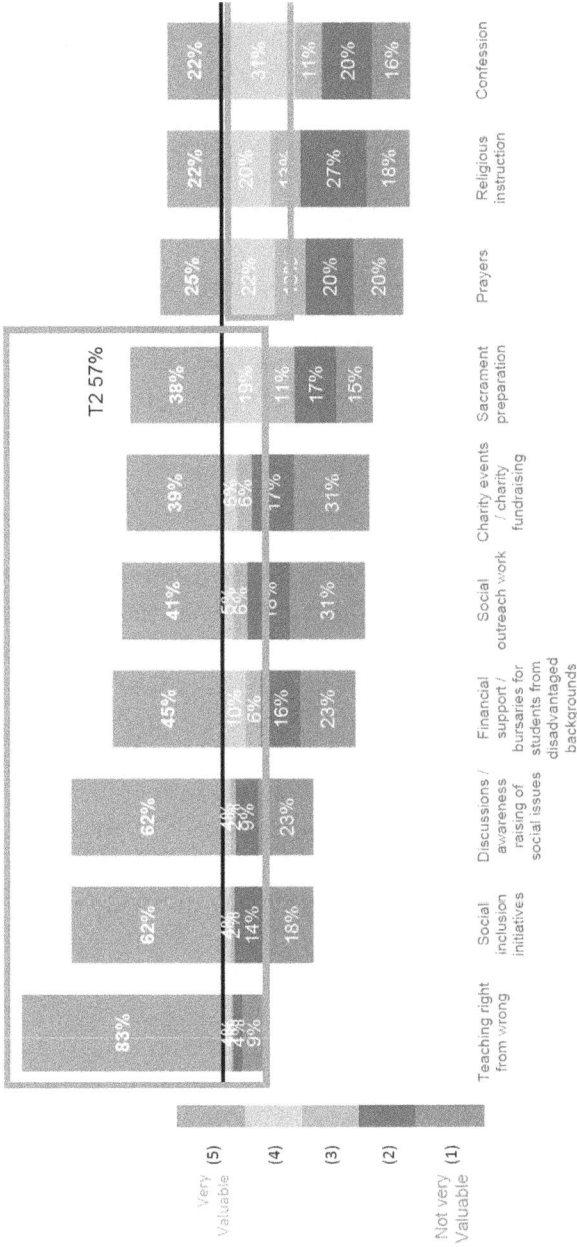

Figure 3.3. Practices and activities valued by parents in a school with a Catholic ethos.

Genesis Report, 2021.

and Chapter 6 on Community National Schools). Thus, a question for Catholic schools is how they will infuse these activities with their faith perspective to demonstrate a point of difference, particularly to the multi- and non-denominational providers. Furthermore, with clear a decline in the level of importance placed on broader religious practices by parents, it is unclear what this means for how Catholic schools talk about and brand themselves to a parent population that is more open to different school types for their children.

The question of what is the 'Catholic school advantage' was explored in the Genesis survey, and it is clear that Irish parents prize highly the moral development of their children. Parents cited a focus on respect, community and faith formation as the three leading advantages of Catholic schools. Interestingly, 'academics' were only cited as an advantage by 20 % of parents in the survey, which may have much to do with the high standard of teaching across the entire Irish primary system, irrespective of patron. Additionally, 20 % of parents thought that Catholic schools had an advantage due to their 'inclusion of students from all backgrounds'.[23] This result is interesting given that Catholic schools are often criticised publicly for not being sufficiently inclusive. Similarly, Educate Together often cites inclusivity as a distinguishing feature of its schools with the implicit suggestion perhaps that others, particularly the dominant Catholic schools, are less inclusive.[24] This view of Catholic schools as inclusive is backed up by a 2012 ESRI report that found Catholic schools to have greater levels of inclusivity than other patrons, when this is understood to encompass race, religion and socio-economic profiles.[25] For parents it would appear their experience of Catholic schools is one of inclusivity, mirroring a reality identified in the ESRI research.

Overall, parents with children in Catholic primary schools appear satisfied with the schools their children attend, although it is less clear what

23   *Articulating New Positioning of Catholic Education in Ireland*, 2021.

24   *Mission and Values*, Educate Together. Available at: <https://www.educatetogether. ie/about/values/>

25   *New Report on Diversity in Primary Schools in Ireland*, Economic and Social Research Institute, 23 October 2012. Available at: <https://www.esri.ie/news/ new-report-on-diversity-in-primary-schools-in-ireland>

is driving this satisfaction. The high quality of education provided in Irish schools, a general focus on teaching right from wrong, and simple convenience of the local school are all certainly factors. The degree to which the individual patronage of their schools is a key driver of satisfaction is unclear. For those advocating for Catholic schools, they cite their distinctive ethos as a factor, as do other providers. A series of five focus groups of parents of students in Catholic schools conducted on by Irish Episcopal Conference (IEC) in 2011 found that 'none actively expressed dissatisfaction' with their choice of a Catholic school and 'no participant expressed a wish for the ethos of that school to change'.[26] A more widely sampled survey by the IEC in 2008, while not backing up the universal consensus of the 2011 research, found that 58 % of parents questioned felt it was 'Important' or 'Very Important' that their school was under Catholic patronage, with just 14 % of parents surveyed indicating that this was 'Unimportant' or 'Very Unimportant'.[27] The 2021 Genesis survey data cited above confirms these findings to a large degree. Among the questions asked in this 2021 nationally representative survey was 'How satisfied are you currently with the school your child currently attends?' 79 % of respondents of primary school-going children indicated that they were 'Satisfied' or 'Very Satisfied' with their child's school, with only 17 % indicating dissatisfaction. On the face of it, given that the vast majority of these schools are Catholic the findings above might lead a passive observer of the Irish primary school system to agree with the IEC's analysis, articulated in the 2011 *Report on Catholic Primary Schools* that 'the Catholic primary school is still valid and valued today and its ethos and values remain relevant in modern Ireland'.[28] This belief of the Irish bishops was echoed again two years later by the Bishop of Kerry, Ray Brown. In his response to the 2013 parental surveys, Bishop

26   *Parental Understanding of Patronage*, Irish Episcopal Conference, 2011. Available at: <https://www.catholicschools.ie/download/parental-understandings-of-patronage/>
27   *Factors Determining School Choice*, Irish Episcopal Conference, 2008. Available at: <https://www.catholicbishops.ie/2008/04/01/factors-determining-school-choice/>
28   *Report on Catholic Primary Schools in the Republic of Ireland*, Catholic Schools Partnership, 2011. Available at: <https://www.catholicbishops.ie/2011/04/06/6-april-2011-catholic-schools-republic-ireland/>

Brown stated that 'in general terms, we saw it as a resounding affirmation of parental desire for denominational education'.[29] While there is some truth in these positive readings of the data, the reality is of course more nuanced. More importantly, what parents want is a more important aspect of determining demand within the educational sector. Overall parental satisfaction of existing schools may have more to do with the quality of academics, discipline and other factors rather than religion or religious ethos. This, too, complicates the reform debates. Many reformers want to make the problem about a lack of non-Catholic schools, but for many parents and families this is not a salient issue. Therefore, the mismatch between the policy problem and policy solution, especially in terms of divestment, helps explain the outcomes unfolding in Irish education reform.

V. The Nature of Demand for Change

There is a demonstrable demand for some change among parents at the primary level. This is borne out in several surveys; however, the degree to which this demand exists is contested on all sides, and it is not helped by large variation and contradictory data in many of the surveys conducted. The 2008 IEC survey on *Factors Determining School Choice* found that less than half (48 %) of parents would choose a school under the management of a religious denomination if all choices were available.[30] A survey a year later (2012) by the Irish Primary Principals Network (IPPN) found that only 23 % of parents surveyed would opt for 'a school owned and managed by a Church which provides for the instruction of its own religion'. In this, a more recent survey than the IEC's, the largest preference among parents (30 %) was for 'a school owned and managed by a

---

29   Michael Sheils McNamee, 'Here Is How Ireland's Bishops Responded to Being Asked to Hand over Their Schools', *TheJournal.ie,* 1 August 2016. <https://www.thejournal.ie/catholic-schools-divestment-ireland-religion-2876185-Aug2016/> (Accessed: 21 March 2021)
30   *Factors Determining School Choice,* 2008.

Vocational Education Committee (VEC) [now called Education and Training Board (ETB)] on behalf of the State'. The second highest preference was for 'a school owned and managed by a multi-denominational group, for example, Educate Together', with schools run by the Catholic Church and Church of Ireland pushed into third place in order of preference.[31] Again, these results conflict with the most recent Genesis survey in which a large percentage of parents (72 %) indicated that they had a choice of school and the school their child attends was their preferred choice. A further 25 % stated that the school represented the only option they had, with 4 % of parents indicating that they were not able to gain a place for their child in their preferred school.[32] The contradictory nature of the data, even within this one survey, is found in a later question in which, when asked if they would have chosen a non-denominational or multi-denominational school for their child had they the choice, 38 % of parents indicated they would have.

One reason for this dizzying level of contradiction within the data concerning the appropriate level of demand for change of patronage at primary level may be due to the term itself, 'patronage'. The IEC's *Parental Understanding of Patronage* report (2011) states that 'patronage is not a word widely known by parents; ethos or the inclusion of religious instruction is more likely to be the understanding of the Church's involvement in primary education.'[33] The report, tellingly, goes on to state that 'the local experience for their child's primary school education is pre-eminent. Systemic concerns with school governance are not centrally important in the parental relationship to their child's education.'[34] The adage about all politics being local in Ireland may be equally true of education in Ireland. The easy question for parents is whether there should be greater diversity

31 IPPN Primary School Research, March 2012. <https://www.ippn.ie/index.php/component/mtree/the-news/press-releases/3899-redc-poll-april-2012-patronage> (Accessed: 11 February 2021)

32 *Articulating New Positioning of Catholic Education in Ireland*, 2021.

33 *Parental Understanding of Patronage*, Irish Episcopal Conference, 2011. Available at: <https://www.catholicschools.ie/download/parental-understandings-of-patronage/>

34 *Articulating New Positioning of Catholic Education in Ireland*, 2021.

of school types available to parents. The hard question is whether they are okay with that change affecting their local school. At a national level, parents seem broadly to agree that there should be a greater degree of school choice (easy), but at a local level very few parents and school communities appear ready to alter their school's patronage – the hard part. Therefore (as we will see in the case studies of divestment in rural, commuter and urban contexts in Chapter 10), there is comfort with divestment at a national level, but when the reality of divestment at a local level becomes apparent, that is to say a possible change of patron in their local school, there can be unease and hostility. Parents, it would seem, agree there needs to be a change, just not in their school.

In 2018, the then Minister for Education, Richard Bruton TD, initiated a new round of surveys in sixteen identified areas as part a new approach to divestment called the 'Schools Reconfiguration for Diversity process'. Minister Bruton stated in a press release at the time that 'the new process will draw on the lessons from the previous model, such as the importance of live transfers and the downsides of having to await closures or amalgamations'. These surveys were part of the Minister's 'plan to deliver on the Government's target to reach 400 multi-denominational and non-denominational schools by 2030'.[35] The surveys were carried out in pilot areas identified by the sixteen local ETBs and conducted by the relevant City and County Childcare Committee on their behalf. The fact that the areas to be surveyed were selected by the ETBs and conducted under their auspices once again raised the issue of conflict of interest given that they are a potential beneficiary of the reconfiguration of denominational schools into multi-denominational schools. While the surveys were conducted during 2018, the results have yet to be made public even though the then Minister for Education, Joe McHugh TD, stated in a response to a January 2019 parliamentary question that the survey results would be published later that year.[36] The results have been seen by some of the key stakeholders

35   Press Release, Dept. of Education and Skills, 28 May 2018. <https://www.education.ie/en/Press-Events/Press-Releases/2018-press-releases/PR18-05-28.html> (Accessed: 11 February 2021).

36   Access at: <https://www.oireachtas.ie/en/debates/question/2019-01-30/114/>

in education, and the indications are that a significant majority of parents surveyed in most areas (75 %+) reported being satisfied with the current level of choice. Some in the Catholic education sector who have seen the data have shared, privately, a belief that the high degree of satisfaction articulated alongside some flaws in the survey methodology may be factors in the results not having been made public.[37]

The view of teachers in relation to the status quo and any potential reconfiguration is somewhat silent in the national conversation. They are, however, an important stakeholder in shaping Irish education policy given the strength of their union, the Irish National Teachers Organisation (INTO). The largest preference in relation to school patronage among teachers is for denominational schools, but the support for such schools is just 28 % (e.g. the Catholic Church).[38] This is followed closely by 27 % who favour a multi-denominational model with religious instruction outside the school day (e.g. Educate Together). The third largest preference is for multi-denominational schools with religious instruction during the school day (e.g. the Community National School model as it was originally conceived). Given the relatively even split in preferences outlined above, it is clear that, like among parents, there is broad agreement at a national level that greater choice should be available, with 80 % stating that parents should have a choice in relation to the ethos of their preference. However, deciphering a way forward based on the stated preference of those working in schools is unlikely to lead to a clear path to divestment or reconfiguration. While there has been a clear fall off in the level of teacher comfort with the place of religion in Irish schools, teachers still see a place for schools under religious patronage.[39]

The Irish primary school system is working well and enjoys high levels of satisfaction among parents. This is not necessarily a factor of the schools

---

37 In private conversation with the authors.

38 David O'Sullivan, *Religion and Ethos in Primary Schools*, Irish National Teachers Organisation, 2013.

39 According to the O'Sullivan/ INTO data teachers who teach RE willingly has fallen from 61 % in 2002 to 49 % in 2012. Similarly support for preparation of students for the sacraments within school has fallen from 66 % to 47 % in the same period.

being predominantly Catholic, as all schools are staffed by well-trained and committed teachers. They enjoy the same levels of funding, albeit most stakeholders will state that they are underfunded.[40] In this context, it is unlikely that one can expect a major push from parents to disrupt the system through a large-scale divestment process. Indeed, there is little significant evidence of a simmering discontent with the status quo among most parents. What is in evidence is a small but vocal minority of parents, along with stakeholders including Educate Together, Education Equality and some of the political parties on the left, who desire greater access to multi- and non-denominational education. This acceptance of the need for wider choice is also supported by the Catholic Church, the largest patron at primary level. What is less agreed upon, however, is a sustainable and agreed pathway for reaching a plurality of provision. The road ahead lies firmly with the views of the middle ground parents, those for whom there is an openness to plurality but not a burning desire to see it implemented if it affects them. The fight for who speaks for them and how powerful they are in moving the majority to some form of a tipping point remains a contested space in Irish education. In the interim, the Department of Education continues to drive the policy agenda, perhaps in time far enough to make such debate irrelevant. As we will explore in Section 3 of this book, those demanding a greater diversity of school types, as well as changes within existing schools under Catholic patronage, have had some success already. Such successes indicate that the Church's ability to influence what is happening in its schools is declining, and its once monopolistic control of Irish primary schools is disappearing.

40   <https://www.into.ie/2019/09/10/primary-schools-remain-overcrowded-and-underfunded/>

PART II

Key Actors in Primary Education Reform

.

CHAPTER 4

The Catholic Church and Education Reform

I. Introduction: The Multiple Layers of the Church as an Organisation

The institutional decline of the Catholic Church and growing secularism within the Irish population represent critical aspects of Ireland's unfolding modernisation. For centuries, the Irish Catholic Church provided the very DNA of Irish national identity – forging a culture of resistance to British rule. In the wake of the 'Devotional Revolution' in the late nineteenth century and the creation of a quasi-confessional state in the 1920s and 1930s, the Catholic Church permeated every aspect of Irish society through the twentieth century.[1] All meaningful networks of association, norms of behaviour and relationships of reciprocity – the essential elements of social capital – found their source and substance in the Church.[2] However, over the past several decades, the Church's dominance has waned significantly.

Education has been one of the most important areas of the Church's mission within Irish society, even as Ireland modernised. In the well-known book, *Moral Monopoly: The Rise and Fall of the Catholic Church in Modern Irish Society,* Inglis argues that the Church has always fought hard to maintain control of education in Ireland. For decades, it was treated as a mortal

---

1   Emmet Larkin, *The Historical Dimensions of Irish Catholicism.* Washington, DC: Catholic University of America Press, and Dublin: Four Courts Press, 1984.
2   See Robert Putnam, *Bowling Alone: The Collapse and Revival of American Community.* New York: Simon and Schuster, 2000, for a thorough definition and discussion of the concept of social capital.

sin for Catholics not to send their children to a Catholic school.[3] As modernisation and secularisation gained steam, there was a fear that once the Church lost control of education and religious leaders were no longer responsible for educating, disciplining, moralising and caring for Irish Catholics, adherence to institutional Catholicism in Ireland would rapidly decline.[4] In many ways, this fear has motivated many religious and lay leaders to defend the Church's role within education as a key, final stand before Ireland gives way completely to the forces of secularisation.

To better understand how the Catholic Church has responded to educational reforms in Ireland, it is important to think about what we mean when we discuss the Church. First, the multivocal and multi-layered nature of the Catholic Church in Ireland, and around the world, is often overlooked. In contrast to many Protestant denominations that are highly decentralised, the Catholic Church is perceived as being extremely hierarchical. Hence, the 'Home Rule is Rome Rule' chants used in Northern Ireland for generations to decry any attempts to create a united Ireland that might come under the influence of the Vatican. Yet, the Church is not a unitary actor; instead, it is best conceptualised as a complex institution consisting of many layers and actors that do not always act in concert. The pope, bishops, priests, lay pastoral agents, lay Catholic leaders and parishioners each have their own interests and role in maintaining and interpreting how the Church best translates its teachings in the political arena. The Church acts similarly to other interest groups in trying to ensure its survival, increase its influence in politics and society (education, morality, tax status, etc.) and maintain control over its members.

Many scholars and media pundits nevertheless tend to focus on the hierarchical nature of the Church and miss the complex, loosely coupled organisation that it is. Even from the hierarchical perspective, various roles are often misunderstood or ignored. For instance, the pope as Bishop of Rome is primary among, but not over, his fellow bishops; hence, the pope's authority over the other bishops is not monarchical but is more a

---

3   Tom Inglis, *Moral Monopoly: The Rise and Fall of the Catholic Church in Modern Irish Society*, 2nd edn, Dublin: UCD Press, 1998, 58.
4   Inglis, 1998, 52.

'first among equals'. Ever since the doctrine of papal infallibility was declared in 1870, many scholars have exaggerated the pope's influence, which is limited to *ex cathedra* papal announcements of doctrine regarding faith and morals. Because bishops, pastors and individuals possess power and rights to themselves, the pope's influence ultimately depends on both the respect for his office and his ability to foster unity with people and offices in the Church. As leader of the Catholic Church worldwide, the pope also has a number of bureaucratic offices that support him in his efforts, which include the Roman Curia (administrative offices of worldwide Church); the College of Cardinals (official advisors); the Synod of Bishops (elected bishops of the world who consult the pope about issues affecting local churches); the Pontifical Commission of Vatican City (oversees the Vatican City nation-state); and the Vicar of Rome (responsible for administering the Rome diocese).[5]

At the next level of hierarchy, there are 4,700 dioceses worldwide – and 26 in Ireland – that are each placed under the authority of a bishop, who is appointed by the pope and has legislative, executive and judicial authority for ministries of sanctifying, teaching and governing in his diocese. Each bishop is a papal appointment, but every bishop has relative autonomous authority to conduct his diocese as he chooses. The pope can restrain the powers of a bishop in specific circumstances of more universal significance, but the pope cannot eliminate the bishops' authority. In addition, there are also more than 219,000 parishes worldwide – over 1,000 in Ireland – that are administered by parish priests who are appointed by the local bishop to be the sacramental leaders and administrators of a parish staff and councils. Increasingly assisted by lay administrators and pastoral associates, these parishes are the heart of the Church because this is where the Church lives out its mission through the individuals whose membership is necessary for the Church's existence.[6] In addition to these geographically organised ministries, there are dozens of religious orders that have historically responded to key needs within the Church, in particular education.

---

5   See Greg Miller, 'Financial Reporting in the Catholic Church', Harvard Business School, N9-104–057, 6 November 2003, 1–4, for a helpful overview of the Catholic Church's institutional structure.

6   Miller, 2003, 3–4.

As the numbers of religious orders have dramatically declined since the 1990s in Ireland, many religious orders have created trusts to ensure the founding legacy and ethos of their schools are passed on to lay Catholics who are increasingly entrusted with leading these institutions. Last, there are the significant numbers of lay Catholic associations and organisations that each serve different purposes and functions, but ultimately serve to unite and mobilise individuals within the Church. Again, these multiple layers, each with their own interests, are key to thinking about the changing role of the Catholic Church in Ireland.

A second key feature when thinking about the Church is that Church ideology and doctrine are not static beliefs, nor are the ways institutional Church leaders engage political systems. For example, whereas the 1864 papal encyclical *Syllabus of Errors* reacted against religious freedom and critiqued all forms of liberal democratic politics, one hundred years later Vatican II declared its support for democracy in its *Decree on Religious Freedom* and in some contexts has been an important institution for extending and consolidating democracy. In Ireland, there have been dramatic shifts in terms of how the institutional Church seeks to place its stamp on Irish politics. Indeed, there has been significant change since 1937, when the Irish Constitution began with the words 'In the Name of the Most Holy Trinity'! In 1953 during the debates on health legislation, Bishop of Cork, Dr Lucey noted that 'their [the bishops'] position was that they were the final arbiters of right and wrong even in political matters'.[7] By the 1970s, the bishops articulated that 'there are many things which the Catholic Church holds to be morally wrong, but it has never suggested should be prohibited by the State'.[8] In more recent campaigns in the 2010s, the bishops' voices were rarely heard. As the institutional Church's role and impact on Irish politics and legislation has evolved, other religious organisations and individuals have sought to insert their own influence on political outcomes. The Church's position was now just one among the many voices being heard.

7   Inglis, 1998, 80.
8   Statement from the Irish Bishop's Conference on Proposed Legislation Dealing with Family Planning and Contraception, 1978.

Later chapters will describe in more detail how the Church has responded to calls for divestment, admissions and curriculum reforms. However, to fully appreciate the Church's response, it is helpful to review the evolving landscape of the various organisations within the Church that have been seeking to provide, enhance and reform the Church's educational mission. Once we have a fuller appreciation of the multiple layers and actors within the Church seeking to influence education policy, the chapter then outlines the key obstacles to the Church responding to educational reforms in any real or comprehensive way. Chapter 10 will provide three case studies of how the Church has responded to divestment in rural, commuter and urban contexts. This later chapter illustrates how the multiple layers and actors within the Church help local interests and communities shape how the Church deals with divestment concerns. The triumph of the local that dictates Church decisions and implementation is similar to the broader syndrome within Irish society and politics where local relationships, ideas, concerns and vested interests bend outcomes towards their perspective.[9] In this way, the Church reflects and embodies trends that persist in almost every aspect of Irish life.

II. The Changing Landscape of the Church's Educational Organisations

Media commentary on the Catholic Church often represents the Church as a unified body that can be expected to act as one, implement or resist change as one, or assent to established principles as one. The media's reporting in relation to issues of perceived control in education, and more specifically divestment, likely reinforces this view in the minds of the general public, politicians and other civic actors. Headlines such as 'Citizens' Assembly should debate church control of education' and 'Church hands over just 11 schools despite diversity drive' exemplify such framing, with

9   Sean McGraw, *How Parties Win: Shaping the Irish Political Arena,* Ann Arbor: University of Michigan Press, 2015.

the focus on a singular 'Church' rather than on the reality of an interconnected network of Church actors.[10] The perception of a singular Church, however, does not match the reality of the Catholic Church, perhaps nowhere more than in the education sector. To understand why key issues relating to Catholic primary schools such as divestment, admissions and curriculum have played out as they have, it is important to fully understand the complex and interconnected Church context in which Catholic primary schools operate.

The mixture of national, diocesan and school-level organisations leads to overlapping roles and responsibilities within the educational sector. Given the strong sense of localism in Irish society and politics, it is not surprising that national organisations generally have more of a representative role, whereas the real locus of power rests with individual bishops. The primacy of the Irish Episcopal Conference (IEC), on all matters relating to Catholic education, through its Council for Education is worth noting. The Council 'articulates policy and vision for Catholic Education in Ireland, North and South, on behalf of the Episcopal Conference [and] it has responsibility for the forward planning necessary to ensure the best provision for Catholic Education in the country.'[11] Due the importance of collegiality among bishops all policies, including in education, that are adopted by the IEC must be passed with the agreement of all bishops.[12] At the local level individual bishops are the official patrons of primary schools, and therefore they own schools and oversee their governance. As mentioned in Chapter 2, this governance responsibility is shared by local boards of management in each school, who in turn are responsible for operational control of schools with principals (see Table 4.1).

In terms of understanding the role of 'the Church' in education, it is sufficient to know that these various layers of responsibility exist within the Church's educational sector. For those interested in more detail, the following sections outline the specific groups and bodies at the national,

---

10   Carl O'Brien, 'Citizens' Assembly Should Debate Church Control of Education', *The Irish Times,* 29 May 2018; Elaine Loughlin, 'Church Hands over Just 11 Schools Despite Diversity Drive', *Irish Examiner,* 15 May 2018.

11   <https://www.catholicbishops.ie/education>

12   Pope John Paul II, *Apostolos Suos,* 1998.

Table 4.1. Authority and responsibility within the Catholic primary school landscape

	Ownership	Representative	Management	Governance	Operations
Irish Episcopal Conference (IEC)		✓			
Catholic Education Services Committee (CESC)		✓			
Catholic Education Partnership (CEP)		✓			
Catholic Primary Schools Management Association (CPSMA)		✓	✓		
Association of Patrons and Trustees of Catholic Schools		✓			
Individual Diocese/ Archdiocese	✓	✓	✓	✓	
Religious Congregations	✓	✓	✓	✓	
Trust Companies	✓	✓	✓	✓	
Boards of Management			✓	✓	✓
School Leadership					✓

diocesan and school level that seek to fulfil the Church's educational mission. The various actors assume greater levels of responsibility depending on the task at hand. We will sketch out which actors have authority for ownership, representation, management, governance and operations in the primary sector. After this detailed section on the stakeholders within the Church sector, in the concluding section of this chapter we discuss the obstacles confronting the Church as it engages educational reform issues. A recurring theme in that final section of this chapter is the lack of coherence within the Church due to the prevalence of local dynamics and the inability of the multiple layers to align their interests and actions to provide a unified front in the face of calls for change.

A. Ownership of Catholic Primary Schools

The ownership of Catholic schools rests with one of three actors: a local diocese or archdiocese, a religious congregation, or a trust company operating on behalf of a single or many religious congregations. The vast majority (95 %+) of Catholic primary schools are owned by the diocese in which they are situated, with a smaller number being owned by, or under the trusteeship of, a religious congregation or a trust company. At secondary level, the situation is reversed as religious congregation(s) and/ or trust companies are patrons for the largest percentage of Catholic secondary schools. The establishment of trust companies began in a significant way in 2007 when five religious congregations, including the Presentation Sisters and the Sisters of Mercy, transferred ownership of 110 secondary schools to an independent lay company called the Catholic Education an Irish Schools' Trust (CEIST).[13] This trust was formed in response to dwindling numbers of vowed religious women and out of a desire to maintain the founding ethos and spirit that these religious communities had imbued their schools.[14]

---

13   The Loreto Sisters had transferred their primary and secondary schools to the Loreto Education Trust in 2003.

14   CEIST Charter. Available at: <https://www.ceist.ie/wp-content/uploads/2019/04/Ceist-Charter-Latest.pdf>

Since 2007, more religious congregations have adopted the trust company model. In some cases, individual religious communities transferred ownership of their schools. The Christian Brothers established the Edmund Rice Schools Trust (ERST) to own and operate its schools. In other cases, religious communities joined together to establish a trust to oversee their schools as was done by the fifteen congregations that established the Le Chéile Schools Trust in 2009. Most of these trusts do not operate primary schools – with some notable exceptions including ERST, which operates thirty-three primary schools out of its total of ninety-six schools, and the smaller Jesuit Education Trust that has three primary schools in its eight-school network. In the primary sector, the individual trust company is the legal owner of the school property, but the local bishop serves as the patron. This layer of complexity is not experienced at secondary level where these trustees act mainly, but not always, as both trustee and patron. While most congregations have now transitioned to the trust company model, it has not been universal as some congregations have continued to own their schools directly.[15]

Notwithstanding the presence of these trusts in a small percentage of primary schools, the vast majority are owned by the local diocese, with the bishop serving as patron of all Catholic schools in his diocese. The role of the patron includes the appointment of the board of management for each school, responsibility for the characteristic spirit (or ethos) of the school, ultimate liability for industrial relations, oversight and responsibility for financial matters and decisions on school status such as growth, amalgamation or closure.[16] The nearly 3,000 Catholic primary schools in Ireland all operate under this patronage model, but they should not, as referenced above, be viewed as one collective body. They are not controlled out of

15   Religious orders with small numbers of schools including the Vincentians and the Society of the Sacred Heart retain direct ownership of schools. Many are likely to transfer their schools to the trust company model in the near future, as the Society of Jesus did in 2021.

16   Department of Education, 'Patronage Assessment Report Primary Schools (2021)', February 2021. Available at: <https://www.gov.ie/en/policy-information/866bf0-establishment-of-a-new-school/#patronage-of-new-primary-schools> (Accessed: 2 November 2021).

one central office, rather responsibility for patronage rests in twenty-six separate dioceses, each headed by a different bishop.[17] Each bishop, acting as patron, has authority for the schools in his diocese, and the authority to close, amalgamate or divest any of these schools is ultimately his alone. Therefore, when it comes to the issue of the Church agreeing to divestment, it is not one decision, but rather twenty-six individual decisions made independent of each other.

B. Representative Structures in Catholic Education

The primary representative voice for Catholic education at a national level is the Irish Episcopal Conference (IEC). Under the Code of Canon Law, an individual bishop (as the appropriate ecclesiastical authority within a diocese), has responsibility for, among other things, giving consent for schools within the diocese to use the title Catholic School and to exercise oversight of these school.[18] Not surprisingly bishops often hold differing views on what is most important in fulfilling these responsibilities. Even when they agree, they often have diverse views on the best strategies to achieve commonly held goals. Although each bishop is autonomous in his own diocese, the quarterly meetings of the IEC enable 'the Bishops to exchange views and share their wisdom and experience in order to promote the common good of the Church in Ireland'. Furthermore, the IEC 'seeks to build effective consensus among the Bishops, thereby contributing to the unity of the Church'.[19] The IEC has several councils with responsibility for designated areas that report to it, including one for education. The Council for Education is made up of three bishops and 'articulates policy and vision for Catholic Education in Ireland, North and South, on behalf of the Episcopal Conference'. Furthermore, this Council

17   Two dioceses, Down & Connor and Dromore, are fully within the border of Northern Ireland and do not hold the patronage of any primary schools in the Republic of Ireland.
18   Code of Canon Law (1983). (English translation) The Canon Law Society Trust. London: Collins, 803–6.
19   <https://www.catholicbishops.ie/about/> (Accessed: 6 April 2021).

has responsibility for the forward planning necessary to ensure the best provision for Catholic Education in the country. It liaises with other Catholic Education Offices, the Department of Education & Skills … [and] advises the Conference on all Government Legislation as applied to education. It responds and acts as spokesperson for the Conference on issues related to the work of Education. It seeks also to develop long-term strategies in education for the Episcopal Conference.[20]

Since 2017, a delegation of the IEC meets annually with the Irish Government, under a structured dialogue process established by then Taoiseach Leo Varadkar, for a bilateral meeting on issues of mutual interest. Perhaps unsurprisingly given the Church's presence in the sector, education has been an item on the agenda of such meetings.[21] More regularly, however, the Council for Education engages officials from the Department of Education to discuss issues of common concern, including legislative and policy issues related to patronage such as divestment, admissions and curriculum, as well as practical matters such as investment in school buildings.

The bishops, despite their predominant place within the Church's educational policy hierarchy, are only one group among many that have formed over the last couple of decades to represent various religious communities and school leaders (see Figure 4.1).

Religious congregations have historically also performed key ownership and representative functions within Irish education. To facilitate cooperation among the multitude of religious congregations and bishops on a full range of educational issues, the Catholic Education Service Committee (CESC) was established in 2010. The CESC was initially composed of twelve members – six from the IEC and six from the leadership of the religious congregations (the Association of Missionaries and Religious of Ireland). The make-up of the CESC was reconstituted in 2021 to include two representatives of the trust companies and one representative from the Catholic third level sector.

---

20   <https://www.catholicbishops.ie/education/> (Accessed: 6 April 2021).

21   Irish Catholic Bishops Conference, 'Delegation of Bishops Meet the Taoiseach and Government Ministers', 31 August 2017. <https://www.catholicbishops.ie/2017/08/31/delegation-of-bishops-meet-the-taoiseach-and-government-ministers/> (Accessed: 6 April 2021).

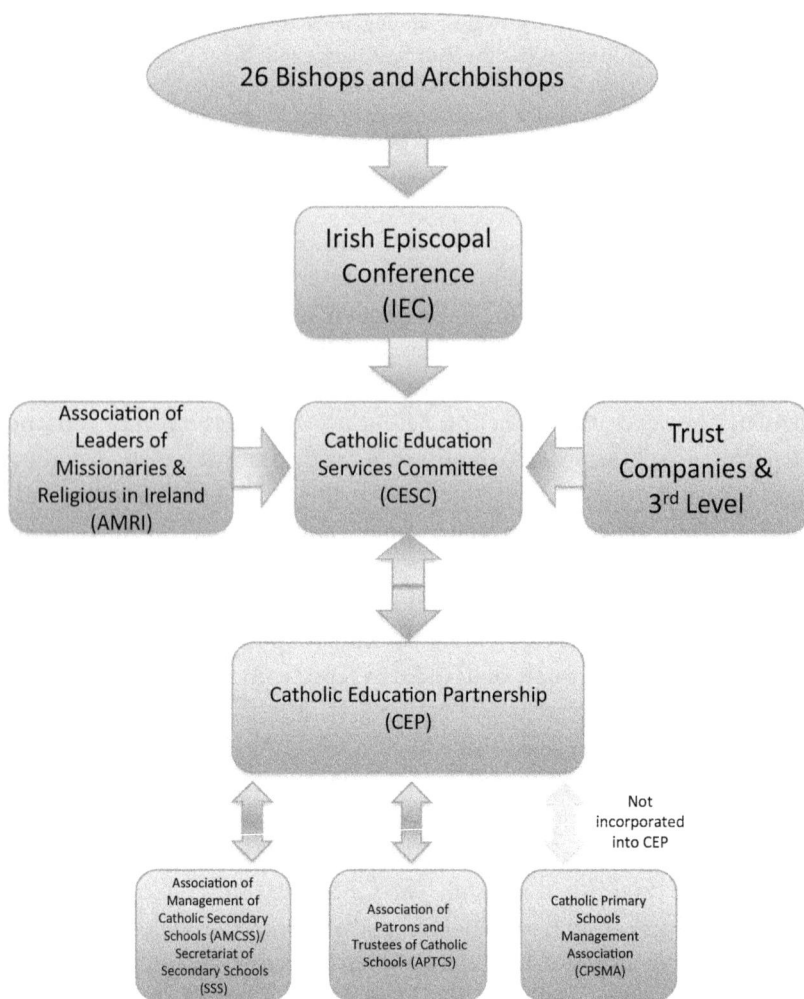

Figure 4.1. Overview of the representative bodies in Irish Catholic education.

To add more complexity to understanding the layers of voices and responsibilities, the CESC established the Catholic Schools Partnership (CSP) in 2010 to augment the representational role of the Church in the educational sector. The purpose of the CSP was to serve as an 'umbrella body providing strategic thinking on major issues facing Catholic schools', and it drew together twenty-two representatives of all the stakeholders in Catholic education on its governing Council.[22] Its aims were to foster coherence, provide a unified voice, support teachers in core activities of teaching and learning, and support governance, trusteeship and management. The CSP was originally led by a full-time executive chairperson, Fr Michael Drumm. However, when Drumm resigned this position in 2016, he was replaced by a part-time chief executive, who had the support of a part-time research officer. The reduction in staffing undoubtedly limited the ability of CSP to achieve its ambitious aims.

In 2020, the CSP was replaced by yet another body, the Catholic Education Partnership (CEP). This latest attempt to coordinate Catholic school efforts in the broader educational sector did not reduce the numbers of actors involved. It did, however, seek to bring greater coherence to the landscape between those involved in patronage and trusteeship of schools (dioceses, religious congregations and trusts) and those with responsibility for providing management supports to schools. The sponsoring body, CESC, hoped to achieve greater coherence by incorporating into the CEP, the Association of Management of Secondary Schools (AMCSS)/Secretariat of Secondary Schools (SSS) and the Association of Patrons and Trustees of Catholic Schools (APTCS).[23] The remit of the CEP includes all levels of education, primary, secondary, third level and adult education.

22 <https://www.catholicschools.ie/csp/> (Accessed: 6 April 2021).
23 For information on the APTCS see <https://www.aptcs.ie/> and for information on AMCSS/SSS see <https://www.jmb.ie/>.

It is notable that CEP does not currently include the Catholic Primary Schools Management Association (CPSMA) under its umbrella, which is the key management organisation that represents all primary school boards of management.[24] The CPSMA 'provides advice and support for principals and chairpersons of boards of management in over 2,800 schools. It collaborates with other management bodies and negotiates on behalf of these schools with the Department of Education and Skills and other education partners.'[25] Mirroring the existing patronage model at primary level, the CPSMA is organised at a diocesan level through elected diocesan councils, which feed in to a Provincial and Central (national) Council. A board of directors oversees the organisation, which is run by a professional staff. The CPSMA represents the patrons in providing management support to schools at a local level, but it also represents Catholic schools in negotiations with Government on a range of issues pertaining to school management. CPSMA does not have decision-making authority on an issue like divestment, which is made by local bishops. These efforts by various Church organisations to centralise and coordinate their efforts have largely been driven by the perceived need for the Church to better respond to evolving challenges from the State and society.

C. Management of Catholic Primary Schools

The Catholic Primary Schools Management Association trains and supports local boards of management throughout the country. This is a herculean task given that there are over 25,000 volunteers on these boards. These volunteers require significant support to help them fulfil their governance and operational oversight duties. One of the CPSMA's most

24   It is possible that the CPSMA may be incorporated into the CEP at a later date.
25   <https://www.cpsma.ie/about-cpsma/> (Accessed: 6 April 2021).

time-consuming roles is offering an over the phone advice service that principals and chairpersons of boards of management can access to obtain relevant legal advice and guidance on issues that arise in their schools. The team of experienced educators, many with school leadership experience, is headed by a general secretary, Seamus Mulconry.[26] According to Mulconry, one of the biggest challenges for both the CPMSA and Catholic schools more broadly is trying to sustain the Catholic ethos within schools. Many board members, chairs and principals lack significant theological training nor are steeped in rich Catholic experience, which makes it difficult for them to enhance the Catholic ethos of their primary schools. Add to this the exponential growth of the bureaucratic demands the State places on principals and boards of management, and it is no wonder, Mulconry contends, that school leaders are feeling embattled and with little time to dedicate to supporting the Catholic mission. It would take over 105 hours to simply read the twenty-nine circulars the Department of Education publishes annually; let alone the amount of time and expertise it requires to deal with State rules and regulations regarding everything from child protection and teaching hours to everything that small businesses are required to complete in terms of taxation and financial reporting.[27] It is the role of the CPSMA to support school principals and chairpersons in meeting these complicated realities.

D. Governance of Catholic Primary Schools

Another layer of complexity in the education context is the local governance responsibility for primary schools. In Ireland, that governance responsibility is vested in the local voluntary board of management by the patron. For Catholic primary schools, the bishop is the patron of all schools within the diocese, but direct governance falls to the local boards of management. The *Governance Manual for Primary Schools* states that

---

26   <https://www.cpsma.ie/whos-who/> (Accessed: 6 April 2021).
27   Seamus Mulconry, General Secretary of the Catholic Primary Schools Management Association, Personal Interview, October 2019.

'it is the duty of the Board to manage the school on behalf of the patron'. Furthermore, 'in carrying out this duty the Board is obliged to consult with and keep the patron informed of decisions and proposals of the Board. The Board is also accountable for upholding the school's characteristic spirit.'[28] Boards of management are appointed for 4-year terms and consist of eight members (two patron nominees, two parent nominees, the principal and one other teacher and two community nominees).[29] The board of management has responsibility for the hiring of staff in the school and is the employer of school staff, although teachers' and special needs assistants' salaries are paid by the Department of Education. Many schools employ a school secretary, caretaker and cleaners, either on a part-time or full-time basis with the board again as employer, with additional funding being made available through the Department, but managed locally by the school. Boards of management do not have the authority to make their school available for divestment if they decide that the local conditions merit it. As has already been established earlier, this authority continues to rest with the patron.

E. Operational Authority

A next layer of complexity is that each local board of management is tasked with managing the school, but they delegate this duty to the principal, who has the responsibility 'for the day-to-day management of the school, including guidance and direction of the teachers and other staff of the school, and is accountable for that management'.[30] The job of leading a primary school in contemporary Ireland is a complex one, where a principal's range of responsibilities includes leadership of teaching and learning, administration of finances and buildings, compliance with various Department of Education circulars and legislation, as well as promoting the school ethos. The growing number and complexity

---

28   *Governance Manual for Primary Schools 2019–2023*, Dept. of Education, September 2019.

29   One of the patron's nominees serves as Chairperson.

30   *Governance Manual*, 2019.

of demands that principals face is making it more difficult to attract the next generation of leaders.[31] In the context of an overburdened leadership, coupled with falling levels religious practice amongst staff, some principals report a lack of 'professional competence' in meeting the faith needs of their school community. A doctoral research study found that greater numbers of teachers and principals are seeking additional financial and pedagogical resources from their patrons to support the ethos in their schools.[32] However, a lack of resources and ongoing support from patrons often leaves individual schools up to their own devices to meet the concrete needs they are experiencing in their schools. This dynamic further consolidates the strong local character of education despite the presence of diocesan and national leadership directives and goals.

F. *Catholic Secondary Education*

The profile of secondary schools is more diverse with just under 50 % of schools under Catholic patronage.[33] The increased diversity of patronage at secondary level helps explain why more attention is directed at reducing the role of the Catholic Church within the primary sector. The profile at secondary also differs from the primary level in that many Catholic secondary schools are under the patronage of the lay Trust companies rather than the bishops. The Trust companies have established central offices which provide programmes and professional services to schools in their various national networks rather than serving schools within one diocese. Although the role of the Catholic Church in secondary education may

---

31 *Irish Schools Face Shortage of Principals as Role's Managerial and Administrative Duties Deter Teachers from Stepping up to Leadership Role*, Irish Primary Principals Network, 8 March 2017.

32 Elaine Mahon, 'Investigating the Perceptions of Primary School Communities in the Republic of Ireland Regarding Their Catholic Identity', Dublin City University, January 2017.

33 Catholic Schools Partnership, *Catholic Education at Second Level in the Republic of Ireland: Looking to the Future*, Dublin: Veritas, 2014.

become a bigger issue in the future, for now it seems to be a relatively uncontested space.

G. *Catholic Institutions at Third Level*

The Catholic education landscape at third level is much smaller than the primary and secondary levels, but it is involved in the formation of teachers for primary school and, thus, adds another voice among the many within the Church. The largest Catholic third level institution is Mary Immaculate College in Limerick, which has a satellite campus in Tipperary, and it is primarily involved in training primary school teachers. Marino College of Education in Dublin is also engaged in teacher training and is, following the incorporation of St Patrick's College of Education and the Mater Dei Institute of Education into Dublin City University (DCU) in 2016, the only Catholic third level institution in the capital city. As part of the incorporation, DCU established the Mater Dei Centre for Catholic Education. The activity of the Centre is complementary to the common programmes of DCU and includes input on the formation of teachers for Catholic primary schools through the Certificate in Religious Education. The other notable Catholic institution at third level is the Pontifical University, St Patrick's College in Maynooth, which is primarily involved in the delivery of theology and philosophy programmes, but also has a role in the delivery of Religious Education courses to student teachers in the adjacent National University of Ireland, Maynooth. All three of these Catholic third level institutions, plus the Mater Dei Centre, are involved in the formation of future teachers for Catholic primary schools. In this way, they are an important set of actors when considering issues of Catholic primary education.

H. *Concluding Thoughts on Catholic Bodies in the Educational Sector*

At a national level, the number of actors and the level of interconnectedness between them is quite significant. The various bodies have clearly delineated roles and responsibilities, with many of them interfacing with the State and the Department of Education on a range of issues. The desire of those in Catholic education to establish a more cohesive structure in support of Catholic trusteeship, patronage and management is understandable when one seeks to understand the range of actors currently involved.[34] The degree to which the current structures are fit for purpose notwithstanding recent efforts, through the establishment of the CEP, to bring coherence to the sector, remains unclear. What is clear however is that the perception of the Church as a single actor, responsible for and with the ability to direct the future of Catholic primary schools as it sees fit, is somewhat off the mark and misses the level of complexity and distributed authority across the system.

III. Obstacles to the Church's Response to Emerging Issues in Education

As the previous section underscored, there are many layers and actors within the Catholic Church in Ireland, especially within the educational sector. The strong sense of localism within Irish culture and politics, discussed further in Chapters 9 and 10, has been nourished by the experience of how the Church lives out its life in varied ways through its local incarnations. Therefore, despite the perceptions of wealth and shared beliefs and practices, the Catholic Church has lacked unity, resources and an overall will to address difficult issues in decisive ways during this time of dramatic transformation within Ireland and the Church.

The experience of divestment reveals these challenges within the Church. As Chapter 10 on divestment will discuss in greater detail, there is widespread agreement in Irish society and among the major educational actors and institutions that the Church should divest the patronage of many of its schools so there are real alternatives and choice for parents and

34 Marie Céline Clegg IBVM, 'Policy and Partnership', *Studies, an Irish Quarterly*, Spring 2019, Vol. 108, No. 429.

students. However, there are few individuals or organisations – including religious, secular and State leaders – that have any clear proposals or plans to implement the historic change required in the patronage of primary schools. Church leaders, including bishops and many religious communities, are willing to divest in principle, but no path to achieve this has been implemented on a sufficiently large scale to facilitate change.[35] The bishops have a formal meeting annually with the Taoiseach and the Department of Education and Skills, but it is then up to each diocese to develop their own approach to divestment and to maintain their own individual relationship with the Department of Education. There is little, if any, discussion across dioceses about how the Church could coordinate a plan on divestment because each diocese is its own patron.[36] This lack of cross-diocesan coordination and planning further fragments the Church's ability to speak with one voice. There is no question that increasing diversity of school types at primary level would benefit broader Irish society, especially the growing numbers of individuals from minority religions and who have no faith that are requesting access to non-denominational schools. Similarly, providing additional school types could also allow Catholic schools to more authentically live out and promote their ethos without fear of diluting their mission to meet the needs of growing numbers of non-Catholics in their schools. Yet, the incentives to divest are not in place at the local level.

Divesting is a risky business. The few places where change through divestment has been proposed there has been significant local opposition, sometimes for religious reasons, but also because few local communities have overwhelming and concentrated demand to force change in their local schools. As Chapter 3 described, although many parents may no longer practice their Catholic faith, they still desire the values of a Catholic school for their children, and many want their children to receive the sacraments. In this climate, it is no wonder that the bishops have not united to implement a plan to divest. Declining numbers in Church attendance and continued loss of confidence in the Church as an institution have weakened

---

35   Rev Paul Connell, Personal Interview, October 2019.
36   Monsignor Dan O'Connor, Education Secretary for the Catholic Archdiocese of Dublin, Personal Interview, July 2020.

the willingness of Church leaders to act decisively for fear of alienating those that remain active within the Church.

A primary challenge facing the institutional Church is that it lacks cohesion and speaking as one voice.[37] The lack of unity is even more important given the changes in society and calls for reform in the media and among civil society actors. Given the lingering effects of the sexual abuse crisis, many Church leaders feel under attack. As a result, many Church leaders are reluctant to speak on behalf of the Church within public debates on virtually any issue, including health and education. The lack of speaking as one voice means that it is difficult to respond quickly and coherently when challenges arise. The slow pace in responding, combined with inability to articulate a coherent policy approach, often leaves the Church lagging leading reform advocates who masterfully engage the media to advance their agenda. For example, the chapter on curriculum describes in more detail how ongoing, and often subtle, changes to the primary school curriculum being implemented by the National Council on Curriculum and Assessment (NCCA) may end up pushing Catholic schools to the point where they no longer are able to teach Religious Education, or integrate it across the curriculum in meaningful ways.[38] In addition to falling behind in the public debates, the lack of unity leads to local concerns overpowering national policies or approaches. Although the bishops are the patrons of nearly 90 % of primary schools across the State and religious communities in some cases owning the land and buildings of primary schools as their trustees, they rarely work together directly to generate a shared vision nor pool resources to meet concrete needs. Such collaboration, such as it is, is ceded to representative bodies that are significantly under resourced given the scale and needs of the network they represent. As a result, local dynamics, not a coherent national plan or vision, are what shape outcomes.

In addition to lacking coherence within the Church sector, the bishops and religious communities are facing declines in the number of religious personnel and financial resources. These declines translate into significantly

37   Rev Paul Connell, Personal Interview, October 2019.
38   Maeve Mahon, Coordinator for Primary Education in Kildare and Leighlin Diocese, Personal Interview, October 2019.

less numbers of people who are financially supporting the Church's educational work, and there is little history, culture or experience of philanthropy in Ireland due largely to a lack of personal resources, which also undermines Church finances. The increased strain on parish and diocesan finances imposed by the COVID-19 crisis has added additional pressures in this area. Therefore, at the very time when the Church needs to be channelling greater financial resources and personnel into the area of Religious Education and Catholic school leadership so that Catholic schools can provide a real model and alternative to Educate Together, Community National Schools and Irish-language schools, they are in dire straits financially.[39] The plethora of urgent issues facing bishops, including the ongoing fallout of the abuse crisis, declining vocations and legal and bureaucratic battles over property and personnel issues, often push education further down the agenda. This lack of urgency surrounding education also undermines cooperation and mutual support among bishops to divest schools and engage other educational issues.[40]

Leaders within Catholic education highlight how these financial challenges and lack of a sense of urgency make it difficult for them to reform the Church from within. Prominent educational leaders within the Church argue that they are fighting an uphill battle. There is a dearth of financial resources within the Church needed to train and educate Catholic school teachers, principals, boards and ultimately students and parents about how to authentically teach and live the Catholic ethos. Additionally, a perceived rise of financial and organisational support within the Department of Education for Educate Together, Community National Schools and Irish-language schools in recent years also siphons resources away from Catholic schools, further limiting the ability of Catholic schools to adapt to an evolving environment.[41]

In the past, the Catholic Church did not have to invest heavily in Religious Education and sacramental preparation because this always

---

39   Rev Paul Connell, Executive Secretary for Education to the Irish Bishops' Conference, Personal Interview, October 2019.

40   Bryan O'Reilly, Patrons' Secretary for Primary Schools in Kildare and Leighlin Diocese, Personal Interview, October 2019.

41   Maeve Mahon, Personal Interview, October 2019.

occurred in schools. Other religious denominations have decades of experience in creating Religious Education and faith formation programmes outside of schools because the needs of their followers required it. Educate Together and Community National Schools have been facilitating religious education and faith formation outside of school hours led by volunteers or paid educators for some time. Thus, it is only in the era of declining numbers of Catholics and the growing diversity of primary school patrons, that the Church has had to be more intentional about religious instruction and faith formation – both for its teachers and its students. Again, at the very time when resources are needed to support Catholic education, these resources are lacking, and the model is under threat despite its overall dominance in numbers.

Catholic school leaders identify several areas of reform within the Church to make their schools more authentically Catholic as well as capable of deepening their commitment to create diverse and inclusive schools. On a practical level, training young teachers who are increasingly less religiously literate is the first step that will require additional resources from the Church. Second, devising a new integrated curriculum for Catholic schools would require considerable time, personnel and resources, and few within the Church appear to be well positioned to do this. The alternative is that Catholic school educators and leaders must find ways to adopt the national curriculum and then tailor it for Catholic school contexts. This could be done, but it would require a more coherent approach and a proactive use of resources to build capacity among teachers, principals and parents.[42] Third, the patrons, or an agent acting on their behalf such as CPSMA, would need to financially support and resource boards of management so they can better prepare new principals, who also often lack religious training and formation, for the responsibility of leading a faith-based school. As seen in Chapter 2 on control, preparation of primary school leaders is directed by the State through the Centre for School Leadership and is non-denominational in ethos. Furthermore, building the capacity of voluntary boards of management for the role of selecting school leaders, who have the competence to lead teaching and learning as

42   Maeve Mahon, Personal Interview, October 2019.

well as be the pastoral leader of the school, is an area in need of strengthening. One leading educator highlighted that in her experience on several boards, there was no support or preparation when hiring a new principal, especially in terms of what it means to lead a Catholic school. In contrast, Educate Together provides a full binder, a course and administrative help to support the process of hiring a principal in their schools. For Dr Anne Looney, the Executive Dean of the Institute of Education at Dublin City University, the Catholic sector is lagging far behind Educate Together in this regard. Ultimately, Looney claims that this could lead to de facto divestment as Catholic boards become less prepared and their principals are less able to deliver an authentic Catholic education, thereby abdicating their leadership role in ensuring the ethos of Catholic schools.[43]

All these efforts require financial resources. For some within the Church, the issue greater than the lack of one voice, a coordinated response and necessary financial resources for training and on-going support, is a lack of will to take responsibility for religious education and faith formation in schools. According to Kate Liffey, former Director of Catechetics for the Irish Catholic Bishop's Conference, the Church needs to stop blaming everyone else for the challenges it faces and instead coordinate the work better. She argues that the Church is well positioned to shape the quality of Religious Education in its schools, but it must articulate what a Catholic school really is. Furthermore, Liffey argues that the Church must prioritise appropriate levels of financial and personnel resources to religious education. There are currently diocesan advisors in most dioceses, and they are tasked with overseeing religious education in all Catholic schools. However, recent research has pointed to the need for greater clarity in relation to the job description, the need for a full-time commitment (many are part-time), and an increase in initial and ongoing training and support.[44] In addition, there are often inadequate numbers to cover the large number of schools in a diocese. In county Dublin, for

43   Anne Looney, Executive Dean of the Institute of Education at DCU, Personal Interview, October 2019.
44   Catherine McCormack, *Using Visible or Invisible Maps? A Case Study of the Role of the Diocesan Advisor in Voluntary Catholic Secondary Schools in the Republic of Ireland*, Dublin City University [EdD thesis], 2020.

instance, there are 350 Catholic primary schools, served by just three diocesan advisors. In practice this means schools often go more than a year without a visit. As a result, it is unclear whether programmes and ideals established at the national or diocesan levels are sufficiently resourced to allow them to be implemented and practised at the level of individual schools. In contrast to the State's corps of inspectors that have high and clear expectations and the authority to sanction teachers and schools with sub-par performance and outcomes, diocesan advisors often have no clear mandate. As a result, these religious education leaders can sometimes be ignored by teachers and school leaders. This also undermines the bishops in their role as patrons. If Church leaders and their designated deputies on the ground are not taking seriously the importance of Religious Education, then it is unlikely that individual school leaders and teachers will place much importance on it either. Whereas in previous generations the Church could take for granted that followers would comply en masse, Liffey argues that the Church must now lead by persuasion and inclusion, convincing would-be followers that there is a clear and worthwhile model that exists within Catholic schools.[45] Thus, while the lack of resources is a real challenge for the Church, perhaps the greater challenge may be a lack of will to develop and implement a concrete strategy for religious instruction and faith formation in schools and parish communities.

The combination of this lack of a unified voice, resources and a coordinated will ends up placing the onus of responsibility and effort to reform on to local communities and schools. The fact that bishops and educational leaders within dioceses rarely coordinate and mutually plan their efforts reinforces the highly local nature of how the Church lives out its mission within Ireland.

The highly local nature of the Church affects how it responds to divestment. It is easy to criticise the Church's inaction on divestment and other areas of education reform. It has continually expressed its willingness to divest schools in principle, but it has not initiated, devised, or implemented a plan on any large scale throughout Ireland. The Church, in

45   Kate Liffey, former Director of Catechetics for the Irish Catholic Bishop's Conference, Personal Interview, October 2019.

this sense, is once again mirroring broader dynamics within Irish society whereby national and local experiences are remarkably different. It is one thing to support reform and the protection of individual rights, especially when it helps those who have been experiencing discrimination and alienation. It is quite another thing to support reform and change when it affects you, your family and children, and your local community in ways that may require sacrifice on your part. Everyone supports equality and inclusion in principle! It is more difficult to support these rights when your local school is being asked to change to benefit broader aspirations within society. Schools are deeply entrenched in local communities where they have rich histories and traditions, but where they are also evolving with the community as it changes too. The fact that Church is unwilling to upset local dynamics without the support of the community is virtually identical to politicians who are constantly defending local interests even if they must oppose their party or larger national trends. The State, too, has national goals, but often struggles to implement them equally in diverse settings throughout the country.

Therefore, the Church's deference to local interests and demands is consistent with the strong localism that pervades Irish society. This is not meant to exonerate the Church from any responsibility to reform, but it is to acknowledge that there are deeper, well-established currents within Ireland that influence how the Church addresses difficult issues during a period of dramatic shifts in society. The Church's highly decentralised nature within Ireland helps explain the lack of one voice, clear lines of accountability and willingness to undertake a costly and coordinated response. This fragmented experience of the Catholic Church also helps explain why national commitments and ideas are lived out in radically different ways depending on the local contexts in which Church leaders operate. A subsequent chapter employs case studies to illustrate how divestment has been addressed in urban, commuter and rural Catholic dioceses. These case studies demonstrate the highly localised nature of reform even within the Catholic Church.

IV. Conclusion

The Catholic Church has undergone a dramatic transformation in the last several decades. The Church was once the leading institution that helped forge a new national identity and undergird Irish familial, community and national life. The early Irish State depended greatly on the Church to provide education, health care and social services. In addition to relying on the Church as a leader in providing social services, the Irish State and broader society depended on the Church to be the moral compass for the nation. Much of this has changed in recent years. The combination of rapidly evolving attitudes and behaviours among Irish Catholics, growing numbers of non-Catholics and non-religious and a swift collapse of the Church's moral authority in the wake of the sexual abuse crisis have transformed the Church and Irish society. In an increasingly diverse contemporary Ireland, the Church is now just one group among many, albeit one that remains a significant stakeholder due to its ongoing ownership and oversight of large numbers of institutions.

In this context of rapid change, the Church is seeking to re-invent itself as a set of believers, leaders and institutions. As this chapter has highlighted, the Catholic Church in Ireland is a multi-layered and multivocal institution that has been reeling from its declining moral authority and place within Irish society. The multiple layers and voices create a lack of unity and an inability to establish a coordinated voice in response to changes in society challenging the Church's ability to maintain its leadership role in the educational sphere. The declining numbers of religious personnel and financial resources have also undermined the Church's ability to provide educational leadership during this time of change. Growing divisions within the Church and broader society have also made it difficult to establish a coherent vision for what the Church's role should be in the educational sphere. The uncertainty of what an authentic Catholic school should look like and how it should live out its ethos have led to highly charged debates among various stakeholders at the national and local levels within the Church.

An overwhelming sense of loss pervades how many leaders and people within the Church are reacting to this period of unprecedented change.

The loss of status, influence, numbers, resources, moral authority, national identity and overall sense of itself as a community of believers makes it difficult for Church leaders to offer hope and clarity. Bishop Tom Deenihan of Meath, a leading voice in the Bishops' Conference on education, has argued consistently that the Church must prepare its students and families to live within a more diverse, modern Irish society. To do this, Deenihan suggests that the Catholic Church must create a vision for its schools, but the Church must also commit to increasing the diversity of patrons, otherwise Catholic schools will be Catholic in name only. He describes divestment of Catholic schools as one key step to meet this change, but he also fears that this is a further nail in the coffin of the Church within Ireland if remaining Catholic schools are not permitted to be authentically Catholic. 'Divesting, as painful as it may be, might be comparable to sacrificing the limb to save the body. At this stage, we need the Minister [of Education], to reassure us that the painful operation of divesting will actually save what remains.' Deenihan concludes that 'radical intervention, brave decisions and new treatment' are needed otherwise 'all will be lost'.[46] Thus, there is a palpable realisation within the Church that change is necessary, but this coexists with the fear that any change will further undermine the Church's future ability to shape the lives and institutions entrusted to its care. Irish Catholic education may benefit from recent insights in England, where there is a 'renewal of the concept of partnership to include church, *school* and state, as well as re-visioning how *all* Catholic educators contribute to the narrative of Catholic education, fit for purpose in the twenty-first-century world'.[47]

The Church, perhaps for the first time since the founding of the Irish Free State in 1922, understands what it means to experience loss. Ironically, certain demographic groups within Irish society, such as ethnic and religious minorities, women and LGBTQ individuals, have been experiencing loss, distrust and mistreatment for decades and have only recently had their

---

46   'Our Schools Need the Freedom to be Truly Catholic', *The Irish Catholic*, 31 October 2019, <https://www.irishcatholic.com/our-schools-need-the-freedom-to-be-truly-catholic/> (Accessed: 1 March 2021).

47   Margaret Buck, *Renewing the Church-State Partnership for Catholic Education, Engaging with the Challenge of Academisation*, Oxford: Peter Lang, 2020, 2.

experience recognised and protected. Experience in other countries has shown that periods of significant social change accompanied by increased diversity can lead to lower levels of trust not only across different social and demographic groups, but within them too. In the United States, for example,

> inhabitants of diverse communities tend to withdraw from collective life, to distrust their neighbours, regardless of the colour of their skin, to withdraw even from close friends, to expect the worst from their community and its leaders, to volunteer less, give less to charity and work on community projects less often, to register to vote less, to agitate for social reform *more*, but have less faith that they can actually make a difference, and to huddle unhappily in front of the television. Note that this pattern encompasses attitudes and behaviour, bridging and bonding social capital, public and private connections. Diversity, at least in the short run, seems to bring out the turtle in all of us.[48]

Given Ireland's growing diversity, and the pace with which such change has occurred, it is not surprising that there has been growing distrust towards the Church and within the Church. The sense of change and loss, as well as the significant reimagining and adapting that these shifts elicit, underscore the uncertainty of the contemporary period. It will be helpful to keep these realities in mind when reading subsequent chapters to more fully appreciate how the various actors, institutions and communities within the Church are seeking to respond to calls for change.

---

48   Robert Putnam, '*E Pluribus Unum*: Diversity and Community in the Twenty-first Century', *Scandinavian Political Studies*, 2007, Vol. 30, No. 2, 150–1.

CHAPTER 5

Educate Together

I. Introduction

The Forum on Patronage and Pluralism in 2011, which is discussed in greater detail in Chapter 10, ushered in a period of renewed calls for reform in Irish primary schools. To fully understand the changes that led to this more recent period, it is enlightening to examine the rise of Educate Together; originally a group of parents seeking to create a non-religious educational experience that has now become Ireland's leading multi-denominational school patron. Outside the Catholic Church, Educate Together is the largest single influence in Irish primary education over the past forty years. President Michael D. Higgins extols and legit-imises Educate Together's place at the heart of the educational system and Irish society: 'There can be no doubt, as a society, we have travelled far from the Ireland of 1978 when the Educate Together movement first took root. Today, that pioneering vision has taken its rightful place in our edu-cational system, growing, flourishing and enabling a further generation of citizens to benefit from the generous and participative ethos which defines Educate Together.'[1] In addition to this presidential endorsement, by 2020, most political parties and members of the media paint Educate Together as the beacon of hope for Irish schools and educational reform more broadly.

Despite its 'star status' in the contemporary period, Educate Together has developed slowly, incrementally and practically over the last forty years, and it has had to overcome significant obstacles. It is instructive to recall the critical steps leading civil society organisations in Ireland have taken in

---

1   <https://www.educatetogether.ie/about/history/> (Accessed: 6 August 2020).

the previous same-sex marriage and abortion campaigns to better understand Educate Together's mission and strategic development. First, like
other civil society groups, the founders of the Educate Together Movement
had a vision for an Ireland with vastly different values, laws and systems
than what existed in Ireland in the 1970s. To counter the strength of the
Catholic Church and the entrenched bureaucracy that undergirded Ireland's
denominational educational system, Educate Together had to articulate
a bold vision, but started small and locally to prove that this alternative
model was possible and that it would not undermine the current denominational system. The founders sought to convince the broader public that
this project 'in no way threatens the rights or interests of those who wish
to have denominational education for their children, and indeed not one
of the Regulations for National Schools would have to be changed to accommodate a school along the lines they have suggested.'[2] Second, Educate
Together had to build on its founding vision and ideology by establishing
an effective national organisation. This organisation helped establish new
schools first at the primary level (1978), then at the post-primary level
(2014), and have been seeking to influence teacher training at third level
(2018). Additionally, Educate Together slowly, strategically and methodically reduced the barriers to educational reform through influencing key
legislative changes regarding patronage, funding for school land and property, admissions and enrolment policies and even curriculum. As the movement demonstrated the effectiveness of its schools and ability to deliver
a strong educational experience, it started to attract media attention and
political party support, all of which combined to slowly shift hearts and
minds about how the system as a whole could change. After forty years
of chipping away, Educate Together may be on the verge of creating the
tipping point necessary to lead to more systematic change. Its rhetoric of
equality has struck a chord among many within Irish society in similar
ways that ultimately led to radical change in same-sex marriage and abortion legislation.

---

2   Áine Hyland with Desmond Green, *A Brave New Vision for Education in
     Ireland: The Dalkey School Project 1974–1984*, Áine Hyland self-published, Dalkey,
     2020, 37.

II. Birth and Development of a Model

Although Educate Together's history has become well-known, it is worth reviewing its growth as a school model and essential civil society actor. Educate Together started, as many movements do, with a few parents who wanted something different for their children and who were willing to fight for it. After the 'integrated curriculum' was established in 1971, it was difficult for parents who did not want their children to be exposed to faith-based values or to take religious instruction courses to find a school free of these influences. Given the constitutional right for parents to oversee their child's education (Article 42.3.1), this original, highly motivated group of parents wanted to provide an education that was not rooted in any particular denomination or religious philosophy. In seeking a 'less pervasive' school ethos, the parents first enrolled their children in a Church of Ireland school in Dalkey, a beautiful seaside south Dublin suburb, in the mid-1970s. Growing enrolments at St Patrick's National School led local Church of Ireland leaders to restrict admission to students of Church of Ireland faith or other Protestant denominations, which fuelled parents who were desirous of a multi-denominational school experience for their children to work even harder to form a new school.[3] By 1978, the Dalkey School Project established a multi-denominational, co-educational school that focused on a child-centred pedagogy and had a managerial body that was democratic in character. These founding principles remain at the core of Educate Together's mission.[4] Thus, the focus on equality and the right to non- or multi-denominational education has been essential to the Educate Together mission from the outset.

The Dalkey School Project inspired imitation in other parts of Dublin – first in nearby Bray in 1981 and then again in North Dublin in 1984. In that same year, Educate Together was formed as the umbrella organisation to represent the interests of this emerging sector. Over the

3   Hyland and Green, 2020, 33–8.
4   John P. Lalor, *Educate Together: An Inclusive Response to the Needs of a Pluralist Ireland?*, PhD thesis, Dublin City University, Dublin, Ireland, January 2013, 22–3.

next six years, Educate Together developed its Charter, which served as the template for this new model. Although the instinct of the founders was to seek a non-denominational education, the 1971 curriculum guidelines integrated secular and religious curriculum and assumed that a denominational ethos would permeate the day. This 'effectively meant that all primary schools were denominational in ethos'.[5] Thus, Educate Together had to work within the existing system, but it also sought to be different.

Educate Together's four guiding principles helped establish it as an alternative school model to the predominant Catholic school model. These four principles were and continue to be: multi-denominational, co-educational, democratically run and child-centred.

First, if it had to be denominational, Educate Together decided to be multi-denominational, and they advertised that their schools would teach students of all faiths and none. The Dalkey School Project conducted a survey in 1976 of local residents to determine the levels of support for the proposed school's three main elements: co-educational, multi-denominational national schools under democratic control. After weighting the results based on the 1,900 adults that completed the survey (816 of which were parents of young children) and the number of non-respondents in the area, 64 % of all adults and 68 % of all parents reported a preference for multi-denominational national schools, 78 % of adults preferred co-education, and 73 % of adults preferred democratic control. These results encouraged the Dalkey School Project leaders that there was sufficient demand for this new school model.[6]

Not everyone was pleased with the proposed multi-denominational approach. During the founding era, Ireland was still overwhelmingly Catholic in name and practice, as over 90 % of Irish citizens were Catholic, and roughly this same percentage reported attending mass weekly at that time. Some Catholics at the time believed the multi-denominational mission was an attack on the Church and the status quo. A report on one of the early Dalkey meetings in 1975 described 'the threat posed by multi-denominational schools to the traditional upbringing of our children.

5   Lalor, 2013, 115.
6   Hyland and Green, 2020, 260–5.

The result being that the State could dictate the philosophy to be taught to our children. This means, as happened in other countries, that the State sponsors courses on Marxism and other subversive subjects.'[7] Other reports at the time indicated fears of atheism: 'Atheistic interest in the Dalkey School Project is clear. Ireland's system of education is denominational by Constitutional guarantee. "We submit that there is no need for such a school as this which can only be divisive. It can only be hostile to religion in an age when it was never more needed... Dalkey could be a precedent for major trouble in other areas." '[8] At that time, most Irish would have defended the Church against attack and proposals to undermine its authority.[9] It was not until the mid-1990s when the child sexual abuse scandal initially emerged, and then with growing frustration and anger over the institutional Church's handling of this abuse over the subsequent decades, that there were increasing calls for a diminished role of the Church in education. By the twenty-first century, Educate Together had consolidated its multi-denominational ethos. Furthermore, as public support for equality within Irish society gained momentum, so too did support for Educate Together. Curiously, the 2015 Annual Meeting voted to replace multi-denominational in the Charter because it was increasingly misunderstood and replaced it with the term 'Equality-based' education. Since then, the descriptive terms 'Equality-based' and 'Equality and Human-rights-based' have been used in all the organisation's public statements.[10] This change occurred at the same time Ireland's same-sex marriage referendum was in full swing and 'equality' was the driving sentiment gaining steam among growing sections of Irish society.

7   Deaghlan O. Torain, 'Letters to the Editor: Subversive Marxism', *Irish Press,* July 18, 1975. <https://archive-irishnewsarchive-com.proxy.bc.edu/Olive/APA/INA.Edu/SharedView.Article.aspx?href=IPR%2F1975%2F07%2F18&id=Ar00811&sk=AC63C5C4> (Accessed: 7 August 2020).

8   'Educate Together Now Country's Fastest Growing Educational Movement'. *Irish Independent*, 17 September 2008.

9   Tom Inglis, *Moral Monopoly: The Rise and Fall of the Catholic Church in Modern Irish Society*, 2nd edn. Dublin: UCD Press, 1998.

10 <https://www.educatetogether.ie/news/lively-engagement-at-educate-together-agm-2015/> (Accessed: 6 August 2020).

Second, all Educate Together schools are co-educational. This was not the norm in the 1970–80s. In 1976, only 46 % of primary pupils were taught in co-educational classrooms, whereas by 2020, this number was up to 89 %, with 91 % of all Catholic primary schools now teaching in co-educational contexts.[11,12] Therefore, at its founding, Educate Together was once again positioning itself to be different and appealed to parents who wanted a different experience for their children. According to Educate Together, they believe that co-educational schools do a better job of encouraging students to explore their full range of abilities and opportunities.

Third, Educate Together schools are democratically run with active participation by parents in the daily life of the school, whilst positively affirming the role of teachers.[13] Similar to primary schools under other patrons, parents became involved through participation on committees and Boards of Management of schools, where there are two parent representatives. Since its founding, Educate Together schools have sought to involve parents in every aspect of learning, community building, extra-curricular activities and administration. The very existence of the original schools depended on parental advocacy, and their charter sought to institutionalise this partnership of parents with the professional educators in the schools. In practice, once schools are established, parental involvement appears to revert to more normalised levels of interaction even though the organisation prides itself on this aspect of its model. For example, a '2012 ESRI report indicated that levels of attendance at formal parent-teacher meetings were high across all school sectors (Catholic, minority faith schools and multi-denominational schools) and the extent to which parents approached

11   See Muiris O'Connor, 'Sé Sí, Gender in Irish Education', Department of Education (2007). Available at: <http://www.sdpi.ie/other_des_publications/des_stats_ SeSiGender_in_Irish_Ed_contents_overview.pdf> and Central Statistics Office, (Accessed: 2 November 2021).

12   Available at <https://www.gov.ie/en/collection/primary-schools/> (Accessed: 27 January 2022).

13   Educate Together, 'Ethical Education at Primary Level', 2021. Available at: <https:// www.educatetogether.ie/about/ethical-education/primary/> (Accessed: 2 November 2021).

teachers informally to discuss their child was higher in minority faith and multi-denominational schools than in Catholic schools.'[14]

Educate Together schools sought to portray themselves in stark contrast to the hierarchical nature of the Catholic Church and schools by emphasising their democratic and participatory culture. Fostering democratic participation and a focus on equality among all students, parents, teachers, staff, etc., are at the heart of the Educate Together model. Parents work together with teachers and staff on the Board of Management, the Parent-Teacher Association and ad hoc parent-teacher committees that address various issues within the school. Boards of management in Educate Together schools, like those in other primary schools, are responsible and accountable for upholding the characteristic spirit of their patron. The difference from Catholic schools is that 'Educate Together maintains an ongoing dialogue with its members on how such accountability should best be implemented in keeping with the organisation's commitment to participatory democracy'.[15] Furthermore, children are encouraged to have a voice in different aspects of the school. 'Examples of democratic practices in the schools included situations where children were often involved in making group decisions, in evaluations, in determining the direction their learning took and were involved in devising procedures for classroom management and models of positive behaviour.'[16] More recently, Educate Together schools have learned from the experience of Latin American schools that have moved away from student council elections to a practice whereby students are selected by lottery. All students are expected to exercise a position of responsibility in the school, which also teaches and inculcates good citizenship traits.[17] In each of these varied ways, Educate Together

14   Merike Darmody, Emer Smyth, and Selina McCoy, *School Sector Variation among Primary Schools in Ireland*, Dublin: Economic and Social Research Institute (ESRI), 2012, 48.
15   <https://www.educatetogether.ie/app/uploads/2019/01/Educate-Together-Patronage-Manual.pdf> (Accessed: 6 August 2020).
16   Lalor, 2013, 5.
17   Paul Rowe, former CEO of Educate Together, Personal Interview, October 2019. Rowe started his work for Educate Together as a volunteer in 1988 when his eldest son started in the North Dublin National School Project NS. He was elected Secretary of Educate Together in 1996 and became Chairperson of its first Board

schools seek to embody their democratic nature and, once again, position themselves in opposition to how things are conducted in Catholic schools.

The democratic and participatory culture is an ideal that can be difficult to fulfil in practice. The biggest challenge to fully implementing democratic principles is that the demands on the school and principal are so high, and there are such high expectations to deliver a strong education whilst meeting growing state bureaucratic requirements, that principals must increasingly act decisively on their own. A recent study of Educate Together suggests that 'it is worth considering whether it is always possible to manage and run large, complex organisations such as primary schools in ways that abide by meaningful democratic and participative principles. The evidence from this research is inconclusive in that regard.'[18] An additional challenge is including representatives of immigrants and foreign nationals and, to a lesser degree, low-income families. Despite growing numbers of students from different nationalities in Educate Together schools, evidence suggests that there is a lack of representation of these multitude of nationalities on boards of management and committees. Most parent leaders and community representatives are White and Irish-born. Principals interviewed in the study spoke about the difficulties involved in securing meaningful parental involvement for reasons of language and cultural barriers, restrictions on engagement on religious grounds, class and even being new to the community. 'All of these reasons militated against parental involvement at this level in the schools. This is an issue for the Educate Together network given their espoused and clearly articulated commitment to parental involvement.'[19] Despite these real and important challenges to fulfilling its democratic ideals, Educate Together works hard to position itself as different from other schools based on its participatory and non-hierarchical structure.

The fourth guiding principle is a child-centred approach. Ironically, all Irish primary schools have a 'child-centred' approach in their pedagogy

---

of Directors upon its establishment as a limited company in 1998. Paul oversaw the establishment of the full-time National Office in 2002 at which time he was appointed the organisation's first Chief Executive and he served in this role until 2020.

18   Lalor, 2013. 137.
19   Lalor, 2013, 133–4, 175.

and curriculum. However, Educate Together has monopolised this type of language, which is another sign of how strong their brand has become. The philosophy and practice of the Educate Together model is to provide inclusive, intercultural education where difference is celebrated and where no child is an outsider. All children have equal rights of access to the school, and children of all social, cultural and religious backgrounds being equally respected and co-educational and committed to encouraging all children to explore their full range of abilities and opportunities.[20] According to Paul Rowe, founding CEO of Educate Together, 'The idea is to transform the learning experience of all, of the way in which individual children are treated, and no child chooses their parents, their social background, their ethnicity. And so children fundamentally should not be treated differently or marginalised based on their background, whether that's ethnic, social or religious.'[21] He adds, that teachers and parents alike consider Educate Together schools as liberating environments in which they can be themselves as they serve the individual needs of their students. 'Teachers can teach to the educational needs of the children, whatever that is. They can very consciously treat children of different religious backgrounds equally, which increasingly lots of young teachers see as an absolute critical social deliverable in the education system.'[22]

There are several concrete practices that Educate Together schools do to support this underlying principle of a child-centred approach. In addition to the previously mentioned ways children are included in democratic decision-making in their classrooms and the school as a whole, there is constant focus on treating students as individuals. First, there are no school uniforms, which is different from most other Irish primary schools. Not only does this eliminate the need for costly uniforms that may low-income families and immigrants cannot afford, it also symbolises the importance of individuality. Second, students call their teachers by their first name. According to Rowe, 'What we've learned is that both those things acknowledge the individuality of the child or the learner. But it also creates, if you

---

20   Lalor, 2013, 4, 26.
21   Paul Rowe, Personal Interview, October 2019.
22   Paul Rowe, Personal Interview, October 2019.

like, a family or a big sister/big brother type of environment between the teacher and the taught. And that's one of the things which we have found, tested and our movement as a whole has adopted.'[23]

The most important way Educate Together schools fulfil their child-centred mission is through their Ethical Education Curriculum. From its founding, the original leaders implemented a curriculum that sought to move away from a denominational orientation where religion was infused into every aspect of the school day and curriculum. The Dalkey School Project founders believed that 'the decision to teach a child religion belonged firstly to that child's parents or guardians' and that each school management committee in multi-denominational schools would determine what form religious education would take so that it would reflect with the wishes of parents and the principles of the school.[24] The Educate Together core curriculum contains four key elements: Moral and Spiritual Development, Justice and Equality, Belief Systems and Ethics and the Environment.[25] Critically important within this approach is that Educate Together promotes religious diversity by teaching about the major religions of the world without promoting any one denomination. Additionally, by linking the curriculum to a regular practice of celebrating festivals, holidays and other traditions of various religious, Educate Together schools seek to enhance 'the links between religious and cultural expression and the development of children's identities. This *(approach)* values a range of identities and attempts to dispel preconceptions and prejudice.'[26]

As part of this core principle of providing a child-centred education that promotes and celebrates individuality, Educate Together schools promote diversity, inclusion and equality. What started in the 1970s to deal with the integrated curriculum in a non-religious – or multi-denominational – way, and thereby consolidate itself as an alternative to Catholic schools, has become a model with broad appeal in Irish society in 2021. A parent of a student in an Educate Together school captured this sentiment of wanting to see this model implemented across Ireland. 'Just

23   Paul Rowe, Personal Interview, October 2019.
24   Hyland and Green, 2020, 273.
25   <https://www.educatetogether.ie/about/ethical-education/>
26   Lalor, 2013, 26–7.

the way the children learn about different things and they learn to respect different cultures and religions in a positive manner. And to be confident in their own beliefs as well. Or where they come from. So, I would like to see that in every school in Ireland. I think schools in general have a very important role in that and the ethical curriculum that Educate Together have is quite a model for it.'[27]

The implementation of a new curriculum during a time of rapid social, economic and cultural change has not been without challenge. From its inception, *Learn Together,* Educate Together's curriculum, was designed so individual schools would adapt it to local contexts to address varying school environments and the wishes of parents. Although this flexibility has been useful, it also makes it harder to deliver a uniform product in ways that the model and network touts. The Ethical Core Curriculum is challenging for teachers because it takes considerable time and energy to translate that into something that they can use in a structured coherent way, which reflects the four strands of the curriculum within their classrooms.[28] Several principals also suggested that those elements of the curriculum that are harder to teach and required more critical treatment due to their controversial or problematic elements often receive less attention. There is also the natural tendency to dilute some of the more difficult material when teaching it, which weakens the effectiveness of the planned curriculum. There may not be as much oversight to ensure that what is supposed to be taught is in fact being taught.[29] The difficulty of delivering the curriculum is further exacerbated by the fact that prior to the mid-2010s there were no dedicated courses on intercultural and multi-denominational education on initial teacher education programmes in Ireland. Therefore, new teachers are often unfamiliar with the approaches used in Educate Together schools.

Developing a model and a new curriculum during a time of social change also means there is generally less consensus on what the school philosophy means in practice. For example, studies have shown that some parents believed that Educate Together schools were

27   Lalor, 2013, 117.
28   Lalor, 2013, 141.
29   Lalor, 2013, 141.

non-denominational, and others used the terms of non- and multi-denominational interchangeably. This can lead to markedly different understandings about how religion should be taught and learned and to varied desires about whether religion should be involved at all. Although the model emphasises a multi-denominational, child-centred, and ethical approach to learning about religion, it is not the case that all students who attend Educate Together schools, or their families, are secular or non-religious.[30] In fact, in Educate Together schools over 50 % of the students are Catholic, and among these, there can be varied beliefs about the role of religion in the classroom, school and broader society.[31] Among those who are non-religious, there are also divisions. Some students and parents who identify as non-religious are ideologically secular and anti-religious, whereas others are totally fine with those who are religious and want to exercise their beliefs. Besides religion, there can also be uncertainty about what diversity means within individual Educate Together schools. As one parent reported, 'Everyone has their own view about what diversity means. Everybody has their own view of what multiculturalism or interculturalism is, so I do think it can get to the stage where it is, you are catering for individuals needs and sometimes it is the strongest voice that gets heard.'[32] For all the praise Educate Together receives for its model and overall approach, it is important to realise it is not without its own problems. Educate Together so often pits itself in opposition to Catholic schools, when it faces many of the same challenges of implementing a curriculum during a time of social change where there is no consensus on virtually any topic. Ultimately, the diversity that Educate Together promotes, one where students of all religions and none are treated with respect, is the ideal, even if there are a myriad of views on what real diversity is.

A challenge facing Educate Together as it continues to develop its model is how their schools integrate into the local communities where they serve. Change is never easy, especially in the tightly knit context of local

30   Lalor, 2013, 131.
31   Darmody, Smyth, and McCoy, 2012.
32   Lalor, 2013, 131.

communities in Ireland. Ironically, some of the very elements that make Educate Together attractive, such as its multi-denominational, inclusive and democratic nature, can also increase the distance between the school and its immediate community. 'Because some parents are attracted by these principles as opposed to making their choice of school on the basis of proximity and convenience, this can result in a school-going population being drawn from outside the local community within which the school is located. This can lead to … a sense of disconnection between the school and its immediate community and this can serve to create a burden on the schools in their attempts to integrate into new and existing communities.'[33] Educate Together schools serve a high proportion of ethnic minorities and immigrants because they are predominantly located in urban areas. Additionally, Educate Together schools also serve higher percentages of students from wealthy, middle-class and highly educated families who are generally more likely to make active school choices and are less likely to be deterred from travelling farther to attend these school types.[34] As a result, Educate Together attracts strong parental support, but their schools also experience certain divisions and tensions within local communities because they are a 'choice' school.

Educate Together's four guiding principles, as described above, were developed initially to offer a model of education that was markedly different than the predominant Catholic school experience. Irish society has been utterly transformed in the period since the Dalkey School project was established in 1978. By the 2010s, the values that have been deeply imbued in Educate Together's mission are now commonly accepted and idealised. Values such as diversity, inclusion, tolerance, multi-culturalism and even secularism are increasingly at the heart of what it means to be Irish, replacing Irish nationalism of the past that was rooted in being White, Catholic, Irish-speaking and not English! Like the dynamics in Irish partisan politics, whereby Ireland's larger parties often absorb the salient and popular policies of minor parties, Educate Together's approach and values were being

33 Lalor, 2013, 130.
34 Darmody, Smyth, and McCoy, 2012.

adapted by many other actors and institutions in the broader educational system. As Chapter 12 will discuss, the National Council for Curriculum and Assessment (NCCA) has adopted many of Educate Together's key features in relation to the national curriculum. As others adopt their model, Educate Together may lose some of its distinctiveness, but they may also have a greater impact on the system as a whole. As Educate Together's model has become mainstreamed, it is well placed to influence future changes in Irish education. However, this model and its relevant ideology would not have been possible without strong organisation locally and nationally to make it a reality.

III. Organisational Growth and Educational Reforms: Flooding the Zone

Complex problems, such as poverty, health, climate change and even education, require equally complex solutions. As a result, U.S. political commentator David Brooks suggests, one must flood the zone to attack problems from multiple perspectives. He argues that critical issues entail a complex system of negative feedback loops, which need an equally complex and diverse set of positive feedback loops to address them. 'You have to flood the zone with as many good programs as you can find and fund and hope that somehow they will interact and reinforce each other community by community, neighbourhood by neighbourhood.' Brooks also suggests that maximum success is dependent on allowing for a maximum diversity to help build an 'ecosystem of positive influences'. This diversity means including left- and right-wing groups, religious and secular groups, government and non-government institutions and so on to create a culture and web of relationships that will positively influence lives of citizens, especially young people.[35]

35   David Brooks, 'Flood the Zone', *The New York Times*, 6 February 2012.

The 'flood the zone' approach is often adopted within an organisation seeking to address a complex issue. Instead of seeking one solution, an organisation is often more successful in creating major reform or systemic change by adopting many smaller, incremental changes that over time combine to make larger change possible. This has been Educate Together's strategy – or at least this is how they have grown organically if not intentionally. Educate Together has grown organisationally incrementally by sector. As it developed within the primary, post-primary and university/third level sector, Educate Together also expanded its outreach to influence key education legislation concerning a range of issues from patronage, land and property ownership, equality rules, admissions policies and curriculum. Evidence presented in Chapter 7 on the media will demonstrate that Educate Together started to attract greater media attention in 2000 and rises from mentions in fifty articles per year in *The Irish Times* in 2010 to over an overwhelming 200 articles per year by 2019. Educate Together gained more attention, and more positive coverage, than any issue within the education sector, thereby confirming its status as a key voice engaging educational reform. A review of these developments will demonstrate that Educate Together has grown and addressed its main concerns in remarkably similar ways that leading civil society actors have done in altering the role of religion in Irish policy and society.

A. *Educate Together in Primary, Secondary and Third Level Education*

As mentioned, Educate Together originally formed as an umbrella organisation of several individual multi-denominational schools in 1984. At that time there were three primary schools. By 1995, there were fourteen schools in the network and the organisation decided to establish a national office to formalise their efforts. The growth accelerated as the organisation became more established, growing to forty-three primary schools in 2007 and to ninety-two primary schools by 2019.

Rowe argues that Educate Together was largely unknown until 2007 when, over two weeks, Educate Together started an emergency school in temporary facilities to respond a population surge in North County

Dublin.[36] Upwards of seventy students, mostly non-White immigrants, did not have placements to begin the school year. Educate Together stepped in to start this emergency school in a matter of days instead of what typically would have taken at least eighteen months to establish. The network's responsiveness demonstrated its ability to deliver and respond to Ireland's rapidly changing society. Educate Together basked in the national spotlight and capitalised on the opportunity to underscore its model. Paul Rowe commented that Educate Together 'aims to meet a growing need in Irish society for schools that recognise the developing diversity of Irish life and the modern need for democratic management structures'. He said, 'In particular, Educate Together guarantees children and parents of all faiths and none, equal respect in the operation and governing of education.'[37] *The Irish Times* added that 'since the announcement of the imminent opening of Educate Together's emergency school in Balbriggan, the school has received an additional sixty applications, with the figure increasing daily. Rowe envisages that its ultimate intake will, like other Educate Together schools, reflect a diverse ethnic spread.'[38]

The events in Dublin highlighted Educate Together, but they also elicited a hotly contested national debate about Irish society, racism, the Catholic Church, the State and educational reform around admissions and patronage. For some, the lack of school placements for immigrants was an example of a racist Catholic Church that was not willing to serve non-Catholic children in need. There was real anger that the Church prioritised Catholic students and failed to respond to these poor, non-White immigrants, which fuelled the debate about acceptable admissions policies. For others, this was an example of the State failing to plan and deal with the significant population growth associated with Ireland's Celtic Tiger economy. Catholic Archbishop of Dublin, Diarmuid Martin, was critical of the State's lack of planning and for one of the first times stated: 'I would be very happy to see a plurality of patronage and providers of education. I have no ambition to run the entire education system in Dublin.'[39] These

---

36   Paul Rowe, Personal Interview, October 2019.
37   Rosita Boland, 'Faith Before Fairness', *The Irish Times*, 8 September 2007.
38   Rosita Boland, 8 September 2007.
39   Rosita Boland, 8 September 2007.

comments sparked further discussion about patronage in the primary sector and underscored the need for greater diversity. Finally, these events also generated heated discussions about equality legislation and whether Ireland was adhering to UN and other international standards on racial and religious discrimination. State defence of the status quo in the educational system further frustrated many within Irish society. As the next chapter will describe, it was at this same time that the State established the Community National School model, run by local Education and Training Boards (ETBs), to offer another type of multi-denominational education.

The highly public and contentious nature of these events and subsequent discussions elevated Educate Together's status within Ireland, helping to paint it as the reformer par excellence. Their proven track record in delivering a quality education over three decades made them a popular option for those seeking to establish a new school. The very next year, 2008, Educate Together opened twelve new primary schools and was in the midst of developing a business plan to open twenty new schools per year. Ireland's economic crisis that started in the fall of 2008 quickly delayed this ambitious growth plan. By 2009, Batt O'Keefe, the then Minister of Education and Science, stopped the demand-driven model for recognising and establishing new schools. From 2010, new schools were only established when the Department decided there was a demographic need for them. In addition to obvious financial limitations imposed during the economic crisis, Educate Together leaders argued that there was also fear within the government that Educate Together was becoming too popular and powerful and the growing demand would create an over-supply of schools.[40] Irrespective of the motives, the state greatly restricted the numbers of new schools and initiated the process whereby existing schools could transfer their patronage to multi-denominational schools. This decision led to the Forum on Patronage and Pluralism and the plan to divest schools, as we will discuss further in Chapter 10.

Another key stage of Educate Together's growth occurred when it expanded into the post-primary sector. Educate Together campaigned for nearly a decade to become a recognised patron at the post-primary

40   Paul Rowe, Personal Interview, October 2019.

level. During this time, Educate Together received significant financial
support (i.e. €1 million) to employ a project manager who spent seven
years researching best practices of secondary education all over the world
and coming up with a blueprint that extended the network's multi-
denominational, ethics curriculum from 1st class through the Leaving
Certificate. The pedagogy and delivery of the curriculum integrated
subjects to facilitate project-based learning rather than teaching every subject separately.[41] Educate Together first applied formally to the Department
in 2007 for patronage status and was granted this recognition by the State
in 2011 on the recommendation and support of Minister for Education
Ruairí Quinn, TD, who believed that Educate Together was a successful
model. His proposal surprised even members of his own Labour Party,
who had close ties with the VEC (Vocational Education Committee)
schools that would be challenged by greater competition in this sector.
These VEC schools were secondary schools originally designed to be non-
denominational, but which had long been influenced by or had close relationships with the institutional Church and its lay leaders.[42] These schools
historically focused on preparing students for employment in trades, manufacturing, agriculture, commerce and other industrial pursuits.[43] Quinn's
support was even more critical given this history.

In 2014, Educate Together opened two post-primary schools in Dublin
and one in Drogheda, Co. Louth.[44] Formal entry into the post-primary
sector provided Educate Together with a more formal seat at the table as
reforms in Junior Certificate curriculum were being engaged. Furthermore,
these new schools helped Educate Together extend its vision and mission.
For example, the focus on democratic participation and child-centred
learning were enhanced as Educate Together got state approval to have
students represented on their boards of management.[45] Although this is a
seemingly minor reform, it illustrates yet another way Educate Together

41   Paul Rowe, Personal Interview, October 2019.
42   Ruairi Quinn, former Minister for Education (2011–14), Personal Interview,
     October 2019.
43   Tuohy, 2013, 243–7.
44   <https://www.educatetogether.ie/about/history/> (Accessed: 7 August 2020).
45   Paul Rowe, Personal Interview, October 2019.

is altering the educational landscape by being relying on different voices to determine how their schools are run.

Now that Educate Together is serving in primary and post-primary education, there is an incentive to become more involved in third level education and, in particular, with initial teacher education at the undergraduate and graduate level. As late as the early 2000s, teacher training in Ireland was dominated by the denominational tradition as 'all five of the Third Level Colleges of Education…are denominational, with four being Catholic and one Church of Ireland [when] Irish society and culture are experiencing radical change and heterogeneity, with increasing immigration and significant shifts in the attitudes of indigenous Irish people towards religion and the Church'.[46] As Chapter 2 described, the twenty-first century has witnessed dramatic change in third level institutions. As of 2020, only two of the five third level institutions training primary school teachers are denominational (Mary Immaculate in Limerick and Marino Institute in Dublin). The other three (NUI Maynooth, Dublin City University and Hibernia) are secular. Hibernia College, founded in 2000 as an online, blended-learning college, is now the largest producer of primary teachers in Ireland. Hibernia is the only 'for profit' teacher training institution and, as a result, does not come under the remit of the Department of Education and Skills and receives no resources from the State.

Educate Together is seeking to alter this third level landscape in three ways. First, in 2013, Dublin City University (DCU) established a diploma programme in Ethical and Multi-denominational Education to prepare teachers for Educate Together and Community National Schools. The course explores 'the theory and practice of multi-denominational and ethical education, democracy and education as well as investigating pluralist pedagogy in curriculum'.[47] It also engages the newly proposed national curriculum in Education about Religions and Beliefs (ERB) and Ethics that has been developed by the National Council for Curriculum and Assessment. Relatedly, Educate Together is negotiating a deeper involvement in DCU's

46 Lalor, 2013, 4.
47 <https://www.dcu.ie/courses/Postgraduate/institute_of_education/Professional-Diploma-Education-Ethical-Multidenominational> (Accessed: 7 August 2020).

Institute of Education to better prepare the greater numbers of teachers who will be teaching in multi-denominational settings and will have to engage students and parents in different ways than is required in Catholic schools. Finally, Educate Together entered a partnership with DCU's Centre for Evaluation, Quality and Inspection (EQI) to develop a national Quality Framework for Ethos in Educate Together Schools. 'The framework involves setting out standards and statements of effective practice which schools will use as part of a self-evaluation process to evaluate practice, and to plan and implement improvements in the school.'[48] Through this effort, Educate Together hopes to overcome the insular nature of teachers and schools only being concerned about their work. In particular, Educate Together with the help of DCU seeks to take advantage of its growing network and a greater use of new technologies to promote quality and innovation among its many members and schools. The ultimate hope is to enhance the whole educational system by fostering a growth mindset, constant evaluation and regular sharing with others so that best practices become the norm. Although Educate Together is least developed in the third level, one can see how it is slowly advancing its mission and overall vision by creating new programmes that address concrete needs in other sectors. Thus, the first way Educate Together is 'flooding the zone' is by becoming fully engaged in teaching at every level within the Irish educational system.

B. Shaping Educational Reform via Legislation and Policy-making

The second critical way Educate Together has 'flooded the zone' in the educational sphere has been by methodically chipping away at legislation and policy that affect how schools operate. Paul Rowe, long-time CEO of Educate Together, admits that the organisation was focused more on building an educational movement than a political movement in his thirty years of involvement. The founding members of the Dalkey

---

48   <https://www.dcu.ie/news/news/2019/Nov/DCU-EQI-commissioned-develop-new-framework-for-Educate-Together-schools.shtml> (Accessed: 7 August 2020).

School Project 'were careful to ensure that the campaign for multi-denominational education never became overly associated with any one political party'.[49] With the goal to educate and increase awareness in the political sphere, early leaders focused on the 1974 local elections and the 1977 general election campaigns to inform political parties and canvass support from the candidates. Apparently, these campaigns were successful because three of the four TDs in the local constituency after the 1977 general election were members of the Dalkey School Project. Despite attracting important support among elected officials and parties, the early leaders worked hard not to allow integrated education and multi-denominational schools to become a political football that became overly politicised. Their primary goal at the time was to establish new school model.[50]

Rowe argues that under his leadership the organisation continued this founding approach of not spending significant time, money, or personnel on explicitly lobbying political actors, although they consistently sought to build cross-party support for their efforts. Rather, Educate Together focused on delivering their core educational principles and strong ethical curriculum to more and more children with the ultimate aim of providing a tipping point. For Rowe, this tipping point will occur when Educate Together serves 10 % of all Irish students in the primary sector, and then serve this same percentage of students in the post-primary sector. In 2019, Educate Together was serving approximately 30,000 Irish students, and they would need to get closer to 50,000 to meet their goal.[51]

Educate Together has not focused heavily on explicitly lobbying to secure changes in the educational sector, but they have benefitted significantly from changes in legislation over the last forty years. We know that correlation is not causation, but Educate Together has developed its model and evolved in ways that map closely with changes in Irish education at each level. Like understanding Educate Together's growth by sector, it is

49   Hyland and Green, 2020, 20.
50   Hyland and Green, 2020, see 63, 135 and 149.
51   Paul Rowe, Personal Interview, October 2019.

instructive to highlight a few of the legislative and regulatory changes that
help explain the organisation's growth.

Between 1995 and 1998, Educate Together built a national office to
help systematise the model and oversee its development and registered as
an educational charity and a company limited by guarantee. Prior to its
establishment as an official, national patron, all Educate Together schools
were required to be their own separate, independent patron. Since then,
each new school becomes part of the Educate Together network (and
only nine of their ninety-two primary schools have remained under independent patronage). This official status as a network and its rapid growth
in membership combined to help consolidate Educate Together's place as
key stakeholder in Irish education.

One of the legal requirements associated with being a nationally recognised patron was that Educate Together had to develop its own patrons
programme to meet national standards. Thus, between 1999 and 2004,
Educate Together developed its *Learn Together* curriculum, which forced
the organisation to systematise its core principles of multi-denominational
and ethical education into a concrete curriculum. By 2005, *Learn Together*
had become recognised by the EU as an example of good practice in multi-
cultural education.[52] The development of this core curriculum would not
have occurred had the organisation not first received official State recognition as a patron. Once legitimised by the State, it solidified its model
and sought to further distinguish itself from other patrons, especially the
Catholic Church. Again, its insider and stakeholder status, gave Educate
Together a seat at the table for further educational reforms and policy
decisions. As debates about ethics education and teaching about religion
rather than from or into religion became more common, Educate Together
had already established some appeal and legitimacy in this area. Chapter 12
will discuss how Educate Together has attempted to shift the curricular
debates to help move Ireland closer to a secular educational system where
religious instruction is not taught during the regular school day and the
role of religion is altogether limited in all Irish primary schools.

52   Paul Rowe, Personal Interview, October 2019.

A second key policy change that altered Educate Together's trajectory was the decision in 1998 by the State to abolish the requirement for patrons and local communities to provide their own land/sites and to pay 15 % of the building costs for all new schools.[53] Prior to this change, it was customary for the Catholic Church to organise the financing of schools in areas where a new school was needed and to provide a site, often from its own lands. This system placed those small groups of parents in urban areas who wanted multi-denominational education for their children at a disadvantage, since they lacked Church support. Furthermore, it usually took five years for new multi-denominational schools to be recognised by the Department of Education: only then would they be entitled to an 85 % building or renovation grant. The system was also discriminatory since the State provided full funding for new *gaelscoileanna*, schools where the medium of instruction would be Irish. In the eleven years up to 1997, while only two new Catholic schools were recognised by the Department of Education, fifty-six *gaelscoileanna* and thirteen multi-denominational schools were recognised.[54]

The land and capital issue had been a significant impediment to Educate Together's growth because finding property for schools was difficult and expensive. In fact, it took six years for the original Dalkey School to raise sufficient funding and to acquire the necessary planning permission before it moved from its original temporary facility to a new building on a new site in 1978.[55] In today's terms, patrons have to put forth approximately €5 million to establish a school and the network, and parents and communities seeking to establish new schools could rarely meet this requirement. According to Paul Rowe, Educate Together had numerous conversations with then Fianna Fáil Minister of Education (and later Taoiseach), Micheál Martin, TD, in the lead-up to this decision where they had made him aware of the systemic constraints on growth that these property and building costs were posing to the network. According to Rowe, the State abolished the local contribution requirement once they realised that there

53   Lalor, 2013, 24.
54   Bill Kissane, 'The Illusion of State Neutrality in a Secularising Ireland', *West European Politics*, 2003, Vol. 26, No. 1, 73–94, DOI: 10.1080/01402380412331300207.
55   Hyland and Green, 2020, 210–32.

were constitutional issues concerning ownership of the land and buildings if patrons owned part and the State owned part.[56] This subtle, but key policy shift paved the way for Educate Together to expand the number of schools much more rapidly. This hurdle in relation to land ownership is a central challenge to the State's ability to accelerate the speed of divestment.

A third, and more encompassing, policy area that was deeply aligned with Educate Together's core principles was the increased attention given to equality legislation beginning in the late-1990s. The Employment Equality Act (1998) protected Irish citizens from being discriminated in the workplace based on gender, civil status, family status, sexual orientation, religion, age, disability, race and membership in the Traveller community.[57] The Equal Status Act (2000) further prohibited discrimination in the provision of goods and services, accommodation and education based on the same nine distinctions.[58] By the time the same-sex marriage referendum was passed in 2015, the phrase 'Yes Equality' had become a mainstreamed phrase and accepted ideology within Irish society and law. Despite these legislative developments and broader social changes, the series of equality legislative acts exempted religious organisations, including Catholic schools and hospitals, from these guidelines.

Educate Together capitalised on these legislative changes to consolidate its brand as an alternative to the Catholic Church and marketed itself as the 'place of refuge for every type of minority family that Ireland has experienced'.[59] It had already been the place for minority religions and the increasing percentage of non-religious and secular Irish citizens. Next, when the growing numbers of ethnic minorities were immigrating to Ireland in the 2000s, the newly passed equality legislation provided a legal framework for them to gain access to education and work, and they were

56   Paul Rowe, Personal Interview, October 2019.
57   <https://www.citizensinformation.ie/en/employment/equality_in_work/ equality_in_the_workplace.html>
58   <https://www.ihrec.ie/guides-and-tools/human-rights-and-equality-in-the- provision-of-good-and-services/what-does-the-law-say/equal-status-acts/ #:~:text=from%20IHREC&text=The%20Equal%20Status%20Acts%20 2000,membership%20of%20the%20Traveller%20community>
59   Paul Rowe, Personal Interview, October 2019.

welcomed into Educate Together schools as the 2007 emergency school openings demonstrated. Finally, as legislation around sexual orientation advanced, Educate Together once again positioned itself as the 'only safe place for openly LGBT community to openly work and not be discriminated against'.[60] It is worth noting, however, that there has not been one case brought against a Catholic school for discrimination on the grounds of sexual orientation nor has anyone been fired from a Catholic school on the basis of their orientation as has happened in U.S. Catholic schools. In many Irish Catholic schools, the marriage of a gay staff member is openly celebrated. Nevertheless, Educate Together has captured the rhetoric in public discourse to expand its appeal and pit it as an alternative to official Catholic teachings on contentious moral issues such as same-sex marriage.

Educate Together has fought hard to preserve its image as the embodiment of an equality-based and human rights education. For example, Educate Together was critical of the Community National School (CNS) model that was established in 2008 and had the potential to compete with Educate Together as a provider of multi-denominational education in Ireland. As discussed in greater detail in the next chapter, these Community National Schools were the first attempt by the State to own and operate primary schools rather than supporting private patrons in their efforts to provide primary education to Irish children. These schools were designed to offer multi-denominational education, but they originally separated children out based on their religion so they could be taught religious instruction within the context of their own faith. Unlike Educate Together schools where students learn about various religions, the CNS model teaches each student from within their own religious perspective while also learning about other faiths. Educate Together and other critics argued that as State schools, the Community National Schools needed to abide by the Equal Status Act and could not have exempted status as religious schools did.

Thus, Community National Schools had to demonstrate that they were treating all students equally. The implication was that if children were being separated out based on religion there was a danger of discriminating against those of no religion – a criticism often directed at Catholic schools.

60   Paul Rowe, Personal Interview, October 2019.

Additionally, if these schools were providing faith formation classes within the school day – opposed to teaching about religion – they would need to have fully qualified teachers with certificates from third level institutions to teach in those areas.[61] The Community National Schools altered their approach to multi-denominational religious education after a few years and began to teach about religion and to offer religious instruction courses and faith formation outside the school day. Rather than tackling critical, and often contentious, issues like whether religious education should be taught inside or outside of the regular school day or whether students should learn about religion rather than from or into a religious perspective, Educate Together capitalised on equality legislation to alter a competing patron's approach to these issues. Once again, Educate Together was consolidating its brand and positioning itself as the leading alternative to Catholic schools in the primary sector.

The Forum on Patronage and Pluralism in the Primary Sector in 2011–12 provided Educate Together with an important opportunity to increase its visibility and to advance its cause both to a targeted set of political and state actors as well as to the media and Irish society more broadly. Similar to ways in which the Citizens' Assembly and Constitutional Convention brought together experts, civil society actors, politicians and members of Irish society and raised awareness and salience of particular issues, the Forum on Patronage and Pluralism did this for education reform. Educate Together made numerous formal and informal submissions as part of these proceedings. In addressing the key issues of establishing new schools in areas of growing population, divesting patronage in areas of stable population but shifting demand, and promoting more inclusive schools everywhere, Educate Together got to lobby for its model and propose broader systemic change.

The Forum helped Educate Together consolidate its key role within the educational sector. Its formal submission begins by claiming that it is 'the' representative of multi-denominational schools in Ireland. This ignores the fact that Community National Schools are also providing a multi-denominational education to Irish students, albeit on a much smaller

61   Paul Rowe, Personal Interview, October 2019.

scale than Educate Together. The submission reiterated Educate Together's four core principles and underscored its claim that it is the only patron providing an equality-based education within Ireland. It highlights its ethical education *Learn Together* curriculum and approach to teaching about religion that it believes lead to better learning outcomes but also leads to greater appreciation of diversity and inclusion among its students.[62]

To appeal to those worried about moving towards an entirely secular system, Educate Together argues that it celebrates religious diversity rather than restricting it. Not only is moral and spiritual development actively taught through the *Learn Together* curriculum, it argues, but different religious and non-religious festivals are also regularly celebrated by the school community to develop understanding and respect for different traditions.[63]

Educate Together's submission went on to criticise the denominational system. The submission concludes that 'there are well-documented difficulties in providing equality for children in an environment where one religious ethos permeates the school programme, controls the power structure and has 30 minutes of each compulsory school day devoted to its world outlook. Educate Together believes that it is impossible to provide for diversity unless there is at least one school in an area which provides the same level of equality as is provided in the Educate Together Model.'[64] Therefore, Educate Together argues that it is the best model and that the Irish educational system can only be reformed and improved if this model is accessible to children throughout Ireland.

Given the glacially slow progress on divesting schools since 2011, Educate Together's greatest achievement from the Forum on Patronage and Pluralism may have been the Advisory Group's recommendation that all Irish primary students receive an Education about Religions and Beliefs

62   <https://www.education.ie/en/Press-Events/Events/Patronage-and-Pluralism-in-the-Primary-Sector/Progress-to-Date-and-Future-Directions-Forum-on-Patronage-and-Pluralism-in-the-Primary-Sector.pdf> (Accessed: 12 August 2020), 12.

63   <https://www.educatetogether.ie/sites/default/files/patronage_forum_submission.pdf> (Accessed: 12 August 2020), 2.

64   <https://www.educatetogether.ie/sites/default/files/patronage_forum_submission.pdf> (Accessed: 7 April 2021), 11.

(ERB) and Ethics.[65] This was an official recognition by a recognised political body that Educate Together's model was worthy of imitation and could
shape the entire primary sector. In Chapter 12, we discuss Ireland's primary
school national curriculum and address in greater detail this push to implement a national ERB and Ethics curriculum. For now, it is sufficient to
highlight how Educate Together maximised opportunities to showcase its
model and to seek ways to get the Irish system to reflect its principles and
ultimate goals. At each turn, Educate Together has sought to lower barriers
to reform and adopted incremental changes in part because the political
will was not at the level necessary to attract media attention, shift public
opinion, nor pressure political actors to bring about more dramatic policy
change. This incremental approach to policy change was evident in the
previous LGBTQ and abortion campaigns and appears to be at work here.

Educate Together's Forum submission offered several other policy and
regulatory suggestions that, in effect, demand an increased role for the State
in ways that benefit Educate Together and undermine competing patrons.
For example, the focus on State ownership of property and buildings was
an attempt by Educate Together to alter how the State funds education.
First, if the State owned school land and buildings, the Catholic Church,
which is the largest owner of school land and buildings in Ireland, would
be greatly limited in its power. Rather than attacking the Church's power
head on, Educate Together argues for a shift towards all new schools being
under State ownership. 'Educate Together is firmly of the view that all
new school buildings and sites should be the property of the State which
can then allocate facilities according to community demand, and that the
current legal terms in which the State funds school buildings on privately
owned sites should be reviewed. This review should ensure that the State
is able to insist that unused space is re-allocated to address changing educational demands as they emerge in the community.'[66]

---

65   <https://www.education.ie/en/Press-Events/Events/Patronage-and-Pluralism-
     in-the-Primary-Sector/Progress-to-Date-and-Future-Directions-Forum-on-
     Patronage-and-Pluralism-in-the-Primary-Sector.pdf>   (Accessed: 12   August
     2020), 12.
66   <https://www.educatetogether.ie/sites/default/files/patronage_forum_submis-
     sion.pdf> (Accessed: 12 August 2020), 4.

Furthermore, Educate Together called for cost-neutral divestment of existing schools, which the Advisory Group for the Forum appreciated. In fact, the Progress Report on the Forum (2014) placed a lot of responsibility on patrons, especially the Catholic Church, to divest their schools and to assume the costs. Although the State would not force the Church to give over schools, 'existing patrons are expected to contribute to the process in a way that is cost-neutral to the state'.[67] Such proposals placed financial responsibility of divestment on the patrons and tapped into public anger of the Church's handling on the sexual abuse crisis.

As mentioned earlier, the Church was being asked to return financial resources that the State had been giving to it for decades. One analyst of the Forum's proceedings suggested that there existed a moral obligation on the part of patrons to divest their property with little or no cost to the State. The Forum's Advisory group, which adopted many of Educate Together's arguments, implicitly expected the Church to behave in a different way than might be expected of any other property owner in comparable circumstances who would receive market-based remuneration for their property. 'The rhetoric is couched in terms of the common good, with a demand that the church groups forego their rights to property.'[68] Such an approach underestimates how previous philanthropy and donations of individuals, parishes and religious communities helped support these schools for generations. Irrespective of the Church's past transgressions, or the fact that these private institutions had received State funding for decades, the demands for cost-neutral divestments and new patrons were oversimplified.

The other reason Educate Together argued for greater State ownership of school land and buildings is that it would give the State more control in deciding how various patrons could operate within different facilities. Again, the fact that the Catholic Church owned a vast majority of school property made it difficult for patrons like Educate Together to acquire land. Therefore, Educate Together stood to benefit from a new system wherein all new schools would involve the State owning the land and buildings and leasing them to patrons.[69] If the whole goal was to diversify

67 Tuohy, 2013, 262–3.
68 Tuohy, 2013, 293.
69 Tuohy, 2013, 296.

the primary sector, Educate Together was well-positioned to become the leading patron for new schools.

Greater State ownership and oversight could also potentially benefit Educate Together in divestment cases as well because the State would have an incentive to respond to changing needs within local communities. Existing patrons, especially the Catholic Church, had less incentive to divest their schools if they would not be remunerated for past investments or current value. Educate Together, by contrast, wanted to take over more schools but faced too many barriers to entry. Although Educate Together had previous experience of taking over property and school buildings when previous schools closed or vacated the premises because of amalgamations or relocation, they believed that if the State had more control over how all buildings were being used, the State would increasingly choose Educate Together as the patron.

One such proposal called for the State to demand unused space in larger schools to be shared with additional patrons so two schools could operate in one space. This would allow the buildings to be used to serve all the needs and demand for diversity of school types in an area in a more cost-effective manner. In such a scenario, if the State owned the land, buildings, and provided most of the other financial support to operate the school, it might also place additional conditions on patrons in return for this financial support. This might be appealing in the short term, but what if things changed? It is 'one thing to suggest that schools share a campus or building when the Department of Education and Skills is the owner of the property and manages the lease. However, it would be a different issue to have two schools in the one building and one patron has a different right to the building because they own it .... What to do when demographics change, and patrons want different things?'[70] Ultimately, such proposals sought to lower the barriers to entry for new Educate Together schools.

Subtle arguments about greater State involvement relate to Educate Together's broader goal of altering denominational education and tying everything back into Ireland's growing equality legislation. For example, the Educate Together submission states that when negotiating the divestment

70   Tuohy, 2013, 295.

arrangements, 'far greater legal weight than ever before should be given to the State grant aid involved in the building, maintenance and daily operation of schools that are privately owned. We believe that it is reasonable for the State to seek assistance in meeting changing community needs in return for the continuance of such comprehensive support.'[71] In other words, if schools are going to receive State aid of any kind, they should be forced to use these resources in ways that the State defines. Additionally, Educate Together argues that 'new legislation should be introduced that regulates the privileges of patrons of schools and requires that these privileges are exercised with full regard to changing community needs.'[72]

One of the novel suggestions Educate Together proposed at this time was creating a national register of the school type preference of parents of preschool children. As part of this proposal, an independent state body would oversee a transparent process of school placement in every local area thereby wresting control of enrolment/admissions policies from individual schools. 'Numbers from this register should be public and should be used to generate local consensus on such allocations. For this to happen, it is essential that the body undertaking the survey has no interest in the running of schools and is – and is seen to be – impartial and fair.' As a result, Educate Together argued that 'the State will have a reasonable profile of parental demand for differing school types in an area. This should form the basis of allocation of facilities and resources…' and will also 'ensure that local school provision is matched as closely as possible to community demand.' Finally, 'this local body should allocate places and resources in schools according to this register and should have the authority to ensure that minimum standards of inclusion are attained by all schools. The independent body must not have any involvement in the patronage or management of schools. It is recommended that it could be properly part of the functions of a reformed system of local government or educational

71   <https://www.educatetogether.ie/sites/default/files/patronage_forum_submission.pdf> (Accessed: 12 August 2020), 8.
72   <https://www.educatetogether.ie/sites/default/files/patronage_forum_submission.pdf> (Accessed: 12 August 2020), 9.

authority.'[73] The State adopted this approach and placed local ETBs in charge of the process. Unfortunately, this placed ETBs in awkward situation where they were both acting as the state regulator to determine local demand for various patrons, while also competing with other patrons to be selected by the State to run new schools. This conflict of interest further complicates the process.

This change potentially solves several problems at once for Educate Together. First, there will be a clear and ongoing awareness of parental demand in every area of Ireland. Educate Together has long argued that there is more demand for their schools than is being met. Second, there will be greater weight given to ensuring that a diversity of options was available to parents in every geographic area. This, too, would help guarantee more school placements for Educate Together schools and prevent individual denominational schools from blocking change in their area. Third, elevating the State's ability to oversee enrolment in schools will further limit the power of denominational patrons, especially the Catholic Church, in the primary sector. Additional suggestions for greater State control in overseeing patrons, devising curriculum, training, and hiring teachers, combine with this proposal on enrolment to bolster Educate Together's ability to deliver its equality-based educational model and ultimately to alter the system. The cumulative effect of these arguments points towards a new system whereby Educate Together is the system! As the next chapter reveals, the emergence of the Community National Schools creates real competition for Educate Together as to which one is dominant and potentially serves as a model for what could serve as the foundation of a new secular primary school system.

While Educate Together was maximising its domestic political lobbying during the Forum on Patronage and Pluralism, it was also making its argument to international bodies. In particular, Educate Together submitted a summary description of the Irish education system to the United Nations' Human Rights Council, which provides the opportunity for each State to declare what actions they have taken to improve the human

---

73   <https://www.educatetogether.ie/sites/default/files/patronage_forum_submission.pdf> (Accessed: 12 August 2020), 5, 9, and 13.

rights situations in their countries and to fulfil their human rights obligations.[74] The submission rehearses the common case for discrimination within the Irish system, underscoring how Irish schools discriminate against minority students and those of no religious belief. The report also argues that equality legislation allows religious schools to 'discriminate on a wide range of religious grounds in matter of selection, promotion and employment of teachers'.[75] The report also highlights how various UN reports have confirmed how Ireland's educational system undermines the civil and political rights of children, as well as racial and religious minorities. These UN Committees have repeatedly called for Ireland to increase diversity within its educational system and provide more equitable enrolment policies as well to deal with its rapidly changing demographic situation. Like earlier campaigns advocating for LGBTQ rights and abortion rights for women, Educate Together sought and received international support and 'legitimacy' for its rights-based arguments.

By shifting from describing itself as offering multi-denominational education to now offering 'an equality-based education' as it did in 2015, Educate Together situated itself as '*the*' patron that was fulfilling Irish equality legislation and meeting international standards. As growing numbers of Irish citizens embraced equality in all things, Educate Together attracted greater attention and popularity for its model and overall approach. Furthermore, Educate Together capitalised on the growing support for equality legislation within Irish society to push its agenda as the leading educational patron and to push for reform on admissions policies and curriculum changes. We will come back to Educate Together's role in the admissions and curriculum review in later chapters, but it is helpful to recognise its increasingly accepted model and how it leveraged its popularity to consolidate its ideological positions and to push reforms.

74 <https://www.ohchr.org/en/hrbodies/upr/pages/uprmain.aspx> (Accessed: 12 August 2020).
75 <https://www.educatetogether.ie/app/uploads/2019/01/Irish-Human-Rights-and-Education.pdf> (Accessed: 12 August 2020).

C. *Attracting Financial Support and Lobbying for More*

A critical concern for many civil society actors is attracting reliable financial resources. As an educational charity, Educate Together relies on membership dues, state funding and private donations from foundations and individuals. These sources each amount to roughly one-third of the national organisation's revenue. In terms of membership schools, each one pays the national office €15 per pupil per annum, which meant that Educate Together received about €400,000 in 2019.

Second, Educate Together's national office receives a core management body grant from the Department of Education each year. The national office was receiving €144,000 per year until 2009 when this grant was cut to €133,000 per year. Although the office has doubled the amount of work it is providing its schools in this latter period, Educate Together has not received additional funds from the State.[76] This means that effectively the grant is only 22 % of its 2006 level – from €19.20 per pupil in 2006 to €4.31 per pupil in 2020.[77]

Third, Educate Together relies on foundations and donors to cover the remaining costs. Like other civil society groups, this funding source has been helpful but inconsistent and unreliable. Paul Rowe claimed that Atlantic Philanthropies was one of its biggest donors. It provided an initial seed grant to Educate Together to help organise its part-time front office in 1994. In 2001, Atlantic Philanthropies awarded Educate Together €1.14 million to support its permanent national office. Although Educate Together was under the impression that this was the first of several three-year grants to underwrite its organisational needs, they only received the one grant because the Atlantic Philanthropies reorganised its office and funding priorities to focus on human rights and diversity.[78] Atlantic Philanthropies had donated almost $8.8 million in grants between 2004 and 2011 to four civil society organisations that had been seeking to change laws and attitudes so that LGBTQ people could enjoy the same rights and protections as their

---

76   Paul Rowe, Personal Interview, October 2019.

77   <https://www.educatetogether.ie/campaigns/state-funding/>   (Accessed: 10 August 2020).

78   Paul Rowe, Personal Interview, October 2019.

fellow citizens. Among the outcomes of their advocacy was the 2010 passage of a civil partnership law and the Citizens' Assembly which recommended a national referendum on same-sex marriage that was ultimately passed in 2015.[79] Educate Together was unable to convince Atlantic Philanthropies at the time that their work was ultimately all about human rights and access.

The One Foundation, a foundation that spent €85 million in ten years, picked up where Atlantic Philanthropies left off, and became Educate Together's largest support, providing the national organisation with over €8 million between 2006 and 2013. In addition to these generous financial resources, the One Foundation provided periodic consultants to assist with business and strategic plans, as well as marketing and a plethora of other services.[80] Educate Together had convinced the One Foundation of its goal of expanding its inclusive approach to education to a tipping point whereby the Irish educational system would change. The One Foundation helped Educate Together to scale up its network by doubling the numbers of primary level students and schools it was serving, to enter into the post-primary sector and to initiate third level programming at DCU – all of which it believed was making inclusive, multi-denominational education a more real option in Ireland. Ultimately, the partnership with the One Foundation helped Educate Together drive policy change and lead practice in relation to a pluralist offering of schooling in Ireland and is now an innovative force in Teacher Education.[81]

This support was obviously incredibly helpful to Educate Together, but the One Foundation has since limited its activity and is no longer engaged in large-scale grant-making. Paul Rowe reported that Salesforce had given Educate Together €1 million in grants and promised an additional €400,000 over the next couple of years before reorganising their funding goals and foregoing on these promised gifts. This created a shortfall for this

79   'Marriage Equality: Lessons for Advocates', <https://www.atlanticphilanthropies. org/insights/insights-books/advocacy-for-impact#marriage_equality> (Accessed: 10 August 2020).

80   Paul Rowe, Personal Interview, October 2019.

81   <http://www.philanthropy.ie/backup/wp-content/uploads/2017/07/One10-2004-2013-Impact-Report-The-One-Foundation.pdf>

amount over the next two years and underscores the precarious funding situation that Educate Together, like other non-profit groups, face.

The limited and precarious nature of financial resources has encouraged Educate Together to lobby the State for additional resources to fulfil their mission, which they argue is transforming the Irish educational system. First, they continue to lobby the Department of Education and politicians for greater numbers of new schools under their patronage. In the 2016 election, they argued for 300 primary schools and thirty secondary schools to be run by Educate Together. This would increase their membership dues, but it would also, they argue, mean that 'all families would have access to an equality-based school within 30 minutes travel time from their homes'.[82] Second, they lobby for additional funds from the State for capitation grants for new schools. They argue that the Department of Education grossly under-pays the patron of a new school to cover the costs of setting up the school. It is currently set at €15,000 per new primary and €25,000 per new secondary school, whereas the average costs to Educate Together for opening a new primary school is €62,000 and a new second-level school is €102,000. Educate Together is calling on the Department to triple the level of the grants to patrons to €45,000 and €75,000 respectively and to agree that Educate Together may invoice the Department for its costs in excess of these figures in relation to its work on the provision of school buildings.[83] In an environment with limited funds, these demands will likely go unheeded, but one can see how Educate Together is increasing its lobbying reach into all aspects of the educational system.

As Educate Together's brand has evolved and become mainstreamed, so has its political support. Paul Rowe has consistently argued that Educate Together has been more of an educational movement than a political one, and as a result, it has very consciously maintained a cross-party approach in its political outreach. During its early years, Educate Together was seen as more of a disruptor than a reformer, and therefore most politicians avoided it. However, as the network expanded its reach and proved its

82   <https://www.educatetogether.ie/app/uploads/2019/01/General-Election-2016-Educate-Together%E2%80%99s-Essentials-for-Education.jpg>.

83   <https://www.educatetogether.ie/campaigns/state-funding/>   (Accessed: 10 August 2020).

ability to deliver a quality education, greater numbers of local politicians were supportive as individuals and would have been aware of Educate Together's work in specific schools. According to Rowe, 'at the end of the day, there were no votes in Educate Together. What's happening now is that there are votes in Educate Together.' During a recent public event to determine the patronage of a new secondary school in City West, Rowe states that 'local TDs lined up supporting Educate Together. That would not have happened. So, it's sort of an indication of the brand appeal of Educate Together today.'[84]

Evidence from party election manifestos and programmes for government confirms the growing support for Educate Together and multi-denominational schools among political parties and not just individual local politicians. Sinn Féin and Labour have included references to supporting Educate Together at both primary and secondary levels in their election manifestoes since 2011 as they both support increasing choice of school types for Irish parents and students. Fine Gael does not explicitly reference Educate Together in its election manifestoes, but it reiterates its commitment to increasing the number of multi-denominational schools in Ireland since its 2016 manifesto and includes this commitment in programmes for government in both 2016 and 2020. Likewise, Fianna Fáil signed on to support multi-denominational education in the 2020 Programme for Government. Fianna Fáil is slightly more hesitant in its support because it recognises the divisive and unhelpful divestment debates that they argue have 'distracted from the important issues which need to be discussed in the context of divestment: We will provide a one-stop information platform within the Department of Education to provide clear, non-biased information on the consequences of divestment and to provide responses to specific claims.'[85]

84   Paul Rowe, Personal Interview, October 2019.
85   Fianna Fáil, *An Ireland for All, 2020 Election Manifesto*, <https://www.inmo.ie/tempDocs/Fianna%20Fail%20GE%202020.pdf>, 79.

IV. Conclusion

This chapter has described and explained the development and expansion of Educate Together as the leading non-denominational educational provider in Ireland. Educate Together, which started as a group of activist parents trying to give their children a non-denominational educational experience, has grown into a network of schools and powerful lobbyist that is at the heart of every key educational issue within Ireland. Educate Together has developed slowly, incrementally and practically over the last forty years, consistently overcome obstacles to its growth. In addition to establishing schools at primary and secondary level, increasing its influence within third level teacher training colleges, and building a national organisation, Educate Together strategically and methodically reduced the barriers to educational reform by influencing key legislative changes regarding patronage, funding for school land and property, admissions, enrolment policies and even curriculum. After forty years of chipping away, Educate Together may be on the verge of creating the tipping point necessary to lead to more systematic change. Although it still operates a very small number of schools within the entire primary sector, it appears to be paving the way for larger, potentially top-down reform. Áine Hyland, in her reflection on the founding decade of the Educate Together movement, concluded that 'the failure of the Church of Ireland to continue with the multi-denominational "experiment" in St Patrick's N. S. Dalkey might well be regarded as providential, because as Michael Johnston wrote more than thirty years later: "what came later – the Dalkey School Project and Educate Together – was a much more important and radical development for the Irish education system".'[86]

Educate Together's rhetoric of equality has struck a chord among many within Irish society in similar ways that ultimately led to radical change in same-sex marriage and abortion legislation. A potential barrier to this trajectory is the degree to which the State may choose to become involved

86   Hyland and Green, 2020, 55.

directly in the primary sector in the same way it has been for decades at the secondary level. In this regard the emergence of the Community National School model, which we examine in the next chapter, is one that has potentially significant implications for the future growth of Educate Together.

CHAPTER 6

Community National Schools

I. Introduction

Another twist on the joke of the farmer giving directions is the famous Irish saying: 'I don't know where you're going, but you can't get there from here!' This has often been said about the Irish educational system. For many, Irish education is so ensconced within a denominational system that it is difficult to see how real change can occur. The fact that the State, from its inception, has chosen to 'provide for' a free primary education by financially supporting private patrons in their delivery of education rather than the State itself providing an education has limited the State's reform options. The emergence of the Community National Schools (CNS) model is largely a response to the need for a different model, one in which the State owns, operates and controls every aspect of the educational experience. Furthermore, the model was specifically designed to provide a markedly different educational experience than both the dominant Catholic school model and its primary alternative, Educate Together schools.

The surge of immigration in the mid-2000s led to a need for more capacity in the system and concurrently increased the demand for different types of primary schools in Ireland. Between the period 1998 and 2007, the number of immigrants doubled from 7.8 % to 15.7 % of the population with Ireland having 'the most abrupt and intensive migration pattern among OECD countries during that period'.[1]

In the aftermath of the widely publicised 2007 incident in Dublin where large numbers of non-Irish, mostly non-White immigrants were unable to secure places in oversubscribed primary schools, the State felt

---

1   Dympna Devine, 'Value'ing Children Differently? Migrant Children in Education, *Children & Society*, July 2013, Vol. 27(4), 282(13).

compelled to respond. There had been some conversations around that time about how the primary sector could replicate the diversity of provision that existed at the secondary level, especially by offering something like the well-established multi-denominational Community School model. In parallel, the rising percentage of Irish citizens with no faith also was driving demand for different types of provision beyond the largely denominational model. The CNS model was viewed as a means of enabling the State to directly meet these emerging needs of both increasing capacity and choice without having to depend on existing primary patrons.[2]

Fianna Fáil Minister for Education Mary Hanafin (2004–08) acted swiftly in 2007 when she announced the intention to establish the Community National Schools with the local Vocational Education Committees (VEC), now known as Education and Training Boards (ETB), as their patron, but she did so without any published documentation or rationale provided from the Department of Education. Under this framework, ETBs are statutory authorities that have responsibility for education, training and youth work. Education and Training Boards Ireland (ETBI) is the representative patron body for the sixteen ETBs around the country as of 2021. Thus, Community National Schools were born out of a ministerial pronouncement without an attendant process or consultation period. They were created to be publicly managed State schools providing a multi-denominational education that caters for the diversity of religious faiths represented in the area served by the school. Given that Educate Together was another private patron, this new model was created to be State-run and multi-denominational in ethos to cater to children of all faiths and none.[3]

According to Minister Hanafin, 'Provision will be made within the school setting for the religious, moral and ethical education of children in conformity with the wishes of their parents.'[4] A 2012 *RTÉ* report found

2   Marie Griffin, former Acting-CEO of County Dublin VEC, Personal Interview, September 2020.
3   Marie Griffin, Personal Interview, September 2020.
4   Mary Hanafin, '*Minister Hanafin Announces Intention to Pilot New Additional Model of Primary School Patronage*'. Available at: <https://www.education.ie/en/PressEvents/Press-Releases/2007-Press-Releases/PR07-02-17.html> [Accessed: 1 May 2021].

that 'the Catholic bishops, in return for their support for Community National Schools, required faith formation to be provided during the school day for Catholic students, which would in turn allow Catholic students to prepare for the sacraments of Reconciliation, First Communion and Confirmation during school time. This was described by Church officials as "a minimum non-negotiable requirement" and was significant in establishing the belief-specific teaching within the multi-belief programme that was developed.'[5] The support of the bishops for this new model may have been based on a commitment by the State that the new model would 'provide Catholic pupils with the same programme of religious education as offered by Catholic Primary Schools'.[6]

There are several noteworthy elements of the CNS model that distinguish it from Catholic and Educate Together schools. First, Community National Schools are State-owned and operated. Had such a model existed in the 1970s it is unlikely there would have been the need or desire on the part of parents to create the alternative to Catholic schools, which led to the creation of Educate Together schools. As we have observed, the State has assumed greater involvement and control in many aspects of education in recent decades, including overseeing the curriculum, teacher training, continuing professional development, guidelines for boards of management and issues related to land, property, buildings and other financial concerns. By establishing its own schools, the State would further consolidate its role in the primary sector and begin to eliminate some of the overlapping or competing interests between the State and private patrons, especially over legal and financial responsibilities, but also over issues related to ethos. Proponents of the CNS model argue that principals and teachers can get back to focusing on delivering excellent curriculum and instruction and

5   Aiveen Mullally, '"We are Inclusive but are we being Equal?" Challenges to Community National Schools Regarding Religious Diversity', PhD, Dublin City University, 2018, 22.
6   Emma O' Kelly, *State Gives Commitment to Catholic Church on Education*. Available from: <https://www.rte.ie/news/special-reports/2012/0328/315388-educationfoi/> (Accessed 1 May 2021).

leaving the growing bureaucratic demands associated with human resources, taxes and benefits and properties to the State.[7]

A second distinguishing feature of Community National Schools is that they were designed to be a truly multi-denominational education that would respond to growing diversity of religious beliefs and practices in Ireland. There is an over-abundance of placements for children seeking a Catholic education, where religious education is essentially faith formation or learning *into* a specific faith. Additionally, Educate Together schools are often perceived as being multi-denominational in name only. In principle, Educate Together adopted an approach that taught *about* religion that was essentially non-denominational and sidelined any religious instruction and faith formation to outside of the school day. In contrast, the CNS model originally sought to be authentically multi-denominational. They designed a curriculum whereby children of all religions and none could learn together, but not in a 'neutral' or about religion approach. Rather, the *Goodness Me, Goodness You* (GMGY) curriculum was initially designed to provide an education *from* within each student's religious perspective that allowed each child to deepen their own faith while also appreciating and learning to understand the religious or philosophical beliefs of other students. In this conception, the hope was that there would be a more genuine treatment of faith as well as an appreciation of growing religious diversity. GMGY was developed as a 'faith and belief-nurturing programme' rather than an 'ethical-moral programme' in the mould of Educate Together's *Learn Together* curriculum.[8] Again, supporters of GMGY argued that the Educate Together model was really more non-denominational or even secular, whereas the GMGY curriculum sought to be truly multi-denominational in its approach. Thus, the CNS approach saw itself as being even more respectful, diverse and inclusive, but also, at the outset, offering faith formation within the school day.

The GMGY curriculum was designed to combine faith development and greater knowledge and respect for the religious and/or philosophical

---

7   Seamus Conboy, Personal Interview, October 2019.
8   Clare Maloney, 'Community National Schools and Faith', *The Irish Times*, 10 June 2016.

beliefs of others.[9] To do this, Community National Schools originally included a core programme about religious beliefs that children of all religious beliefs and none took together for 80 % of their time in Religious Education (RE) courses. The remaining 20 % of time was devoted to Belief Specific Teaching (BST) where over four weeks each year children were differentiated into various belief groups, namely Catholic, Christian, Muslim and Humanist/Buddhist/Hindu (HBH) in accordance with the wishes of parents. During these specific belief modules, the faith and practices associated with relevant traditions were nurtured. The overall goal was to combine learning 'about' faith for most of the time with a learning 'from' or 'into' a faith perspective for the other part of the time.

The Community National Schools approach to teaching religion also sought to better engage parents and the local community. As all schools do, CNS acknowledges parents as the primary educators of their children, especially in terms of religious education. 'Each lesson includes an overview for parents that can be downloaded from the GMGY website with a suggested activity that parents can engage in with their child at home while relating the content to their own faith or belief perspective.'[10] Therefore, the goal of the model was for each child to develop their own faith and to bring this learning back into the classroom and school where all faiths and beliefs interact. Community National Schools also refer to sacramental education, rather than sacramental preparation, which is left to parents and the local parish. The goal was to reinforce what parents want and complement what takes place in school with the traditions, values and faith/beliefs that are being learned at home.

In terms of community engagement, 'The number of groups and the faith/belief targeted in the groups is proactively managed in each school and reflects the composition of faiths/beliefs in the school and the resources available to each school. The purpose of grouping the children according to their faith/belief traditions is to enable them to engage with the unique aspects of their faith/belief tradition.'[11] Again, this exposure

---

9   National Council for Curriculum and Assessment, '*Goodness Me, Goodness You! Programme for Junior Infants to Second Class Review Report: The Experiences of Stakeholders*', May 2018, Dublin: NCCA, 8.

10   Mullally, 2018, 12.

11   Mullally, 2018, 11–12.

to one's own faith, as well as those of other beliefs, was designed to foster diversity and inclusion. By originally hiring faith specific teachers to teach these belief-specific courses rather than classroom teachers, the goal was to provide a more authentic teaching of each religion or set of beliefs. This approach sought to distinguish itself from non-denominational or secular approaches as well as denominational education that focuses solely on one faith perspective.

II. From Aims to Reality in Pursuit of a Model

The Community National School model was barely over 10 years old in 2021. Thus, there is not a significant body of research that has examined the real impact of these schools. Nevertheless, the findings of a recent doctoral study – and a couple other studies – of the Community National School model point to the tension between ideals and aims on the one hand and implementation and practical realities on the other. The findings from the doctoral study are based on the results of a parental survey with nearly 170 responses and interviews of principals and teachers in seven different Community National Schools over the course of an academic year and published in 2018. Ironically, at the time of publication, Education and Training Boards Ireland (ETBI), the representative body for Community National Schools, introduced significant changes in the model based on some of the tensions underscored in this study, especially around how religion is taught in the schools.

Community National Schools are inclusive and multi-denominational, and many parents choose these schools for this reason. When asked whether CNS's inclusive ethos and catering for all faiths and beliefs were important to them when choosing the school for their children, 76 % parents in the study stated Yes, with only 17 % reporting that this was not important to them when choosing the school.[12] Additionally, a majority of parents were 'in favour of their children being exposed to different beliefs (83 %)

12   Mullally, 2018, 99.

and that Community National Schools should nurture their child's belief (82 %)'.[13] Similarly, most parents were in favour of their children participating in celebrations of different religious festivals (84 %) and secular festivals (87 %) in the school.[14] Thus, there was widespread support among parents, but also among teachers and principals, for the guiding principles that undergird the CNS model.

Nevertheless, there were significant challenges that Community National Schools faced when seeking to implement this diverse, inclusive and equal model. The diversity of views within and across religious and secular communities makes implementing these ideals exceedingly difficult – especially during a time when beliefs have been changing so quickly and dramatically. As critics suggest, how many students, parents, teachers, or principals need to object to how faith or beliefs are taught for this approach to feel exclusionary and unequal, thereby undermining the overall aims of the school? There have been conflicts in almost every aspect of how these schools seek to teach and celebrate diverse religious beliefs and those with no religious beliefs.

For starters, there were several challenges to implementing the *Goodness Me, Goodness You* (GMGY) curriculum, the cornerstone of the multi-denominational approach. A significant portion of GMGY depends on a narrative approach that nurtures a child's own sense of religious faith, belief and identity. This approach also relies on parents engaging students at home to deepen and integrate their children's sense of identity. The model encourages honest and open inter-faith conversations in the classroom as well. Although these are laudatory aims, they are hard to implement.

First, evidence from parental surveys suggests that there is mixed experience and knowledge of this programme among parents. Many teachers interviewed in the study did not think parents were engaging the GMGY curriculum at home. Results from the parents' surveys indicate that 49 % of parents agreed with the statement that they were 'very aware and engaged with the material at home', whereas 38 % of parents agreed with the statement that they were 'vaguely aware but do not discuss GMGY at home',

---

13 Mullally, 2018, 83
14 Mullally, 2018, 91–2.

9 % were 'unaware', and 4 % were 'uninterested'.[15] An overwhelming 95 % of parents surveyed agreed that they were the primary educators of their child in terms of values, beliefs and practices.[16] So even if these parents were not fully aware of what was going on with their children's religious education in the CNS (and many were not!), they took responsibility for their children's overall beliefs, whatever those might be.

A second major finding of this study was that many teachers, principals and parents were unclear about what nurturing religious beliefs meant. Consistent with other 'public school' models, the CNS model intends 'to provide an equality of religious education for all children, educating them together and fostering a respect for difference'. This conforms to teaching and learning *about* and *from* different beliefs rather than instruction or nurture *into* a particular worldview or religious belief.[17] Despite these stated goals, for many teachers and parents, nurturing beliefs equated with faith formation or instruction into faith, which is not the aim of Community National Schools. Thus, there was disagreement over what 'nurturing' meant and whether it was really the task of the school to enrich students' faith. In one school, there were over 100 complaints from parents of minority faiths about the content and approach to how their faith was being taught that the principal suspended the teaching of GMGY in that school.[18]

A related challenge is that most teachers, principals and parents involved in the study recognised that it is difficult to nurture the beliefs of all faiths. Teachers indicated that they did not have the knowledge, training, expertise, or comfort level to engage students' narratives about their own faith, let alone facilitate inter-faith conversations when the teachers and students lacked the religious literacy to have meaningful conversations. Most teachers are trained for denominational settings and historically there has been little training for pre-service teachers in a multi-denominational setting, so it is not surprising that many CNS teachers felt ill-equipped to teach the multi-faith and belief-specific aspects within Community

15   Mullally, 2018, 75.
16   Mullally, 2018, 116.
17   Mullally, 2018, 115.
18   Mullally, 2018, 76.

National Schools.[19] While support was provided to teachers as part of the introduction of GMGY there was still a perceived lack of training reported amongst teachers which made them uneasy in the classroom for fear of disrespecting or misrepresenting various beliefs, which often led them to shying away from or avoiding 'difficult conversations'.[20] A common criticism of Community National Schools is that 'while the so called multi-denominational, pluralist approach may seem attractive and inclusive in a more diverse Ireland, "the celebration of difference makes all religions, in the end, a matter of indifference" and will inevitably fail'.[21]

In addition to challenges with the multi-denominational portion of the curriculum, there were considerable obstacles in the Belief Specific Teaching section of the curriculum. This part of the junior infants to second class curriculum originally included four weeks of the year where students were separated into various belief groups and were taught by employed teachers at the school from a faith perspective on their particular religion or belief system. In principle, this was appealing to many parents, but there have been problems in implementing the programme. These problems raise issues for the model as a whole because they undermined the ability of CNS to provide both faith about multiple religions and about belief specific teachings, which was a key original feature that was meant to distinguish CNS from Educate Together schools.

First, there is an 'inequality of provision' within and across beliefs. For example, a majority of students are Catholic, and therefore more attention is often given to teaching the Catholic faith. This can make other, non-Catholic students feel as though they are missing out on something that a majority of children are experiencing. Previous research found that children in Community National Schools generally preferred not to be separated into belief-specific classes. For most non-Catholic students, they already learned about their faith at home or outside of schools in their respective religious communities.[22] Furthermore, a parental study of the content of the stories included in the GMGY programme found that 83 %

---

19   Mullally, 2018, 119.
20   Mullally, 2018, 77.
21   Mullally, 2018. 197.
22   Mullally, 2018, 107. See also Daniel Faas, Aimee Smith, and Merike Darmody, 'Children's Agency in Multi-Belief Settings: The Case of Community National

of the stories made sole reference to Christian beliefs, which underscored how many minority religious and non-religious parents felt that the curriculum was biased against them and inconsistent with an inclusive and equality-based curriculum.[23]

Additionally, many teachers and parents questioned how the 'Hindus, Buddhists and Humanists' could all be lumped together. As one parent noted, 'For a programme that claims to be so into equality and inclusivity, I don't think it really delivers that in belief-specific teaching.'[24] Another parent said that 'there is a perception in the school that religion is part of everyday life, a message that a religion, no matter what it is, is good. However, this does not support the children who are being raised in a non-religious environment. We automatically are lacking and different. I would prefer there to be no religious instruction in schools and no division of children. Religion should be taught in the appropriate religion's community of worship, not school.'[25] This captures the broader frustration of atheists and humanists that there exists a 'predisposition to the existence of God in the schools and that their children would be perceived as different or lacking due to their lack of belief in a God. They argued that religion should not be taught in public schools and is a private matter.'[26] Given the fact that the Primary Curriculum emphasises the role of schools in tending to spiritual formation as part of the holistic development of children, teaching religion was in keeping with this standard.[27]

Educate Together was also deeply critical of this separating of children based on their beliefs and argued that separate can never be equal. 'This raises serious legal difficulties for a State body, which must fully comply with our current equality legislation and constitutional obligations in relation to religious discrimination. If such practices are allowed, these schools will

---

Schools in Ireland'. *Journal of Research in Childhood Education*, 2018. <https://doi.org/10.1080/02568543.2018.1494645>.

23   Mullally, 2018, 108.
24   Mullally, 2018, 79.
25   Mullally, 2018, 83.
26   Mullally, 2018, 114.
27   Government of Ireland, *Primary School Curriculum*. Dublin Stationary Office, 1999.

be the only part of our State services in which separate treatment according to religion is permitted.'[28] These beliefs underscore the challenges facing the CNS model when seen through the lens of the human rights of the children. Slow motion images on national TV of non-White students huddled in a corner while the rest of the children – White and Irish – walked into other rooms as part of this religious segregation during the school day, stoked criticism of the CNS model in the early days.[29] Although the model was meant to be multi-denominational, it was portrayed as very Catholic and unequal in many public contexts.[30]

Further challenges associated with Belief Specific Teaching included teachers feeling ill-prepared and uncomfortable, divisions within faith and belief traditions, and logistical issues. The model shifted from originally seeking the assistance of experts in the various faith communities to lead the BST classes to eventually relying on regular classroom teachers to teach these courses as well. Although the teachers were not meant to be specialists or experts in the various faith or belief groups and felt ill-equipped to form children in their individual faith, they often became more faith-formation teachers than facilitators and felt uneasy about this role. Even though the original designers of the curriculum were excellent at facilitating inter-faith conversations, teachers on the ground struggled to realise the vision of the curriculum in the classroom. This would have required far more Continuing Professional Development (CPD) which was simply not possible in the context of the already overloaded curriculum and set of expectations placed on teachers. Add to this the changing faith life of teachers whereby increasing numbers had no religious affiliation, which also made it difficult to lead such faith conversations.[31]

The faith formation role was especially relevant for those teaching Catholic children, many of whom lack real knowledge of their faith because

28 Mullally, 2018, 34.
29 RTE, *Prime Time*, 8 April, 2010.
30 Seamus Conboy, Personal Interview, October 2019. See also Hyland, Á. and Bocking, B.. Religion, Education, and Religious Education in Irish Schools. *Teaching Theology and Religion*, 2015, Vol. 18, No. 3, 252–61.<https://doi.org/10.1111/teth.12292>.
31 Seamus Conboy, Personal Interview, October 2019.

they do not get much teaching at home.[32] This is due in part to the central role denominational schools have played historically in meeting this need. Within religious denominations, there are also significant differences in terms of beliefs, practices and overall value systems, which further complicates how teachers present the various religions in the classroom. It is not uncommon for parents of the same faith as the school patron to complain to the school about aspects of what is being taught in various classrooms, for example, in the area of Relationships and Sexual Education. Finally, there were logistical issues as well when in some schools there were forty children in one religious education class and in another classroom there were only three students. How to facilitate the classes and assign students became both a logistical, resource and political nightmare for administrators.[33]

Another major concern for all Community National Schools was how they dealt with sacraments. The CNS model originally adopted a sacramental education approach wherein students learned about the sacraments or key religious rites and rituals within school but participation in these religious rites of passage was facilitated outside of school by their respective religious groups. The Belief Specific Teaching for Catholic students nurtured their faith and understanding about the sacraments, but parents and parishes were supposed to prepare the students explicitly for the sacraments of Reconciliation and First Communion. In reality, there was significant variation in terms of how this was implemented across Community National Schools, and the implementation was largely dependent on the level of catechetical support available from local parishes. Unlike minority religions that have long been conducting religious education classes outside the normal school day, there is much less experience of this in Catholic parishes. In areas where local parishes had strong faith formation programmes for young people, the Community National Schools did not have to engage faith formation during the school day. However, in many schools, some form of sacramental preparation occurred during the school day, which was beyond what the GMGY programme outlined.[34]

32   Mullally, 2018, 80. See also Faas, Smith, and Darmody, 2018.
33   Mullally, 2018, 81.
34   Mullally, 2018, 85.

Irrespective of how sacramental education was delivered, there was a sense by most parents and teachers that there was a bias towards the Catholic faith.[35] Not only were Catholic students the only ones receiving sacramental preparation during school, but there appeared to be more support and emphasis on the Catholic faith compared to other religions or secular beliefs.[36] Recall that the Catholic Church insisted on faith formation during the school day as a non-negotiable requirement for Catholic children when they supported the creation of Community National Schools in 2007. As the curriculum dictates 2.5 hours for the patron's programme in all schools, children in Catholic schools have Religious Education for 2.5 hours per week, whereas the students in Community National Schools only had four weeks of more faith specific Religious Education. This contributed to Catholic bishops indicating that they did not consider CNS religious education sufficient faith formation for Catholic children.[37]

The CNS model also struggles with how to address religious festivals, symbols and ethos in a context that promotes diversity, inclusion and equality. It would be difficult for every religious or secular festival or belief to be celebrated or displayed within the school. In addition, Mullally argues that there is also plenty of diversity within religious traditions that makes it difficult to determine how and when festivals should be celebrated, and which symbols exhibited.[38] Some schools have over sixty different nationalities and twenty religions represented among their student body. Who decides which festivals or symbols gain prominence? Huge debates emerged within every school about how to deal with Christian holidays like Christmas and Easter or other holidays like Halloween, which is explicitly banned by Jehovah's Witnesses and Pentecostal churches. For some, there is enough about Christmas within broader Irish society that these schools should not be spending their time on this when there are so many other things to cover. As a result, Christmas is often replaced with a 'Winter Festival/Assembly' in schools. Others believe that this 'dumbing down' of Christmas in attempt to avoid offending non-Christians is unfair

35 Faas, Smith, and Darmody, 2018.
36 Mullally, 2018, 86–7.
37 Mullally, 2018, 118.
38 Mullally, 2018, 89.

to Christian students who celebrate the festivals of other religions and secular beliefs.[39] Curiously, when parents were asked to participate, lead and explain various religious and ethnic festivals, Hindu, Muslim and other minority religious parents jumped at the opportunity. In contrast, many White, Irish Catholics were unwilling or unable to explain the significance of the Nativity in front of others![40]

A challenge that emerged for Community National Schools was that minorities often felt even more different and exposed as the school sought to engage minority faiths or ethnicities. Comparative evidence suggests this has occurred in other countries as well. According to Mullaly, there is a 'tendency to emphasise minority belief celebrations more than majority celebrations [which] can result in an exoticising of minority cultures. It can actually contribute to emphasising that they are different and foreign to the norm.'[41] The lack of consensus about what festivals and symbols are most important, or about what the process is for making such choices should be, often leads to confusion and widely different results across Community National Schools. There ends up being more emphasis on cultural and secular aspects of religious festivals via artwork, food and traditional dress. As one teacher stated, 'This keeps things as secular and as diluted as possible and as child-centred and as fun and as inviting and as community-based as possible.'[42] Ultimately, Community National Schools seek to be non-exclusionary of any belief or religion while balancing and reflecting the beliefs of the children attending the school as the Forum on Patronage and Pluralism proposed.[43]

Community National Schools are State-run schools that are bound by equality legislation. Therefore, there are cases when religious beliefs are

---

39   Mullally, 2018, 91–2.
40   Seamus Conboy, Personal Interview, October 2019.
41   Mullally, 2018, 111.
42   Mullally, 2018, 91.
43   Mullally, 2018, 112 and *Forum on the Patronage and Pluralism in the Primary Sector: Progress to Date and Future Directions*, July 2014, 7 <https://www.education.ie/en/Press-Events/Events/Patronage-and-Pluralism-in-the-Primary-Sector/Progress-to-Date-and-Future-Directions-Forum-on-Patronage-and-Pluralism-in-the-Primary-Sector.pdf>.

superseded by established State law and this means some beliefs are valued more than others. For example, some Muslim and conservative Catholic parents have complained about same-sex marriage and how it was being supported within their Community National School. In this case, the State's laws take precedence over the religious beliefs of several religious traditions. Principals encourage parents to deepen whatever values they want their children to have at home, but also ensuring that their children are comfortable enough to be able to hear other perspectives and see other perspectives without totally taking it on. 'Therefore, in Community National schools, parents are encouraged to instil their family values, as well as their religious identities, within their children and are assured that their child has the right to express these values, once it is done in a respectful way.'[44] Like other public schools, Community National Schools seek to educate children in the shared values of justice, equality and rationality, and these values can and do come into conflict with some parents' beliefs. The schools must 'provide a forum for open and respectful sharing and debate, rather than seeking consensus', and it us up to the parents to impart their desired values.[45]

Most Community National Schools have become progressive in their attitudes and values, which is not ultimately neutral in that they do not support many views of more conservative faiths. Yet, because CNS are multi-denominational and emphasise equality, they often attract students of minority religions even though many of these students' parents have more conservative views. For example, prior to changes in the admissions legislation, Muslim parents may have had much more in common with the values and ideology of an all-girls Catholic school than a Community National School, but they would have ended up sending their children to a CNS because Catholic schools were oversubscribed.[46] Once Catholic schools could no longer accept children based on their faith, families of minority religions had more school options. Anecdotal evidence suggests that the combination of single-sex education and a more conservative set of values

---

44   Mullally, 2018, 100.
45   Mullally, 2018, 113.
46   Seamus Conboy, Personal Interview, October 2019.

often entices Muslim parents to send their children to Catholic schools over CNS where co-educational classes and acceptance and promotion of more progressive views is less appealing. Again, multi-denominational does not mean that all beliefs are accepted equally. In many ways, CNS are more about equity than equality – where equity is defined as seeking 'to understand and provide people with what they need rather than the same thing as everyone else'.[47]

Many Community National Schools set up physical spaces in prominent locations in their schools to manifest and engage their ethos. One principal described a CNS in CityWest in Dublin wherein as you entered the school there was a multi-belief wall opposite an equality wall. The multi-belief wall provided a place where parents and students could bring in images or objects that best represented their core beliefs and display them publicly. These objects ranged from crowns to crucifixes to love hearts (the latter placed there by atheist parents). There was even a public ceremony to ritualise these images and celebrate the diversity. On the opposing equality wall, there were words and images representing the nine grounds for discrimination in equality legislation to represent that all children and their families are treated equally regardless of their ethnicity, religion, orientation, beliefs, etc. According to this principal, the images on these walls would often conflict with one another and tensions would heighten. In many ways, these physical manifestations of religious and non-religious diversity created more tension and conflict than the GMGY curriculum did.[48] These tensions underscore the challenge of being both diverse and inclusive, let alone equal.

Given the challenges of engaging all religious beliefs and trying to be all things to all people, the leaders of the Community National Schools in ETBI conducted an eighteen-month review of its model. The process included school leaders, teachers, educational experts and parents. As mentioned, there was growing disaffection among Catholic leaders who thought that students in CNS were not receiving adequate faith formation. Likewise,

---

47   Clow, B., Bernier, J., Haworth-Brockman, M. and Pederson, A., *Rising to the Challenge: Sex-and-Gender-Based Analysis for Health Planning, Policy and Research in Canada*. Nova Scotia: Atlantic Centre of Excellence for Women's Health, 2009.
48   Seamus Conboy, Personal Interview, October 2019.

many parents from other faiths, especially Muslims, thought that their faith was not being taught well either. A growing sense emerged that cultivating or forming faith was not really occurring for any religion. As a result, the decision was made to move all religious formation outside of the school day and students were no longer separated into Belief Specific Teaching groups for four weeks each year for junior infants to second class programme.[49] The NCCA also carried out a review of the original GMGY programme that took into consideration the views of ETBs, school leaders, teachers, parents and children of their experiences of the programme. This led to the GMGY curriculum being revised to become less explicitly focused on religious diversity and became 'more accurately described as a values and ethics curriculum rather than religious.'[50]

The vocal complaints of Muslim parents about how religion was being taught concerned the Department of Education officials who desperately wanted to avoid further public scrutiny over accusations of mistreatment of Muslim and other minority students in Community National Schools. As one former VEC leader reported, separating students for religious education 'became the rock on which the religion programme foundered.'[51] Initially sacramental preparation was suspended in some schools but ultimately a decision was taken by ETBs to do no more sacramental preparation during the school day.

As a result of these decisions, CNS developed four strands within its Patrons Programme curriculum to broaden its attempt to be both multi-denominational and equality-based. These strands are beliefs and religions, values, philosophy and identity. The beliefs and religions portion teaches about various religions, but also maintains learning from religion by keeping the family project as a key part of the curriculum. The values section focuses on issues of right and wrong and explores Irish, EU and international (i.e. United Nations) values and sought to teach children about individual versus societal values. The philosophy portion of the curriculum exposes

49 Seamus Conboy, Personal Interview, October 2019.
50 Daniel Faas, Aimee Smith, and Merike Darmody, 'Between Ethos and Practice: Are Ireland's New Multi-denominational Primary Schools Equal and Inclusive', *Compare*, 2019, Vol. 49, No. 4, 602–18.
51 Marie Griffin, Personal Interview, September 2020.

children to different ways of thinking about the world and emphasised developing skills in dialogue and appreciating pluralism. Finally, the identity section engages issues such as race, language and sexual orientation in addition to religious beliefs.[52]

ETBI leaders report that the new curriculum, which was developed by the NCCA, freed teachers up from focusing solely on nurturing faith and religious beliefs to a broader exposure to different sets of values. This helped teachers move beyond the fear of not knowing what to say to students when they did not know what they believed or what the various faith taught on various issues. No longer bound to what religious leaders or others in society determined what was right, many teachers found their own voices and could more readily listen to the voices of the students – one of the goals of the story/narrative approach. However, the rapidly changing nature of Irish society and the growth of various sets of beliefs that have become acceptable means that there is no clear direction of what ideas, values and beliefs should be included in the curriculum and which should not.[53] For leaders of this model, the reliance on the narrative approach and heavy parental involvement, in combination with the diverse set of festivals, celebrations and symbols present within CNS, helps these schools be truly multi-denominational and equal in their approach.

The leaders within ETBI were pleased with the changes brought about as a result of the review processes but were unsure how these decisions would be received throughout their network of schools. Although Community National Schools were seeking to develop a model, their organic growth meant that each school was slightly different in how they sought to implement their approach to meet local needs. Therefore, ETBI encouraged all Community National Schools to incorporate these changes to the curriculum and the move to facilitating any faith formation outside of normal school hours, but they did not force the schools to make this change immediately. ETBI leaders were surprised that all of their schools adopted these changes within one year, rather than the eight years that they were

---

52   Megan Whyte, Educational Policy and Development Officer, ETBI, Personal Interview, October 2019.

53   Megan Whyte, Personal Interview, October 2019.

allotted. In fact, many of the more rural schools were most eager to make the change, which was surprising given the higher levels of religiosity in more rural areas. Many teachers within smaller, rural schools that often had to combine classes were thrilled that sacramental preparation would no longer dictate the schedule for all students, let alone those in 2nd (First Communion) and 6th class (Confirmation). Additionally, a majority of parents were also convinced that these changes would help overcome the demands of the overall curriculum and better help students of all religious beliefs and none deal with the challenges of religious diversity.[54]

Almost overnight, this model of seeking to engage faith-based education within the school day was dramatically altered and there was virtually no push back. Although there remains some variation across Community National Schools because they each seek to meet local needs and all the schools face different demographic realities, there was uniformity on the fundamental issue of how and when religious beliefs would be engaged. This was a key stage in Community National Schools' development. Although there had been attempts to nourish all faiths and none, this proved nearly impossible. The shift to teaching *from* religion to teaching *about* religion was something Educate Together had done early in its model as well. The difference this time was that Community National Schools were a State model and this could impact the expansion of Educate Together and other patrons over time as it continues to develop.[55]

Not everyone has celebrated this critical shift in the CNS model. An educational leader from the then VEC reported that there was real excitement about Community National Schools in the beginning. There was real hope that a model that brought together children of all faiths and none, including Catholics, could foster new learning and community building in the new diverse Ireland. The pressure of logistics, training and management of its implementation combined to undermine the original vision.

Public pressure on the model may have also contributed to this shift. A 2010 *Prime Time* report on RTÉ by education correspondent Emma O'Kelly featured criticisms of the way religious education was carried out

54   Seamus Conboy, Personal Interview, October 2019.
55   Marie Griffin, Personal Interview, September 2020.

in the new Community National Schools. During the segment, Labour's Education spokesman Ruairí Quinn, TD, claimed the pilot programme schools had been hijacked by the Church and was highly secretive. The Broadcasting Authority of Ireland (BAI) upheld complaints against the programme and faulted it for failing to fully and accurately represent the views of the Department of Education and vocational education commit-tees that were running the schools.[56] Despite this ruling, sufficient damage appeared to have been done to challenge the credibility of the new model.

The straw the broke the camel's back was the targeted pressure by Muslim parents to school leaders that their children were not being taught properly. The desire to avoid the charge of discriminating against Muslims or any other minorities (or the fear of being accused of such discrimination), hastened the shift in the CNS model, leading CNS to look much more like Educate Together schools than it had originally planned.[57] The with-drawal of Church support for the model happened almost simultaneously with the change in the CNS model. The ETBI attempted to establish an acceptable alternative with the Church to make divestment by Catholic patrons to the ETB's Community National School model more attractive.[58] Ultimately this was unsuccessful, but as Chapter 10 will describe, this has not been a barrier to the CNS model dominating in the divestment space.

III. From Developing a Model to Building a Network

The organic growth of how Community National Schools modified its curriculum and adapted its ethos model is just one key stage in its overall development. The State was dipping its toes in the water, testing the tem-perature and how well it could survive the changing educational and social

---

56   Paul Cullen, 'Complaints Upheld as Authority Rules "Prime Time" Report Lacked Balance', *The Irish Times*, 30 June 2010.

57   Marie Griffin, Personal Interview, September 2020.

58   Kate Liffey, former Director of Catechetics for the Irish Catholic Bishop's Conference, Personal Interview, October 2019.

environment. The other critical step in Community National Schools' development is how the organisation has grown both locally and nationally. As stated previously, Community National Schools are State-owned and operated schools that are under the authority of local Education and Training Boards and, therefore, have certain benefits and obstacles. Unlike Educate Together, CNS has the benefit of being a 'late developer'. According to famous economic historian Alexander Gerschenkron, there can be a benefit to emerging after others have paved the way. Later developers can learn from their predecessor's mistakes and often skip stages of growth and expansion because new technology, resources and insights make such rapid development possible. There is often an increased pressure on later developers to grow more quickly in order to survive. As a result, later developers often receive significant state support to expand more swiftly.[59]

As State-owned schools, Community National Schools have certain benefits. In particular, CNS rely on their patron ETBs to resolve many of the managerial, bureaucratic and facilities issues confronting schools. Most Irish primary schools are dependent on voluntary boards of management to oversee important, and often time-consuming, matters such as hiring and firing of personnel, as well as managing other human resources, maintenance and building-related demands of schools. Community National Schools have an in-built State system that oversees many of these executive management type of issues that occupy large percentages of time that principals and boards in most other schools must address. According to one ETBI leader this led some parents and local communities in existing schools under other patrons to seek out Community National Schools as their patron because they wanted the State – not private providers – to be the patron (and thus the employer) so the State could deal with teachers and principals in more professional ways.[60] This allows leaders and boards in Community National Schools to focus on enhancing their school's curriculum and instruction so they can provide the best possible education for

---

59 Alexander Gerschenkron, *Economic Backwardness in Historical Perspective*. Cambridge: Harvard University Press, 1962.
60 Seamus Conboy, Personal Interview, October 2019.

their students rather than getting bogged down in dealing with overflowing toilets, leaks, repairs, dilapidated classrooms, overcrowded lunchrooms and, of course, personnel complaints.[61] Many parents perceived this new model as a good thing, feeling assured that as a state school, Community National Schools would provide better oversight and feel a lot like the Community Schools at the secondary level that had already proven themselves.[62]

It is not all roses! One downside for CNS is that they have higher levels of regulation, accountability, and transparency due to their public status and this often creates considerable bureaucratic paperwork, which can be time-consuming and distracting. Nevertheless, the access to State resources and personnel to deal with running schools is an advantage CNS have over other patrons. More detail on how this has worked in specific schools in Kerry that divested patronage to stay alive will be discussed in Chapter 10 on the Church's response to these educational reforms.

The existence of a pre-established administrative supports has been an attractive selling point for schools seeking new leadership. Of the twenty-seven Community National Schools established up to 2021, eleven were divested from existing patrons (Catholic Church, Church of Ireland and Steiner). Surprisingly, Community National Schools have emerged more in rural and commuter areas and less in large, urban and diverse settings where one might have expected higher demand for multi-denominational education due to greater levels of racial and religious diversity. Declining populations, shifting demographics and a desire to differentiate themselves from other local schools have been commonly given reasons for seeking CNS patronage. Although ETBI has encouraged local ETBs to accept many of the invitations to take over schools that they have been given, they have also been cautious to avoid assuming leadership of failing schools that are merely seeking a last resort by the local community to salvage their school. Given the pressure to prove its ability to deliver a strong educational experience, ETBI must make the most of opportunities to succeed.[63]

61   Seamus Conboy, Personal Interview, October 2019.
62   Marie Griffin, Personal Interview, September 2020.
63   Seamus Conboy, Personal Interview, October 2019.

Community National Schools have benefitted greatly from their access to State resources and personnel. However, the fact that real authority lies with the sixteen individual Education and Training Boards (ETBs) and not with the representative body, Education and Training Boards Ireland (ETBI), complicates how the model works in practice. The sixteen ETBs replaced the thirty-three Vocational Education Committees (VECs) that had been overseeing education since the 1930s. The reform was designed to streamline the annual planning process and to give the Minister of Education more direct authority. For example, the Minister could require an ETB to establish a school or other education or training institution or permit an ETB to jointly operate education facilities with other bodies and, in certain circumstances, to provide support services to other education or training providers.[64]

While enhancing the Minister's authority, this reform also perpetuated and consolidated local officials' authority over education. Nevertheless, unclear lines of authority have made it difficult to know who is in charge and made it more difficult for ETBI to ensure its evolving model would be implemented. For example, in addition to the Chief Executive, every ETB has several additional leaders on its staff, including the Director of Schools, Director of Further Education and the Director of Organisational Services. Additionally, each ETB is comprised of twelve local authority representatives (i.e. elected county councillors), two staff representatives, two parents' representatives and five members from bodies representing local community and business interests.[65] When legal questions emerge, it is uncertain whether the chair of the ETB, chief executive, or one of the directors has ultimate responsibility. Ironically, the State has essentially replicated a challenge facing the Catholic Church, whereby the national and local aims may not always align. Like the Church where each individual bishop is the patron of schools in his diocese and, within the confines of State curriculum, legislation and regulation, has a large degree of autonomy in the exercise of their patronage even if it contradicts national

---

64   <https://www.education.ie/en/Press-Events/Press-Releases/2013-Press-Releases/ PR-%202013-%2007-%2001.html> (Accessed: 4 September 2020).

65   <https://www.education.ie/en/Press-Events/Press-Releases/2013-Press-Releases/ PR-%202013-%2007-%2001.html> (Accessed: 4 September 2020).

goals set out by the Bishops' Conference, each ETB can make its own decisions about how to run their schools. This undermines speaking with
one voice and ensuring a consistent model that ETBI has been working
hard to develop. The practice of some ETBs at secondary level entering
joint patronage arrangements with Educate Together may also contribute
to undermining the idea of a consistent model and values unique to ETB
multi-denominational schools.[66]

Finally, there are also competing interests for individual members
on the ETBs and the Board as a whole. It is not uncommon to see a local
County Councillor cutting the ribbon for new school buildings of various
patrons in their area because they seek to attract attention for being involved in delivering a new school to the local community. Meanwhile,
the same County Councillor may be a member of the local ETB that is
responsible for advancing the interests of Community National Schools
in the same area. The desire to be perceived as the broker and deliverer of
goods and services from the State to the local constituency has been and
continues to be the bread and butter of successful politicians and state officials. This can entice local ETBs to assume leadership of schools so they
can get credit for saving schools without real attention to safeguarding
the model. For example, some ETBs have started Community National
Schools but due to the local context they have essentially remained Catholic
in practice. Concerns about this practice at secondary level have been well
documented.[67] This may allow members of the ETB to get credit for serving
local needs, but it may undermine the overall model and prevent further
growth of CNS given they are designed to be multi-denominational in
nature. It appears as though local ETBs may need to be reminded of the
model so they know that religion is taught outside of school hours and
that local parishes must respond to the faith needs of their communities.

Last, the ETBs were tasked by the Department to gauge the parental
demand for various primary school patrons in their local areas. Although
many surveys were conducted in 2018–19, none of the results have been

66   Kate Liffey, former Director of Catechetics for the Irish Catholic Bishop's
      Conference, Personal Interview, October 2019.
67   Emma O'Kelly, 'Documents Reveal Catholic Influence in State Schools', *RTE.ie*,
      15 October 2017.

published. The fact that ETBs have been tasked with both regulating local educational matters in their areas and promoting and providing the CNS patronage model reinforces the competing institutional roles this model encompasses. As discussed in Chapter 2, it is unclear whether the blurred responsibilities contributed to these delays and conflicting reports concerning the data.

These factors leave ETBI fighting an uphill battle as they seek to consolidate and expand their model. Complex dynamics on the local ETBs make it more productive for ETBI to focus their efforts on the directors and principals of specific schools because they are the ones on the ground doing the work. Despite the occasional attempt by ETB members to grab the spotlight in the local community for their involvement in CNS, it appears as though these members tend to defer to principals' and ETBI leaders' educational expertise on most day-to-day operational matters. However, these lines of authority often remain murky and force ETBI to persuade and convince key stakeholders of the importance of the model.

Although local ETBs have considerable financial and personnel resources to support local Community National Schools, there are only two ETBI staff members paid for by the State supporting CNS at the primary level. Additionally, ETBI's budget is determined each year by the Department with little attention to medium- and longer-term strategic goals. There is plenty of rhetoric by politicians and political parties of Ireland having 400 multi-denominational schools by 2030, but there is very little attention given to how the State, as a specific patron, will contribute to achieving this goal. This budgetary structure undermines ETBI's ability to strategically plan for the future.

Another key structural limitation is that Community National Schools (and therefore ETBI) are often treated as one patron among many competing for state resources for new and existing schools, which hinders large-scale growth in the number of schools it can operate. Unlike Educate Together, which has a national office of nearly twenty-five staff members and over forty years of experience lobbying parents to demand new primary schools in local areas, ETBI has a small staff focused on primary schools and limited central resources.[68] The fact that ETBI has never been formally included in State planning about new schools, let alone a longer-term vision for the primary sector, reinforces that despite the Community National Schools being State-run schools, the individual ETBs remain just another patron.

A striking feature of the development of Community National Schools is that it was an innovative response to a dramatically shifting demographic reality within Ireland. On the one hand, the State was responding to the growing demand for diverse primary school patrons, especially non-Catholic school alternatives. The State directly providing education rather than relying on private patrons to deliver primary education could lead to longer-term, potentially dramatic changes in the system. On the other hand, the State realised that the Church, despite its declining moral authority among large numbers of the population, retained control over 90 % of all primary schools and it would not divest large numbers of its schools without some sense that the faith needs of its young followers would be addressed in some way. This different way of offering a multi-denominational education softened Church opposition to this reform and helped diversify school patrons. The CNS model was initiated at the very time Ireland's Celtic Tiger economy was collapsing, which greatly restricted the financial resources available to build up the network of schools. In the end, the reliance on local ETBs allowed the state to serve local needs, but it also made implementing a coherent national model more difficult. This classic 'Irish solution to an Irish problem' demonstrated a certain degree of responsiveness and meeting local needs, but it also created competing interests with limited resources to make longer-term, lasting change more likely.

It is unclear what the medium- and longer-term impact of the shift in how Community National Schools deliver a multi-denominational education will affect their appeal among the Irish public. Initially, the unique selling point for CNS's model versus Educate Together's model was that faith formation and instruction was offered during the school day. As CNS shifted, their model appears similar in approach to that employed in Educate Together schools. Leaders within ETBI would still argue that

---

68   <https://www.etbi.ie/about-etbi/etbi-team/>

the relationships with parents and local communities and the incorporation of faith-based and secular festivals and symbols within Community National Schools represents a qualitatively different educational experience. This embrace of the local community is also at the heart of the Educate Together network however, and both patron programmes share a focus on ethics, equality and the diversity of belief systems (and associated rituals) active in society. If the CNS model is to continue to grow it will likely need to continue to clarify its model and differentiate itself within the multi-denominational sector.[69]

Critics of the CNS model argue that these schools are merely responding to market sentiment and that the model lacks clarity and conviction. If such a core element of the model and one of the salient points of difference with other school patrons was ditched so quickly, detractors wonder how strong of a school model this really is. There is a risk that a market-driven evolution could continue to transform the model given strong local demands and variation among ETBs in terms of the type of education they wish to deliver. Although there is a sense that Community National Schools have become more pluralist than multi-denominational as a result of their change to religious formation and/or instruction occurring outside of school, they have intentionally not adopted this language. Though Educate Together officially changed their charter and now describe themselves as offering an equality-based education, they end up speaking publicly in terms of being multi-denominational because that is what people know and recognise. Again, whether people like it or not, religion continues to define the system and the nature of all patrons, and a school is known for being denominational or multi-denominational even if it is more secular or pluralist in reality.

Proponents of Educate Together argue that they have consistently delivered a strong ethical education and that their model has withstood the test of time. Educate Together's unique selling point has also been that their 'movement' enlists a high degree of parental involvement, particularly

---

69   *Learn Together, an Ethical Education Curriculum for Educate Together Schools,* Educate Together, 2011 and *Goodness Me, Goodness You, Curriculum for Community National Schools,* NCCA, 2018.

at the initiation stage through grass roots organising of a local campaign to open a school. This initial strong reliance on parents to demand a school in the first place stands in contrast to the state bureaucracy of ETBs. This can be spun in different ways. For Community National Schools, their schools are different in part from Educate Together because of the financial and administrative resources they obtain from the State. Community National Schools are also experiencing a smoother transition into the secondary education sector because of the large, and growing, number of schools in the ETB sector. The ETBs are joint patrons, with largely Catholic groups, of Community Schools and Community Colleges, schools that were previously under the former VECs. They also hold patronage of non-designated Community Colleges which were historically called 'Techs' under the old VECs. Thus, ETBI, as the representative patron body for all ETBs, is seeking to link the model of education at the primary level to what it does or will provide at the secondary level. Similar to Educate Together, such a goal is another step in the development of their model and attempt to attract students from junior infants all the way through to the Leaving Certificate. The growing competition to attract parental support at all levels elicits such behaviour and helps explain why the different patrons are growing in similar ways.

Although there is a complex relationship between Community National Schools and the Department of Education and Skills, the Department appears to be growing in their support for CNS as evidenced by the numbers of new schools established between 2014 and 2019. From 2014 to 2016, Educate Together was given patronage of thirteen new schools, while ETBs opened just 5. In the subsequent three years (2017–19), there was a noticeable shift in new school patronage. In this latter period, Educate Together was granted patronage of eleven new schools and the ETBs just one behind with ten new schools. The growing preference of parents for the CNS model, expressed through the parental preference surveys discussed in Chapter 3, should not be discounted in explaining this growth of new schools also. Over this same three-year period, if you include divested schools the ETB/CNS number of new schools jumps to twenty new schools, with Educate Together schools remaining static at 11. Such trends point to growing competition between Educate Together and Community

National Schools in the coming years as to who will open more schools. The current Government's commitment to 'expand and prioritise the transfer of viable schools to Community National Schools' signals strong support from legislators that the CNS is at the heart of the next chapter of Irish primary education.[70]

One leading educational policy expert reported in 2019 that there had been high-level talks among leaders of the Community National Schools/ ETBI, the Catholic Church and the Department about divestment of over 200 some schools. It is long been perceived that Church leaders preferred divesting their schools to Community National Schools compared to Educate Together Schools. The presumption is that CNS is more amenable to learning and promoting the faith of their students, whereas Educate Together schools are far more secular in their approach.[71] Such an agreement has not materialised, but if it did, this would greatly accelerate the reforms in this area and help overcome the lack of concrete implementation to achieve the Forum's original goals. The changes to the original CSN model whereby in-school faith specific education was removed from the model undermined some level of trust by Church leaders towards the emerging model at the primary level. Nevertheless, the long-standing partnership between the Church and the ETBs at secondary level as co-patrons points to future possibilities between these two stakeholders.

IV. Conclusion

This chapter has reviewed the creation and development of the Community National Schools (CNS) model of multi-denominational schools. The emergence of the CNS model is largely a response to the need for a different model, one in which the state owns, operates and

70 *Programme for Government: Our Shared Future*, October 2020, <https://www.gov.ie/en/publication/7e05d-programme-for-government-our-shared-future/> (Accessed: 6 January 6, 2021).

71 Personal Interview with leading Irish educational policy expert, October 2019.

controls every aspect of the educational experience. Furthermore, the model was specifically designed to provide a markedly different educational experience than both the dominant Catholic school model and its primary alternative, Educate Together schools. The State has assumed greater involvement and control in every aspect of education in recent decades, including overseeing the curriculum, teacher training, continuing professional development, guidelines for boards of management and all issues related to land, property, buildings and other financial concerns. By establishing its own schools, the State has further consolidated its role in the primary sector and has begun to eliminate some of the overlapping or competing interests between the State and private patrons, especially over legal and financial responsibilities, but also over issues related to ethos. Proponents of the CNS model argue that principals and teachers can get back to focusing on delivering excellent curriculum and instruction and leaving the growing bureaucratic demands associated with human resources, taxes and benefits and properties to the State. For some, Educate Together never would have had to be developed had the Community National Schools existed back in the 1970s. The existence of this new model has created greater competition among non-Catholic school patrons, but it has also provided a sneak preview of what a State-led secular school system might look like in Ireland in the years ahead if support for more radical educational reforms continues to grow and the Community National School model becomes the default choice of the State for new and divesting schools.

CHAPTER 7

Irish Media and Primary Education Reform

I. Introduction

The media has continued to grow in importance in Irish society in recent decades. Political analysts often credit the Irish media with challenging the authority of the Church and the State, as well as promoting or elevating progressive concerns about equality and inclusion in a rapidly changing Irish society. This chapter provides original analysis of media coverage of key educational issues, actors and institutions over the past several decades to show precisely how the media engages educational reform. We assess the extent to which the media defines how educational problems are framed and what possible solutions are available. Given the media's important role in the marriage equality and abortion campaigns, it is informative to observe how the media engages the politics of educational reform. We were curious whether the media is merely the arena wherein educational debates occur, or whether it operates as another key actor that has its own set of interests and goals within these key reform debates.

The chapter begins with an overview of the media landscape in Ireland, offering both a historical overview of the media landscape and a more focused review of how the media engages the contemporary Irish political process. The bulk of the chapter reports results from a longitudinal examination of how Ireland's two leading newspapers, the *Irish Independent* and *The Irish Times*, engage primary education issues. After a quick look at the overall issues covered in these leading papers, we focus on the issues discussed within our policy case study chapters in the final section of the book: divestment, admissions and curriculum. We highlight the frequency in which actors and issues are covered, and we also examine the sentiment associated with this coverage. This sentiment analysis allows us to explore the tone associated with various actors and issues to gauge whether the media has its own biases or whether it provides a balanced perspective of the debates. We find that the media is certainly a key actor within the Irish political system because it informs and shapes the nature of the debate. Nevertheless, the coverage of the educational debates was balanced with fairly equal treatment of the various sides of the debate both in terms of frequency and tone of the coverage.

II. Political Reporting and the Irish Media Landscape

The Irish love their news! Ireland's high literacy rates and levels of educational attainment, combined with Irish citizens' social nature and love of being in the know, make them active consumers of news in all its forms. Like most advanced countries, Ireland's media landscape has grown and diversified over the last century evolving from print to radio to television to social media. With each stage of development, the earlier predominant forms have not been entirely eclipsed. According to one study, 'television remains the most popular platform for accessing the news in Ireland, at 73 %, followed by online media (70 %). RTÉ has the greatest reach at 64 %, followed by the Independent News and Media at 44 %, *The Irish Times* at 37 % and breakingnews.ie at 24 %. Just over half (52 %) of Irish people say they use social media platforms as a source of news each week. Nevertheless, traditional print media remains an extremely important source of political information for the Irish public.'[1]

A 2020 Reuters Institute for the Study of Journalism published a Digital News Report with slightly different findings. This report suggests a greater structural decline for TV and print media and much stronger role for online (including social media) sources in terms of where people

---

1   Michael Breen, Michael Courtney, Iain McMenamin, Eoin O'Malley and Kevin Rafter, *Resilient Reporting: Media Coverage of Irish Elections Since 1969*. Manchester: Manchester University Press, 2019, 22.

living in Ireland get their news.[2] Between 2015 and 2020, the report indicates that TV declined as a source from 76 % to 64 % and print from
50 % to 32 %. In terms of social media, 80 % of respondents claiming they
get their news online in 2020. This is potentially misleading because many
Irish get their news from the online outlets of print or TV sources. Nearly
70 % read their news on their smart phones, which helps explain the great
decline in physical print sources. There exists far greater diversity of sources
in the online outlets.[3] Irrespective of the platform, Irish news gatherers
report having the greatest trust in the traditional sources. RTÉ (76 %),
The Irish Times (75 %) and the *Irish Independent* (73 %) were rated as the
three most trusted sources of Irish news according to the Reuters Report.
Additionally, a 2020 communications research study found that of the top
100 journalists in Ireland based on six different measures, 58 % were print
journalists, 29 % were broadcast journalists and 13 % were online journalists.
In this study, *The Irish Times* had the most journalists in the top 100 with
24, followed by RTÉ with 17 and Independent News and Media with 14.[4]
Despite the persistence of traditional sources, younger people are certainly
accessing news in different ways, and the rise of online sources, and in particular social media, were deeply influential during the same-sex marriage
and abortion referenda campaigns as Chapter 8 will underscore. The importance of social media has increased over the last decade, but it is still an
emerging phenomenon. Given our interest in examining how educational
issues have been addressed over the last sixty years, with a particular focus
on reforms since 2000, an analysis of print media is more valuable than a
detailed study of social media trends.

When television emerged in the 1960s, circulation of all Irish national newspapers was about 216,000 per week. Irish newspaper readership peaked at 1.24 million in 2009 and has dropped over the last decade
to about 736,323 in 2018. Therefore, at its peak readership just a decade

2   <http://www.digitalnewsreport.org/survey/2020/ireland-2020/>
3   For example, respondents report weekly use of *The Irish Times* print (18 %) and
     online (17 %) and *Irish Independent* print (20 %) and online (31 %). Therefore,
     where Irish citizens are getting their news is a little less clear than the numbers
     portray.
4   <https://www.murraytweetindex.ie/>

ago, a quarter of Ireland was getting their news from national papers. The *Irish Independent/Sunday Independent* and *The Irish Times* are the two leading national papers, with readerships of 513,487 and 265,058 respectively in 2018.[5]

In addition to diversifying the types of media, and the numbers of sources within each medium, the overall character of political reporting has changed. According to a recent study, *Resilient Reporting: Media Coverage of Irish Elections Since 1969,* Irish media was partisan and deferential to priests and bishops and to politicians and their parties during the early period of the Irish state. Reporters covering politics before the 1960s generally relayed what happened in parliament and not much else. It was not uncommon for Catholic bishops to edit key stories or government ministers to squash articles they deemed unhelpful or harmful. *Resilient Reporting* authors indicate that there was a shift in the 1960s towards weaker partisanship of ownership and a more critical approach to authority in what they call 'critical impartiality' among reporters. Rather than deferring to politicians, priests and bishops, media began to engage leaders in debate and hold them accountable for their actions, as well as offering their own analysis and comments on the events they covered. The rise of television is often credited with this shift, but the authors of *Resilient Reporting* argue that, in reality, the Broadcasting Act of 1960 removed the Government's ability to intervene directly in broadcasting. This act committed the national broadcaster to impartial coverage of politics and other controversial issues, but it allowed a new generation of eager journalists to stop merely reporting verbatim what politicians had said in parliament and to introduce a more critical and dialogic approach to journalism.[6] Although this legislation pertained more to the national television and radio station, RTÉ, print media is perceived as also having maintained this critical impartiality as well.

The rise of social media has created a new phenomenon whereby journalists become very vocal, and perhaps more outspoken in their opinions on their personal platforms than they are in their professional writing in

---

5   Breen et al., 2019, 24; <https://newsbrandsireland.ie/data-centre/circulation/>.
6   Breen et al., 2019, 21–2.

media outlets. Popular journalists like Fintan O'Toole and Una Mullaly often expand on their professional positions when posting personally online in a tone that shifts from journalist to campaigner or advocate. Emma O'Kelly, the RTÉ Education Correspondent, has been criticised for being explicitly critical of the Catholic Church's role in education in her official coverage, and she is even more outspoken in her personal tweets, which are often picked up by other news sources.[7] The rising popularity of annual awards for the most influential Irish journalists on Twitter confirms the growing significance of online journalism. As a result of this dual personal and professional reporting, most informed consumers of the news will understand where journalists' ideological home is despite the impartiality of most professional reporting. Although taking a closer look at this critical distinction is worth understanding in greater detail, this lies outside the scope of this study.

Unlike patterns in many other advanced democracies dominated by significant market competition in the media sector, Ireland's media has not succumbed to 'hypercritical infotainment' to sell their products and increase their profit margins. *Resilient Reporting* concludes that Ireland's media system is guided by enduring and relatively strict norms of critical impartiality, whereby the media plays a positive role in conveying political information and encouraging public debate. The authors argue that most political reporters do have their own personal views, but they do present them in non-partisan ways. At least in terms of party-political competition, Ireland's political journalists have usually restricted themselves to providing an arena for debate instead of taking sides. Therefore, Irish journalists do not generally express their political opinions through their reporting.[8]

7   The Catholic Primary Schools Management Association (CPSMA) filed an official complaint against RTÉ concerning Ms O'Kelly's reporting. According to the BAI Code of Fairness, Objectivity & Impartiality, Rule 21, 'A news presenter and/or a reporter in a news programme may not express his or her own view on matters that are either of public controversy or the subject of current public debate.' CPSMA argued that all 20 of Ms O'Kelly's RTÉ stories between January 2015 and May 2017 on the theme of religion, education and the state portrayed the Catholic Church negatively. The report also argues 91 % of Ms Kelly's personal tweets during this same period on this same theme were also negative in tone.

8   Breen et al., 2019, 21, 58.

The bulk of political reporting and commentary in Ireland focuses on elections and parliamentary activity. The sheer number of political journalists has grown dramatically from less than 12 in 1969 to over 130 in 2016.[9] In general, political reporting concentrates on political parties and their leaders, elected officials, candidates and policies. In recent years with the increased reliance on referenda to deal with controversial issues such as abortion and same-sex marriage, there has also been focused media coverage during these campaigns. The targeted and concentrated nature of these campaigns tends to elevate media attention on the specific issues covered in referenda. Rather than media driving the debate, Ireland's journalists seem to follow the rhythm of political competition.

Unlike elections where parties and candidates draw most of the attention, referenda campaigns often highlight other civil society groups and voices. The extra-parliamentary character of referenda has provided Ireland's major parties with an institutional vehicle for turning contentious issues over to voters without exposing themselves to the realignment risks of a general election. Although minor parties have used referenda as a bully pulpit to challenge major parties, the nature of referenda as second-order campaigns focused on single issues has limited the longer-term electoral consequences of minor parties. The overall effect has been to keep electoral and referenda competition distinct from one another. Referenda have provided insulation for the major parties, protecting them from having to alter their winning formula of sustaining strong partisan attachments, instead allowing them to offer broad, catchall ideological appeals during general elections.[10]

The very existence of referenda provides major parties with a powerful tool when forced into the predicament of taking sides on controversial issues. Not surprisingly, over 80 % of TDs in McGraw's 2007 and 2011 Parliamentary Surveys admitted that they campaigned less during referenda than in general elections. Ireland's major parties have increasingly – and deliberately – ceded the referenda domain to single-issue groups, who, in

9   Breen et al., 2019, 27.
10   Sean McGraw, *How Parties Win: Shaping the Irish Political Arena*. Ann Arbor: University of Michigan Press, 2015.

turn, mobilise unattached voters. These single-issue groups are less likely to take their cues from political parties. Winning or losing referenda appears to be less crucial to the major parties than ensuring that the issues – once in referendum – do not spill over into the electoral arena. Major parties often choose not to adopt decisive positions, sometimes even declining to actively campaign during referenda. This gives organisations within civil society an opportunity to win votes not available to them during general elections.[11]

Given the historically minor involvement of political parties in Irish referenda, the media has been the main arena for referenda as the campaigns unfold on television, local and national radio and opinion pieces in local and national newspapers.[12] The referendum campaigns concerning hot-button social issues in the 1980s and early 1990s, and once again in 2015 and 2018, have been intense and emotionally charged. The next chapter will discuss media coverage of the marriage equality campaign revealing how stories of individuals and activists dominate these campaigns. For example, the nationally televised interview with drag artist and activist Rory O'Neill, aka Miss Panti Bliss, and the subsequent speech at the Abbey Theatre, high-lighted the challenges of being gay in Ireland and the pressures of ongoing homophobia. Additionally, several high-profile politicians and popular TV and print journalists sharing their 'coming out' stories sparked further interest in print and social media.[13] In addition to the Yes campaign's clear and consistent messaging, Yes Equality, which was the umbrella group that led the Yes campaign, also conducted a flashy national bus tour, a strong merchandising strategy with bilingual Yes/Tá badges and apparel, a disciplined voter registration effort, a national door-to-door canvassing campaign and a sophisticated social media campaign.[14]

Although *Resilient Reporting* concluded that social media was still not a major factor in general election campaigns, at least according to Ireland's

11 McGraw, 2015.

12 Johan A. Elkink, David M. Farrell, Theresa Reidy and Jane Suiter, 'Understanding the 2015 Marriage Referendum in Ireland: Context, Campaign, and Conservative Ireland', *Irish Political Studies*, 2017, Vol. 32, No. 3, 361–81 (366).

13 Grainne Healy, Brian Sheehan, and Noel Whelan, *Ireland Says Yes: The Inside Story of How the Vote for Marriage Equality was Won*, Kildare: Merrion Press, 2016.

14 Elkink et al., 2017, 365.

established media outlets, social media was essential during the 2015 marriage equality campaign.[15] Many young, first-time voters were disengaged with traditional media but were very engaged on social media. The youth sector perceived referenda as more important than elections because they were voting on issues they cared about and ones that political parties were not actively engaging.[16] Leaders of the Yes Equality campaign worked with national and regional newspapers and radio to mobilise their message. Social media was perceived by many as being more dramatic, exciting, professional looking, positive and respectful, and this seemed to have a significant impact. The #HomeToVote phenomenon was noteworthy for the ways it activated significant numbers of young people from abroad to travel home to register their vote. This approach was present, albeit to a much lesser extent, during the 2018 abortion referendum as well.

A disconnect emerged during the campaign whereby traditional national media characterised the Yes campaign as quiet and inactive, but they missed the proliferation of social media mobilisation and on-the-ground canvassing.[17] In contrast to the highly organised and visible Yes campaign, the No campaign focused almost exclusively on radio because of strict rules about 50:50 balance of airtime during referendum campaigns. The No side also paid for many YouTube advertisements, which fell outside the rules on political advertising.[18] Ultimately, the traditional media outlets kept emphasising the 'silent no voters' that never materialised and largely missed the social media activity. Twitter and Facebook were widely used to remind voters to cast their ballots on polling day and to facilitate other voters getting to the polls through an extensive system of carpooling and other schemes.[19] The growing importance of social media during these campaigns may eventually undermine the 50:50 rule of providing equal time to both sides of an issue if greater numbers of citizens and political actors are waging their debates via social media.

15   Breen et al., 2019, 58.
16   Healy et al., 2016, 41.
17   Healy et al., 2016, 67, 78.
18   Elkink et al., 2017, 365.
19   Elkink et al., 2017, 366.

The media undoubtedly plays a critical role in elections and referendum campaigns. However, media tends to track key events and follow where politicians, party leaders and civil society actors focus their attention; the media does not set the agenda per se. *Resilient Reporting,* for example, argues that the growing concentration of media attention on political party leaders during elections is due more to the choices and emphases of political parties than it is to the media driving the agenda.[20] Similarly, we know that media follow stories that are politically salient. As the next chapter highlights, the numbers of newspaper stories on abortion depends on the political process. On average, there were less than 100 articles per year in the *Irish Independent* on abortion since 1970, except for years when there was a referendum or key legislative case as there was in 2013, and then there were closer to 500 articles in those years. Despite regular coverage of this important issue, the media dramatically increased their attention when there was a specific political event on which to focus their attention.

Ireland's deliberative experiments with the Constitutional Convention (2012–14) and Citizens' Assembly (2016–18) are further examples of political institutions focusing public, and therefore, media attention on salient issues of political, social and economic reform. The overwhelming support that emerged out of the Constitutional Convention for same-sex marriage and the intense media interest that surrounded the proceedings and recommendations all but forced the otherwise conservative Taoiseach, Enda Kenny, to call for a referendum. The Labour Party, Enda Kenny's government coalition partner, had been promoting this agenda for years. The increased media attention given to same-sex marriage and abortion grew out of the Constitutional Convention and Citizens' Assembly, respectively. The inclusion of citizens, politicians, experts and civil society leaders and activists during the Convention's 'careful, measured and informed deliberation' was critical.[21] The process informed policy-makers and advocates about the nature of the debate and how citizens would react, and the media had a front row seat from which to report to the broader Irish society.[22]

20   Breen et al., 2019, 111.
21   Elkink et al., 2017, 364.
22   Elkink et al., 2017, 364.

Ultimately, the Irish media are critical to facilitating debates within Irish society. Nevertheless, they do not act in a vacuum and are very dependent on leaders within political parties and civil society to give them something engaging to report.

Media coverage of Irish policy-making outside of elections, referenda and formal deliberative institutions is much less focused and predictable. There have been few studies about how the media, and newspapers specifically, have covered key policy areas within Irish politics. Therefore, we seek to parallel previous media studies by examining how Ireland's leading daily newspapers, the *Irish Independent* and *The Irish Times*, cover educational issues in the primary sector. As one would expect, education more broadly and primary school policy more specifically are not covered as much in the news because these issues are rarely at the top of the agenda during elections, and they have not yet been the subject of a targeted referendum campaign. Media coverage of education is more varied than comparable coverage of abortion or same-sex marriage. For starters, the previous reform campaigns concentrated on a single issue and whether it would legally alter the Constitution.

Although abortion and marriage equality are not entirely religious matters, the battle between religiously motivated and secular arguments was more targeted when discussing these topics. Within minutes of the 2018 abortion referendum outcome being announced, calls for eliminating or reducing the role of the Church in education were pronounced. Labour Party leaders claimed that 'people always ask what's next and our view from a constitutional framework is that the next big question for people to address is the relationship between the Church and State in education'.[23] Four days after the abortion referendum, Róisín Shortall, TD, of the Social Democrats brought a proposal to the Dáil to take religion out of the school day, thereby creating a secular school system.[24] Thus, momentum for secular change appeared to be growing and getting the Church out of Irish schools was the next domino activists wanted to fall in Ireland's march

---

23   Elaine Loughlin, 'Labour Calls for Removal of Link between Church and State in Education', *Irish Examiner*, 29 May 2018.

24   Róisín Shortall, 29 May 2018. Available at: <https://twitter.com/SocDems> (Accessed: 18 February 2021).

towards secularisation. Despite such calls for change, educational reforms seeking to secularise the primary school system have been minor and slow.

The differences between religious and secular concerns are much more diffuse within education debates. There are multiple contentious issues within the overall educational sector, and these are often broken down among third level, secondary level and primary level. For example, third level is engulfed in battles over State funding, student fees and hiring capacities. Religion has not been much of an issue at third level ever since the founding of the National University system in 1908 when the British State guaranteed the Catholic hierarchy that religion would not be part of the university curriculum. One issue that has emerged at third level in recent years relates to the qualifications teachers are required to earn to teach in denominational settings. There has been criticism that State-funded teacher-training colleges were advising students to take the certificate in religious studies (CRS) to boost their chances of getting a job irrespective of their beliefs. The CRS qualifies students to instruct pupils in either the Catholic or Protestant faith. Educate Together has since developed an ethics course that can be done as a secular alternative to the certificate.[25]

There is greater diversity of types of schools at the secondary level where only 48 % of schools are Catholic, which may explain why many of the most controversial debates at secondary level focus on such issues as the fairness and importance of the junior and leaving certificate exams, and less on religious themes.[26] There has been a growing debate in recent years about the Relationships and Sexuality Education (RSE) curriculum, with special concern by secular advocates that Catholic schools will not implement the changes. The 2020 Programme for Government responds to this secular concern by stating that the governing coalition will 'develop inclusive and age-appropriate RSE and SPHE [Social, Personal and Health Education] curricula across primary and post-primary levels, including an inclusive programme on LGBTI+ relationships and making appropriate

25 <https://www.irishtimes.com/news/education/quinn-advises-teachers-to-study-re-to-boost-their-job-prospects-1.1840363>.
26 <https://www.education.ie/en/Publications/Statistics/Data-on-Individual-Schools/Data-on-Individual-Schools.html>.

legislative changes, if necessary'.[27] Such proposals openly challenge Church teachings and imply further secular standards being implemented at the secondary level.

There are far more religious vs. secular debates at the primary level. This is largely because there is much less diversity in this sector, where nearly 90 % of schools are Catholic. Changing demographics and growing demand for non-denominational educational opportunities have emboldened requests for a change in the role of religion in primary schools. The fact that these religious vs. secular debates occur more intensely in only one sector of the overall educational sphere diffuses attention given to these debates within Irish society.

Thus, newspaper attention on secular vs. religious debates within educational sector is much less frequent and salient than they were in the same-sex marriage and abortion campaigns. The abortion and marriage equality campaigns convinced many Irish citizens that changes in legislation would protect others' rights to choose how they live in ways that did not impinge on the choices or lifestyles of others. If someone wanted to have an abortion, or to enter a same-sex marriage, this impacted those involved but would not directly affect others. By contrast, proposed educational reforms do affect other individuals and local communities because changes in school admissions, curriculum, or type of ethos, influence the formation of all students and indirectly their families and the local community.

Primary schools are critical sources of social capital within every community, so minor changes that alter how they function can have ripple effects in their respective communities, often eliciting local hostility to proposed adjustments. There is a rich history of academic research that underscores the importance of Catholic schools in the United States as a source of social capital and cohesion in their local communities.[28] Recent

27   'Programme for Government: Our Shared Future', June 2020, 95. <https://www.documentcloud.org/documents/6944741-Programme-For-Government-June-2020.html>.

28   Coleman, J. S., *Foundations of Social Theory*. United Kingdom: Belknap Press of Harvard University Press, 1994; Lee, V. E., Bryk, A. S. and Holland, P. B., *Catholic Schools and the Common Good*. United Kingdom: Harvard University Press, 2009; Putnam, R. D. and Campbell, D. E., *American Grace: How Religion Divides and Unites Us*. United Kingdom: Simon & Schuster, 2012.

research demonstrates the disastrous impact of Catholic school closures on neighbourhoods – and there have been 1,800 Catholic school closures in the past two decades in the United States. *Lost Classroom, Lost Community* illustrates that Catholic schools build trust and social cohesion in their neighbourhoods, and once closed and not replaced, their absence triggers higher levels of disorder, crime and an overall decline in community cohesiveness.[29] The Irish educational system is different; schools are not closing, they are either transferring their patronage via divestment or new schools are being established in areas of demographic growth and change. In addition to demographic change, changes in admissions policies have elicited some local backlash. Thus, any change in admissions policies alters local community dynamics. Irish primary schools are key local institutions that engender social capital and civic engagement; therefore, any changes to these community institutions affect everyone. This explains why the NIMBY ('not in my back yard') phenomenon is prevalent in the educational reforms in ways that were not present in the marriage equality and abortion campaigns that focused much more on individual rights. The multiple and varied ways that educational reforms affect local areas helps account for lower frequency of attention nationally as debates are framed in local terms, which further fragments how these controversial issues are addressed in the media.

III. Methodology

To better understand the frequency and nature of newspaper coverage of key debates in educational reform at the primary level, we studied the *Irish Independent* and *The Irish Times* in the period since 1960. Although the *Irish Independent* is perceived as slightly more conservative and historically has reached a broader social spectrum, and *The Irish Times* is perceived as being more progressive leaning and reaching a more advanced

---

29   Margaret F. Brinig and Nicole S. Garnett, *Lost Classroom, Lost Community: Catholic Schools' Importance in Urban America*. United Kingdom: University of Chicago Press, 2014.

socio-economic clientele, the two papers have become more similar in their political reporting.[30] According to analysis in *Resilient Reporting,* these two papers have become remarkably parallel in terms of their overall framing and sentiment of election reporting. Since 1989, both papers have been less neutral and more critical and negative in their tone of elections, but this has been driven more by social and cultural change in Ireland rather than by specific market pressure. The *Resilient Reporting* authors argue that both papers gave clear preponderance to policy over political competition in their electoral coverage, which confirms their perception that mainstream print media seeks to provide balanced reporting of elections and political competition.[31] Our study of primary school educational issues in the main newspapers seeks to analyse whether such balanced or neutral coverage exists outside of elections, referenda and national deliberative institutions.

Our research team conducted thorough searches of coverage in the two leading national papers, *The Irish Times* and the *Irish Independent.* The Appendix provides detailed descriptions of what searches produced our results. In general, we examined key issues and actors within primary education by searching for all articles that included several words related to a particular theme or group of people rather than only having specific words or phrases in a set order.[32] The results vary in the two papers, and

30   For a thorough historical overview of Irish media see John Horgan, *Irish Media: A Critical History Since 1922.* London: Routledge, 2001.

31   Breen et al., 2019, 120–7.

32   The following explains the overall search approach employed in both newspapers. *The Irish Times* website separates into two types of search tools: one through 'IrishTimes.com', which has digital copies of articles published in text and online from 1996 through the present, and the other through 'the Newspaper', which has photographs of articles published in text and online (when applicable) from 1859 through the present. Access to the 'IrishTimes.com' search tool is free, while access to 'the Newspaper' search tool requires a subscription provided by Sean McGraw. Using this database meant entering a key term or phrase into the desired search bar. When an exact phrase was desired, rather than the presence of the words within the article 'EXACT-WORD' was entered rather than 'EXACT WORD' for example 'primary-curriculum-review' versus 'primary curriculum review'. For articles from 1996–2019, 'IrishTimes.com' was used, while for articles from before 1996 'the Newspaper' was used. When searching for articles on a yearly basis, limiting

it is unclear whether such differences are due to the quality of the search engines for both papers and/or the substantive emphases the two papers have in their education reporting. Although we were very diligent in our approach, we do not pretend to be experts in media and content analysis. Nevertheless, we report our findings as a basic measure of frequency in hopes of contextualising how the media is addressing critical religious and secular themes in primary education.

We first examined the frequency of key issues associated with educational reform dating back to 1960 and were able to identify a range of topics based on this initial, open-ended search. Next, our research team established the themes and actors most frequently discussed within the key issues of divestment, admissions policy and the curriculum. For this part of the research, we limited ourselves to articles published since 2010 for these three themes. In this part, we first read all the articles within each theme and identified the most common issues and actors. As a team, we discussed and agreed upon the acceptable categories.

Second, we employed a web-based application called Voyant to do a computer-generated quantitative analysis of all the articles that addressed divestment and admissions (<https://voyant-tools.org/>). Voyant recorded the frequency of words and phrases for all the articles we uploaded from both newspapers that address our relevant themes.[33] Our individually

---

the data range to 'January 1, YEAR – December 31, YEAR' was used. The *Irish Independent* has partnered with Irish Newspaper Archives to hold the archive of all their articles dating back to 1905. Access to this database was provided through Boston College's library website. Searching this database always starts with filtering for just the title 'Irish Independent 1905-current'. While both the categories of 'ALL of these words' and 'This EXACT word or phrase' where used when trying search terms, most frequently the search terms were entered in the 'This EXACT word or phrase' search and search terms such as 'primary' or 'school' were added in the 'ALL of these words' search to specify results when needed. Limiting the date range was also used for most search terms.

33 This user-friendly resource helps determine the frequency and context of specific words in relation to the larger text. It is known for its good ease of use, the documentation that provides good instructions for users, the simple interface, and the ability to export data. The primary limitation of Voyant Tools is the occasional prolonged text-loading time and the challenge of gathering information using some visualisation tools (e.g. Knots, Lava, and Mandala) configured in the Voyant Skin

generated coding produced virtually identical lists of key actors and themes as Voyant, which confirmed the validity of our human coding. However, we found our coding scheme and results more useful, especially when seeking to discuss and understand complex issues (see Appendix for additional notes).

As one last step, we also employed an additional web-based application, MeaningCloud, to help us conduct a rudimentary sentiment analysis of the critical actors engaged in these debates.[34] MeaningCloud is known for using a semantic analytics approach, grounded on an advanced understanding of text, to enable the extraction of deep insights from complex documents and interactions. The application is recognised as more accurate and far superior to other applications because it allows, besides associating words with polarities, defining these polarities considering modifiers, the context and the function of every word at every moment.[35] After uploading all the relevant articles on divestment and admissions, MeaningCloud categorises the tone of text as positive, neutral, negative or none. Rather than allowing the application to determine the overall tone of each article, we chose to use this application to analyse the tone of the coverage on the most frequent actors we had already identified. Given the number of topics, sub-topics, different speakers and sentiments potentially included within each article, we thought our targeted approach was less confusing. For example, if we employed a more general evaluation approach an article may be listed as having a negative attitude, but it would be unclear whether this means that it was negative towards the divestment process or towards the Catholic Church, the Department of Education, or even one specific school. Therefore, we employed MeaningCloud to measure what percentage

---

Builder. See Megan Welsh, 'Review of Voyant Tools', *Collaborative Librarianship*, 2014, Vol. 6, No. 2, 96–7. <https://go-gale-com.proxy.bc.edu/ps/i.do?id=GA LE%7CA393876396&v=2.1&u=mlin_m_bostcoll&it=r&p=AONE&sw=w> (Accessed: 2 July 2020).

34   <https://www.meaningcloud.com/>.

35   'MeaningCloud Provides Entirely Customisable Sentiment Analysis to Get Maximum Accuracy'. ICT Monitor Worldwide, 19 April 2016. Gale General OneFile, <https://link-galecom.proxy.bc.edu/apps/doc/A449972722/ITOF?u=mlin_ m_bostcoll&sid=ITOF&xid=059d936f> (Accessed 2 July 2020). See also <https://www.prweb.com/releases/2018/05/prweb15471871.htm>.

of coverage specific actors received that was positive, neutral, or negative. The goal of this multiple-step investigation is to understand whether the media has been playing the same critical role in shaping debate as it did in framing the same-sex marriage and abortion debates.

IV. Coverage of Primary Education Reforms in the *Irish Independent* and *The Irish Times*

A. Overall Frequency of Issues

We focused on how religious and secular concerns are covered in the Irish media to gauge how the secularisation process is unfolding in this sector since 1960. The initial, open-ended search discovered that the theme of curriculum was the most common, averaging about 100 articles annually in each paper (see Figures 7.1 and 7.2). There was a brief, but dramatic uptick in coverage on the curriculum in the *Irish Independent* to about 330 articles per year in the late 1970s and again to 250 articles per year in the late 1990s when the 1999 curriculum replaced the previous 1971 curriculum.

'Primary school curriculum' is a broad topic that includes anything that is taught in Irish primary schools from the core curriculum to religious education, ethics education and sexuality and relationships education. Outside of curriculum, there was generally no significant coverage of any single issue within the primary sector in either paper that achieved 100 articles per year. There were more than fifty articles per year several times in the *Irish Independent* for religious education. Sexuality and religious education in *The Irish Times* never obtains above fifty articles in a year and averages closer to fifteen per year throughout the period from 1960–2019. In the *Irish Independent,* there are about forty-five articles per year on religious and sexuality education since 1960.

The hot-button issues within the primary sector do not receive much attention, and when they do receive greater consideration, it is generally

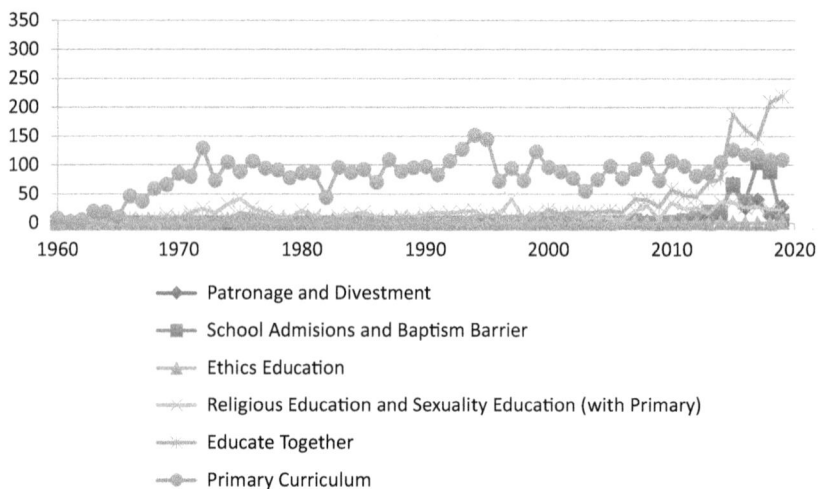

Figure 7.1. *The Irish Times* primary education key issues and actors: 1960–2019.

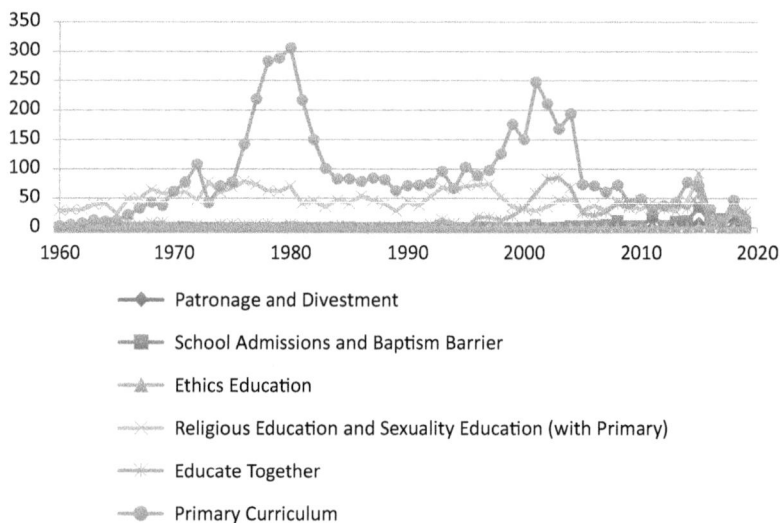

Figure 7.2. *Irish Independent* primary education key issues and actors: 1960–2019.

associated with a particular political process such as the Forum on Patronage and Pluralism in Irish Schools in 2011 or the Education (Admissions to School) Act of 2018. The divestment/patronage issue was first mentioned in *The Irish Times* in 2007, and it peaked in 2015 with seventy articles. A combined total of nearly 120 articles over a two- to three-year period when the issue was being hotly contested is significantly less than previous contentious social and moral issues. School admissions and the 'baptismal barrier' gained attention beginning in 2015 and peaked with approximately 100 articles in 2017 and ninety articles in 2018 when legislation was being debated and ultimately passed. Although sexuality and religious education average around fifty articles per year until 2010 when they increase to approximately 100 per year, coverage of ethics education is essentially ignored in *The Irish Times*. In terms of key actors, Educate Together is the most striking as it begins to gain traction in 2000 and rises from mentions in fifty articles per year in 2010 to over an overwhelming 200 articles per year by 2019. Educate Together gained more attention than any issue within the education sector, thereby confirming its status as the key educational reformer. A similar search in the *Irish Independent* reveals even smaller numbers of articles on these key issues and actors within the primary sector. For example, there are approximately twenty-five articles per year since 1960 on sexuality and religious education, about forty articles per year on Educate Together since 2000, and only a handful of articles on the other primary education themes.

A deeper analysis of divestment, admission and curriculum coverage in *The Irish Times* and *Irish Independent* provides greater insight into what the real issues are within each of these topics and which actors are driving the debate in these areas. Debates about reforming Ireland's primary sector, and the Church's role within in it, escalated in 2011 when the new Fine Gael-Labour Government initiated the Forum on Patronage and Pluralism in the Primary Sector. Ruairí Quinn, TD, Labour Minister for Education (2011–14), was the catalyst for the Forum. 'Creating more diversity and inclusiveness was the flagship enterprise of former minister for education Ruairí Quinn. He set up the Forum on Patronage and Pluralism in the Primary Sector on his first full day of office, and at one stage promised to wrest half of the State's 3,100 primary schools from Catholic Church control.'[36] Quinn knew this was his last term in office and decided to be bold in seeking reform because everyone thought it was necessary but no one was willing to tackle it because of the layers of complexity and number of vested and competing interests. The overall goal of the Forum was to offer suggestions and devise a plan for how Ireland could increase both the diversity of school types within the Irish primary sector (i.e. increase the number of non-denominational or multi-denominational schools) and respond to the level of diversity of children within schools so students of minority religions or no faith at all had sufficient options available to them and were not discriminated against in any school they attended. Despite widespread agreement in favour of increasing diversity and breaking the Church's near monopoly on primary school patronage, little change has occurred.

Divestment has proven difficult, as we will discuss more fully in Chapter 10, because local communities, parents, educational leaders and politicians support change in principle but not in their specific contexts. The glacial change in diversity of patrons may explain why there was a groundswell of support to abolish religious background as an admission's criterion for Catholic schools that culminated in the Education Act of 2018. Overnight, this legislation denied Catholic schools from giving preference, through their admissions policies, to Catholic students in hopes that all Irish schools would become more diverse internally. This Act did not affect minority faith schools who are still allowed to give preference to students of the same faith as the school patron in their admissions processes. Advocates seeking to protect the rights of minority religions and those of no faith viewed admissions reform as a more immediate fix while they continued to fight for the creation of greater numbers of multi- and non-denominational schools within the overall system. Curricular changes were the other more immediate or medium-term reform on which advocates of greater diversity within the primary sector have focused their attention. For many reformers, the goal has been to remove religion from being taught in primary schools altogether. If this cannot be achieved, secular

---

36   Joe Humphreys, 'Segregation Concerns Over Transfer of School Patronage', *Irish Times*, 1 January 2015.

reformers have sought to use curriculum to limit the impact of religious education and to increase the focus on ethics and other alternative forms of values-based education independent of faith formation.

The subsequent sections explore the extent and nature of national newspaper coverage of these themes to get a sense for how the media is covering the religious vs. secular debate and to compare this to previous media coverage of same-sex marriage and abortion reforms.

B. Divestment and Patronage

Consider divestment. There were ninety-five total articles on divestment and patronage from 2010 to 2019 in the *Irish Independent* and *The Irish Times*. These articles focused the greatest amount of attention on parents, then on individual school patrons, various aspects of the State and finally other local actors. As mentioned, there has been near universal support for greater diversity of school types in the Irish primary school sector in recent years. Nevertheless, decisions about divesting schools of their patronage affects parents in local communities in more tangible and important ways than the public at large. The Irish Constitution guarantees that the State will 'provide for' a primary education for all Irish children, but it also gives parents the right to choose what type of education they want for their children. Therefore, it is not surprising that parents were mentioned in fifty-four articles on divestment, the most of any actor (see Table 7.1).[37]

The next most popular actors in divestment articles were the specific patrons: forty-five articles for Education and Training Boards who oversee Community National Schools, forty-one articles that reference Catholic bishops and thirty-five articles that highlight the role of Educate Together. Given that seven out of eleven of schools that divested their patronage were Catholic schools, and ten out of eleven of the new patrons of these divested schools were Community National Schools run by local ETBs, it is not

---

37 Ireland. Bunreacht Na HÉireann = Constitution of Ireland. Dublin: Oifig an tSoláthair, 1945, Article 42.4.

Table 7.1. Actors in *Irish Independent* and *The Irish Times* divestment articles: 2010–19

Actor	Number of Articles
Parents	54
Education Training Boards/Community National Schools	45
Bishops (Catholic Church)	41
Educate Together	35
The Forum on Patronage and Pluralism	22
Minister for Education[a]	20
Boards of Management	16
Multi-denominational Schools	10
Non-denominational Schools	7

[a] The Department of Education has had several names over the years: 1921–97 Department of Education; 1997–2010 Department of Education and Science; 2010–20 Department of Education and Skills.

surprising that these patrons gained the most media attention. Although Educate Together has greater visibility overall within the primary sector during this period, they were focusing their efforts more on establishing new schools rather than taking over divested schools. Educate Together were selected as patron for 24 % of all new primary schools in Ireland for the period 2000–10 and 53 % in 2011–19 (Department of Education data). For a comparison, the Catholic Church was selected as the patron of 54 % of new primary schools in 2000–10 and *zero* in 2011–19, whereas ETBs were selected as patron for 4 % and 28 % of new primary schools in these respective periods.

Although the media concentration on patrons is perhaps obvious, some argue that this focus is misplaced. For example, some defenders of Catholic schools argued that 'research clearly establishes that patronage is not the main issue in determining school choice for parents. The issues of most immediate concern are the proximity of the school, its educational standards, and family connections.'[38] The implication is that, though patronage is important, there are other factors that more specifically determine school choice for parents and students. For others, the counterexample was argued. Namely, parents are inherently forced to compromise their religious beliefs to secure their child's spot in a primary school. In places where there are waiting lists, parents are scouting their children's school years in advance. If there are no other alternatives, and the choice is between baptising their child despite a lack of belief in the Church, or not having their child enrolled in a school, parents may choose the former, especially if they do not have the financial means to pay for transportation to schools farther away.[39] Irrespective of the various sides, the patrons are the gatekeepers to reform and must therefore be part of any change that might occur.

Media attention also focused on various state actors and local community leaders. The Forum on Patronage had twenty-two articles and the Minister of Education was mentioned in twenty articles. Given the media's tendency to cover political actors and events, it is unsurprising that these State-sponsored bodies and actors gained considerable attention. These were followed by sixteen references to boards of management, which consist of patron representatives, school leaders, teachers and parents. The newspapers also mention multi-(ten) and non-denominational (seven) schools several times. These more generic citations underscore that there are several models available within the primary sector, but each type is named in relation to the overall norm of denominational schools, which date back to the 1830s. One cannot escape religion in Irish primary schools because even the names and models note whether there is one religion, multiple religions, or no religion in each school.

As alluded to earlier, Ireland's media is known for being impartial, critical and challenging in their reporting. The most frequently addressed issues in the national newspapers regarding divestment accurately capture the key concerns of the various actors participating in the debate.

---

38   Michael Drumm, 'In My Opinion: Variety of Patronage is Called for to Meet the Demands of Parents'. *Irish Independent*, 12 October 2011.

39   <https://www.irishtimes.com/life-and-style/people/i-became-one-of-those-parents-i-used-to-read-about-and-snigger-1.1354270> (Accessed: 24 July 2020).

Table 7.2. Top issues in *Irish Independent* and *The Irish Times* divestment
articles: 2010–19

Issue	Number of articles in which it appears
Slow Progress	42
Religious Curriculum	33
School Ethos	26
Local Hostility	24
Human and Constitutional Rights	18
Changing Social Demographics	15
Property Ownership/Compensation	15
Catholic First Admissions Policy	9
Inclusivity in Catholic schools	6

Given the pace of change, it is not surprising that two of the top four categories discuss the limited progress and high degree of local hostility (see Table 7.2).

There were forty-two articles in the two papers that highlighted the complex reasons why progress on divestment of more schools was not going faster. According to one commentator, 'Observing the process of divestment of school patronage from religious institutions is like watching an uphill slow bicycle race on a glacier. Pouring water onto the already slippery slope.'[40] There was plenty of blame for the pace of divestment to go around as some articles blamed the Department of Education while others blamed the patrons of school. One author suggested that encouraging Catholic bishops to divest their schools was 'a bit like asking turkeys to vote for Christmas'.[41] Additional articles called for specific actors to take more action to speed up the extremely slow process.

40   Rob Sadlier, 'School Patronage', Letter to the Editor, *The Irish Times*, 16 January 2015.
41   Sean O Diomasaigh, 'Patronage System and Education', Letter to the Editor, *The Irish Times*, 11 November 2015.

In addition to frustration over the pace of change, the fourth most discussed issue was 'local hostility' (twenty-four articles). The prevalence of negative reaction by local leaders and communities to the potential change to their children's schools reveals the NIMBY nature of educational issues. John Coolahan, leading scholar on Irish education policy and Chair of the Forum on Patronage, captured the importance of localism:

> It is understandable that local communities have a sense of loyalty and identity with their local school, which may have been built up over generations. In the light of local debate, it seems that there can be a general agreement on the principle of divestment, but it should apply to another school, but not ours! There is a need for better communication and proactive advocacy and leadership by key partners such as the local patron, the teachers' union, the National Parents' Council and local politicians to help unlock local perspectives and attitudes in the interest of the common good.[42]

Again, the overall assumption is that change is necessary, but there remains significant opposition to how this change will be implemented. The communal impacts of proposed changes distinguish these reforms from the individual rights-based arguments prevalent in marriage equality and abortion campaigns. These educational reforms affect the entire community and involve more complicated discussions, which helps explain the slower rate of change than on these previous secular policy reforms.

The second and third most popular issues discussed within divestment articles were religious curriculum (thirty-three articles) and school ethos (twenty-six articles). Concerns about religious curriculum are diverse. In addition to basic descriptions of the different religious and ethics education taught by different patrons, many articles debated whether the Department of Education or the patrons should have control over religious education. Additional articles within this category focused on how non-religious students have difficulty avoiding religious education in schools. One reason is that creating acceptable opt-outs for religion classes is tough because of the integrated nature of education in primary schools.

Many articles addressing the school ethos underscore reasons why Catholic schools should be allowed to maintain their religious ethos,

---

42 John Coolahan, 'Comment: We Need to Pick Up the Pace to Revitalise Our School System', *Irish Independent,* 2 July 2014.

reinforcing how a school's ethos can attract students, families and teachers who share a particular ethos. The argument is that reducing the number of Catholic schools could help the remaining ones to be truly Catholic rather than compromising their ethos to keep non-practicing parents and teachers satisfied, which is a growing reality given changes in belief and practice. There was some concern over the extent to which Catholic schools can truly be autonomous given that the State dictates employment, admissions and curriculum policies.[43] Defenders of patrons' rights consistently under-score to anyone who will listen that their rights to preserve their ethos are enshrined in the Constitution.[44] On the other end of the spectrum, there were also articles that addressed ethos in a very negative context, arguing that Equal Status Act (2000) 'gives State-funded schools a license to dis-criminate against children on the basis of religion'.[45]

Several divestment articles focused on human and constitutional rights (eighteen) as a main concern. There was specific reliance on the United Nation's criticism of Irish education as a human rights abuse which im-pinges on the rights of parents and students of minority or no religion who must attend Catholic schools because they have no other option. The constitutional right of parents to choose the religious education of their child was employed by actors on both sides of the debate, highlighting the complexity of determining which rights take precedence when there are multiple and competing claims to constitutional protections. Patrons of schools also have constitutional protections to help them protect and fulfil their ethos, which adds a further layer of complexity to these competing constitutional rights within this sector.

Although a common complaint of Irish Catholic primary schools by those advocating most vociferously for change is that they are not very in-clusive of non-religious or minority religious students, this topic was only mentioned in six articles. This is one of the few categories where the two papers were slightly different in their coverage. The articles and opinion

---

43   David Quinn, 'Letters: You'll All Miss Value of Catholic Ethos if It Goes'. *Irish Independent,* 18 March 2011.

44   Ireland, 1945, Article 44.2.5.

45   Patrick Monahan, 'Do We Want to Discriminate against Children based on Their Religious Status?', *Irish Times,* 21 August 2015.

pieces in the *Irish Independent* highlighted positive aspects of how inclusive Catholic schools already are, implying that legislative change was unnecessary. In contrast, *The Irish Times* posited the opposite, namely that Catholic schools tend to be more exclusive in terms of who they admit and how they treat minority students. Curiously, a 2012 Economic and Social Research Institute (ESRI) report found that there was greater socio-economic diversity among pupils in Catholic primary schools than in those under different patronage. Similar evidence has been presented about the numbers of Travellers in Catholic schools.[46] Educate Together and others argued that these numbers were misleading because they controlled such a small number of schools and therefore had fewer opportunities to serve these various communities in ways that Catholic schools did.

The debates over divestment have gotten intense and emotional, especially for those who feel they have the most to gain or lose by such change. Nevertheless, the overall treatment of the various actors involved seems balanced. According to our rudimentary sentiment analysis conducted by MeaningCloud, the tone of most coverage of key actors in the divestment articles is primarily positive, with much less negative or neutral reporting (see Table 7.3).[47] The results in MeaningCloud refer to the number of times each actor was mentioned in the cumulative text file that contained all articles on divestment and patronage. This explains why the frequencies are different than the results obtained from the coding and counting scheme we devised on our own and was discussed previously. MeaningCloud also includes a fourth response category, 'None', which we do not include here. This explains why the numbers do not add up to 100.

---

46 *New Report on Diversity in Primary Schools in Ireland*, Economic and Social Research Institute, 23 October 2012. Available at: <https://www.esri.ie/news/new-report-on-diversity-in-primary-schools-in-ireland>.

47 We conducted the sentiment analysis only on actors and not on issues. It was too cumbersome and time-consuming to devise a set of words and phrases that would be conducive for MeaningCloud's sentiment analysis. The complex nature of the issues involved in divestment – and later admissions – would have made this a much larger project than was reasonable given the role of the media section within the scope of the overall book project.

Table 7.3. MeaningCloud sentiment analysis of actors in divestment articles *Irish Independent* and *The Irish Times*: 2010–19

Actor	Positive (%)	Neutral (%)	Negative (%)	Total Mentions
Minister of Education	27.91	4.65	8.14	86
Patron	35.29	1.18	16.47	85
Parent(s)	36.84	6.58	11.84	76
Catholic	28.77	2.74	16.44	73
Educate Together	48.08	5.77	13.46	52
Community	31.11	0	8.89	45
Department of Education	25.00	4.55	11.36	44
Bishop/Archbishop	36.59	4.88	9.76	41
Community National School/Education Training Boards	36.36	4.55	4.55	22
Board(s) of Management	8.33	16.67	0	12
Forum on Patronage and Pluralism	20.00	0	10	10

None of the actors received more negative- than positive-toned reporting according to this textual analysis. Even Catholic bishops and other Catholic leaders, who are often perceived more negatively in public discourse, had far greater positive than negative attention in this analysis. For example, 37 % of news coverage in the *Irish Independent* and *The Irish Times* on Catholic bishops was positive in tone, compared to only 10 % that was negative in tone. When 'Catholic' was mentioned, 29 % of the coverage was positive and 16 % negative. Boards of management were the only actors that received more neutral (17 %) than positive (8 %) coverage in the divestment articles – and no actor had a plurality of negative coverage. There is only slight variation in the tone that the various actors received. For example, Educate Together received the most positive coverage (48 %), whereas ETBs, bishops, parents and patrons had approximately 35 % positive coverage. These findings reinforce the critically impartial nature of Irish media reporting. The media may have influenced the debate on divestment more because of the frequency in which it covered actors and issues as opposed to the tone in which they covered the leading actors within the debate.

The case studies in Chapter 10 highlight the intensely local nature of divestment. Perhaps not surprisingly, there are some differences between how local and national media cover specific cases of divestment. The national media appears more inclined to cover divestment when it involves Catholic schools because that is the overwhelmingly dominant patron. Curiously, when the three Steiner schools transferred their patronage to another multi-denominational patron in the form of Community National Schools, there was barely a mention at the local or national level. The process of divesting Two Mile Community National School, Brannoxtown Community National School and Faughart Community National School – all Catholic schools becoming multi-denominational schools – received on an average fifteen articles per school, whereas the divestment of the three Steiner schools overall attracted one sentence in one article and the Galway Steiner National School was covered in only one other article.[48] The Steiner schools were in no danger of closing. In fact, the enrolments were growing in each as the schools continued to gain support from parents who were looking for a less competitive and more creative environments for their children, as is the goal of Steiner education.[49] However, the Board of Lifeways Ireland, which was the patron of the Steiner schools, had reviewed its future and found that 'in the current climate it is not possible for

48   Sarah Burns, 'Four Religious-Run Schools Switching to Multi-Denominational Model'. *The Irish Times*, 27 August 2019. <https://www.irishtimes.com/news/ireland/irish-news/four-religious-run-schools-switching-to-multi-denominational-model-1.3998803>; Briain Kelly, 'Galway Steiner NS Becomes GRETB Community School'. *Galway Daily*, 14 August 2019. <https://www.galwaydaily.com/news/galway-steiner-school-becomes-gretb-community-school/>.

49   Shauna Coen, 'Different Class: Families Opt for Steiner Path as an Alternative to Traditional Route Through Education'. *Connacht Tribune*, 13 April 2018.<https://archive-irishnewsarchive-com.proxy.bc.edu/Olive/APA/INA.Edu/SharedView.Article.aspx?href=CTT%2F2018%2F04%2F13&id=Ar03400&sk=E2B53390>.

a voluntary body such as Lifeways to provide the broad range of necessary supports to the growing number of schools that wish to teach using Steiner methodology'.[50] Thus, the company transferred patronage of the schools to the local Education and Training Boards. Since there was no change in the overall diversity of denominational and multi-denominational schools, the media appeared uninterested, and these divestments occurred without much notice.

C. Admissions Policies

Next, we turn to an analysis of how admissions and the so-called 'baptismal barrier' were addressed by the leading national papers. Whereas there were ninety-five divestment articles between 2010 and 2019 in the *Irish Independent* and *The Irish Times*, there were 299 articles on admissions during the same period. Once again, when there is a more clearcut political process or debate, the media tends to focus more of their attention on the issue. The question at hand was whether, in cases where schools had a waiting list, they could use religious background as a criterion for admittance. The issue of oversubscription and its extent, especially outside fast-growing, urban context, was hotly debated. 'While an ESRI study has indicated that about 20 percent of schools are oversubscribed, Archbishop Diarmuid Martin estimates just 5 % of Catholic primary schools in Dublin are oversubscribed.'[51] Despite the uncertainty of how many are affected by this issue, many parents were stressed about

50   'Galway Steiner National School to Become a Community National School under the Patronage of GRETB'. Galway & Roscommon Education & Training Board, July 26, 2019. <http://galwayroscommon.etb.ie/latest-news/galway-steiner-national-school-to-become-a-community-national-school-under-the-patronage-of-gretb/>; 'Two County Clare Steiner National Schools to Become Community National Schools under Patronage of the Authority'. Limerick and Clare Education and Training Board, 26 July 2019.<https://lcetb.ie/two-county-clare-steiner-national-schools-to-become-community-national-schools-under-patronage-of-the-authority/>.

51   Carl O'Brien, 'Keep 10 % of Catholic school places for unbaptised, says group'. *Irish Times,* 24 July 2016.

how this might affect them and decided to take steps to ensure a place-ment. One activist reported that 'parents can never know from year to year which schools will be oversubscribed so the safest thing to do is play it safe and baptise your child'.[52] Declining numbers of believing and practicing Catholics, some of whom, like the parents mentioned in this article, had their children baptised to get them accepted into their local primary school, and overall demographic changes caused many to ques-tion admissions policies in Catholic schools.

Although there was widespread recognition that reform and change were needed, considerable differences existed about how to achieve change and what the real problem was. For secular reformers, it is all about indi-vidual rights. 'The right to education and the right to religious freedom are individual rights. They do not depend on the existence of critical mass. It is no answer to say that few children are affected; even one single child being denied access to an accessible school based on religion is unaccept-able in a pluralist democracy. It is a violation of rights guaranteed by our Constitution and by international human rights law – nothing less.'[53] For Church leaders, it is often more about a lack of placements in schools – an issue for Educate Together schools as well. Archbishop Diarmuid Martin of Dublin said, 'It is not fair to blame the Church', especially when 'the vast majority of them (Catholic schools) had a reputation for being a good educator and so everybody wants to go there leading to oversubscription'.[54] From this perspective, the real issue is that the State is not adequately planning and providing education to offset changing demographics, not that the Church is discriminating against non-religious and minority reli-gious students in their primary schools. According to the Catholic Primary Schools Management Association (CPSMA), the number of oversubscribed schools was as low as 6 % of all Irish primary schools, and in the greater

52 Paddy Monahan, 'Patronage System and Education', *Irish Times*, 11 November 2015.
53 Conor O'Mahony, 'In My Opinion: New Minister Must Act Quickly on Denominational Schools Issue', *Irish Independent*, 11 May 2016.
54 Sarah MacDonald, 'Archbishop Defends Right of Schools to Put Catholics First in Queue'. *Irish Independent*, 5 August 2015.

Dublin area, where the issue is most acute, only seventeen of forty-two oversubscribed schools involved non-Catholics not gaining admission.[55]

Given the complexity and intensity of the issues related to admissions, it is useful to note the frequency of actors and issues included in news coverage just as we did for divestment. Many of the same actors are showcased in these articles. Parents, school patrons and local boards remain relevant. However, the admissions debate was much more targeted because of specific legislation under consideration. As a result, State/Government actors and institutions, political parties and civil society actors were far more prevalent in these debates. Many of these more politically driven actors were absent, or minimised, during the Forum on Patronage discussions. The consultative, open-ended nature of how divestment was engaged intentionally sought to include often under-heard voices within society and those most affected by proposed changes. Primary school admissions' policies were more narrowly framed within the context of a specific legislative act and addressed within a tighter time period. This demonstrates that how and where debates are conducted influences the types of actors engaged, as well as subsequently shaping how they are covered in the media.

Table 7.4 summarises the key actors that the *Irish Independent* and *The Irish Times* included in their coverage of articles on primary school admissions policies from 2010 to 2019.

Government/State actors garnered the most attention, with a combined 367 articles. The Minister for Education and the Department as whole combined for nearly 300 articles. The Taoiseach (twenty articles) and Attorney General (seventeen) were also critical to passing legislation and ensuring the legality of the ultimate solution. Institutions within the State, the Forum on Patronage (twenty-six) and the Equality Tribunal (sixteen), also proved essential to the debate and, therefore, received some attention.

Like the divestment debates, individual patrons and types of patrons were essential to the discussions. There were 250 articles that mentioned the various patrons. Though bishops are the patrons of over 90 % of Irish primary schools, they barely topped the polls for most articles on admissions

---

55   <https://www.cpsma.ie/cpsma-responds-to-minister-brutons-decision-to-remove-religious-criteria-from-catholic-school-admissions/>.

Table 7.4. Actors in *Irish Independent* and *The Irish Times* admissions articles: 2010–19

Actors	Total # Articles
State/Government	367
Minister for Education	199
Department of Education	89
Forum on Patronage	26
Taoiseach	20
Attorney General	17
Equality Tribunal	16
Patrons	250
Bishops	63
Educate Together	61
Multi-denominational	50
Non-denominational	33
ETB/CNS	28
Gaelscoils (Irish)	15
Parents	226
Political Parties	128
Labour	47
Fine Gael	37
Fianna Fáil	36
Sinn Féin	8
Community-Based Groups	83
Boards of Management	46
Community	21
Past Pupils	9
Joint Managerial Board	7
Civil Society	72
Equate	34
Education Equality	26
Teachers' Union	12

policies among the various patrons with sixty-three articles, closely followed by Educate Together with sixty-one articles. Community National Schools (twenty-eight) and Irish schools (fifteen) were mentioned in considerably fewer articles. By most standards and perceptions, Educate Together has been the leading alternative to Catholic primary schools. Although they have been in existence since the 1980s, Educate Together schools have dramatically increased in numbers since 2000, and they are the standard bearer for non-denominational schools in Ireland with ninety-five primary schools and nineteen secondary schools by 2020.[56] Although Educate Together schools are primarily urban, they have opened a number of schools outside Dublin and the commuter belt in recent years; only thirteen of their 109 schools are west of the Shannon River, which is often the geographic marker for rural Ireland. Educate Together had an incentive to engage the admissions debate because many of their schools had waiting lists. The admissions criterion in all their schools was a 'first-come, first-served' approach, which was one of the criteria that the Department of Education was considering abolishing in the bill. Thus, Educate Together was lobbying the government to allow their admissions policy to continue while also requesting State support to open more of its non-denominational schools. In contrast, Community National Schools do not have one single admissions policy that all their schools implement, nor do they have many schools with waiting lists, which could explain less attention on them during this debate. The higher profile of Educate Together certainly contributed to their enhanced coverage in these articles, but the fact they were specifically involved in one of the issues being debated focused their energies. Once again, key actors engaging the political process and advocating shifts in line with growing public sentiment attracts greater media attention. This debate further consolidated Educate Together's public profile as 'the' alternative to Catholic schools.

Like divestment, parents were essential in the admissions debate. There were 226 articles that highlighted parents and their concerns about how their children are accepted into schools. Similarly, the importance of local concerns was also for a significant part of the admissions debate. There were

56   <https://www.educatetogether.ie/schools/parents/> (Accessed: 9 April 2021).

eighty-three articles that referenced local actors: boards of management (forty-six), community (twenty-one) as a generic reference to the locale, past pupils of schools (nine) and the Joint Managerial Body (seven).

Unlike divestment, the admissions and 'baptismal barrier' articles included more references to political parties and key civil society actors advocating reform. Among the political parties, Labour received the most attention with forty-seven articles, which is not surprising given that they have most consistently argued for removing religion from schools altogether. Fine Gael, Labour's coalition partner, had the second most mentions in admissions articles. Richard Bruton TD, Fine Gael Minister for Education and Skills (2016–18), spearheaded the debates, including offering four different possible solutions, before finally passing legislation that banned Catholic schools from considering religious background of students in their admissions processes. The governing parties' leadership on this specific legislation, and secular reforms more broadly, elicited greater attention by the media.

The high number of articles with views and comments from leading civil society groups advocating change and the end to religious influence in Irish primary schools is noteworthy. Chapter 11, which provides a detailed analysis of the admissions issue, underscores the critical role these civil society groups and advocates had in raising awareness on the issue and mobilising support for this focused reform solution. The two leading advocate groups, Equate and Education Equality, received considerable attention in the media. Equate was mentioned in thirty-four articles, Education Equality in twenty-six articles and teachers' unions in twelve. The absence of easily recognisable civil society groups defending the role of religion in education, other than Catholic bishops, and to a minor extent, Church of Ireland leaders, underscores that most actors discussing admissions policy sought change and they ultimately achieved it. Like trends during the same-sex marriage and abortion campaigns, civil society actors are visible, and can be successful, when they have political decision points such as referenda, deliberative bodies, or specific legislation on which to focus their efforts. Such political focal points help keep the media's attention on critical issues, which outside these key political touchpoints tends to go unnoticed.

It was much more difficult to code and count the issues within the admissions/baptismal barrier theme. On the one hand, the decision over whether to allow religion as an admission criterion is clear-cut: it is either acceptable or not. On the other hand, many actors used this debate to include any or all reform-based issues within these debates. In many cases, the issues had nothing do with religion at all. In fact, there were 785 articles on admissions between 2010 and 2019 in the *Irish Times* and *Irish Independent* that tackled non-religious issues,[57] compared to 575 articles that spoke about religious or secular-related issues.[58] Non-religious issues ranged from hiring and firing practices to funding for various programmes to Irish-language requirements. These were not related to the religious vs. secular debate. Issues such as religious education, protection of minority students' religious rights, and whether a child has been baptised are examples of issues that clearly fall within the religious vs. secular debate.

57   This category includes the following issues: the appeals system, cherry picking the best students, oversubscription and not enough places for children, 'first-come, first-served' admissions policies, admission of special needs pupils and funding for their programs, guaranteeing places to children of past pupils, catchment areas (as both a problem and a potential solution), discrimination against Travellers, transparency of admissions policies, fee-paying schools (State funding and State control of admissions policies at them), guaranteeing places to siblings, soft barriers to enrollment, legal/constitutional barriers to change, discrimination against immigrants, discrimination against newcomers to an area, charging admissions fees, who hires and pays the salaries of teachers, discrimination against students from disadvantaged backgrounds, guaranteeing places to teachers' children, feeder schools, location-based schooling driving housing, gaelscoil's prioritising students who speak Irish, entrance tests, and prioritising students based on parents' occupation/financial situation, lack of funding, soft approach, and education inclusive of LGBTQ+ children.

58   This category includes the following issues: school ethos and traditions, human right to education, religious education (whether it can be opted out of and whether the government should be involved in it), the changing demographics of Ireland, the possible solution of the nearest school rule, parents baptising children just to get them into schools, lack of choices among school types for parents, protections for minority religion schools, divestment not being enough, ban on religion in admissions entirely, raising church-state tensions, the autonomy of Catholic schools, a watered down Catholic ethos, quotas for prioritising religious pupils, the Church wanting divestment over admissions policy changes, Catholic schools being inclusive, faith formation as a private matter, guaranteeing places based on baptism barrier, and state-funded network of secular schools.

We devised an alternative way of coding the various sub-issues within the debate on admission to provide broader insight into the nature of the debate. First, there were 726 articles that discussed admissions criteria and concrete processes at the school level. These articles focused on such things as whether siblings, geography, 'first-come, first-serve' criterion, fees, entrance exams, Irish-language proficiency, and of course, faith should have anything to do with school admission. This sub-topic also included references to the four proposals Minister Bruton published about admissions criteria within the legislative debate:

- A catchment area approach, banning religious schools from giving preference to children of their own religion who live outside the catchment area ahead of non-religious children who live inside the catchment;
- A 'nearest school rule', allowing religious schools to give preference to a religious child only where it is that child's nearest school;
- A quota system, which would allow a religious school to keep a certain number of places for children of that religion;
- An outright ban on schools using religion for admissions. Church schools might be allowed to require parents to indicate respect for the ethos of the school.[59]

The last criterion was ultimately passed, so religion could no longer be used to determine admittance in Catholic primary schools. However, minority religious schools maintained their right to admit students based on their religion to help bolster and preserve the overall ethos.

The second most common sub-topic focused on social change and the processes for dealing with it. There were 440 articles in this category. This includes references to a broad range of issues including insufficient placements, the appeals system, the human right to education, transparency of admissions policies, the changing demographics of Ireland, lack of choices among school types for parents, legal/constitutional barriers to

59   Kitty Holland, 'Removing the Baptism Barrier Is Largely Meaningless', *The Irish Times*, 20 January 2017.

change, increasing Church-State tensions, watered-down Catholic ethos, a State-funded network of secular schools, a lack of funding for new schools and maintaining the status quo.

The third and final category focused on what specific demographic groups should be considered for admittance. This category had 148 articles that referenced whether students from minority groups such as Travellers, minority religions, immigrants, newcomers to an area, lower socio-economic status, the LGBTQ+ community, or those with special needs should receive special consideration in admission policies.

From the breadth and complexity of these issues, we can infer that many actors behaved as though this may be their only time to air their concerns. Like second-order elections when candidates or smaller parties use campaigns to increase visibility for themselves and their preferred policies rather than dealing with the issue at hand, actors used the admissions debate to raise a diverse set of educational reform concerns. The contentious legislative debates provided concerned citizens and groups a key political forum in which to air their views and mobilise supporters.

A brief sentiment analysis relying on MeaningCloud once again confirmed that news coverage of the actors at the heart of the admissions debate was largely balanced and more positive than negative. In terms of sentiment and tone, Table 7.5 reveals that most actors received more positive than negative coverage during the admissions debate.

There are a few minor differences in these results compared to the sentiment analysis for the divestment articles. First, despite overall positive support, several categories had a much narrower gap between their positive and negative coverage. This gap was between 4 % and 12 % for Parents, all mentions of Catholic that are not bishops, Bishop/Archbishop and the Labour Party. The other actors tended to have over 15 % more positive than negative coverage, with Educate Together gaining the most positive coverage; with a whopping 48 % overall, and 36 % more positive than negative coverage. The Educate Together school model has clear and widespread support in the media. The second difference is that Boards of Management and Past Pupils received slightly more negative than positive coverage during this debate. For divestment articles, no actor had greater negative-toned coverage than they had positive- or neutral-toned coverage.

Table 7.5. MeaningCloud sentiment analysis of actors in admissions articles *Irish Independent* and *The Irish Times*: 2010–19

Actor	Positive (%)	Neutral (%)	Negative (%)	Total mentions
Minister for Education	32.56	9.30	17.83	258
Parents	29.39	9.21	22.81	228
Catholic	24.34	4.61	19.74	152
Department of Education	24.10	3.61	9.64	83
Patron	30.67	0	10.67	75
Community	23.61	4.17	8.33	72
Educate Together	48.28	3.45	12.07	58
Bishop/Archbishop	32.08	9.43	20.75	53
Labour Party	31.91	10.64	27.66	47
Fine Gael	31.25	3.13	25.00	32
Board of Management	16.13	0	19.35	31
Past Pupil	3.33	0	6.67	30
Teacher	44.00	12	20.00	25

The primary implication of these findings is that the leading newspapers appear to provide more positive and neutral coverage rather than negative coverage when discussing the contentious educational issues. Rather than judging or attacking the actors involved, the leading newspapers influence the debate more in terms of the frequency in which they mention various actors and issues. There are strong and competing views included in these educational debates, but the media appears to record and highlight rather than dictate the nature of the debate. This conclusion confirms earlier research on election coverage that the leading newspapers provide an essential arena for competing sides to persuade public opinion to their preferred outcomes rather than leading the charge for change in a particular direction. That slightly more attention has been given to reform and change, and to high-profile actors like Educate Together, tracks with the broader demographic changes in Irish society supporting change in that direction. As the numbers of practicing Catholics diminishes and the numbers of Irish citizens and immigrants who claim to be either no or a minority religion increases, the media highlights these changes, which alters the character of educational debates and enhances momentum calling for change.

D. Primary School Curriculum

Examining how *The Irish Times* and *Irish Independent* covered curriculum proved more challenging. Curriculum is a broad term that deals with how subjects are categorised, scheduled, taught, assessed, etc. For example, curriculum addresses which subjects are part of the 'minimum state curriculum', like mathematics and languages, and which subjects are part of 'flexible time', such as religious education, patron's programmes and physical education. Recent debates have considered whether there should be a two- or three-stage model for how the curriculum helps children learn in developmentally and pedagogically appropriate ways that move from subject-based learning to thematic-based learning.[60] There are also key differences in how the curriculum is devised and structured depending on whether dealing with junior/senior infants or first through sixth class, or in disadvantaged areas that are designated as Delivering Equality of Opportunity Schools (DEIS), or with students with special needs; or with all boys or girls or co-educational contexts, or in a denominational, non-denominational or multi-denominational school and so on. Issues that pertain to the curriculum are boundless.

In terms of the religious vs. secular debates, recent shifts in the curriculum and proposed changes could dramatically alter or end the role of religion in Irish primary schools. Curricular changes are a more subtle form of change than divestment or admissions and, therefore, seem to

---

60   See *Primary Developments: Consultation on Curriculum Structure and Time*, Final Report, National Council for Curriculum and Assessment, January 2018.

receive different, and often less, news coverage. The sheer number of curricular changes in recent years has crowded the schedule and teachers struggle to teach all subjects during any given week. Recent additions to the curriculum include Social, Personal and Health Education (SPHE); the Social, Environmental and Scientific Education (SESE); and the proposed curriculum for Education about Religions and Beliefs and Ethics (ERB and Ethics). These three programmes each have some overlap with religious education, pressing teachers to choose how they want to realistically spend their time. ERB and Ethics, for example, 'helps pupils to know about and to understand the cultural heritage of the major forms of religion, belief traditions and world views which have been embraced by humankind. It is not focused on nurturing a belief or practice system of any one religion, instead it focuses on fostering an informed awareness of the main theist, non-theist, and secular beliefs including key aspects of their cultural manifestations.'[61] The Religious Education Curriculum for Catholic schools also teaches learning, respect and toleration of other religions and secular beliefs. Like other subjects, this curriculum takes a spiral approach, whereby themes/ topics build on each other as the child progresses through the curriculum.[62] As a result, other religions are not confined to one point in the curriculum but are revisited throughout in parallel with children's growing engagement with, and understanding of, their own Catholic faith.

The real challenge is how to adjudicate the critical differences that persist between those who want religious education to be eliminated from Irish primary schools and those who want to preserve it. Underpinning these ultimate goals are real and impassioned differences in perspective about whether schools should teach about faith (i.e. facts, history, etc.), teach from faith (i.e. values, beliefs, creed, etc.) or teach into faith (i.e. faith formation and sacramental preparation). Those who support religious education believe in the importance of all three types of faith education.

---

61 National Council for Curriculum and Assessment, 'Education about Religions and Beliefs (ERB) and Ethics in the Primary School: Consultation Paper', November 2015. <https://ncca.ie/media/1897/consultation_erbe.pdf>.

62 Irish Episcopal Conference, *Catholic Preschool and Primary Religious Education Curriculum for Ireland*. Dublin: Veritas, 2015.

They wish to teach and form students in the faith and believe that information and knowledge in the religious education curriculum are conveyed in an objective, critical and pluralistic manner in Catholic primary schools. Those who are opposed to teaching religious education believe that it is only acceptable to teach about faith in schools. They argue that the non-religious outlook on life is not respected and even discriminated against in denominational schools. Proponents of this perspective argue that changing the emphasis to a history of religion would be less discriminating towards non-religious pupils and would help these students feel less isolated and excluded.[63] Irrespective of the validity of the arguments, and despite the emotional intensity felt by those on both sides of the debate, discussion concerning curriculum can often become quite technical. As a result, these discussions are followed more closely by teachers, academics, professionals and defenders of either side, and less by the broader public. Changes in this area may be more subtle and fly under the radar of significant media exposure.

Curricular issues become more relevant for the religious vs. secular debates when discussing concrete plans to change the time devoted to teaching religion or plans to remove religious education from the school day altogether. A recent proposal from 2019 under consideration by the National Council for Curriculum and Assessment (NCCA), the main statutory body that advises the Minister for Education on all curricular issues, is to reduce the time allotted to teaching religion in primary schools from 150 minutes per week (thirty minutes per day) to 120 minutes (twenty-four minutes per day) has gained considerable traction. 'A survey by the Irish Primary Principals' Network found that the vast majority of principals felt less time should be spent on teaching religion in the classroom and more on subjects such as maths, English and physical education.'[64] Another proposal seeks to shift religion class to the first or last period of

63   Caroline Renehan and Kevin Williams, 'Religion, education and conflict in the Republic of Ireland', *Journal of Theories and Research in Education*, 2015, Vol. 10, No. 1, 67–87. Special Issue. *Religion, Conflict and Education.* Edited by Stephen McKinney and Federico Zannoni.

64   Carl O'Brien, 'Parents Leaving It to Schools to Prepare Children for Sacraments', *The Irish Times*, 15 May 2019.

the day to facilitate those students who wish to opt-out of religious education instruction. Still others propose eliminating religion altogether from schools, thereby ending the ability of schools to integrate religion and faith-related activities throughout the school day, which has been the established norm since 1971.

Ironically, many Irish parents who are open to having less Church involvement in Irish schools and society more generally do not want to move sacramental preparation outside the school day because this would require a greater time commitment on their part! Regular mass attendance may be down, but do not dare to take away the revered 1st Communion or Confirmation ritual that fosters family and community engagement! 'Many teachers say they have noticed a deterioration in children's religious knowledge over the years. Some talk of how they end up having to re-teach students how to receive Communion in their Confirmation year. One recalls a recent First Holy Communion ceremony where the amused congregation were unaware of when to sit, stand or kneel at any point during the Mass. It's clear that many parents are not engaging with church practices – though they expect it of their schools.'[65] For many of these parents, they feared the loss of this important family and cultural event more than they considered this an attack on their faith or religious practice. 'I'm doing it so we can have a fun day out with friends and family. I'll admit that I'm more focused on food, drinks and music than I am on the Christian sacraments and the admission of my child into the Christian Church. Yes, it's flaky, fair-weather and extremely hypocritical of me, but I'm not the only one. As Christians, many of us partake in milestone ceremonies despite a very obvious lack of faith.'[66]

The Church was accused of seeking to scare parents into believing that not only would there be no more sacraments if there was a change in patronage, but other things would go as well. For example, secular civil society activist Paddy Monahan argues that 'they have conducted a campaign to incite fear, uncertainty and doubt among parents, making claims

65   O'Brien, 2019.
66   Barbara McCarthy, 'Despite a Lack of Faith, I Can Still Find a Place for Religion in My Life', *Irish Independent*, 27 July 2015.

that switching to an unknown patron would result in the removal of book clubs, garden fetes, and Christmas celebrations'.[67]

Irrespective of some motivations, a recent study reports that access to sacramental preparation was cited by parents as the fourth most influential factor when choosing a primary school for their children, with 47 % stating it was important or very important in making their choice. It was preceded only by location, academic reputation and reputation for discipline, in that order.[68] Nevertheless, many non-denominational schools support faith formation and sacramental preparation after school and have found it to be successful. Catholic Archbishop Diarmuid Martin of Dublin and others have been calling for parents and local parishes to play a much greater role in preparing children for sacraments outside of school, which could have dramatic effects on whether religion remains part of Irish primary schools in the medium term.[69] Such proposals could also reduce the numbers of children receiving the sacraments, but they may actually increase the proportion of committed Catholics.[70] Additionally, if sacramental preparation was moved outside of school for all children, some parents admitted they would be less concerned about having their school become multi- or non-denominational because their children would not miss out on this rite of passage. This shift might also get parents more involved in their children's faith formation.[71]

For secular advocates, these changes to sacramental preparation still fall short of the radical change they deem necessary. 'It is important to note that the plan to move sacramental preparation outside the classroom will not affect the daily thirty minutes of religious faith formation that takes place in virtually every primary classroom in the country. Nor will it change the

---

67   Paddy Monahan, 'It's Self-serving for Church to Move Sacraments out of School Hours', *Irish Times*, 11 December 2019.

68   Genesis, *Articulating a new positioning for Catholic education in Ireland*, September 2021.

69   Jack Horgan-Jones, 'Parents Not Schools to Lead Communion Preparations, Says Archbishop of Dublin', *The Irish Times*, 3 December 2019.

70   O'Brien, 2019.

71   'South Roscommon School to Meet to Consider "Change of Ethos" '. *Shannonside News*, 19 June 2019. <https://www.shannonside.ie/news/local/roscommon/south-roscommon-school-meet-consider-change-ethos/>.

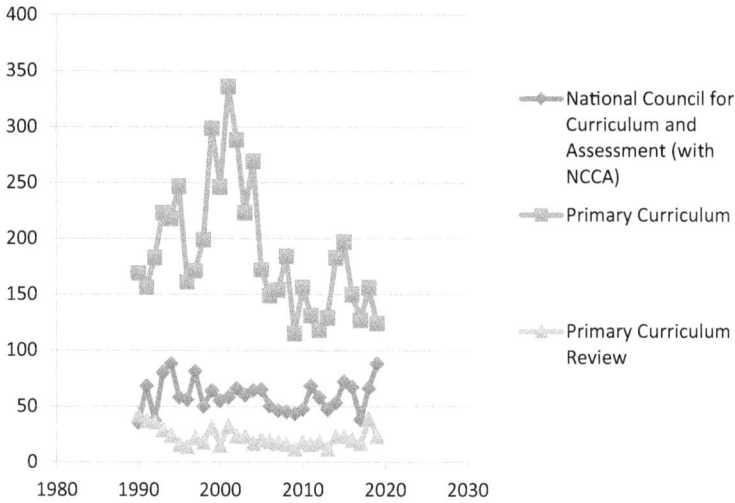

Figure 7.3. Combined curriculum articles in *Irish Independent* and *The Irish Times*: 1990–2019.

standard practice in these schools of segregating children from the "wrong" religious background for this period every day. That's right, shockingly it is the norm throughout Ireland for children not of the Catholic faith to be singled out every day in the classroom from four years of age to sit alone at the back of the class while their peers receive faith-formation.'[72]

A quick glance at the numbers of articles on primary school curriculum demonstrates that the broad category receives regular attention in *The Irish Times* and *Irish Independent* (see Figure 7.3).

From 1990 to 2005, there were between 150 and 340 articles annually on the primary curriculum. This number drops to about fifty articles per year from 2005 to 2019. The NCCA was mentioned in approximately fifty articles per year in the *Irish Independent* and *The Irish Times*. The several years around critical curriculum reviews and changes, such as in 1999 and 2016–18, did not gain much attention in the media even though this was all-consuming for teachers, advocates and academics during these years.

72   Monahan, 11 December 2019.

Figure 7.3 shows that there were on average twenty articles per year in the two papers on the various curriculum reviews.

If one explores more specific themes within the primary school curriculum, one finds that no one issue gains that much attention. Religious education in primary schools, which is sometimes discussed as a curricular issue and other times covered as a theme in its own right, is the most popular specific topic and averages forty-three articles per year in the *Irish Independent* and thirteen articles per year in *The Irish Times* since 1960. In contrast, there were only three articles on Sexuality Education in primary schools per year in both the *Irish Independent* and *The Irish Times* over the same period. Additionally, there were less than fifteen articles total between 2009 and 2019 on Ethics in the primary curriculum in both papers. The highly touted ERB and Ethics curriculum has been much discussed in professional circles as a result several articles published on the theme by the NCCA and Ireland's ESRI; however, during this same period, it received virtually no news coverage.

The multitude of issues contained within curriculum debates are often discussed in the same articles. As a result, issues related to religious education and religious schools often get buried and do not receive as much attention as other church-state issues. Even though curriculum is the most common topic overall within primary schools, the issues most relevant to the secularisation of schools are less common. The lack of one, clear-cut issue – or even venue – in which to engage the religious vs. secular debate within curriculum reform, forces curriculum into detailed conversations that get lost in the weeds or left to academics to discuss and journalists to ignore.

V. Conclusion

Media coverage of educational reforms has been less frequent and generally less intense than those in the marriage equality and abortion campaigns. The sheer multiplicity of issues, as well as the countless numbers of individuals, groups, institutions and levels affected by policy reforms in different ways depending on the issue, often dilutes or diffuses the nature of the debate. Therefore, the framing of the problem and set of solutions associated with each aspect of educational reform influences the type of attention it attracts. The hot-button issues within the primary education sector do not receive much media attention, and when they do receive greater consideration, it is generally associated with a particular political process such as the Forum on Patronage and Pluralism Schools in 2011 or the Education (Admissions to School) Act of 2018.

Again, how issues are framed and what solutions are offered matters. In divestment, the debates are intensely local. As a result, there has been a strong NIMBY phenomenon present within these debates that was not present in the marriage equality and abortion campaigns that focused much more on individual rights. The multiple and varied ways that educational reforms affect local areas helps account for lower frequency of attention nationally as debates are framed in local terms, which further fragments how these controversial issues are addressed in the media. Our analysis found that the overall treatment of the various actors involved was balanced and the coverage was largely positive towards all the actors.

The coverage of admission policies included more reporting on State/government actors and institutions, political parties and civil society actors because they were more directly involved in the specific legislation under consideration. Many of these more politically driven actors were absent or minimised during the Forum on Patronage discussions. The consultative, open-ended nature of how divestment was engaged intentionally sought to include often under-heard voices within society and those most affected by proposed changes. Those impacted by the different policies was crucial as well. Whereas divestment affected parents, schools and communities, the framing of admissions had less impact on many of these actors and therefore did not elicit the same level of concern or opposition. This too influenced the nature of the media coverage.

Ironically, the recent shifts in the curriculum and proposed changes could dramatically alter or end the role of religion in Irish primary schools, but there has not been that much coverage in the media. Since curricular changes are a more subtle and are often addressed by bureaucrats and educational specialists and professionals, they receive less attention than more visible issues like divestment and admissions. The fact that religious education and religious schools often get combined with other curriculum changes means that they often get buried and do not receive as much attention as other Church-State issues. This may benefit those advocating change, because it may allow them to gradually reform the system and create far more lasting impact without attracting too much attention. Sometimes, less attention can be beneficial to avoid elevating the salience of issues that have the potential to divide and mobilise individuals and groups with competing interests. Ultimately, upcoming reforms could lead to the types of change that become difficult to reverse and eventually lead to a completely secular educational system.

The media have provided a key arena in which individuals, groups, communities and institutions have engaged educational reform issues. Our analysis suggests, that perhaps differently than in previous policy areas, the media has been quite balanced, neutral and overall positive in its treatment of the education debates. In Part III of this book, we shift from focusing on the main actors individually and begin to look towards the three policy issues in more detail. To bridge the gap between this focus on actors and our more careful examination of how the policy process unfolds, we turn to an overview of political parties and their positions on education reform. Political parties are the final arbiters of all policies within Ireland. Even though Ireland's major parties often defer to civil society groups or wait to act more decisively in policy processes until there is consensus within Irish society about proposed policy solutions, they are the key actors that ultimately determine whether policies become law. Chapter 9 will reveal recent trends in party support for the various education issues.

PART III

The Politics of Primary Education Reform and Policy Case Studies

CHAPTER 8

Policy Evolution: LGBTQ and Abortion Rights as Precursors of Educational Reform

I. Introduction

Few countries have been enmeshed in a dynamic and changing environment like the one that resulted from the unprecedented social, cultural and economic transformations experienced by the Republic of Ireland from the late 1980s onward. The economic boom of the 1990s and the first decade of the twenty-first century utterly transformed Irish society. The boom altered incomes, the nature of the workforce, levels of educational attainment, the structure of family life, the percentage of immigrants, and even where people lived. Significant shifts in attitudes and voter preferences among the electorate have occurred simultaneously. The social, cultural and racial homogeneity that once characterised Ireland has become less prevalent, hollowing out the consensus that had eased the forging of the broad, cross-class appeals so vital for many of Ireland's political parties.

Ireland's dramatically altered social and economic landscape has transformed the country's policy landscape as well. Not all social changes lead to change in policy outcomes, but shifts on the scale experienced in Ireland have opened up policy spaces previously unimaginable just decades ago. In particular, the Catholic Church's loss of its moral monopoly has created a new space within the policy sphere that civil society activists have taken advantage of to redefine how issues are framed. These activists mobilised media attention and influenced public opinion, which in turn prompted major political parties to revise their positions and support important policy changes. The noteworthy results of the marriage equality referendum in 2015 and abortion referendum in 2018 are often portrayed as miraculous events because Irish society's attention was 'suddenly' focused on these issues, which then ushered in a period of radical policy shifts. However, these results were the culmination of decades of hard work that laid the foundation that eventually led to these much-acclaimed outcomes. The passion, energy and ensuing momentum that emerged from these campaigns encouraged activists and significant segments of Irish society to demand similar change in the educational sphere. The thought was that if the once dominant Catholic Church could be sidelined and defeated on these hot-button moral issues, perhaps the Church's influence in education could be greatly reduced or even eliminated altogether.

A recent study of educational policy reform in the United States reinforces the idea that politics is not just about who gets what, when and how, but is also about who wants what and why![1] This study offers a helpful roadmap for how policy evolution has and may continue to develop in Ireland. Based on their studies of American politics, Wolbrecht and Hartney describe how framing issues influence their salience, place on the agenda, meaning and significance, and what policy alternatives are available to policy-makers to address these issues. They argue that how issues are framed and addressed evolves, which can help explain how major policy changes occur. They contend that issue redefinition rarely, if ever results from a single cause, but usually occurs because changed social realities interact with policy entrepreneurs who actively seek to define policy problems and solutions in ways that can lead to change.[2] The experience in the United States reveals that a 'change in issue definition may lead groups with established positions to reconsider and revise their position or abandon the issue entirely. Alternatively, issue redefinition may motivate groups not previously active in the debate to develop a preference.'[3] For Ireland, as in many places, increased salience of issues can undermine previous monopolies of understanding about how things should be done and newly active groups often gain influence in shaping policy debates. Additionally, elected

1   Christina Wolbrecht and Michael T. Hartney, ' "Ideas about Interests": Explaining the Changing Partisan Politics of Education', *Perspectives on Politics*, American Political Science Association, September 2014, Vol. 12, No. 3, 603–30.

2   Wolbrecht and Hartney, 2014, 605.

3   Wolbrecht and Hartney, 2014, 606.

representatives are constantly evaluating the perceived utility of issue positions to help them attract and secure sufficient electoral support. As issues are redefined, party elites balance party ideology, voter interests and their own preferences, which often leads them to re-evaluate and change their views on issues.[4]

Wolbrecht and Hartney's study of shifting partisan attitudes and policy preferences towards educational reform builds on the experience of issue redefinition in the area of LGBTQ rights in the United States. The issue was reframed within a broader equality and inclusion movement. This shift altered the individuals, groups and parties that favoured the respective policy choices. For example, 'Over the last 30 years, public discourse about homosexuality shifted from a focus on sexuality and a distinctive gay counterculture to an emphasis on equality and inclusion into such well-regarded social institutions as marriage and the military.'[5]

In the United States, similar reframing of educational issues altered partisan support for salient educational reforms. Education was previously framed as a 'choice between federal funding to address perceived inequalities, and leaving schooling to states and localities', and more recently it has been defined in terms of teacher quality, standards and accountability. A key implication of this shift was that the Republican's position radically changed. In the latter framing, the Republicans opposed unions and favoured the application of business principles to public functions. For Wolbrecht and Hartney, 'The important point is that not only has the shift in issue definition led the parties to favour (or oppose) new education policy proposals, but issue redefinition has contributed to a change in the parties' positions on long-standing policies.'[6] Their analysis reveals how shifting preferences and expanded group participation by various groups – including teacher unions, civil rights organisations and education reform advocacy organisations – redefined the problem and set of solutions that the public and parties eventually supported. Therefore, educational policy, and how issues were redefined in the face of evolving social conditions and

---

4   Wolbrecht and Hartney, 2014, 606.
5   Wolbrecht and Hartney, 2014, 622.
6   Wolbrecht and Hartney, 2014, 621.

strategic choices by policy and party elites, mirrored what occurred within the LGBTQ movement in the United States.

There has been similar policy evolution in Ireland. This chapter will provide a brief summary of how the marriage equality and abortion referendum campaigns were the culmination of decades of civil society groups advocating for change and organising and mobilising to achieve their goals. Advocates of change redefined the issues within a broader equality and inclusion agenda, which allowed them to overcome the previous monopoly the Church had maintained in Irish society and to attract new actors and groups to their agenda. In the process of redefining the issues, reformers took advantage of changed attitudes and new coalitions within Irish society to encourage political parties to support change. In the wake of marriage equality and abortion policy reforms being achieved, many Irish civil society advocates and party elites asked 'What's next?' as a way to signal their ambition to dramatically limit or eliminate the role of religion in Irish education.

In this chapter, we summarise and explain the key developments in these previous campaigns to determine what lessons can be learned and applied to the educational reform campaign – which will be discussed more explicitly in the next chapter. Although many reformers talked about educational reform as though it would just happen in the wake of these momentous policy victories, this is unlikely. In fact, educational reform has been underway for decades, but our analysis will demonstrate how it may not be as far along the path to change as these other policy areas. The more we can understand how the Church, civil society actors, the media and ultimately politicians behaved during these other policy reforms, the more we will be able to understand how educational reforms are being framed and addressed and what outcomes are likely to unfold. These previous campaigns shed light on how policy problems have been framed, which in turn influenced the policy alternatives available to Irish policy and party elites in the past. The ways in which previous issues have been defined and then engaged through the courts, citizens' assemblies and legislative contexts are also relevant. Ultimately, this chapter sets the stage for how we will examine how educational reform has evolved in Ireland, with a similar view to how actors and institutions are interacting to engage these critical reform issues.

II. The Evolution of LGBTQ Rights in Ireland

Several key court cases and legislative reforms dating back to 1988 ultimately led to the passing of the same-sex marriage referendum in Ireland in 2015. Legislation aimed at penalising homosexuality dated back to 1861 and 1885 British laws that essentially 'criminalised homosexuality'. These laws remained in effect until 1993. The journey to overturn this legislation began in the 1970s when a leading gay rights activist, Professor David Norris of Trinity College Dublin, organised the Sexual Liberation Movement (1974), which subsequently led to the formation of the Dublin University Gay Society and the Campaign for Homosexual Law Reform.[7] Mary McAleese and Mary Robinson, both law professors and eventual Presidents of Ireland, helped advise the Campaign for Homosexual Law Reform in the late 1970s and early 1980s.

David Norris lost his original case in the Irish Courts (*Norris v. Attorney General*) in 1983, which sought to overturn the 1861 and 1885 laws. He then took his case to the European Court of Human Rights in 1988, and he won a ruling that declared Irish laws breached the Convention's rules on respecting the private lives of individuals. Successive Fianna Fáil governments had avoided enacting legislation to honour the court mandate. Only when Labour entered a coalition with Fianna Fáil was the 1993 legislation passed. The age of consent that was established was equal to that between men and women.

The Gay and Lesbian Equality Network (GLEN), originally formed in 1988 to fight for inclusion of lesbian, gay, bisexual and transgender individuals in Irish society and to ban discrimination based on sexual orientation,

---

7   Connor Hayes, 'Outing the Party: Irish Political Party Engagement in the 2015 Same Sex Marriage Referendum', Senior thesis, Department of Political Science, University of Notre Dame, 1 April 2016.

was critical in passing the 1993 legislation. GLEN, which ceased operations in 2017, maintained its legal focus since its inception and influenced all subsequent legislation in this area. For example, they lobbied successfully to include sexual orientation in the Employment Equality Act (1998) and the Equal Status Act (2000). There were key exemptions within these acts for religious organisations, including Catholic schools and hospitals, but equality was becoming more widely accepted within Irish society and its legal framework.

In addition to the exemptions within the equality acts, a judicial setback for the LGBTQ community occurred when the High Court in *Zappone v. Revenue Commissioners (2006)* ruled against Katherine Zappone and Ann Louise Gilligan in their attempt to have their 2003 Canadian marriage recognised in Ireland so they could submit joint tax returns. The High Court decision prompted greater commitment and action by gay rights' activists seeking to legalise civil unions, such as increased financial backing to fight for equality legislation. Atlantic Philanthropies, a US-Irish foundation, spent $8.8 million in grants, primarily to four organisations that each in their own way sought to advance rights in this area. These included GLEN, Marriage Equality (which was founded in 2008 in the aftermath of the *Zappone* case), Transgender Equality Network Ireland (TENI) and LGBT Diversity (which sought to help people outside of Dublin). Atlantic Philanthropies supported these varied groups because at the time there was no consensus as to the best tactical approach to achieve judicial and/or legislative reform.[8]

Although each of these groups performed key roles in advocacy and shaping public opinion, GLEN was particularly instrumental in passing the Civil Partnership Act (2010). This act granted some legal privileges of marriage, though not all, such as adoption, to gay couples. GLEN leaders had close contacts with many Fianna Fáil politicians who, in the face of criticisms over the collapsed Irish economy, were eager to achieve something legislatively. Some gay rights' groups, especially Marriage Equality,

---

8   Eric Brown, *Yes: Marriage Equality's Path to Victory in Ireland*. Available at: <https://www.comnetwork.org/insights/yes-marriage-equalitys-path-to-victory-in-ireland/> (Accessed: 7 April 2021).

were upset that this legislation did not achieve complete recognition for gay couples because they believed that civil unions would slow progress towards full marriage recognition. In contrast, GLEN had feared that Fianna Fáil would never go for full marriage rights or that the same-sex rights would be taken off the agenda altogether. Like its strategy in the 1998 and 2000 Equality Acts GLEN recognised that 'gay rights were the third rail for rural Irish politics'.[9] Therefore, they pursued a patient, subdued and incrementalist approach, which proved successful. The 2010 legislation passed unanimously in the Dáil and was a major milestone for the LGBT community. Not only had twenty years of equality legislation shifted public opinion, but the next two years' experience of civil unions raised visibility and awareness that homosexual couples were as loving and committed as heterosexual couples, and this paved the way in the lead-up to the referendum.[10]

The 'earthquake' general election of 2011 ushered in further change as the new Fine Gael and Labour coalition government had strong views in support of change. Labour had been supportive of equality legislation for gay individuals dating back to the 1970s and had supported 1993, 1998 and 2000 legislation. Likewise, Fine Gael had been the first party to support civil unions in 2004. The new coalition's Programme for Government highlighted equality and promised a Constitutional Convention within twelve months to engage the issue of same-sex marriage.[11]

The Constitutional Convention is an example of Ireland's major parties addressing key issues facing Irish society via extra-parliamentary institutions within the Irish political system to avoid disrupting the entrenched advantage of historic parties and advancing the electoral interests of challenger parties.[12] This Constitutional Convention was established in 2012 by the Fine Gael-Labour government to deal with a range of issues ranging from more mundane issues, such as presidential elections and

9   Hayes, 2016, 13.
10   Grainne Healy, Brian Sheehan and Noel Whelan, *Ireland Says Yes: The Inside Story of How the Vote for Marriage Equality was Won*. Kildare: Merrion Press, 2016, 5–6.
11   Healy, Sheehan and Whelan, 2016, 3.
12   Sean McGraw, *How Parties Win: Shaping the Irish Political Arena*. Ann Arbor: University of Michigan Press, 2015.

terms, voting age and Dáil reform, to hot-button issues like same-sex marriage.[13] The Convention consisted of 100 members, including sixty-six citizens, thirty-three politicians and one chair. After months of deliberations, a 79–21 vote recommended that the State change the Constitution to allow for same-sex marriage. GLEN, Marriage Equality and the Irish Council for Civil Liberties (ICCL) were among the presenters in support of the proposition and gained visibility and legitimacy for their role in the nationally televised broadcast. After months of increased pressure, the Government announced in November 2013 that it would hold a referendum in the spring of 2015.[14]

Over the next eighteen months, those in favour of constitutional change combined their efforts to generate widespread support that ultimately resulted in 62 % of voters in the 2015 referendum supporting same-sex marriage. There were several key reasons for this outcome. First, the leading civil society groups overcame their tactical differences and formed a united front in the Yes Equality campaign. GLEN, Marriage Equality and ICCL working together led a focused, positive and methodical campaign that combined traditional and new methods. Their more traditional 'ground game' consisted of a massive 'get the vote out' campaign, a door-to-door grassroots effort that canvassed every house in Ireland *twice*, and a national bus tour with prominent local leaders from around the country. Yes Equality also mastered a modern social media campaign that won over the hearts and minds of new and old voters alike by reframing how Irish people defined family and defended rights. In particular, the Yes side maintained an incredibly positive tone that emphasised personal stories demonstrating that LGBTQ individuals and couples were part of broader families that represented the values of the new Ireland rooted in equality and fairness. High-profile parents with LGBTQ children, including former President Mary McAleese and her husband Martin, the father of the then Minister of

13 See David M. Farrell and Jane Suiter, *Reimagining Democracy: Lessons in Deliberative Democracy From the Irish Front Lines*. Ithaca and London: Cornell Selects, 2019.

14 Eric Brown, *Atlantic Insights: Advocacy for Impact*, Atlantic Philanthropies, 2016, <AP_Advocacy-Impact-Insights.pdf> (<atlanticphilanthropies.org>). In particular, see 'Yes: Marriage Equality's Path to Victory in Ireland', 66–88.

Health, Leo Varadker, who recently announced that he was gay, and Tom Curran, the Secretary General of Fine Gael, epitomised the positive, family-based approach. Yes Equality learned from lost state-wide campaigns in the United States and chose not to run traditional LGBTQ issue campaigns that focused on mobilising their base. Instead, the Yes side engaged with the concerns of mainstream/middle voters that generally believed that 'if it matters to them and has no consequence for me, sure why not?'[15] The ability of the Yes Equality campaign to mobilise the mainstream prevented the extremes on either side of the issue from dominating the debate.

A second key feature of the campaign was the role of political parties. Historically, political parties have campaigned much less during referenda campaigns than they do in general elections. Some argued that this was the case in this referendum as well because only Sinn Féin and the youth wings of Fine Gael and Labour were active in their public campaigns. However, the parties did influence the campaign in multiple ways, even if in more indirect and informal ways. The parties were essential in training Yes Equality in their canvass and poster strategies.[16] GLEN's leading lobbyist, Tiernan Brady (who had been critical in the passing of the civil unions legislation), worked intensively with the general secretaries of all the political parties and linked in local county councillors, youth wing members and party activists, tying them all to the Yes Equality efforts.[17]

Additionally, party leaders coordinated their efforts with the Yes Equality so that they would launch their party campaigns closer to the actual referendum so they could be more effective and focused. Yes Equality was even able to get opposition parties to focus on the referendum and not on anti-government sentiments. For example, one campaign slogan was '2015 Vote for Equality, 2016 Vote Against Austerity'.[18] The governing parties strategically helped keep the debate focused on same-sex marriage by clarifying uncertainty around the controversial issue of same-sex couples' rights to adopt children. The Children and Family Relationships Bill in

15   Healy, Sheehan and Whelan, 2016, 44.
16   Hayes, 2016; Healy, Sheehan and Whelan, 2016.
17   Healy, Sheehan and Whelan, 2016, 36–7.
18   Healy, Sheehan and Whelan, 2016, 70–1.

2014 addressed these concerns and dropped proposals to regulate surrogacy, which had been another controversial issue.[19]

Finally, political parties were key actors in the national print media. A study of all coverage in *The Irish Times* and the *Irish Independent*, the two leading national newspapers, between January and May of 2015 reveals that political party leaders and politicians were leading spokespersons during the campaign. In fact, of all articles reporting on the referendum during this period, 42 % of all quotes were by politicians and party leaders, which was well ahead of advocacy and community organisations (19 %) and Catholic Church leaders (15 %). Given the cross-party support, it is unsurprising that nearly 70 % of all commentary by politicians and party leaders in the newspapers supported the Yes side.[20]

A third key feature during the campaign was that the Catholic Church and conservative Catholic groups were unable to mobilise support in ways that they had in previous referendum campaigns. The No side sought to mobilise what they thought was the 'silent majority' of more conservative voters and therefore focused their efforts on the rights of children to a mother and a father and the unforeseen consequences and changes in social fabric that same-sex marriage would unleash. Although Archbishop Diarmuid Martin of Dublin assumed a quieter approach in an apparent attempt not to alienate moderate and progressive Catholics, Archbishop Eamon Martin of Armagh was more outspoken. As Primate of All Ireland, the Archbishop of Armagh had a message read at all the Sunday masses weeks before the referendum that explicitly stated that the Catholic Church would not 'support an amendment to the Constitution which redefines marriage and effectively places the union of two men, or two women, on a par with the marriage relationship between a husband and wife which is open to the procreation of children'.[21] The Yes Equality leadership publicly expressed disappointment at the tone of this latter message and for the failure to distinguish between religious and civil ceremonies, but they

---

19   Healy, Sheehan and Whelan, 2016, 19.
20   Hayes, 2016, 18.
21   Archbishop Eamon Martin, 'A Message on the Marriage Referendum', 1 May 2015, <https://www.catholicbishops.ie/wp-content/uploads/2015/05/2015-May-02-Care-for-the-Covenant-of-Marriage.pdf>.

ultimately felt that the Church hierarchy was not having much impact on the middle ground.

Differences in the Catholic Church's position emerged as prominent priests like social justice campaigner Fr Peter McVerry offered Yes positions. Furthermore, high-profile lay Catholics also offered an alternative faith-based perspective. For example, Ursula Halligan, a leading TV journalist, gave older voters permission to vote yes as she acclaimed that 'as a person of faith and a Catholic, I believe a Yes vote is the most Christian thing to do. I believe the glory of God is the human being fully alive, and that includes people who are gay.'[22] And Tom Curran, the Fine Gael General Secretary, whose son was gay, stated publicly that 'as a Catholic, seeing creation as being born out of love, I couldn't see how he was different to my other two sons or daughter.'[23] Additional efforts to personalise stories of adult children of same-sex couples and to get grandparents to accept younger gay individuals altered the sense of what an acceptable family was, which undermined the Church's previous attempts to speak on behalf of families.

The overwhelming Yes vote in the 2015 referendum was the culmination of years of civil society activism that changed legislation and influenced public opinion. There had been a dramatic evolution in Irish attitudes towards homosexuality in the last quarter century from a solid majority expressing the belief that homosexuality was 'always wrong' to a majority expressing the belief that it was 'never wrong'. For example, those who reported that homosexuality was 'always wrong' declined from 59 % in 1981 to 23 % in 2006, whereas those who reported that homosexuality was 'never wrong' went from 3 % in 1981 to 53 % by 2006.[24] Even the nature

---

22   Healy, Sheehan and Whelan, 2016, 101.

23   Healy, Sheehan and Whelan, 2016, 110.

24   Data for 1981 is taken from the World Values Survey, and the data for 2006 is from the 2006 Irish Study of Sexual Health and Relationships (www.dohc.ie/publications/pdf/ISSHR_Main_Report.pdf?direct=1>, 101–4). The WVS used a 1–10 scale with 1 = never justifiable and 10 = always justifiable. In order to compare with the 2006 data, we converted the WVS responses into the categories used by the 2006 survey. Thus, WVS responses 2 to 4 were labeled as 'homosexuality is nearly never justified'; and the responses 6 to 9 were combined to create the category 'homosexuality is sometimes justifiable'. The categories for the 2006 ISSHR

of the question changed as these shifts occurred to the point where Irish citizens started to be asked their views on civil unions, same-sex marriage and same-sex adoption rights. In 2006, over 80 % reported that same-sex couples should have some legal recognition; 64 % supported extending current rights afforded to heterosexual couples (e.g. tax and inheritance privileges) to same-sex couples; and 51 % expressed support for gay marriage. There was some opposition to adoption rights, with only 39 % reporting that same-sex couples should be able to adopt, whereas 50 % were against extending this right to gay couples.[25] There was greater attention on the issue of same-sex marriage between 2012 and 2015, and public opinion in favour of same-sex marriage ranged from 67 % to 76 % during this period.[26]

Although broader changes in society have clearly affected attitudes on all social issues, including homosexuality, there is no doubt civil society groups and activists were critical to ushering in these judicial, legislative and referendum results. The ability to redefine the issue, raise awareness and then mobilise activity around concrete political processes and institutions was essential. The media had a key role in this process. The same study mentioned previously that examined same-sex marriage coverage in *The Irish Times* and *Irish Independent* between January and May 2015 found that 65 % of all articles supported the Yes vote, 29 % supported the No side and only 6 % were neutral.[27] Therefore, despite the TV mandate to provide equal time for both sides of a referendum, this was not the case in print media. The social media campaign was even more skewed towards the Yes side. A simple look at the Facebook presence during the campaign revealed the following numbers of followers for the key groups during the campaign: Yes Equality 66,427; Fianna Fáil 21,536; Fine Gael 22,414; Labour 13,748; Sinn Féin 97,837; Archdiocese of Dublin 1,336; and

---

Survey were: homosexuality is always wrong, mostly wrong, sometimes wrong, and never wrong.

25   *The Irish Times*, 22 October 2006 and 24 November 2006.

26   Red C Polls were published in November 2013 (76 % yes), February 2014 (76 % yes), January 2015 (77 % yes) and April 2015 (72 % yes); IPSOS/MRBI polls were published in November 2012 (53 % yes), April 2014 (67 % yes), October 2014 (76 % yes), December 2014 (71 %), and March 2015 (74 % yes).

27   Hayes, 2016, 21.

Irish Catholic Bishops' Conference 1,976.[28] The Yes side cultivated a much stronger online presence than the Church.

As we have briefly mentioned earlier in this chapter, Ireland's major parties have strategically acted over the years to prevent programmatic differences from rising to the political surface, thereby disrupting long-term patterns in electoral outcomes. They have also sidestepped contentious issues confronting the electorate, often by allowing civil society actors to take the lead during referendum campaigns. These efforts move potentially divisive issues from the electoral and parliamentary arenas to non-electoral institutional domains.

A similar pattern occurred with respect to homosexuality rights. Although all of Ireland's political parties ultimately supported same-sex marriage rights, most of these parties waited until public opinion had shifted sufficiently such that there was no doubt that a referendum and subsequent legislation would pass. Ireland's politicians hesitated even longer than politicians in other countries. A review of other countries reveals that in jurisdictions where parliament passed same-sex marriage legislation, median public opinion was 57 %; and jurisdictions where courts legalised same-sex marriage, the median public opinion was 47 %. Legalisation in Ireland occurred when popular support was closer to 62–65 %.[29] Achieving this threshold of public support was a key factor in determining Ireland's major party backing.

Evidence from surveys during and after the 2015 Marriage Equality referendum underscores the degree of attitudinal change in Ireland over religious and moral issues. There was no question Irish citizens have been becoming more liberal, and the conservative base has shrunk to a one-third minority, and the pace of change is dramatic.[30] These key social trends reveal how dramatically changed realities can create new spaces for individuals, civil society groups, educational reformers and politicians to redefine policy problems and their potential solutions. Policy and party elites certainly

28   Hayes, 2016, 40.
29   Hayes, 2016, 15–16.
30   Johan A. Elkink, David M. Farrell, Theresa Reidy and Jane Suiter, 'Understanding the 2015 Marriage Referendum in Ireland: Context, Campaign, and Conservative Ireland', *Irish Political Studies*, 2017, Vol. 32, No. 3, 375–8.

revised their positions based on changes in society and the ways in which moral issues were being framed.

III. Abortion Rights in Ireland

Abortion has been a salient and divisive issue within Irish society ever since the passage of the 1983 referendum on the 8th Amendment inserted a provision into the Constitution (Article 40.3.3) that provided protection of the life of both the 'mother' and the 'unborn'. Hotly contested referenda in 1992 and 2002 continued the debate over abortion rights, especially over whether the threat of suicide constituted grounds to permit abortions in Ireland. Yet, despite its salience, abortion has been conspicuously absent in most Irish elections. Irish legislators have essentially ignored the issue in parliament until 2013, when the highly publicised death of Savita Halappanavar, an Indian citizen who was living in Ireland, led to intense efforts to amend Irish abortion law. A final referendum was held in 2018 that legalised abortion.

Civil society groups, first conservative and later progressive, led the charge on abortion policy, rather than political parties. The first abortion referendum, in 1983, was held largely due to the influence of the anti-abortion lobby, which sought to ensure that no law or court decisions would make abortion legal. Although abortion was not particularly salient during any of the three elections over the previous eighteen months, leaders of the two leading parties were fearful of losing additional votes during this electorally volatile period. Electoral volatility and increased competition among parties shifts the policy landscape and opens up previously unexplored possibilities. Both major party leaders promised Ireland's powerful 'pro-life' lobby that they would hold a referendum on abortion once elected, and Fine Gael fulfilled its promise once in government with Labour.[31] None of the major parties campaigned vigorously for or against

31   Jane O'Mahony, 'The Irish Referendum Experience', *Representation*, 1998, Vol. 35, No. 4, 225–36.

the measure.[32] Two-thirds of voters supported including a 'pro-life' statement within the Constitution; the referendum passed. The debate, however, was far from over.

Abortion re-surfaced in 1992 because of debates surrounding the European Union's Maastricht Treaty and its effect on Ireland's abortion policy. Attention was also heightened because of a controversial court case, *Attorney General v. X*, in which the Irish Supreme Court determined that a suicidal pregnant teenager possessed the right to travel overseas for an abortion, since it was argued that her life was endangered by the pregnancy. Public and political debate flared over the Court's decision, and legal confusion ensued as to what the Court's decision meant for the availability of abortion in Ireland. The public debate over abortion continued to intensify, leading the government to hold another referendum with three separate questions on the ballot later that autumn. Some members of Fianna Fáil with close ties to leading anti-abortion activists wanted to fight the issue in an electoral context, but party leaders ultimately decided in favour of holding a referendum. Most major party TDs believed that the referendum was the better place to handle the concerted lobbying of the Catholic Church and the 'pro-life' activists.[33]

The three hotly contested referenda held on the same day sought to uphold the right to access information regarding abortion, the right to travel to another country to procure an abortion, but also sought to prohibit abortions from being performed in Ireland on the grounds of suicide risk. Fianna Fáil strategically crafted fuzzy wording, which left voters confused about what constituted a threat to the pregnant woman's health, and the timing of this referendum, powerfully shaped the campaign, its outcome and the longer-term legacy of the abortion debate for partisan politics in Ireland. The choice to hold the three referenda on the same day as the election was a deliberate strategy to permit debate and encourage voting directly on the issue without affecting how people cast their votes for

32 Richard Sinnott, 'Cleavages, Parties, and Referendums: Relationships between Representative and Direct Democracy in the Republic of Ireland', *European Journal of Political Research*, 2002, Vol. 41, 811–26.

33 Brian Girvin, 'Moral Politics and the Irish Abortion Referendums', *Parliamentary Affairs*, 1994, Vol. 47, No. 2, 203–21.

candidates and parties in the general election. Although the eight months before the election had been consumed by trenchant public debate regarding abortion, the parties were mostly silent on the issue during the election campaign itself.

With the issue of abortion still unsettled, yet another referendum followed in 2002, again concerning the removal of the threat of suicide as grounds for legal abortion in Ireland. Despite divisions over whether to hold a referendum, the availability of the referendum as an alternate domain for dispute resolution once again kept abortion out of election campaigns.[34] The referendum battle was intense, but it was also rejected by a narrow margin of 50.4 % to 49.6 %. The result signalled continued deep divisions within Irish society over abortion, despite its lack of salience during elections.

Despite the Court's 1992 ruling and intense media pressure to act, mainstream parties in the Dáil simply refused year after year to legislate on abortion, avoiding the risk of alienating the electorate. The primary exception to this pattern was the passing of the *Protection of Life During Pregnancy Act* in 2013. The introduction of the bill was motivated as a response largely due to the outcry over the death of 31-year-old Savita Halappanavar, who died in an Irish hospital after complications from a miscarriage. This high-profile case brought abortion policy to the forefront again. The case was also partly in response to the European Court of Human Rights judgment in the 2010 *A, B, and C v. Ireland* case that demanded Ireland provide a credible procedure by which a woman could determine whether she is eligible for an abortion in Ireland. Like the evolution of gay rights in Ireland, resorting to ECHR proved helpful for progressive lobbyists seeking to alter Irish law. The 2013 legislation marked the first time that abortion was debated openly and aggressively within parliament. The bill passed, but not before splits occurred within several parties, confirming party leader concerns about succumbing to internal divisions over hot-button issues.

---

34   Fiachra Kennedy, 'Abortion Referendum 2002', *Irish Political Studies*, 2002, Vol. 17, No. 1, 114–28.

Abortion policy did not resonate with voters in the 2016 election. Those candidates who sought to capitalise on their positions towards abortion, irrespective of whether they promoted clearly defined 'pro-life' or 'pro-choice' positions, did not fare well electorally. Unique among the parties was Labour, which advanced a more expansive pro-choice agenda, hoping to catch the cultural winds of the same-sex marriage referendum in 2015 and reverse their dismal standing in the polls. The 2016 results seem to confirm a longer-term pattern that, when it comes to abortion policy in Ireland, parties are more successful in elections when they seek consensus or avoid the issue altogether, leaving it to be addressed within non-electoral domains.

Whereas Labour, Greens, Sinn Féin Social Democrats and Workers' Party made explicit manifesto commitments to hold a referendum to repeal the 8th Amendment in 2016, Fine Gael proposed holding a Citizens' Assembly to engage the issue. Once elected, the minority Fine Gael government funded a second Citizens' Assembly to address abortion and other key issues facing Irish society and its political system.[35] There was overall support within the Citizens' Assembly for change. For example, 87 % voted that the 8th Amendment should not be retained in full, 56 % voted in favour of replacing or amending the 8th Amendment and 57 % voted to replace the constitutional amendment and to authorise parliament to legislate to address termination of pregnancy, any rights of the unborn and any rights of a pregnant woman.[36] Curiously, many participants' positions shifted over the course of the weekends of deliberation, especially those of the conservative and undecided members whose positions became more liberal and supportive of change towards permitting abortion in Ireland.[37] The process of deliberation once again proved essential to redefining issues in ways that shifted public opinion and engaged politicians in critical ways.

A Joint Oireachtas Committee (JOC) on the 8th Amendment of the Constitution met regularly to consider the Citizens' Assembly's

35   Luke Field, 'The Abortion Referendum of 2018 and a Timeline of Abortion Politics in Ireland to Date', *Irish Political Studies*, 2018, Vol. 33, No. 4, 1–21. DOI: 10.1080/07907184.2018.1500461.

36   <https://www.thejournal.ie/people-polled-citizen-assembly-3673017-Nov2017/>.

37   Farrell, Suiter, Cunningham and Harris, 2019.

recommendations between September and December of 2017 under
the leadership of Fine Gael Senator Catherine Noone. Ultimately, the
Government supported the Citizens' Assembly's recommendation to hold
a referendum to repeal the 8th Amendment with an enabling provision that
Parliament would then legislate on the appropriate conditions for when
abortion would be allowed if the referendum passed.[38] The concrete links
between the Government, the Citizens' Assembly and the parliamentary
committee increased the profile of the debates and recommendations and
helped engage the wider public on the issue.[39]

Once again, civil society actors dominated the referendum campaign.
On the Yes side, Together for Yes (the national civil society campaign
to repeal the 8th Amendment) was composed of the Abortion Rights
Campaign (an all-Ireland women-led grassroots effort), the Coalition
to Repeal the Eighth Amendment (an umbrella organisation of over 100
groups including political parties, trade unions and other civil society
groups) and the National Women's Council of Ireland (a 45-year-old
feminist organisation). Learning from the same-sex marriage campaign,
Together for Yes sought to link both national and regional efforts that relied
heavily on both medical arguments and emotional appeals that provided
positive messages about love, compassion and support for anyone 'needing'
an abortion.[40] The Yes side also capitalised on the Citizens' Assembly and
the broader deliberative process to legitimise its arguments. Ailbhe Smyth,
the co-director for Together for Yes, constantly claimed that 'there had
been a very long, democratic process leading up to the proposed legislation' and that the Government was wise to follow the recommendations
of the Citizens' Assembly.[41]

The No side combined the efforts of two main groups, Love Both
(the successor to PLAC from 1983) and Save the 8th (an umbrella group).
The Iona Institute, a conservative Catholic think tank, helped broker the
No campaign. The No campaign argued that the proposed legislation was

38   Field, 2018.
39   Farrell and Suiter, 2019.
40   Fields, 2018.
41   Yasmeen Serhan, 'Ireland's Very Secular Vote on Abortion', *The Atlantic*,
      25 May 2018.

too extreme and highlighted the vulnerable cases such as those with disabilities or conditions such as Downs Syndrome. The No side lacked an organised ground game, and their strong digital efforts were greatly limited when Facebook banned foreign individuals and groups from advertising and Google banned referendum advertising altogether.[42] The tech giants' actions underscored the fear at the time that foreign influences using financial support and targeted campaign appeals might tip the results for the No side as they had affected the Brexit and Trump campaigns.[43]

Perhaps the most striking difference between the 1983 and 2018 referendum campaigns was the explicit role of the Catholic Church in seeking to influence the vote. In 1983, the Church hierarchy and activist lay Catholics were extremely vocal in sharing their religious-based opposition to abortion, and they were also well organised in mobilising voters and pressuring politicians. By 2018, Catholic Church leaders intentionally took a back seat in recognition that in light of the abuse crisis, which has rocked the Church since the 1990s, the exhortations of celibate priests on an issue concerning women's autonomy over their own bodies and their reproductive rights might be counterproductive.[44] Interestingly, both sides of the debate framed their appeals in secular, not religious language. One analyst argued that the Church and its followers were heavily involved in the campaign, but they we deliberately downplaying religious arguments to appeal to a younger generation that is less impressed by and/or shaped by traditional Church teachings.[45]

The 2018 abortion referendum passed with a whopping 66 % of the vote in the fourth highest turnout (64 %) for a referendum in Ireland's history.[46] Public opinion had shifted dramatically since the early 1980s when there was significant opposition against abortion (see Figure 8.1).[47]

---

42   Field, 2018.
43   'Ireland's Abortion Referendum: Don't Mention the Church', *Economist*, 24 March 2018.
44   'Irish Archbishops Say Abortion Vote Shows Church's Waning Influence', *The Guardian*, 27 May 2018
45   *Economist*, 24 March 2018.
46   Field, 2018.
47   Girvin, 1992; Sinnott, 1995.

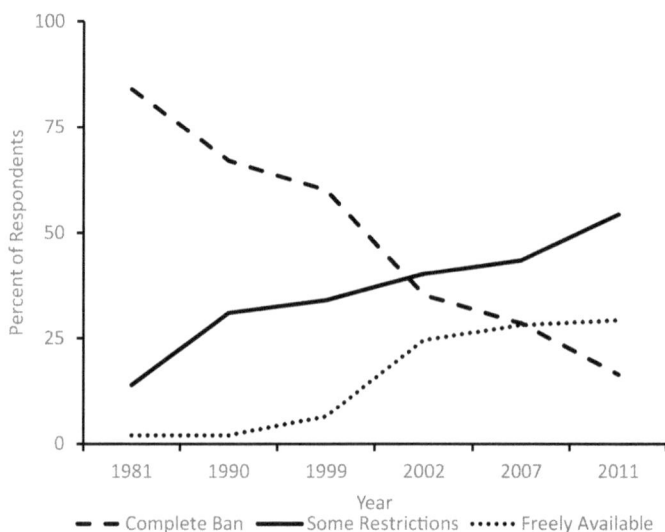

Figure 8.1. Attitudes towards abortion in Ireland: 1981–2011.

Data for 1981, 1990 and 1999 are from the European Values Survey and data for 2002, 2007 and 2011 are from the INES.

Public opinion polls between 2012 and 2018 reported even higher levels of support (i.e. between 80 % and 90 %) for allowing abortions in certain cases, especially when the mother's life is at risk or in cases of rape and incest.

The prevalence of reservations about freely permitting abortion and the fact that opinion polls had narrowed during the referendum campaign led to astonishment when the ultimate vote was so large in favour of legalising abortion. The results were also surprising to many since the proposal before the electorate permitted abortion 'on demand' or without restrictions up until twelve weeks and after that when the mother's health was at risk or in cases of foetal abnormality. Two exit polls suggest that Ireland's progressive shifts are likely to continue growing as the only demographic group that had mostly No voters were those over 65 years old. In all other demographics, there was a majority that supported abortion rights, with women, young and urban voters expressing greater percentages of support for legalising abortion.[48]

48   Field, 2018.

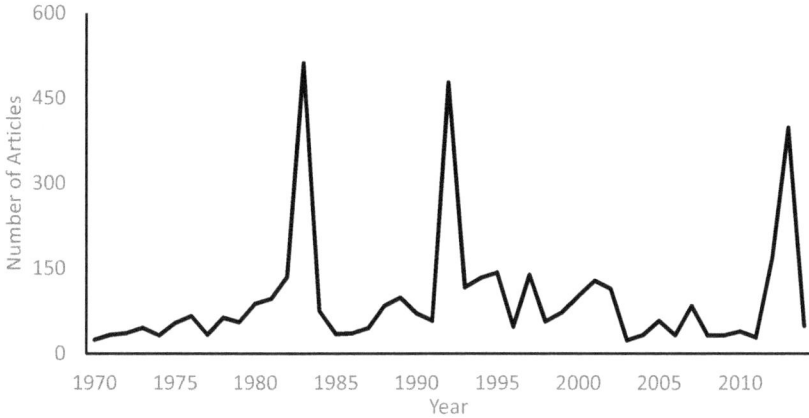

Figure 8.2. Number of newspaper stories in *Irish Independent* on abortion: 1970–2014.

Such trends imply a sense of inevitability whereby it was only a matter of time before the more progressive views would win the day and overturn Ireland's conservative religious and moral policies. Despite this sense of inevitability, it is important to underscore the divisive and highly emotional nature of this issue and how it was engaged within the political arena. The reliance on extra-parliamentary institutions to focus the debate and raise awareness during periods when politicians were reluctant to act on such divisive issues has proven an effective strategy for reformers past, present and future.

A brief snapshot of how abortion has been covered in the Irish media underscores a similar pattern whereby media and public attention increases when there are political processes to focus the debate: abortion assumes greater salience during referenda campaigns and then retreats to the backburner, with only slight increases during elections (Figure 8.2).[49]

---

49   The data for the *Irish Independent* was gathered using the Irish Newspaper Archive. <www.irishnewsarchive.com>. The search included references with the exact word 'abortion'. Articles that only mention abortion to contribute to another topic are not included in these numbers.

Less than 100 stories on abortion were published annually in the *Irish Independent*, the most widely read Irish daily newspaper, in most years since 1980, including election years. Yet, when abortion referendum campaigns heated up, as in 1983 and 1992, coverage increased 500 %. The only comparable spike in media coverage occurred in 2013 when public outcry over the Savita Halappanavar case brought abortion policy to the forefront again. Although abortion clearly matters to Irish citizens, voters are led to engage the issue in the domain of referenda. Abortion is less salient to the public – and to the media – during non-referenda periods, including during elections. These trends suggest that despite media performing a key public role in the abortion debate, and perhaps even highlighting more progressive views in recent years, other actors have been more important in directing the policy-making process.

Consider the politics of abortion for political parties. Ireland's political institutional framework creates different incentives for parties in terms of whether and how they engage abortion. There are several factors that powerfully incentivise party leaders to address abortion differently in elections and referenda. In elections, there exists an imperative to attract broader support among an increasingly heterogeneous electorate. Adopting clearcut positions on abortion could jeopardise support for parties of all stripes during Irish elections, but especially major parties. The challenge for minor parties appears greater as they seek to balance competing incentives during referendum and elections campaigns. On the one hand, minor parties have previously benefited from visibility gained during second-order campaigns like referenda. The potential to mobilise more progressive voters is therefore appealing. On the other hand, doing so might alienate moderate and conservative voters whose lower preference votes may be required by the minor party to get elected in general elections.

Therefore, the combination of Ireland's partisan cleavage structure, PR-STV electoral system and the growing heterogeneity of attitudes towards abortion among citizens and politicians has led most parties to downplay the importance of abortion during elections and instead employ extra-parliamentary institutions, in this case referenda, to block minor parties from capturing newly emerging issues. In this institutional domain, civil society groups take the lead and minor parties can support more progressive or controversial views without jeopardising their electoral fortunes.

Prior to the 2018 referendum, Irish citizens appeared to be divided into similarly sized conservative, liberal and moderate segments on the issue. Thus, neither a conservative nor a progressive policy platform on abortion would capture most of the vote. Likewise, an increasing proportion of Irish citizens expressed the view that abortion was important to them, but only about half of the public turned out in the 1983 and 2002 referenda – implying that about half the population simply did not care enough to vote. Another half of the public holds centrist attitudes, ambiguous attitudes, or simply does not care. This suggests that a progressive or conservative policy platform on abortion is likely to capture no more than a quarter of the vote during an election.

Therefore, the structure of public opinion combines with the incentives created by the electoral system to help explain why major parties have been unwilling to gamble on a realignment that might alienate existing supporters but draw in new ones. A small number of progressive or conservative voters could be drawn to a pro-life or pro-choice platform, but many centrist voters might find the party's focus on abortion alienating or overly strident. Major parties appear to have navigated this political mine field by implicitly mobilising anti-abortion activists through close personal relationships in the 1983 referendum when public opinion was more skewed in that direction,[50] and subsequently politicians have more quietly engaged the issue in later campaigns (even though leaders like former Taoiseach Bertie Ahern maintained anti-abortion positions). Because opposition to abortion in all cases has been falling, allying with anti-abortion activists has become riskier in the contemporary period. Electoral incentives provided by the electoral formula combine with the evolving structure of public opinion to influence both major and minor party strategies on abortion during elections.

Ultimately, a key take-away from these referenda experiences is that this extra-parliamentary institution and process of deliberation focuses public debate on contentious issues and provides various actors with different opportunities to engage or avoid these issues. Civil society advocates and groups, the media, the Church and political parties each take

50   Tom Hesketh, *The Second Partitioning of Ireland?: The Abortion Referendum of 1983*. Laoghaire: Brandsma Books, 1990.

advantage of these political processes to frame issues in ways that advance their interests within a rapidly evolving social context when previously strong and long-standing loyalties and patterns no longer controlled the policy-making process.

IV. Conclusion

The ultimate policy victories for marriage equality and abortion were made possible by decades of grassroots mobilising that altered public opinion. By engaging court cases, citizens assemblies, and legislative acts, reform-minded individuals, civil society groups and eventually politicians capitalised on evolved attitudes to usher in significant policy change. The gradual, incrementalist approach took decades, but ultimately achieved its goals. Reform was possible in part because the response to questions of who wants what and why was quite different in the mid-2010s in Ireland than it was prior to the 1990s. The collapse of the Church's moral authority meant there was no longer a monopoly of views on moral issues. As a more diverse set of attitudes emerged among growing segments of Irish society, new actors gained prominence and long-standing politicians and groups revised their positions to make change possible. As earlier studies of policy redefinition implied, framing marriage equality and abortion rights in the context of equality, human rights and inclusion redefined the problem and its solution.

Key policy shifts have occurred in Ireland over the last decade, but there were intervening developments that made these ultimate changes possible. For example, the Civil Partnership and Certain Rights and Obligations of Cohabitants Act 2010 were a critical preliminary step that paved the way for the eventual passing of the same-sex marriage legislation. Civil Partnership was a tangible victory that delivered real benefits for same-sex couples. This legislative act softened the ground among voters. Those voters who believed that this change would undermine the institution of marriage realised that their lives were not impacted by these new policies. This legislative act was one more step in the decades' long campaign for change, and it established the foundation on which campaigners mobilised support during the 2015 referendum.

Similar incremental changes occurred on the march towards abortion rights being established within Ireland. The Protection of Life During Pregnancy Act 2013 was the final stepping stone in the build-up to the passing of the 2018 abortion referendum. The tragic death of Savita Halappanavar a year previously was the focusing event that led to public outcry over Ireland's treatment of women's health and encouraged politicians to act swiftly to enact change. The 2013 legislation provided only limited circumstances under which abortions could be provided in Irish hospitals, but it was significant, nonetheless. As in the case of the same-sex marriage campaign, the 2013 act went some way towards the ultimate destination for which reformers had sought. It also softened the ground for many voters in the lead-up to the 2018 referendum because abortion was already a reality in Ireland, albeit in limited circumstances, and there did not appear to be dramatic negative outcomes on Irish society as whole as a result.

The developments from these earlier campaigns raise important questions for those interested in educational reform. Although some educational reformers seek the complete elimination of religion from Irish primary schools, a majority within Irish society, and as a result, most Irish party elites, do not appear ready to support this complete policy change. Nevertheless, there appears to be support for less radical and more incremental policy reforms, especially ones that do not personally impinge on one's own beliefs and actions. There is growing public support for increasing diversity of primary school patrons so that growing numbers of non-religious and those from minority religions have access to an education of their choosing. Yet, there are still significant sections of Irish society, especially at the local level, who oppose divesting their Catholic school to a different patron to achieve greater diversity. Not to be deterred, reformers are redefining educational issues in terms of equality, diversity and inclusion, and they are seeking minor educational changes that will not impinge on the educational choices of Irish families and students but will still provide greater opportunities for those seeking non-Catholic alternatives.

Seen in this light, the 2018 Admissions Bill might be the incremental change necessary before any further educational reforms will be supported by greater numbers. It was a tangible win for campaigners who had set their sights on eliminating the 'baptism barrier' so primary schools could no longer admit (or not admit) students based on their religious beliefs and practices. Reformers leveraged public opinion, policy proposals, lobbying and the media to achieve this swift legislative reform and potentially soften the ground for further reforms. For educational reformers, they hope they are on the same policy trajectory as the same-sex marriage and abortion campaigns.

It is too early to tell what the ultimate legislative victory would look like within the primary education sector. Some reformers suggest that the government could propose a constitutional amendment to put an end to the denominational status of Irish schools as happened in the Canadian province of Quebec. In the case of Quebec, their 1995 General Convention on Education concluded that 'we must put an end to the denominational nature of the education system… there is no valid reason any more, other than a historical hang-up, to constrain a public education system on the basis of denominational privileges'.[51] Fischer concludes that Quebec offers us a glimpse of one possible path for the future of Irish denominational education asserting that there are striking similarities with aspects of Irish history and with the main contemporary issues now facing the Irish State and society. The 2020 Programme for Government included a commitment to hold a Citizens' Assembly on the Future of Education, which emboldened reformers because the final impetus to hold referenda on same-sex marriage and abortion emerged out of these citizens' assemblies. Such an approach provided cover to the political class who feared being the sole instigators of such policy decisions for fear of alienating some of its core and potential voters.

For those campaigning for change to the Irish primary school system, an ultimate focus on constitutional change may not prove as fruitful as it did for those who campaigned on same-sex marriage and abortion. Both of those issues were long in gestation with decades of campaigning leading to the victories in 2015 and 2018. The issue of greater plurality of patronage

---

51   Karin Fischer, *Schools and the Politics of Religion and Diversity in the Republic of Ireland – Separate but Equal?*. Manchester: Manchester University Press, 2016.

(or reform of the primary system) has only emerged to any real extent in the last decade. Additionally, a constitutional approach would have to address property ownership, an issue protected in the Irish Constitution. Educational reformers may want to limit such constitutional measures to Church property associated with education. However, any such constitutional amendment would have broader implications beyond education that would be complicated and could potentially create a whole set of new groups that would fight against changes to property ownership. Finally, unlike the same-sex marriage and abortion debates where there was one, clear-cut and binary yes-no decision to make, there are several issues in education. There may be support for some educational changes that limit or alter the role of the Church in education, but there remains insufficient popular support for removing the Church from education altogether. This explains why there is a different framing for each educational issue, and relatedly, there are differing policy solutions to each issue.

As a result, there are also different coalitions of individuals, groups and political parties that support these various reforms. Some reforms might adversely impact supporters of the cause who do not wish to embrace greater choice themselves. For example, someone might support greater diversity of school types to meet Ireland's changing demographics, but also not want their local school to change patrons. If forced to do so, they may consider the cost of reform too high and therefore oppose such change for others too. As the number of educational issues multiplies, so too do the number of positions and coalitions that must be generated to make such policy outcomes passable. The next four chapters will identify and discuss in greater detail how political parties, civil society actors and educational patrons, including the Church, have addressed the issues of divestment, admissions and curriculum to illustrate how the issue definition and redefinition process has evolved within the primary school sector.

CHAPTER 9

Political Parties and Education Reform

I. Background on Contemporary Irish Party Politics

The experience of same-sex marriage and abortion revealed potentially new patterns of policy-making in Ireland. For educational reformers, there was hope that similar dramatic policy shifts may be possible within education. However, the complexity of the constitutional issues associated with educational reform and the differing and often conflicting set of interests among many of the key actors within this policy area means that reforms will unfold differently within this sector. Previous chapters have highlighted the preferences and organisational development of educational patrons including the Catholic Church, as well as other civil society advocates and the media. To round out the cast of key actors and gain a broader perspective of the policy-making process, we now turn to an analysis of political parties. In this chapter, we discuss the nature of Irish political parties and examine how they adopt and adapt policies, compete in elections and form government coalitions influence their positioning towards educational reform. This important background highlights the parameters within which civil servants and government officials can engage policy options within education.

Ireland's two main parties, Fianna Fáil and Fine Gael, and to a lesser extent Labour, have historically followed a flexible, catchall approach that had led them to adopt centrist positions. They are vote-seeking parties that have continuously altered their ideological positions to appeal to a broad cross-section of Irish voters, balancing traditional supporters with new voters. In contrast, Ireland's minor parties have been more policy-seeking in their approach, offering more cohesive, focused and sometimes non-centrist policy views – at least on core issues. The minor parties appear more constrained ideologically, having generally been founded to address issues that major parties were perceived to be ignoring or addressing insufficiently.[1]

In addition to adopting centrist positions and shifting ideological positions as society's preferences on salient issues become clearer, McGraw's previous work demonstrates that major parties have sought to take advantage of their ideological flexibility and catchall appeals by emphasising elements on both sides of divisive issues. For example, the stark transformation of religious and moral values in Ireland over the last thirty years ushered in intense debate that catalysed and ultimately peaked during the marriage equality and abortion referenda. Until a critical mass of public support was reached, the major parties sought to tread lightly in these debates and remained noncommittal to avoid electoral quicksand.

The ability to displace increasingly salient issues to citizens' assemblies and referenda allowed major parties to address issues without jeopardising their electoral appeals, especially on key religious and moral issues. This has allowed major party leaders to affect the salience and ownership of issues, much like when they shift programmatic appeals. During electoral competition, these displacement strategies allow major parties to avoid exacerbating internal divisions over controversial issues, such as abortion, and to focus their energies on issues where they have a proven edge over minor parties, such as delivering for local constituencies and managing the economy. At the same time, these strategies also have permitted the major parties to claim that these contentious issues are being addressed within the political arena. This introduced another means by which major parties had buffered their electoral support as they deprived minor parties of opportunities to mobilise the electorate around salient issues in a rapidly changing social and political environment.[2]

As vote-seeking parties, the major parties have avoided acting on salient issues until sufficient public support was achieved. This threshold was around 60 % in both the marriage equality and abortion campaigns.

1   Ben Mainwaring and Sean McGraw, 'How Catchall Parties Compete Ideologically: Beyond Party Typologies', *European Journal of Political Research*, May 2019, Vol. 58, No. 2, 676–96; doi: 10.1111/1475-6765.12307.
2   Sean McGraw, *How Parties Win: Shaping the Irish Political Arena*. Ann Arbor: University of Michigan Press, 2015.

In both campaigns, the issue had been narrowed to a binary, yes versus no, decision on whether to amend the Constitution. In education, there have been multiple issues and areas where reformers have wanted to reduce or eliminate the role of religion in Ireland's schools. The complexity of these issues and the number of competing constitutional rights has made reform within education less clear-cut than in these other campaigns. Furthermore, proposed educational changes would affect more than just individuals and families as was the case in previous campaigns. Here, whole communities are affected by changes to the patronage and ethos of schools, admissions policies and the overall curriculum. This elevates the intensity of local politics, which are a key dimension of Irish electoral politics.

In the context of general elections, rather than casting their ballots based on intense programmatic battles over increasingly prominent moral issues, the economy, or Ireland's place within the EU, Irish voters generally vote for the candidate who will best serve the local constituency and who they know personally. Irrespective of methodology, surveys and exit polls conducted between 1977 and 2011 confirm that the most significant factor consistently shaping voter preference is the perception that the candidate will best serve the local needs (39 %), followed by identifying with party policies (25 %), electing the Taoiseach (16 %), and, finally, determining government ministers (14 %).[3] As a result, politicians are rewarded for how well they look after local constituency and community concerns and are overly sensitive to defending local interests even at the cost of going against national policies or priorities. It is one thing to adhere to party positions when less tangible benefits are at stake or when extra-parliamentary institutions exist to address contentious issues, but when policies are perceived to conflict with material interests at the local level, Irish politicians regularly jettison national party positions to attract votes locally.[4] The intensely local nature of schools means that even small changes in and to them can have larger ripple effects within their surrounding communities. Highly aware and sensitive politicians work hard to defend these local interests. Add these political factors to the various cultural factors that reinforce a

---

3   McGraw, 2015, 71.
4   McGraw, 2015, 147–8.

strong sense of place and loyalty to one's local community in Ireland, and one can see why educational reforms face an uphill battle – and this just one dimension of educational reform.

There is no question that religious beliefs, practices and identities are rapidly evolving in Ireland, and this affects views of ordinary Irish citizens on the role of religion in education. However, there is not an overwhelming wave of public opinion in support of change on most issues, which helps explain the hesitancy of politicians to act. As discussed in Chapter 3, there is a difference between 'easy' and 'hard' facets of questions in survey research and public opinion polls. Easy questions generally deal with a principle or an overall view, whereas hard questions focus on the implementation of such policies, forcing respondents to choose between specific solutions and policy alternatives.[5] So although there may be growing and widespread support for altering the role of the Catholic Church in Irish schools, an easy question, there is minimal clarity on what concrete and practical steps could be implemented, a hard question, without disrupting local schools and communities. Again, the nature of the issues being debated, and the various individuals and groups effected by proposed changes, vastly alters how these educational issues have been defined and redefined within the political arena.

Not surprisingly, Ireland's minor, and primarily left-leaning, parties have been stronger proponents of educational reforms that reduce or eliminate the role of religion in Ireland's primary schools. In contrast, Ireland's major parties have been more cautious, seeking both to honour the preferences of those seeking to preserve the status quo and those seeking reform. Recognising the difficulty in implementing such changes that so deeply affect local communities, the major parties have supported both sides of the debate and often focused on creating a consultative process that includes all the major stakeholders and leads to change only when most Irish citizens are ready.

5   Pat Lyons, *Public Opinion, Politics and Society in Contemporary Ireland*. Dublin, Ireland and Portland, OR: Irish Academic Press, 2008.

To demonstrate how this process of balancing support for easy and hard facets of educational policy reform has unfolded, this chapter provides a brief analysis of data from party manifestoes, public opinion surveys and original parliamentary surveys. This evidence illustrates how political parties have positioned themselves on the key educational issues over the last few decades as Irish public opinion on the role of religion in schools have changed as well. The lack of clear-cut support for educational reform within Irish public society helps us understand the slow pace of support for reform among Ireland's major parties over the last few decades. This analysis will set the stage to the next three chapters that will explore in more detail how the key reform issues of divestment, admissions and curriculum have been engaged. The varied ways that these issues were defined influenced which actors assumed a greater role in that issue's policy debate and potential reforms.

II. Political Party's General Election Manifestoes on Educational Reform: 1981–2020

A brief analysis of political party manifestoes for general election campaigns reveals broad and growing support for educational reform among Ireland's political parties in recent decades. As mentioned above, the smaller, left-leaning parties have been more outspoken on reform than the larger parties. Ireland's major parties have continued their pattern of trying to protect long-standing interests while also attracting new voters. This entails supporting both sides and emphasising process and consultation on the path towards gradual reform.[6] This pattern suggests a similar, incremental pattern of reform as consensus grows among the political

---

6 In this analysis of party manifestoes, we relied on the following archive: Michael Pidgeon. 'Manifestos by Party'. *Irish Manifestos Archive,* Michael Pidgeon – Dublin City Councilor, 21 February 2020. <www.michaelpidgeon.com/manifestos/index. html> (Accessed: 25 September 2020). For simplicity, further citations will name the party manifesto, year and page number.

parties with the major parties supporting change when sufficient public opinion is achieved.

The Labour Party offered unconditional support for multi-denominational education from the start of the Dalkey School Project in the mid-1970s.[7] Subsequently, Labour was an early advocate of the secularisation of Irish schooling, first pushing for pluralist structures in their 1981 general election manifesto. Although Labour did not emphasise educational reform issues in their general election manifestoes again until 2007, they have been the most outspoken and consistent party on educational reform during election campaigns since then, leading the way on discussions of patronage, multi-denominational schools and sex education. In their 2011 election manifesto, Labour stated that their goal was to 'reform our education system so that it is more democratic and recognises the diversity of ethos within modern Irish society'.[8] In that same manifesto, Labour also announced their plan to establish a time-limited Forum on Patronage and Pluralism. Labour also requested that Educate Together be recognised as an official patron at the secondary level, which would allow the nation's leading multi-denominational patron to create a system of schools from junior infants through the Leaving Certificate. This would consolidate the Educate Together model and could in time challenge the long-standing denominational structure of Irish education as greater numbers demand this type of non-denominational education.

In their 2016 general election campaign, Labour laid out their Admissions Bill proposals, reiterating that 'the emerging evidence of parents feeling forced to baptise their children to ensure a school place is a national scandal which must come to an end'.[9] The 2016 Labour manifesto also highlighted their support of multi-denominational schools as more inclusive and proclaimed their intentions to build a national network of multi-denominational schools. Support for divestment and the establishment of new schools would help create a system where real choices were

---

7   Áine Hyland with Desmond Green, *A Brave New Vision for Education in Ireland: The Dalkey School Project 1974–1984*. Áine Hyland self-published, Dalkey, 2020, 48.

8   Labour Party Manifesto, 2011, 61–2.

9   Labour Party Manifesto, 2016, 94.

available to parents. In the 2020 general election, Labour continued its calls for reform by increasing the pace of divestment, requiring sex education in all schools, ending subsidies for fee-paying secondary schools and developing a national strategy for supporting LGBTQ students and teachers in all schools.[10]

The smaller parties of the left also consistently supported educational reforms over the decade since 2011. The Green Party, which came to national prominence in 1997 by winning two seats in the Dáil, advocated for the growth of multi- and non-denominational schools, Gaelscoileanna, and Waldorf Schools in their 1997 manifesto. In 2007, the Greens pledged to 'equality-proof all curricula' and update present sex education programmes.[11] It is not surprising that this thorny issue of sex education impinges on religion and parental rights, which may explain why it has still not been addressed more fully even in 2021. The Green Party was one of the earliest parties to highlight admissions as an issue when they called for a review of enrolment policies in their 2011 general election manifesto. In 2016, the Green Party proposed to 'end any discrimination at school entry on the basis of religion or special education needs'.[12] In addition to highlighting concern for sex education and LGBTQ+ issues in 2016, the Greens confirmed their commitment to 'ensuring that students' ethnicity and religion (or non-religion) are not barriers to their enrolment and participation in school'.[13]

Likewise, Sinn Féin consistently advocated reform in education with a special focus on attacking inequalities that existed with Ireland's educational and healthcare systems. Like the Greens, Sinn Féin won their first contemporary Dáil seat in 1997, but unlike the Green Party, Sinn Féin did not mention educational reform in their manifestoes until 2007. Then, Sinn Féin introduced its plan to 'review the current system of ownership and management of schools with a view to ensuring equitable education for all, sufficient school places for all pupils wherever they live and the best management of schools'.[14] In 2007, Sinn Féin also proclaimed its support of

10   Labour Party Manifesto, 2020, 22 and 33.
11   The Green Party Manifesto, 2007, 27.
12   The Green Party Manifesto, 2016, 32.
13   The Green Party Manifesto, 2020, 47.
14   Sinn Féin Party Manifesto, 2007, 28.

Educate Together and multi-denominational schools, as well as for greater emphasis on intercultural education in schools, which was often seen as a way to broaden the curriculum beyond just Church teachings. In 2011, Sinn Féin supported Educate Together's recognition at the secondary level and demanded an end to state subsidies of private education.[15] Similarly, Sinn Féin's 2016 election emphatically called for an end to discrimination against children in admissions based on religion and to increase diversification of patronage. 'Huge numbers of children are regularly excluded from their local school based on their religion. Yet the government continues to subsidise private schools with millions in taxpayers' money, further entrenching educational inequalities and a two-tier system.'[16] The party's claims about huge numbers illustrate that the Church's framing of this as an issue that affects only a small number did not have much of an impact or was being ignored to drum up public support. Sinn Féin also reiterated its equality and economic arguments in 2020 when they called for a phasing out of public subsidies to private schools and for more emphasis on LGBTQ+ equality in all Irish schools.[17]

The Social Democrats have also been consistent in their support of more radical reform in education with a particular focus on creating a secular educational system with no involvement of religion, especially at the primary level. Unlike the Greens and Sinn Féin, who are reform-minded, but do not spend much time, space, or energy on education as a policy focus, this was a priority for the Social Democrats. For the Greens, their policy focus is on environment and climate change, while Sinn Féin's policy priorities have been Northern Ireland and economic inequality. In both the 2016 and 2020 general elections, the Social Democrats laid out detailed plans to 'Ensure Pluralism in Education' by amending the Equal Status Act so children cannot be refused admission based on religion. They proclaimed that 'a modern Irish democracy must respect and reflect the diversity of Irish society and the citizens which it serves. The State has a responsibility to ensure that each child has access to a State-funded school within their

---

15   Sinn Féin Party Manifesto, 2011, 28.
16   Sinn Féin Party Manifesto, 2016, 47.
17   Sinn Féin Party Manifesto, 2020, 47.

locality, and that the ethos of the school is inclusive of their family's belief system.'[18] In 2020, they announced their support for establishing a citizens' assembly to make recommendations to the Oireachtas on how to move towards an entirely secular education system. Additionally, they sought to remove faith formation from the school day and provide it as an after-school option and they reaffirm their desire to 'rigorously follow-through on school divestment as per recommendations from the Forum on Pluralism and Patronage'.[19] In 2021, the Social Democrats announced their official position that seeks a complete separation of Church and State, which has obvious consequences for their future policy positions on education.

These highly supportive proposals on educational reform reiterate many of the ideas and arguments that have been propagated within civil society for years. Despite the clarity and consistency of these smaller political parties, longer-term experience in Irish politics suggests that until the major parties openly support policies, real change does not occur. The major parties are often reluctant to assume clear stands on divisive issues due to their tendency to build broad, cross-class electoral support to sustain their predominance. A similar pattern emerges with respect to educational policies for both Fianna Fáil and Fine Gael. They want it both ways. They want to reform education and respect the growing diversity within a changing Irish society, but they also want to honour the preferences of many within Irish society that still appreciate the role of religion within education. Both parties also emphasise the need to develop consultative processes that include various voices in these important discussions on education.

Fine Gael, although supportive of reforms in recent election manifestoes as it has sought to capture the public's appetite for reform and equality, did not address educational reform issues until the 2007 general election. Since 1987, they often reiterated their support for parents as the primary educators. In their 2007 general election manifesto, Fine Gael supported the establishment of non-Catholic schools, which was a nod to diversity in education. Significantly, the language is 'new schools' – implying the creation of new institutions rather than divestment of Catholic ones,

18   Social Democrats Party Manifesto, 2016, 35.
19   Social Democrats Party Manifesto, 2020, 71–2.

which gained traction in 2011. In the decade since 2011, Fine Gael has that the predominance of Catholic schools is not reflective of the needs of Ireland's changing society. In 2011, Fine Gael also supported holding a national forum on education 'to allow all stakeholders, including parents, to engage in an open debate on a change of patronage in communities where it is appropriate and necessary'.[20] They employed language consistent with civil society reformers, calling for greater choice, diversity and standards in schools and inviting parents to assume a greater participatory role in achieving these goals.[21]

Fine Gael strutted its equality credentials and aspirations again in their 2016 general election manifesto:

> Fine Gael will continue to promote a more inclusive, diverse, fair and progressive society. As the first country in the world to vote for marriage equality, Ireland should continue to lead by example. We will promote equal gender treatment in the workplace, recognise the diversity of our communities and assist those with a disability to fully participate in society. Fine Gael will also strengthen parental choice and diversity in our school system, reflecting the need in modern Ireland for new forms of multi-denominational and non-denominational education.[22]

As the largest party, Fine Gael had a much broader set of educational policies in its manifesto to ensure that it had a little bit for everyone. The party reiterated its emphasis on divestment and increasing the number of multi-denominational schools to 300 by 2030, all the while reminding voters that they have a 'road map' for change and are working 'with all stakeholders to facilitate this process'. At the same time, Fine Gael reassures others by confirming their desire to 'safeguard the right of parents to send their children to denominational schools that offer a distinct religious ethos.' Fine Gael also provides concrete plans to fight bullying and offer more choice and support for after-care to meet the needs of young parents.[23] Fine Gael's 2020 general election manifesto repeated many of these promises and increased the number of multi-denominational

---

20   Fine Gael Party Manifesto, 2011, 34.
21   Fine Gael Party Manifesto, 2011, 76.
22   Fine Gael Party Manifesto, 2016, 25.
23   Fine Gael Party Manifesto, 2016, 50, 55, 58, 59 and 108.

schools it sought to establish by 2030 to 400, while still upholding 'the rights of parents to have their children educated in a denominational school. We will protect minority faith schools.'[24]

Fianna Fáil, historically a party that has attracted support from the most traditional and religiously conservative voters in Irish society, was an early adopter of the movement to establish multi-denominational schools. As early as 1975, the then Fianna Fáil leader Jack Lynch argued that mixing students of different religions could lead to a more peaceful society by building a more plural society in the Republic of Ireland and in Northern Ireland. Lynch supported the rights of parents to establish multi-denominational schools where a majority desired this type of school, and he believed that pilot schools, if successful, would determine whether additional multi-denominational schools should be established. He qualified his comments by claiming that his support for pilot multi-denominational schools did not signal his desire to phase out the existing denominational system of schools. In fact, to demonstrate to critics of change that he understood their concerns too, he argued that constitutional protections existed to ensure that students only receive religious instruction approved by their parents.[25] Fianna Fáil's 1987 manifesto mentions its ongoing support for multi-denominational education.[26] They continued calls for multi-denominational schools and increased parental involvement in 1989, when they also discussed a major review of the educational system and the curriculum. At the same time as expressing a desire to use education for a 'world of rapid…social change', their 1989 manifesto highlighted that they saw the Church as an educational partner. Fianna Fáil's inclusive and consensus-building approach was on display in this 1989 manifesto as they proclaimed, 'We have always sought to achieve our objectives in partnership with all those involved in education, and we will continue to do so through our participation with the social partners in the Programme for National Recovery.'[27] During this same period, Fianna Fáil Minister for Education Mary O'Rourke approved the establishment of seven new Educate Together schools between 1987

---

24   Fine Gael Party Manifesto, 2020, 36.
25   Hyland and Green, 2020, see 79–94.
26   Fianna Fáil Party Manifesto, 1987, 54.
27   Fianna Fáil Party Manifesto, 1989, 86.

and 1991, which was a dramatic increase for this school model. O'Rourke also announced in 1990 that children attending multi-denominational schools were entitled to the same school transport benefits of children attending denominational schools. This change facilitated students traveling from greater distances to attend multi-denominational schools, including in areas outside of Dublin.[28]

Fianna Fáil's 1997 platform committed to providing capital grants to multi-denominational schools and supporting Educate Together. It likewise stressed a desire to empower parents to manage their local school. Curiously, Fianna Fáil barely mentioned educational reform issues in 2002, 2007 and 2011 in their general election manifestoes. Instead, the party focused its educational proposals on the role technical and higher education play in economic development, a priority given both their role in Ireland's previously booming economy and its prospects for recovering from Ireland's economic collapse in 2008.

In 2016, Fianna Fáil joined the chorus of parties highlighting Ireland's increasingly diverse society and the need to include all voices in the search for a better and fairer educational system that does not penalise children for their denomination. To this end, the party promised to 'engage with educational partners to set out a consensual approach to roll out further divestment of schools in line with assessed community demand. Reform school admissions based on locality to ensure children have access to their local school regardless of denomination while protecting religious rights. Ensure LGBT students and staff are treated equally in every school.'[29] Note both the emphasis on equality language and the consensual process, but also a defence of local interests. These varied emphases underscore Fianna Fáil's strategy to attract support from across the electoral spectrum. In 2020, Fianna Fáil once again supported change, but it took a step back from radical change by arguing that too rapid of change can be divisive and unproductive:

> The potential divestment of schools has been a subject of controversy in recent years. In some cases, unfounded claims have been made by campaigners which have created

28   Hyland and Green, 2020, 238.
29   Fianna Fáil Party Manifesto, 2016, 49.

confusion for parents. These divisive and unhelpful debates have distracted from the important issues which need to be discussed in the context of divestment: We will provide a one-stop information platform within the Department of Education to provide clear, non-biased information on the consequences of divestment and to provide responses to specific claims.[30]

The party tried to tap into its past image of being the most effective manager of the State bureaucracy. By calling for a reduction in the level of bureaucracy in schools, Fianna Fáil was making a popular appeal to attract teachers and school leaders who often feel under-appreciated and represent a significant voting block during elections. The broad, more consensual approach reveals that Fianna Fáil is supportive of change, but not quite ready to engage radical reforms to eliminate the role of religion in Ireland's schools. Given Fianna Fáil and Fine Gael's desire to support both educational reform and to protect the interests of anyone who might be threatened by change – be they local interests or supporters of faith-based education – the incremental pace of change is likely to persist in the coming years until a clearer majority of public support for secular aims is attained.

Increasing the diversity of primary school patronage by providing greater access to multi-and non-denominational schools emerged in 2007 as a key educational issue in all party manifestos, except Fianna Fáil. This election occurred a few months before the issue would come to national prominence with the shortage of school places in Balbriggan in North Dublin. The issue has been present in all political party manifestos since.

III. Party and Voter Surveys: Attitudes on Educational Reform

Mainstream political parties have often backed reform when there is broad support for change within Irish society. We examined recent voter

30   Fianna Fáil Party Manifesto, 2020, 79.

and partisan attitudes on select educational issues to determine whether a similar pattern exists with education. Evidence from the *Which Candidate* Survey in 2016 and 2020 and McGraw's 2016 Parliamentary Survey provides us with this closer look at voter and candidate views on educational issues in more recent years. First, consider the *Which Candidate* Survey. This is an Irish-based internet application that helps voters identify candidates and parties that hold policy positions consistent to their own. It started during the 2014 Irish local elections and was also conducted during the 2016 and 2020 Irish general elections. In addition to answering questions on a wide range of economic, social, political and moral issues, voters are also asked to share their social demographic and political backgrounds. Each voter is asked the same set of questions as the candidates were. Once finished, the voter is provided with a customised results page containing a ranking of candidates ordered by how closely their answers match. The website calculates the proximity of a voter to a candidate based on all the questions where the voters and candidates both answer the question. If, for example, a voter has a proximity score of 0.5 to a candidate across all shared questions, the overall match with this candidate is expressed as 50 %. The survey factors in the importance of issues to voters by only matching their responses with candidates who also answer questions for which voters are interested. Questions marked as having 'no opinion' are excluded from the proximity calculations.[31]

There were two questions pertaining to the role of religion in education in the 2016 *Which Candidate* Survey and one in the 2020 survey. In 2016, the survey first asked voters and candidates whether religion should be taught in State-funded primary schools. Given that all primary schools in Ireland are State-funded, it is instructive that 'State-funded' is explicitly included in the question. It subtly implies that there may be a conflict between receiving State funding and teaching religion. Respondents could choose from the following responses: No, religion should only be taught outside of school; Pupils should learn about various religions, not one particular faith; and Yes, schools should instruct pupils in line with their religious ethos. Of the approximately 25,000 voter respondents, a third

31   See <http://www.whichcandidate.ie/>.

(33.6 %) responded that religion should only be taught outside of school; a majority (54.9 %) believed that students should learn about multiple faiths not just one; and a small portion (11.6 %) reported that pupils should learn the religion of their school's ethos.

There were only minor differences (i.e. greater than 6 % difference from the overall average) in responses based on a voter's social demographic characteristics. For example, a voter's gender or geographic circumstances (i.e. urban, commuter, or rural constituencies) did not explain much of the variance in answers to this question, whereas there were slight differences in responses based on age and educational attainment. In terms of age, respondents ages 18 to 24 reported higher than average support (66.7 %) for learning about multiple faiths, and respondents ages 55 to 64 and 65 and older reported much higher than average support for teaching religion of their schools' ethos (20.4 % and 31.8 % respectively). Similarly, those with lower levels of education, such as only primary school (35.6 %) or junior certificate (20.4 %), also had higher than average levels of support for teaching religion in State-funded schools.

Political variables also explained little variation on this question about whether religion should be taught in State-funded primary schools. Those respondents who acknowledged being 'not very interested' in politics reported a marginally higher than average level of support for learning about multiple faiths (62.3 %). Not surprisingly, voters who identified themselves as more left-wing on a 0–10 scale, especially those who considered themselves a 2 (47.3 %) or 3 (42.8 %), reported higher than average support for not teaching religion in school. Inversely, those who identified as more right-wing reported higher than average support for teaching religion of one's own faith. For example, those who identified as either a 7, 8, 9, or 10 on the 0–10 Left-Right scale reported between 25 % and 39 % support for students learning about their own faith compared to the overall average of 11.6 % supporting this view. The only other striking finding based on the political background factors is that voters who intended to vote for Fianna Fáil were much more supportive of teaching one's own religion (35.7 %) and much less supportive of not teaching religion in schools (16 %) than the overall averages. This confirms the conventional wisdom that Fianna Fáil supporters are more conservative and that there are far fewer voters holding these positions within the broader society, which may affect the party's longer-term electoral support.

The second question about the role of religion in primary education addressed the admissions criteria for primary schools. Respondents were asked whether schools should be allowed to give preference to children based on their religion. The response options included: No, religion should have no place in school admissions policies for State-funded schools; Yes, but only if there are suitable alternatives (e.g. non-denominational schools) in the area; and Yes, schools should be able to serve their own religious communities first. Nearly 80 % (79.2 %) of respondents reported that religion should not be a valid criterion for primary school admission. An additional 13 % reported that religion could be factored into admission but only when other options were available to students. Only 8 % considered that religious background should be utilised so that faith-based schools could serve the students who belonged to their faith. Thus, two years before the School Admissions Bill of 2018 was passed that forbade Catholic schools from considering religious background as a valid criterion for admittance, there appeared to be overwhelming public support to make this policy shift. The nearly 80 % in favour of changing admissions policies is well above the 60 % threshold that represented a tipping point of public support that encouraged major parties to support legislative change.

Given such high numbers supporting abolishing religious preference or practice as a basis for admission, it is not surprising that there is little variation in social or political demographic factors that shapes respondents' views on this issue. Every single social and political demographic variable had over 50 % support for ending religious background in admissions policy. Older voters and those with lower levels of educational attainment did report higher than average support for permitting religious schools to consider religion, but still over two-thirds of respondents in these categories support ending religion as a valid criterion for primary school admittance. The only category with less than 50 % support for this shift was those who identified as a 9 on the 0–10 Left-Right scale. And even here, 49 % wanted to end religious admission criteria. Like the previous question, voters intending to vote for Fianna Fáil were slightly more conservative than the overall average response: 51 % responded no to religious criteria in admission policies, 24 % stated yes if alternative non-denominational schools were available in the area, and another 24 % supported allowing religious criteria. These results are quite different than those for voters supporting other parties. This, too, suggests that Fianna Fáil is no longer the broad, catchall party it has historically been as it garners support from smaller and smaller sections of Irish society rather than attracting the highest percentage of support from every demographic characteristic as it did from the 1930s to 2011.[32]

There are fewer responses from candidates and parties for these two questions in the 2016 survey. On whether religion should be taught in State-funded primary schools, most candidates (60 %) reported that students should learn about various faiths but not one. Interestingly, whereas nearly a third of voters thought religion should not be taught at all in primary schools, only 12 % of candidates held this view. Likewise, twice the percentage of candidates (24 %) reported support for religious schools teaching about their own faith compared to voters (12 %). The fact that candidates appear slightly more conservative than voters based on evidence from this survey is consistent with the trend in Irish politics. Politicians rarely lead the change but rather shift their positions to adopt popularly held believes, especially on more controversial policies or ones that will require more radical change to the existing system.[33]

It is difficult to infer too much about the differences within parties because the numbers are small, and therefore variation in responses can dramatically alter the results. In terms of party positions, most of the mainstream parties held the view that students should learn about multiple faiths and not just their own. The Anti-Austerity Alliance and the Workers' Party argued for no religion in schools. On the other end of the spectrum, the two more conservative parties, Fianna Fáil and Renua, supported schools being able to teach their own faith within the school day.

On admissions policy, most candidates also supported an end to the religious criteria for primary schools, but the numbers were again much lower than voters. Whereas 80 % of voters supported this shift to ending

32   McGraw, 2015.
33   McGraw, 2015.

religious-based admissions criteria, only 52 % of candidates held this view. Most parties also supported ending religious criteria, with only Fine Gael and Renua supporting religious criteria if alternative schools were available in the area. Fianna Fáil did not offer a position on this policy issue, perhaps because they did not want to alienate their base even though supporting this policy shift might attract broader support on educational policy issues.

There was only one question in the 2020 *Which Candidate* Survey pertaining to education. Unfortunately, the wording of the question is less helpful for this study because it asks voters and candidates to consider whether the Church has too much control over Irish schools and hospitals. Not only does this combine the Church's involvement in both education and healthcare, where the involvement in both sectors is substantively different, but the wording is framed in negative terms. Survey research recognises the phenomenon of acquiescence bias, whereby most people are more likely to agree with statements rather than disagree.[34] To combat that, a survey could ask the question twice in two different formats or word the question in more neutral ways. For example, the survey could have said, 'How much control does the Church have over Irish schools?' and the responses could have been something like 'Too much/The right amount/Not enough'. The existing wording made it easier to support the view that the Church has too much control in Irish schools. Nevertheless, it provides a snapshot of attitudes among a significant sector of Irish society.

The results indicate an overwhelming belief that the Church has too much control over Irish schools and hospitals (Figure 9.1). Of the nearly 115,000 voter respondents, 75 % agreed with this statement, 13 % disagreed and 12 % neither agreed nor disagreed. Like the 2016 survey results, older (55–64 and 65 and older) and those with less education (primary and junior certificate or lower) had much lower levels of agreement – indicating greater support for the Church's involvement. Nevertheless, even

---

34   Paul J. Lavrakas, *Encyclopedia of survey research methods* (Vols 1–0). Thousand Oaks, CA: Sage Publications, Inc., 2008, doi: 10.4135/9781412963947; <https://methods.sagepub.com/reference/encyclopedia-of-survey-research-methods/n3.xml>.

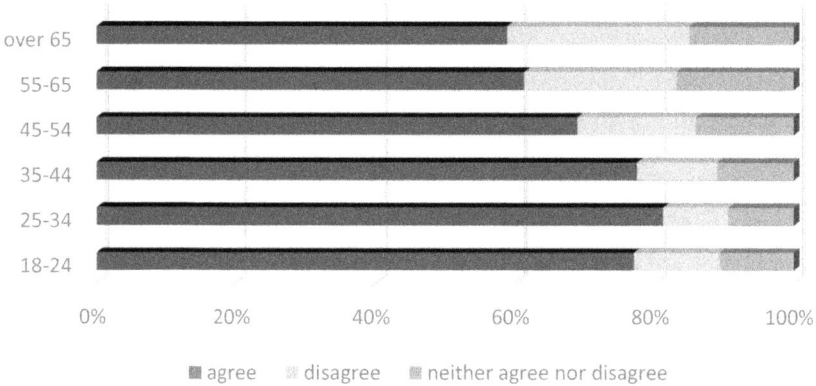

Figure 9.1. The Church has too much control over Irish schools and hospitals, by age.
Data from *Which Candidate* survey.

here most respondents agreed that the Church had too much control. The
results were 61 % of those aged 55–64, 59 % of people 65 and older, 60 % of
those with primary school education and 66 % of those with a junior certificate as their highest educational attainment agreed that the Church had
too much control. Similarly, in terms of political background factors, those
who identified as more left-wing had higher levels of agreement about the
Church having excessive control than those on the right, but most of these
right-wing identifiers still agreed the Church had too much control. Only
those who identified as a 9 on the 0–10 Left-Right Scale had less than 50 %
(47 %) agreement on this issue. Thus, once again, a vast majority of Irish
citizens report that the Church has too much control in Irish schools and
hospitals. As discussed in Chapter 2 dealing with control in Irish primary
education, it is unclear what voters perceive this Church control to be. When
analysed on a case by case basis, the perception may not match the reality
in term of where control actually lies at the primary level. Unfortunately,
there were not enough candidates or parties that responded to this same
question in the 2020 *Which Candidate* Survey to offer a legitimate comparison and a fuller sense of how respondents were engaging the question.

Despite the overwhelming sense that change should occur in the educational sector, with large numbers agreeing that the Church should have less

control, there is no clear sense of what should be done. A 2016 Parliamentary Survey highlights the desire for change but the uncertainty about the path to reform. This originally designed and implemented survey by McGraw interviewed face-to-face 97 of 158 TDs (*Teachta Dála*, members of the Irish Parliament). This was the third such parliamentary survey designed to capture TD and party positions on key issues in Irish General elections.[35]

First, TDs were asked to identify what proportion of Irish primary schools should be operated by the Catholic Church.[36] Overall, the TDs were evenly split on their views on Church patronage. Only 1 % thought the Church should be the patron for all primary schools, whereas 21 % thought the Church should manage most, 38 % about half, 20 % a few and 20 % none (see Table 9.1).

Curiously, there is significant diversity within most parties. Again, Fianna Fáil is slightly more conservative with 42 % supporting the view that the Church should run 'most' primary schools and 44 % 'about half' compared to only 14 % of Fine Gael TDs who thought the Church should run 'most' primary schools. Instead, 55 % of Fine Gael TDs reported that the Church should lead 'about half' and 23 % 'a few' of all primary schools. Sinn Féin is also divided but with a majority reporting views that seeking to limit Catholic patronage: 56 % stated that the Church should run 'a few' schools, and 31 % responded 'none'. Only the Green TDs were united in their views that the Church should control 'about half' of all primary schools, but there were only two Green TDs interviewed.

Second, TDs in the 2016 Parliamentary Survey were asked whether the State should build new schools or divest Catholic schools by transferring their patronage to a non-denominational or multi-denominational

35   Exact survey items can be found online at: <https://github.com/mainwaringb/Ireland_EJPR_2018>. In all three surveys, we sent a personalised letter to all TDs inviting them to participate in the face-to-face survey. We followed up the letter with at least five phone calls to parliamentary assistants to arrange for a time to conduct the interview. The sample in all surveys reflects those who were willing to meet in person to complete the survey.

36   The question was: 'In terms of education policy, do you think churches should be patrons of all, most, about half, a few, or no primary schools?'

Table 9.1. TD attitudes on percentage of primary Catholic schools desired (%)

	Total	Fianna Fáil	Fine Gael	Labour	Sinn Féin	Greens	Left Alliance	Independents
All	1	3	0	0	0	0	0	0
Most	21	42	14	0	0	0	0	29
About Half	38	44	55	67	13	100	20	14
A Few	20	8	23	33	56	0	0	14
None	20	3	9	0	31	0	80	43

patron.[37] Given the trade-off of spending more money during a time of limited government funds or forcing schools to divest/change their patronage and risk alienating local communities and leaders' support, it is unsurprising that TDs were deeply divided in their responses. Overall, 53 % of TDs thought new schools should be built, whereas 47 % reported that they would divest existing religious schools (see Table 9.2).

Only Labour and Green TDs were united in their views, with all Labour TDs supporting building new schools and the two Green TDs advocating divestment. A majority of Fianna Fáil TDs promoted building new schools, whereas most TDs in the other parties favoured divesting existing religious schools. The high levels of division within and across parties underscores the complexity of the problem and the cost of making tough choices that pit limited resources against deciding on whose opinions matter most.

This review of partisan and voter attitudes confirms that there is growing support among voters and parties to limit the Church's degree of control within education. This means that parties must engage potential reforms if they are to reflect evolving attitudes within Irish society. True to form, Irish political parties, especially Fianna Fáil and Fine Gael, have constantly adapted their policy positions to engage local interests, broader societal trends and pressure from minor parties to reform. Similar shifts in policy appear likely in some areas of educational reform.

IV. The Reform Context: Key Political Developments from 2011 to 2021

On his third day as Minister for Education in the new Fine Gael-Labour government in 2011, Ruairí Quinn, TD, decided to usher in a period of

---

37   The question was: 'In areas where there is demand for secular or non-denominational schools, which alternative approach would you prefer the state adopt: to build new schools even though this may be expensive; or to divest schools of their existing religious patronage even though this may be divisive in the local community?'

Table 9.2. TD attitudes on reform: Build new schools or divest existing religious schools (%)

	Total	Fianna Fáil	Fine Gael	Labour	Sinn Féin	Greens	Left Alliance	Independents
Build New Schools	53	59	41	100	47	0	11	71
Divest Existing Religious Schools	47	31	59	0	53	100	89	29

dramatic reform. Despite warnings from Department staff that he was not prepared to speak to an annual meeting of all Catholic primary school teachers, Quinn announced the Forum on Patronage and Pluralism in the Primary Sector. Ireland had changed, and its educational system needed to change with it he argued. Quinn referred to Ireland as a 'post-Catholic' country that needed to provide greater diversity of school types and diversity and inclusion within schools to meet the needs of Ireland's changing demographics. Quinn, an acknowledged atheist, valued the Church's role in Irish education and society, but also believed strongly that its role needed to be curtailed.

Quinn, and his Labour and Fine Gael colleagues, had assumed power in the wake of Fianna Fáil's historic collapse in the 2011 general election when they dropped from seventy-eight to twenty seats. The population was still growing, and financial resources were scarce as Ireland was trying to recover from its worst economic crisis (pre-COVID-19), making it an inauspicious time to enter government. Quinn sought Education and was clear from the outset, that after thirty-four years in parliament, this would be his last ministerial post. He said his two biggest goals from the outset were to alter the junior certificate programme and increase diversity in the primary sector. According to Quinn, the prospect for change in both areas had been gestating for twenty years and 'the ship has finally left the harbour and it will eventually reach its destination. But from my point of view, what I wanted to achieve was to ensure that by the time I left the post, the ship will be so far gone out to sea, that it can never be recovered.'[38] Although Quinn sought radical change, he was quick to point out that he did not want to usher in secularisation in ways that would undermine the school experience of current children. 'You only go to school once' was a common line of Quinn's during his tenure. Therefore, he wanted to avoid making schools a battleground for competing visions of change. Nevertheless, he initiated the Forum to kickstart what he considered long overdue reform.

The common Irish expression, referenced previously, 'I do not know where you are going, but you cannot get there from here!' characterises the

---

38   Ruairí Quinn, TD, former Minister for Education (2011–14), Personal Interview, October 2019.

context in 2011 in which the Forum was announced. There was no doubt that the primary sector could benefit from change, but there were many questions circling at that time. Such as, what type of change? How fast could such change occur? Who would be involved in the process of bringing about the changes? And what would the goal of reform look? Irish society had been dramatically transformed as we have seen in previous chapters. As every aspect of society had changed, there was a growing realisation that education needed to respond to such changes. Changes in wealth and poverty, the rise of non-religious citizens, and the emergence for the first time of large numbers of ethnic minorities and immigrants in Ireland combined to radically alter the children entering Irish schools. Relatedly, there was no consensus on how to deal with these changes, especially because many educational reforms would require either a constitutional amendment or altering legislation in ways that pitted certain constitutional rights against one another, for example, freedom 'of' and freedom 'for' religion, parental rights as primary educators of their children, property rights, etc.

As Irish society grappled with these changes, so too did the Irish educational system. In *Denominational Education and Politics: Ireland in a European Context,* Tuohy aptly described the Irish context in this way:

> Over the past thirty years or so, there has been a growing demand to disentangle the Church from the provision of education yet there seems to have been little political will to do this. The State has continued to expect the Church to become patron in many new primary schools and has actively pursued this partnership. It is only in the last ten years that serious efforts have been made to facilitate new patrons in setting up schools thus providing some diversity and choice within the system. However, there is still a lack of willingness on the part of the State itself to set up and run schools as part of its responsibility to the common good. In this, Ireland is very different from other countries in Europe.[39]

Tuohy suggests that there are three key background factors shaping Ireland's educational reform debate. These include different conceptions of how to deal with social change, how to balance individual rights and the common good and what type of goals and power dynamics are

39   David Tuohy, SJ, *Denominational Education and Politics: Ireland in a European Context*, Dublin: Veritas, 2013, 325.

being pursued. The rapidly evolving social and political context in Ireland meant that there were significant divisions on multiple levels. A quick review of Tuohy's analysis on these three dimensions is enlightening for our upcoming discussions on divestment, admissions and curriculum.

First, there were different schools of thought of how to deal with Ireland's rapid changes.[40] For some, the goal was assimilation, whereby the goal was to treat everyone the same and ignore differences. In this scenario, new groups were often seen as competitors for social rewards rather than as partners in achieving common goals, and competition between majority and minority groups ensued. The implicit expectation is that newcomers had a greater responsibility to adapt to pre-existing conditions. Assimilation essentially eliminates expressions of individual identity because there is still only one vision of society. For others, dealing with change meant seeking accommodation, where the goal would be to protect differences among individuals and groups. In this scenario, compromise is key as each group cedes some of their demands to ensure freedoms for all to pursue their interests, with special attention given to providing a voice for minority groups in decision-making. In education, the accommodation approach entails ensuring that all students have a place and guaranteeing equality of opportunity – if not outcomes/achievement. Here, the challenge is how to balance competing interests when you are seeking to accommodate everyone's interests. Finally, there are still others whose goal is integration and the transformation of culture. For proponents of this approach, individuals, groups, public/government institutions and schools must all work together to achieve greater equality by promoting diversity, inclusion, tolerance and respect among all to transform society. There is not much room in this approach for those who highest priorities are not consistent with the goals of diversity, inclusion and equality. The normative claims and goals of cultural transformation undermine alternative visions of society. In the end, there was no consensus within Irish society in the early 2000s in the period leading up to the Forum on Patronage and Pluralism. As a result, individuals, groups and institutions were operating with markedly

---

40   See Chapter 2 in Tuohy, 2013, for a thorough review of these approaches to addressing social change in the political sphere.

different assumptions, values and goals, and this complicated any political discussion that had to resolve conflict and create agreed upon solutions.

Second, according to Tuohy, there are different ways actors and groups conceive of and employ conceptions of individual rights and the common good.[41] The challenge is whether individual or social needs take precedence when there is conflict. Both perspectives entail normative assumptions and a commitment to lasting and universal values that are not always consistent with one another. For those who focus on rights, the individual trumps everything else, whereas common good advocates value the social context above all. Debates over what constitutes a good life can be deeply unsettling and can also lead to great conflict over the distribution of goods and services and whose voices are involved in decision-making processes. Common Good arguments can end up leaving many individuals and groups feeling excluded and some feeling that they have an unjust burden in meeting society's goals. An over-emphasis on individual rights can also lead to a growing focus on benefits with little attention given to social responsibilities. Not only does it become difficult to balance rights and responsibilities, but it is increasingly difficult to distinguish which rights are of greater importance. Educational reform in Ireland is plagued by competing constitutional rights and obligations as the Irish Constitution protects parents and children's rights, educational patrons' rights, and even the State's right in the educational sphere. The lack of consensus on how to deal with Ireland's increasing diversity has resulted in a lack of consensus on how to adjudicate and balance these competing rights.

Finally, Tuohy argues that within any diverse liberal democracy there are battles over political, economic and cultural goals.[42] He contends that there has been a growing focus on cultural goals, where power is symbolic and there is an emphasis on the moral imperative to value and behave in particular ways. In educational reform debates, the promotion of diversity and pluralism are cultural goals that offer a vision of society that caters for different individual interests and simultaneously promotes high levels of social cohesion. More specifically, debates are framed in terms of religious

41   See Tuohy, 2013, 80–104.
42   Tuohy, 2013, 65.

pluralism that protects the dignity of each person to pursue their own religious or philosophical truths without any interference from the State or other groups. For Tuohy, there is a tendency to use interests and rights interchangeably, but they are different and demand different types of actions. 'If rights are infringed, then the issue is a moral one and it needs immediate legal remedy. If a right gives rise to legitimate interests, then the issue is political, and the solution is found through negotiation. Setting the agenda for negotiating the legitimate interests of minority groups as equal citizens becomes the challenge.'[43] Ultimately, framing the debate in terms of infringement of rights escalates the conflict. It also places everything within a highly normative and moral context where people can be more defensive.[44] The mounting popular support for the cultural goals of diversity, pluralism, tolerance and inclusion highlight the ascendancy of minority religions and non-religious/secular interests and the difficulty of those groups that seek to defend their own religious interests and identities. For the Catholic Church, the challenge is how to deal with their loss of dominance and how to accept being one group among many in a more diverse Irish society. These differing conceptions of the problem represent the various values and groups involved in these educational reform debates. They also set the stage for our review of the evolving views of political parties on various educational reforms. The lack of a consensus on how to implement sufficient reforms points to why major parties have been cautious in their positions on educational issues. Ireland's major parties seek to balance honouring the growing numbers within Irish society that want to reduce or eliminate the role of religion in primary schools with the shrinking, but still critical mass of Irish citizens who want religion to remain part of primary schools for their children.

43 Tuohy, 2013, 333.
44 Tuohy, 2013, 228–31.

V. Case Studies of the Politics of Educational Reform: Divestment, Admissions and Curriculum

The politics of primary education reform are varied depending on how the problem is defined, the solutions being offered and the political climate and national mood within which reforms are engaged. As earlier chapters have underscored, politics is often about who wants what and why. The broad approach to policy-making adopted in this book acknowledges the critical role of civil servants and government officials in crafting and shaping policy reforms. However, this broad approach also recognises that these policy actors depend greatly on the views and interactions of political parties, civil society advocates and groups, the Church and the media as they seek to devise and implement policy. Although demands for greater equality, diversity and inclusion have become widely accepted as Irish society has been transformed in recent decades, different policy solutions create different coalitions of support. In the contemporary electoral environment, where there is minimal party loyalty and high levels of electoral volatility, politics have become more competitive and uncertain. The electoral collapse of Fianna Fáil in 2011, the confidence and supply minority coalition that was pieced together in 2016, and the first ever coalition between Fianna Fáil and Fine Gael (with the help of the Greens) point to the dramatically uncertain and altered political climate in Ireland. Therefore, party elites and candidates are balancing varied, and often competing, interests as they seek to generate sufficient and ongoing electoral support. Additionally, education issues, although important, are not always the top priorities during elections. This helps explain the cautious, wait-and-see approach of Ireland's major parties. They engage educational reform issues in varied ways depending on the specific issue at hand, the proposed solutions being debated, and the impact such changes will have on critical groups within Irish society.

Civil society activists and educational specialists have been working diligently for decades to reduce or eliminate the role of religion in primary schools. These advocates primarily want to increase the number of multi- or non-denominational schools and alter what is taught within all schools, so religion no longer dominates the curriculum and overall experience. These activists and reform advocates have been essential to heightening awareness of key issues, but they rely on individuals, local communities and other groups to demand change from politicians if policy change is to materialise.

The Church has multiple interests depending on with whom in the Church you are engaging. Institutional Church leaders and school leaders want to serve the changing needs of Irish society, but they also want to preserve the ability of Catholic schools to fulfil their ethos and to pass on the faith to the next generation of believers. Individual students, parents, teachers often have mixed views. On the one hand, there is widespread distrust and anger among many Catholics towards the institutional Church for its role in Ireland's sex abuse crisis and its treatment of children and women. On the other hand, many Catholics are eager for their children to learn the faith, receive the sacraments and benefit from the rich tradition of social justice within the Church. Furthermore, many Catholics who are angry at the institutional Church have a positive attitude towards their local and personal experience of Church. The multiplicity of voices, interests and levels within the Church means that who wants what and why is almost always in flux and often in tension.

For parties seeking to attract sufficiently large coalitions of voters, the changes in the Church have complicated their task. Traditionally, Ireland's two historic parties have relied on the steady electoral support of older and conservative voters who have often also been more likely to turnout to vote. As these older and more conservative voters have decreased in number in recent years, the major parties have also sought to attract new, younger voters who often prefer more progressive, secular views. Ireland's smaller, more left-leaning parties have regularly supported more progressive and secular policies within education, and now Ireland's larger parties cannot ignore such appeals if they want to remain competitive in the new electoral context.

Local communities, like the Church, have varied and fluid sets of interests, which can complicate trying to understand who wants what and why. Even though there is nearly universal support for equality, diversity and inclusion within Irish society, local communities often oppose change because it affects them personally. Many Irish citizens prefer to maintain the status quo and, as we will see in the next chapter, are willing to fight to prevent any change of patronage or school type in their local community. In many cases, battles to preserve existing local schools is less about the role of religion in the schools, and more about levels of satisfaction with the current reality. Parents often choose what school their child attends based on location/convenience, academic reputation and good discipline, and not because of deep-seated religious or secular beliefs. As a result, intense local battles over what happens in schools can take on a different tone and level of activity for varied reasons and often for different sets of interests that undergird national debates on education reform. For Irish politicians that depend on generating and maintaining strong local electoral support, there is an incentive to promote and protect local community interests even if these positions conflict with national party positions. Likewise, local Church leaders also defend local interests even if these oppose national directives from the bishops. Therefore, issues that are defined in ways that affect local communities to a greater extent than individuals – or even national interests, are likely to face greater opposition.

The final key group that influences how policies are defined, debated and solved is the media. As Chapter 7 highlighted, the media has become accustomed to challenging the Church, the State and the overall status quo. Less a unified actor that seeks specific changes, the media has focused their attention on describing how various actors and issues interact to engage educational issues. Not surprisingly, media attention is naturally drawn to focus on issues where there is conflict, tension or large numbers of actors and groups are affected. Policy entrepreneurs and reform advocates know this, which encourages them to generate events and programmes that will attract attention. This dynamic has greatly influenced how various policy issues receive attention and what solutions have attracted greater levels of support.

The next three chapters each address one of the key reform issues within the Irish primary sector – divestment, admissions and curriculum. The detailed treatment of each issue illustrates the ways in which the specific issue problem is defined influences the solutions being proposed, the groups most affected by the specific policy proposals, the salience of the issue and the ultimate policy outcome. Issue salience and outcomes vary in these three policy areas despite sharing overall goals. These goals include a desire to increase the number of non-Catholic schools in the primary sector as well as increase the diversity and inclusion within all schools. These reforms have been framed within the broader equality movement which has gained momentum in Ireland in the last several decades. The varied outcomes demonstrates that even though there may be broad support for making schools more reflective of contemporary Irish society given the transformation in recent decades, the politics of each issue is different. These results underscore the varied politics of policy reform.

In the next chapter, we discuss divestment, the process whereby Catholic primary schools transfer their patronage to non- or multi-denominational patrons. This reform area, although broadly supported, has led to minimal actual change. The current imbalance of patrons in the primary sector leads virtually everyone to support greater diversity of patronage in principle. Yet, there is no clear path to achieve this, especially since the solution requires local schools and communities to change their patronage. The intense opposition to change at the school and local community level has left individual educational, Church and political leaders with little incentive to force communities to change their school patronage. Politicians and officials within the Department of Education have consistently chosen to play the long game, not wasting their political capital on upsetting local interests. There is an implicit acceptance that the situation will gradually change in the coming years and a new consensus will emerge that will be more willing to accepting change. As society continues to become less religious, and the Church has fewer personnel and financial resources to devote to sustaining its institutions (as had occurred within the healthcare sector), change will eventually be the only option. In the short term, the Department of Education has focused on establishing new non- or multi-denominational schools where there is a clear need. Over time, the two currents will converge, and the demand for change will outweigh the local opposition that currently exists.

Chapter 11 reviews the recent change in primary school admissions policies. In contrast to the slow, gradual and highly unsuccessful divestment policy, admissions reform achieved swift and significant policy change. Instead of focusing on increasing the number of non-Catholic schools, the admissions reform sought to define the problem in more individualistic, rights-based language as the means to create more diverse and inclusive primary schools. By eliminating the right of Catholic schools to admit or deny admittance to students based on their religious or secular beliefs and identities, reform advocates argued that Irish primary schools would become more diverse, inclusive and equitable. Reformers made extremely effective emotional arguments that the 'baptismal barrier' prohibited non-religious and minority religious students from gaining access to the school of their choice, thereby condoning religious discrimination in State-funded schools. For some this amounted to State-sponsored discrimination that put 'faith before fairness'.[45] This was increasingly unpopular among growing numbers within Irish society. Defenders of Catholic schools unsuccessfully argued that the existence of waiting lists in a few over-populated areas of Dublin was due to the State's lack of planning in dealing with demographic trends and not because the Church was discriminating against non-Catholic students. Ultimately, there was universal support for admissions reform among politicians. No one wanted to be perceived as being against the protection of rights, especially when it relates to protecting children's rights. The smooth passing of this act reveals how a narrow, rights-based framing that ensured the rights of others but had little impact on those who still preferred a Catholic education, helped create a broad coalition of support.

The final policy case study chapter focuses on proposed changes to the primary school curriculum. In Chapter 12, we review how reformers once again seek to reduce or eliminate the role of religion in Irish primary schools, this time by altering what is taught in all schools. In many ways, changes to the curriculum have the potential to create a real transformation in the primary sector. Debates over which subjects are taught, how they are taught and for how long and when during the school day they are engaged often become contested and intense. However, these debates rarely capture media or broader public attention because they are waged by educational specialists, vested interests, academics and government bureaucrats and they deal with fine-grained details. The curriculum debate, like admissions, is also being framed in terms of rights-based arguments that highlight how

45   Rosita Boland, 'Faith before Fairness', *Irish Times*, 8 September 2007.

State-funded schools are discriminating against children. The argument is that children's religious freedom is being infringed upon due to requirements for religious education and weak procedures to ensure that students can opt-out of religion as the Constitution guarantees. Although these rights-based arguments appear to be gaining traction, there are enough parents who still want religious education and sacramental preparation within the school day for their children, which means immediate change is unlikely. Major parties will likely wait until a broader consensus emerges before offering their support for fear of alienating potential voters in a highly competitive and electoral context. Additionally, politicians have consistently deferred to educational experts, Department officials and the National Council for Curriculum and Assessment (NCCA) to deal with curriculum changes. Ironically, recently proposed cuts to the amount of time devoted to Religious Education within the school day and support for a new curriculum on Education about Religion Beliefs and Ethics signal that key reforms are already in development, and more transformative reforms are only a matter of time. The chapter on curriculum reveals the multiple layers and sets of actors involved within each policy issue and helps us understand that some of the most radical changes can be more subtle, bureaucratic policy shifts.

The ideal window of opportunity for enacting policy reform is generally limited. As stated in the introduction, changing social dynamics, rising awareness of a problem or new reality, changes in administration and shifts in the national mood often need to occur simultaneously for policy reform to occur. Furthermore, policy windows can close quickly, but one window closing can also open or encourage pursuit of other policy reforms. The slow pace of divestment underscores the complexity of policy solutions due to the varied sets of interests affected by this policy solution. The lack of progress in this area has encouraged reformers and politicians to focus their attention on other possible solutions for fear that the appetite for reform might wane. The narrow focus on admissions helped reformers achieve a tangible victory that may have paved the way for future reforms. The tension between national, local and individual interests involved in the curriculum debates, reveal that for change to occur, it may take a longer period or may have to result from subtle shifts in bureaucratic guidelines rather than another legislative or contentious public debate. The three policy case study chapters help us understand the politics of educational reform and gain insight into the future of the Catholic Church in Irish primary schools.

CHAPTER 10

Divestment

I. Introduction and Background to the Educational Reform Debate

The demand for change in Ireland's primary sector had become widespread in the 2000s. The imbalance of patrons in the primary sector, with the Catholic Church serving as the patron of nearly 90 % of schools, led virtually everyone to support greater diversity of patronage in principle. The first policy solution that was proposed and focused on in the period from 2011 was divestment, the process whereby Catholic primary schools transfer their patronage to non- or multi-denominational patrons.

The goal seemed simple and straightforward. The Church would respond to changing demographics and demands within Irish society and transfer large numbers of its schools to alternative patrons. The then Catholic Archbishop of Dublin Diarmuid Martin, the largest patron of primary schools in the country, offered early support for divestment. 'From the moment of my appointment as archbishop in 2004, I advocated a process of divestment of a substantial number of Catholic schools to foster a more pluralist presence which would reflect changing demographics. It would also open the possibility of more clearly defining the Catholic nature of Catholic schools.'[1]

On several occasions, Archbishop Martin proposed that the Catholic Church would reduce its patronage of primary schools from 90 % to 50 %. This became so commonly accepted as the goal that one of then Minister

---

[1]   Patsy McGarry, 'Archbishop Martin Proved Right about School Patronage', *The Irish Times*, 12 July 2017 (Accessed: 13 August 2020).

for Education Ruairí Quinn's top advisors encouraged those involved in
the proceedings to stop using the '50 % of schools being divested' figure,
as Archbishop Martin and indeed the Minister himself had proposed,
because many people within Irish society were starting to believe this was
happening when it was far from reality.[2]

This policy solution, although broadly supported, has led to minimal
actual change. The main reason for the lack of progress is there is no clear
path to achieve this transfer of school patronage, especially since the solution requires local schools and communities to change their patronage.
The intense opposition to change at the school and local community level
has left individual educational, Church and political leaders with little incentive to force communities to embrace divestment. Instead of forcing
the issue and coping with strong local opposition in communities, officials
from all sectors, including State and Church leaders, have decided to proceed cautiously, only responding to local communities where there has
been sufficient demand for change. Even here, the demand for change by
local communities was rooted more in a desire to save failing and closing
schools rather than out of an idealistic campaign to provide greater numbers of non-Catholic school opportunities for children in the area.

Divestment has been largely unsuccessful due to these competing
interests. There is an implicit acceptance by those desiring greater diversity that the situation will gradually change in the coming years and a
new consensus will emerge that will be more willing to transfer school
patronage. As society continues to become less religious, and the Church
has fewer personnel and financial resources to devote to sustaining its institutions, change will eventually be the only option goes the thinking. In
the short term, the State has focused on establishing new non- or multi-
denominational schools where there is a clear need, but the State either lacks
or is unwilling to commit resources to do this on a large scale. Reformers
believe that the two currents will eventually converge and the demand for
change will outweigh the local opposition that currently exists.

2   John Walshe, former Education Journalist/Aide to Minister Ruairí Quinn, Personal
     Interview, October 2019. See also Sean Flynn, 'School Patronage Survey Queried',
     The Irish Times, 14 December 2012.

As of 2021, there has been little appetite for change at the local level and, as a result, there has been little progress made to increase school choice via divestment. According to one commentator, 'Why should the church give "some" but not all rural schools away? Which ones? The fact is that there is a majority of Catholic parents in almost all rural communities and a significant minority of non-Catholic parents. In such a situation, arbitrarily picking some schools for divestment is only going to increase the dissatisfaction of both Catholic and non-Catholic parents.'[3] As a result of the various complexities and local dynamics, only eleven schools transferred their patronage between 2011 and 2019: seven Catholic schools, three non-denominational schools (Steiner schools), and one Church of Ireland school.[4] Of these, ten have become Education and Training Boards (ETB)/Community National Schools and one transferred to the Irish medium school network of An Foras Pátrúnachta.[5] Community National Schools are the preferred government model for schools that are being divested by the Catholic Church. In fact, the 2020 Programme for Government by Fianna Fáil, Fine Gael and Green Party promises to 'expand and prioritise the transfer of viable schools to Community National Schools'.[6] The widespread perception is that Catholic Church leaders also prefer Community National Schools to Educate Together schools if they are going to transfer patronage. Again, the public view was that Community National Schools are more accommodating of religion and religious education than the secular approach in Educate Together schools.

Although the government's policy goal is to have at least 400 multi-denominational and non-denominational primary schools by 2030, the current pace suggests that there will only be about 200 multi-denominational

3   James Cruickhank, 'State and Church and School Patronage', Letter to the Editor, *Irish Times,* 26 August 2015.

4   The Department of Education report a further 12 schools that were 'established under the patronage divesting process' between 2013 and 2019 based on the 2013 *Parental Preferences* surveys discussed in Chapter 3. These were new schools, not a result of a transfer of patronage.

5   Data received from the Department of Education, November 2019.

6   'Programme for Government: Our Shared Future', June 2020, 96. <https://www.documentcloud.org/documents/6944741-Programme-For-Government-June-2020.html>.

schools by this target date. In addition to the eleven schools that have divested their patronage between 2011 and 2019, only sixty-four new schools have been built in the same period. Of these, thirty-four are Educate Together Schools, eighteen are Community National Schools, eleven are Gaelscoils (the majority of which are multi-denominational schools), and there is one other.

In this chapter, we will first discuss the formation of the Forum on Patronage and Pluralism in 2011, as well as identifying its key findings and recommendations, especially those focusing on divestment. To illustrate how difficult divestment is to achieve, the chapter provides three case studies of how the Church has sought to engage divestment in rural, commuter and urban contexts. These case studies underscore the strength of local interests and the challenges that these varied interests at local level create for the Church, the State and other primary school patrons. The lack of success in divesting significant numbers of schools demonstrates the importance of how policy solutions are framed. In this case, local communities proved far too powerful in defending their interests that national actors and ideological reformers were no match. The other two reforms examined in this book, admissions and curriculum, offer radically different solutions to the proposed problem of a lack of diversity and inclusion in Irish primary schools. The different framing creates different sets of coalitions that support or oppose these reforms, which helps explain the varied outcomes that unfold.

II. The Forum on Patronage and Pluralism in the Primary Sector

In 2011, the Government established the Forum on Patronage and Pluralism as a one-year process to bring together interested individuals, groups and stakeholders within civil society with politicians and Department of Education and Skills leaders to assess the lack of diversity within the primary sector. The Minister set out the terms of reference for the Forum to advise him as follows:

1. How it can best be ensured that the education system can provide a sufficiently diverse number and range of primary schools
   catering for all religions and none.
2. The practicalities of how transfer/divesting of patronage should
   operate for individual primary schools in communities where it is
   appropriate and necessary.
3. How such transfer/divesting can be advanced to ensure that
   demands for diversity of patronage (including from an Irish-
   language perspective) can be identified and met on a widespread
   basis nationally.[7]

Special attention was to be given to the Catholic Church's willingness to
divest schools and the State's ability to operate the national school system
under the financial constraints of that period.

Although the original task of the Forum was to think critically about
the issue of divestment, the process led to a broadening of the scope of areas
within the primary sector that the Advisory Group decided warranted
reform. Rather than focusing merely on divestment, within months the
Advisory Group had included 'promoting more inclusiveness in all schools,
including 'stand-alone' schools where divesting patronage to another body
is not an option', as one of the key recommendations for reform. For some
this was a natural next step based on the submissions and consultations that
the Advisory Group had accumulated. For others, this focus on inclusion
within schools was not part of the remit of the Forum and represented the
Forum 'slipping its moorings' to the point where it wanted to offer new
guidelines for the internal workings of all schools.[8]

The Forum accepted written submissions from interested individuals
and groups during this year-long process. The vast majority of submissions
(86 %) received by the Advisory Group set up to lead the Forum process

---

7   28 March 2011 – Minister Quinn announces the establishment of a Forum on
Patronage and Pluralism in the Primary Sector, <https://www.education.ie/en/
Press-Events/Press-Releases/2011-Press-Releases/PR11-3-28.html>.

8   Amalee Meehan and Daniel O'Connell, 'The "Deeper Magic of Life" – A Catholic
response to the Forum on Patronage and Pluralism', *The Furrow*, June 2012, Vol. 63
No. 6, 278–85.

were from parents and individuals, but they also received reports from parents' associations, boards of management and key stakeholders.[9] Many of the submissions were not about divestment, and instead focused on issues such as religious education and other curricular concerns. The views in these responses ranged from those who strongly argued that religious education should have no role at all in primary education to others who believed that primary schools in Ireland are already very inclusive and who oppose any change in the current system.[10] Although a wide set of views was sought, the Forum's Advisory Group was not in favour of plebiscites or large town hall gatherings because they were perceived to be divisive and upsetting for communities. From the Advisory Group's perspective, 'the solution, for the common good, needs to be sought in a calm, respectful and reasonable way'.[11]

Again, the Forum was being employed by the Government to find ways to help it create greater diversity of school types, but it quickly included recommendations to foster higher levels of diversity and inclusion within all Irish primary schools. Similar to the deliberative democracy institutions that were so vital in the marriage equality and abortion rights campaigns, the Forum was designed to help voice a wide range of concerns during a time of dramatic change when consensus might be difficult to achieve. Additionally, the Forum sought to devise concrete suggestions that would lead to real policy change. In terms of fostering lively debate, the Forum invited all participants to engage on four overarching issues: 1) establishing new schools in areas of rising population, 2) divesting of school patronage in areas of stable population but with shifting demographics and interests,

9   *Forum on the Patronage and Pluralism in the Primary Sector: Progress to Date and Future Directions*, July 2014 <https://www.education.ie/en/Press-Events/Events/Patronage-and-Pluralism-in-the-Primary-Sector/Progress-to-Date-and-Future-Directions-Forum-on-Patronage-and-Pluralism-in-the-Primary-Sector.pdf>. The stakeholder groups that responded were: Association of Trustees of Catholic Schools; Catholic Schools Partnership/ Catholic Primary Schools Management Association (joint submission); Gaelscoileanna Teo; National Association of Boards of Management in Special Education; Irish National Teachers Organisation; and the National Parents' Council – Primary.

10   Forum Progress Report, 2014, 17.

11   Tuohy, 2013, 276.

3) promoting inclusion within all schools and 4) providing Irish-language schools. As mentioned, the third point about inclusion was not part of the original terms of reference from the Minister, but it became one of the most discussed aspects of the entire Forum, perhaps softening the ground for further reforms by initiating the conversations at that point. Although addressing inclusion does not pertain to finding a mechanism for divestment, it did open the door to discussing the new Education about Religious Beliefs (ERB) and Ethics curriculum and making Religious Education a discrete subject – both of which are discussed in greater detail in Chapter 12.

There were several concrete outcomes that emerged from the process. First, the New Schools Establishment Group (NSEG) was established to oversee the creation of all new schools in areas with growing populations. The goal was to respond to rising parental demand for plurality and diversity of patrons. This new group also conducted surveys of parents in areas with stable populations where there was little hope of a new school unless an existing school divested its patronage to a new patron. The Advisory Group reported that there was sufficient demand for a wider choice of patrons in twenty-eight of forty-three areas, with the highest demand in those areas seeking change for a new Educate Together school.[12] Several Catholic education leaders highlighted the low turnout in parental surveys to argue that demand for change was inflated.[13]

Despite the uncertainty of demand (see Chapter 3), the Government and advocates of change argued that there was a high degree of demand for change, which fuelled intense conflict among the various groups with competing goals and values involved in the process. It was not surprising that there were heated debates over who conducted these parental surveys and how the results would be interpreted. Both Church and State leaders were suspicious of the other and feared that the results would be skewed. Ultimately, there were lower response rates because Church leaders insisted on paper, rather than online surveys.[14] Once the data was collected, even the numbers were disputed. Proponents of change consistently argued that

12   Forum Progress Report, 2014, 13.
13   Flynn, 14 December 2012.
14   John Walshe, Personal Interview, October 2019.

there was overwhelming support for change among parents in five pilot study local areas. However, there was a majority of support in only two of five pilot areas. According to John Walshe, long-time Irish journalist and right-hand man to Quinn during the Forum, what 'clear and sufficient' demand meant was that if there were six schools in each area and 35 % to 50 % of parents reported supporting a desire for greater diversity of school types, then all the parents seeking change could be combined into one school that was divested from being a Catholic school to another type of school. In addition to disputes over how to survey and to interpret the results, Walshe argued that most parents appeared to be satisfied with the overall education of their children based on survey results. As a result, many parents, he argued, did not want to stir things up by demanding huge change.[15] Fr Michael Drumm of the Catholic Schools Partnership pointed out at the time 'that this is not a survey in the ordinary sense of the term as it is not based on a representative sample' and raised questions as to why the Department of Education and Skills would not publish statistics on the percentage of parents who had participated in the surveys.[16]

Although there is a clear preference for new schools, the Forum recognised that this may not be possible in every geographic area due to lack of students to make an additional school viable in the area and because of financial constraints facing the State. Urban contexts offer some degree of choice, whereas in more rural areas there is a preponderance of small, stand-alone schools with no other options in the area. As a result of the lack of a clear path to divestment and establishing new schools, the Advisory Group pivoted beyond its original terms of reference and added a focus on offering recommendations to promote more inclusive schools. Some proposals built on best practices and offered suggestions on how to celebrate religious diversity via religious celebrations, festivals and artifacts. Other recommendations included ensuring that boards of management of denominational schools reflect the diversity of the local community or developing mechanisms for whole-school or self-evaluation by schools on their diversity and inclusionary practices.[17] Still other recommendations

15   John Walshe, Personal Interview, October 2019.
16   Flynn, 14 December 2012.
17   Forum Progress Report, 2014, 12.

about enhancing inclusion within all Irish schools called for specific actions to correct current weaknesses in the system. For example, there was some attention given to how to treat students who may wish to opt-out of denominational Religious Education classes. In many ways, the proposed ERB and Ethics curriculum that suggested teaching students 'about' different religious traditions and ethics made sense for students in these cases but may not be as suited for all students, which reformers advocated. Additional recommendations concerned admissions policies based on religious backgrounds and also curriculum. We will discuss these recommendations in detail in the next two chapters.

The Forum created considerable momentum for educational reform in the primary school sector. Ironically, the Forum did little to develop a plan to divest sufficient numbers of schools to alter the overall system. However, the Forum established a political process and venue for debate about how to increase the diversity of school types and to promote the goals of diversity and inclusion within schools even though this was not the stated goal of the Forum at its founding. The central policy issues of this book – divestment, admissions and curriculum – all stem from the momentum created by the Forum on Patronage and Pluralism, thus demonstrating its critical role in hastening educational reform in the primary sector.

The Forum process had a couple of significant limitations. First, there was no real vision for what the role of the State would be in divested schools. Even the popular notion of divesting 50 % of all denominational schools was not realistic. Instead, as Tuohy argues, 'The debate focused on which private patron should run which school, and there is no clear thinking on what the benefits of this structure would be for the state or the patron taking it on. There are tensions that exist when private patrons take full responsibility for state policy [i.e. running schools in this context] rather than cooperating with it. This runs the danger of either undermining the role of the patron or treating patrons with different philosophies differently, with some philosophies having State preference.'[18] There was almost an implicit understanding – or hope by Quinn and other advocates of

---

18 David Tuohy, SJ, *Denominational Education and Politics: Ireland in a European Context*, Dublin: Veritas, 2013, 335.

change – that diversity could be achieved by finding a different patron, most likely Educate Together, to become a legitimate alternative to the Catholic Church. Nevertheless, there was also a realisation that the Church was still too invested in local communities and schools for such dramatic change to occur so rapidly. Rather than tackle the Church head on, or seek a secular system, the strategy was to seek incremental reform as we will see unfold in the subsequent chapters on admissions and curriculum.

A related issue is that the Forum appeared to favour a more secular version of education in its pursuit of a more diverse and inclusive educational system. As mentioned, there is no clear mechanism to adjudicate among competing rights or to reconcile when individual or group rights conflict with conceptions of the common good. However, 'it would appear from the Forum Report that there would be a greater onus on parents to comply with the conditions set forth by a patron in a "secular school", whereas in a religious school, the onus would be on the patron to accommodate the parent. If this is the case, then it amounts to different treatment of patrons based on religious belief, and it shows a State preference for a particular philosophy. This problem is not dealt with in teasing out the recommendations of the Forum Report.'[19]

Third, there was almost a naïve belief that such large-scale change could be implemented in a cost-neutral basis. The Forum's underappreciation of the costs involved placed undue expectations on the Church to take the initiative to hand over schools without much compensation in return.[20] 'The rhetoric is couched in terms of the common good, with a demand that the Church forego their rights to property.'[21] By framing things in cultural terms, leaders within the Forum process, and supporters of Educate Together's model in particular, oversimplified the compensation process associated with any changes in property rights. Such framing elicited a negative response from many leaders within the Catholic Church, thereby entrenching their opposition to change. It was as if the ideal of creating an 'equality-based education' to better serve Ireland's religiously diverse society

19   Tuohy, 2013, 273.
20   Tuohy, 2013, 319.
21   Tuohy, 2013, 293.

was of such value to Ireland that patrons should be willing, if not excited, to bear the costs.[22] This severely ignored the vast amounts of time, money and personnel resources religious actors and institutions have poured into schools and their communities over decades and centuries. Furthermore, such framing failed to appreciate the strength of feeling amongst Church leaders that their schools were already equality-based and had been effectively serving children from a diversity of backgrounds for decades.

One of the biggest challenges facing divestment and building new schools is finding acceptable space or land for a proper construction site. In cases of divestment, many Catholic school properties have been deemed unfit for purpose as was the case in the Burren, County Clare. In another example, officials in the Department of Education clashed with the Christian Brothers and its educational wing, the Edmund Rise Schools Trust (ERST), over the divestment of a former school at Basin Lane in Dublin to a non-Catholic patron. Records of correspondence from the time show that ERST, which controls the property interests of the Christian Brother schools, refused to surrender the vacant school premises until it had secured financial concessions.[23] There are different obstacles when building new schools. Whereas Catholic schools have a much easier time gaining access to land because local parishes provide land/sites, this is not true for other models. When a school patron is not able to provide land/site for the establishment of a new school, the Department of Education must source a suitable site, purchase it and submit planning permission. Where a school patron can provide the land/site, the above responsibilities lie with the local patron, and therefore there is less of an administrative and financial burden on the State. One consequence of this is that 15 % of new schools from 2000 to 2010 were located in temporary accommodation, with this figure increasing to 55 % between 2011 and 2019, a period when no new Catholic schools were established.[24] Schools also tend to stay in temporary accommodations for lengthy periods. A 2019 report found that in the last ten years, just eleven of the fifty-seven primary schools opened by Educate

22   Tuohy, 2013, 317.
23   Joe Humphreys, 'Christian Brothers Withdrawal Is not First Clash over Divestment', *The Irish Times*, 10 March 2017.
24   Data received from the Department of Education, November 2019.

Together had moved to permanent accommodation.[25] Thus, the sheer administrative and financial costs associated with establishing new schools have also slowed the pace of reform.

Much of the criticism for the lack of progress in divesting schools was directed at the Church. John Walshe reported that John Coolahan, the Chair of the Forum, was deeply disappointed with the bishops. As the largest patron, Coolahan felt that they should have taken a more proactive role in more forcefully encouraging local parish schools and communities to divest schools where appropriate. Leaving such choices almost entirely to local communities helped produce the slow rate of change that has transpired.[26]

As we discussed in Chapter 4, one of the greatest challenges when dealing with the Catholic Church is the lack of a unified voice. It is critical to understand that there are 26 Catholic patrons as each local bishop has authority over schools in his diocese. This is a significant driver at the heart of the paralysis of the Church response, or lack thereof. Not only do bishops often disagree with one another on best the strategies and approaches, but the decentralised leadership structure within the Church hierarchy makes it difficult for other actors, including the State, education reformers and individuals to know with whom to speak when engaging other broader issues in education. The lack of a clear structure and overall sense of transparency can complicate dealing with the Church, but it may also help Church leaders obfuscate or slow the pace of change. Further decentralisation is possible because local communities and parishes do not always share the views of diocesan leadership. For example, there were many local voices declaring opposition to divestment, often for reasons other than preserving a faith-based education, as we will discuss below. Thus, for many Catholics, the strategy became more of a 'wait and see approach'. It was almost as if the Church did nothing, the issue would go away, or in time, there would be enough change in public opinion that reform would be easier when there was a natural consensus.[27] One Church leader cited

25   <https://www.breakingnews.ie/ireland/80-of-educate-together-schools-opened-in-last-decade-still-in-temporary-accommodation-946592.html> (Accessed: 10 July 2020).

26   John Walshe, Personal Interview, October 2019.

27   John Walshe, Personal Interview, October 2019.

U.S. President Reagan's style of leadership as emblematic of how many Irish leaders think. Reagan, when confronted with complex problems, would often not do anything. Reagan believed that many issues would resolve themselves in time.[28] Many within Irish society and the political sphere were shocked by Quinn's boldness. Although proponents of change were delighted to have a minister so actively engaged in reforming the system, opponents of reform on divestment and other issues in education waited patiently until Quinn's retirement in hopes that the momentum for change would wane with his departure. For some, this was more an 'active waiting' that could help stall greater change.[29]

Quinn found it ironic that the Church 'discovered democracy' when confronted with the challenge of divesting local schools. Whereas the Church was supportive of change overall, and leaders like Dublin's Archbishop Martin were outspoken on the need to divest schools, Quinn contends that the Church did little to work for real change. In fact, he suggested that in some local areas, local clergy encouraged parents and activists to voice their opposition to divestment. He cited one example where a local Catholic boys' school could have easily merged with a local Catholic girls' school to free up an existing school building for a new, non-denominational school but local opposition stirred resistance to change. The local pressure was so severe that the local Labour TD sided with his constituents and went against the preferred party position on divestment. In the end, a small cohort of active parishioners, on whom the Church was dependent for its own survival over the medium turn, blocked change from occurring.[30]

Other Forum leaders also expressed disappointment in the Church for not transferring their schools and properties to other patrons or to the State. In one of the earliest negotiations, Walshe reported that the Christian Brothers were demanding more money than the State could offer. The State, fearful of setting a bad precedent, did not meet the demands. Ultimately, the Christian Brothers' Trust (ERST) chose to sell the property and there

---

28 Fr Paul Connell, Executive Secretary to the Council for Education of the Irish Episcopal Conference, Personal Interview, October 2019.
29 John Walshe, Personal Interview, October 2019.
30 Ruairí Quinn, Personal Interview, October 2019.

was no school divestment. It is challenging for the State to induce greater levels of change if they lack the resources to pay either existing patrons for their land/property or to help new patrons secure land/property for their schools.[31] This financial aspect of the divestment process has never been fully appreciated by virtually any actors, especially those seeking change, which also explains the lack of much change in this area.

Years later, Quinn argued that no one was being attentive to the issue of property, which was central to Ireland's educational system. In particular, he argued that more attention should be given to ageing religious communities who could easily sell off all their land and redeploy their assets elsewhere, even outside of Ireland. Even though the State may have outsourced education in establishing the denominational nature of schools, Quinn believes that the State needs to address the issue of property now. According to Quinn, if the State really wanted to be radical, it would pass legislation to ensure that property where schools currently exist could not be sold or re-purposed for non-educational use. This extreme tactic would emphatically demonstrate the State's commitment to education no matter what historical developments transpired to get us to this point.[32] Once again, this represents insightful thinking on the part of reformers, but it does not address the difficulty in making such change happen due to the financial interests involved.

III. Divestment Cases

A. Emerging Issues from the Forum's Recommendations

The public narrative after the Forum and its reports between 2011 and 2014 was that there existed enthusiastic support for divestment of schools. However, only eleven schools had divested their patronage by 2019, which underscores the challenges facing the implementation of

31   John Walshe, Personal Interview, October 2019.
32   Ruairí Quinn, Personal Interview, October 2019.

divestment. The lack of successful cases of divestment may also reveal why reformers quickly broadened the scope of the Forum discussions so as not to close the window of opportunity for additional primary sector reforms. Of the eleven schools that have transferred their patronage, seven were Catholic, three were multi-denominational Steiner schools run by Lifeways Ireland, and one was a Church of Ireland school. Only one school was in an urban area; instead, the majority occurred in more rural areas of Clare, Galway, Kerry, Kildare, Louth, Roscommon and Wexford.

Most of the schools had extremely low enrolments, and many schools faced closures due to declining student numbers. Seven of the eight denominational schools had twenty-six or fewer students, and many of them had dipped into single digits. The largest denominational school, Scoil Náisiúnta Bhrighde in Louth, had declined from 100 students in 2010 all the way down to six students in 2017, before rebounding to seventeen pupils in 2018 and forty-six in 2019 under the new Community National School patronage. Two of the three Steiner schools had enrolments over 100 students, and the third had increased from nine students to thirty-eight students since 2016. These latter schools divested for non-enrolment-based issues.

Faced with the threat of closure, many of these schools were motivated by local parents and community members fighting to save their schools at all costs. Rather than seeking a transfer to a non- or multi-denominational school for ideological or religious reasons, most of these schools sought a change in patronage for pragmatic purposes. In many schools, bad school leadership, weak boards of management and/or bad communication between the schools and families forced students to flee these floundering schools. In County Louth, for example, parents staged a protest during the 2016–2017 school year in which they withdrew their children from the school for one day a week for six weeks to highlight poor standards.[33] These parents repeatedly wrote to various organisations and public representatives,

33 'Uncertain Future for School as Students Do Not Return'. RTE.ie. RTÉ, 29 August 2017. <https://www.rte.ie/news/education/2017/0829/900865-louth-school/>; 'Parents Forced to Withdraw Pupils from Faughart NS'. LMFM, 9 August 2017.

demanding the patron, Archbishop Martin, intervene and seek the resigna-
tion or relocation of the principal or they would be forced to withdraw their
children and the school would be in danger of closing.[34] The Department
of Education claimed they were working closely with the manager of the
school to ensure that the issues raised in the Department's enhanced inspections of the school would be improved upon over the summer.[35] Only
six students returned to the school in September of 2017, and those parents
said it was largely because they could not find another suitable place for
their children.[36] Divestment was ultimately initiated by parents desperately
seeking new management. A new patron was sought because they energetically wanted change and the existing patron had failed to act, not because
they wanted a different ethos. Unlike many of the other cases, once new
management was installed, enrolment numbers quickly increased.

For many of the schools, the goal of transferring to a multi-
denominational patron was initiated to attract more families from a wider
area to boost their enrolment numbers. These schools stood to benefit
by offering a different kind of education than other schools in the area.[37]
There was also a longer-term hope that by providing a wider variety of educational options, more families would move back to the area who might
otherwise stay in places like Dublin, thereby increasing the population of
the entire area.[38]

<https://www.lmfm.ie/news/lmfm-news/parents-forced-to-withdraw-pupils-
from-faughart-ns/>.

34   'Archbishop Martin Urged to Intervene to Save Faughart NS'. LMFM, 11 August
     2017.   <https://www.lmfm.ie/news/lmfm-news/archbishop-martin-urged-to-
     intervene-to-save-faugh/>.

35   Carl O'Brien, 'Department of Education Intervenes to Help Improve Standards at
     Louth School'. *The Irish Times*, 30 August 2017.

36   'Uncertain Future for School', 2017.

37   Toby McCoy, 'Three Irish Primary Schools to Convert from Catholic to
     Nondenominational'. IrishCentral.com, 27 August 2019. <https://www.
     irishcentral.com/news/ireland-primary-schools-non-denominational>.

38   'Kerry ETB Takes over Two More Schools – August 26th, 2019'. Radio Kerry, 27
     August 2019. <https://www.radiokerry.ie/kerry-etb-takes-two-schools-august-
     26th-2019/>.

A key challenge within the divestment process was deciding on the best location to divest a school once a demand for alternative patrons emerged. In a few of the divestment cases, some parents expressed interest in establishing multi-denominational schools to broaden the overall educational experience for their children.[39] In Roscommon, the spokesperson for the local ETB assured families that the Community National School model preserved religious education for children and encouraged any faith community to set up faith formation classes on the school grounds outside of school hours to be led by a member of the community or parish, rather than the school.[40] The Bishop of Elphin, the previous patron of the school in Roscommon, also held meetings with current parents of children in the school and with parents of preschool children in the catchment area to gauge the desire for a multi-denominational school.[41] Based on the various meetings held, the Bishop announced the divestment of the school to the Galway & Roscommon ETB.[42] Thus, Lecarrow Community National School became the first multi-denominational school in the county, which previously had eighty-five Catholic schools and two Church

39   Gabija Gataveckaite, ' "It's Good for Them to Be Taught Inclusion" – Schools Drop Religious Ethos in Bid to Ensure Survival'. *Irish Independent*, 27 August 2019; Emma O'Kelly, 'Three Primary Schools Transfer from Catholic Patronage'. RTE news. RTÉ, 27 August 2019. <https://www.rte.ie/news/2019/0827/1071103-patronage/>.

40   'Religious Education Still Available for St. Joseph's NS Pupils Who Want It'. *Shannonside News*, 25 July 2019. <https://www.shannonside.ie/uncategorised/religious-education-still-available-st-josephs-ns-pupils-want/>.

41   'South Roscommon School to Meet to Consider "Change of Ethos" '. *Shannonside News*, 19 June 2019. <https://www.shannonside.ie/news/local/roscommon/south-roscommon-school-meet-consider-change-ethos/>.

42   'Lecarrow Community National School to Open under the Patronage of GRETB'. Galway & Roscommon Education & Training Board, July 26, 2019. <http://galwayroscommon.etb.ie/latest-news/lecarrow-community-national-school-to-open-under-the-patronage-of-gretb/>. 'Kiltoom/Cam: St John's National School, Lecarrow'. *Westmeath Independent*, 3 August 2019. <https://archive-irishnewsarchive.com.proxy.bc.edu/Olive/APA/INA.Edu/SharedView.Article.aspx?href=WMI%2F2019%2F08%2F03&id=Ar02600&sk=6B6913FA>.

of Ireland schools for the 2018–19 school year.[43] It was opened for the practical reason that it was available and not because it was the best location to meet changing demand for more diverse patrons. Roscommon town, the only locale in Roscommon that was surveyed in 2013, was identified as not having enough demand for a multi-denominational school to make it a viable focus area for divestment.[44]

In other counties, there was a mismatch between demand for alternative patrons and the proper location where divestment could occur. For example, County Louth had not been identified as an area with a particular need for an increased diversity in the patronage of primary schools. Then, when Louth-Meath ETB was asked by the State in 2018 to select an area with high levels of interest in opening a multi- or non-denominational school, they selected an area in County Meath, not Louth, where Faughert National School was ultimately reopened later that year under the patronage of the local ETB.[45] This mismatch between supply and demand underscores the difference between national goals seeking greater divestment and local realities where such change was not always feasible.

As the divestment process unfolded, there was some competition between Educate Together and Community National Schools led by local ETBs over who would assume patronage of these divested schools, but Community National Schools emerged as the clear winner. Educate Together often gained early traction because it has such a well-known brand.[46] However, Community National Schools gained support over

43   'Roscommon's First Community National School to Open in Lecarrow'. Midwest Radio, 27 August 2019. <https://www.midwestradio.ie/index.php/news/33226-roscommon-s-first-community-national-school-to-open-in-lecarrow>; 'Primary Schools 2018–2019', Accessed: 2020.

44   *Report on the Surveys Regarding Parental Preferences*, 2013.

45   *Report on the Surveys Regarding Parental Preference*, 2013; '28 May 2018 – Minister Bruton Commences Plan to Increase Provision of Multi- and Non-Denominational Schools'. Department of Education and Skills, 28 May 2018. <https://www.education.ie/en/Press-Events/Press-Releases/2018-press-releases/PR18-05-28.html>; Emma O'Kelly. 'Louth School to Reopen after Forced Closure Last Year'. RTE.ie. RTÉ, 20 July 2018. <https://www.rte.ie/news/2018/0720/980054-scoil-naisiunta-bhrighde-louth/>.

46   'South Roscommon School to Meet', 2019.

time. It is unclear exactly why such support shifted. ETBs certainly appealed to the promise of effective governance and access to state resources, which would ease the burden on principals in the areas of administration, governance and capital grants. The Wexford ETB announcement of the Community National School, for example, emphasised the benefits that this new form of governance would provide for the staff of the school and the quality of education that would be maintained. Rather than highlighting the multi-denominational ethos, the emphasis was on the new form of governance and on how the ETB support system could provide for a school with dropping pupil numbers.[47] This favouring of the CNS model was feared by Educate Together from the very beginning as something that would block their expansion.

For some, especially many in the national news media, the preponderance of divested schools becoming Community National Schools pointed to the preference for this model by both the Department of Education and the Catholic Church.[48] Educate Together repeatedly complained that there has been insufficient diversity in the divestment process and a biased preference for Community National Schools. Education Equality, a progressive civil society group that seeks the removal of any religion in Ireland's 'state-funded' primary schools, along with Educate Together, argued that parents are not getting adequate choices in school types. They vociferously disagree with the Catholic Church's role in selecting new patrons. They contend that the Church's preference for Community National Schools prevents a true plurality of patrons from forming.[49]

47 'First Community National School in Wexford: Waterford & Wexford Education & Training Board'. Waterford & Wexford ETB, 20 February 2019. <http://waterfordwexford.etb.ie/latest-news/first-community-national-school-in-wexford/>.

48 Kim Bielenberg. 'Discussions to Start Soon on Transfer of Catholic Schools Transfer', *Irish Independent*, 19 September 2018.

49 'Granting Patronage of Killarney School to Local ETB "Not What Parents Want or Deserve"'. *Breaking News*. Breakingnews.ie, 13 June 2017. <https://www.breakingnews.ie/ireland/granting-patronage-of-killarney-school-to-local-etb-not-what-parents-want-or-deserve-793416.html>

We turn, now, to see how these and other factors play out in varied ways depending on the geographic context in which divestment is explored and attempted.

B. *Geographic Factors Shaping Divestment*

An important backdrop to understanding divestment is that Irish society morphed from a relatively straightforward urban–rural dichotomy to a more complex pattern in recent years. Since the 1990s, there has been explosive growth of a significant commuter belt surrounding Dublin, which increased levels of inward migration of people 25 to 44 years old into these commuter zones.[50] In many ways, the eastern third of the country has and continues to grow, whereas the midlands and the west have experienced declining populations. These trends have pressurised delivery of services, especially for schools, transport, childcare, healthcare, retail, housing, etc. The Church, like the State and other national organisations, has had to deal with responding to the emergent needs associated with these changes. For schools, this translates into significantly declining numbers of students in rural schools and growing numbers in commuter and urban schools. The resultant variation in school sizes in rural, commuter and urban settings creates different dynamics for school leaders, as well as for patrons of schools and the Department of Education as they seek to respond to changes and plan for the future.

In addition to the effect of population changes, there exist growing demographic differences among these geographic regions, with rural areas and urban areas on each end of the demographic spectrum and the commuter areas experiencing somewhat of a hybrid or mixed experience. To better illustrate these differences, we conducted a case study in a rural (Kerry), commuter (Kildare) and urban (Dublin) county to see how the Church was responding to social changes in these varied local areas. In socio-economic terms, these three counties encompass a cross-section of

---

50   James Walsh (ed.), *People and Place: A Census Atlas of the Republic of Ireland*. Maynooth: National University of Ireland, 2007, 329.

Irish society, whether measured in terms of population (size, change and density), employment (industries and numbers), educational attainment, religious background, percent of population that are non-Irish nationals, Irish speaking, commuting to work, among other dimensions. For example, Kerry has higher percentages of Irish speakers; native-born residents; Catholics; households with husband, wife and children; and those working in construction, manufacturing and agriculture. Urban areas such as Dublin have lower percentages in each of these categories, but with higher percentages of foreign-born residents, higher levels of educational attainment, and more people employed in trade and commerce. Kildare, characteristic of a commuter county, straddles these other two on most measures.

Of particular interest for our study are the numbers of religious and non-religious in each area, the breakdown of school patrons by county and political preferences on issues related to religion and society. In each category, there is the same continuum of results with Kerry and Dublin on the extremes and Kildare between them, pointing to the differences among rural, commuter and urban contexts within Irish society (see Tables 10.1, 10.2 and 10.3).

According to the 2016 census, 78 % of Irish citizens identify as Catholics. Not surprisingly, Kerry had the highest percentage of Catholics (86 %) and Dublin had the lowest percentage (72 %), and Kildare was in the middle with 81 %, which was still above the national average. Inversely, Dublin had the highest percentage of non-religious residents (15 %) and Kerry had the least (7 %), whereas Kildare had the same as the national average (9.8 %).

Given these numbers, it is not surprising that Kerry has the highest percentage of Catholic primary schools (95 %) and lowest percentage of multi-denominational schools (3 %), and Dublin had the lowest percentage

Table 10.1. Religion demographics by county[a]

	National	Kerry	Kildare	Dublin
Catholic	78.3 %	85.9 %	81.3 %	72.3 %
No Religion	9.8 %	7.3 %	9.8 %	14.5 %

[a]Central Statistics Office, 2016 Census.

Table 10.2. Percentage of Catholic and multi-denominational primary schools by county[a]

	National	Kerry	Kildare	Dublin
Catholic	89 %	95 %	82 %	77 %
Multi-Denominational	5 %	3 %	11 %	13 %

[a]Dept. of Education 2020/21 Individual Schools Data.

of Catholic primary schools (77 %) and highest percentage of multi-denominational schools (13 %).

Once again, Kildare's figures lie between the two extremes with 82 % Catholic schools and 11 % multi-denominational schools. The growth of multi-denominational provision in Dublin has been driven exclusively by a surge in new schools, opened to meet the growing population in recent decades. Of the seventy new schools opened in Dublin between 2000 and 2019, fifty-four (77 %) opened under multi-denominational patronage.[51] Just over half of these schools were Educate Together schools, which means that 10 % of Dublin primary schools are now run by them. By contrast Educate Together operates only 3 % of primary schools nationally.

The data on school sizes is consistent with these figures as rural Kerry's schools are extremely small, with 57 % enrolling less than 100 pupils, well above the national average of 40 % for this size. By contrast, only 9 % of Dublin's schools and 39 % of Kildare's schools have less than 100 pupils, and nearly half of all schools in Dublin (48 %) can be considered large schools with more than 300 students. Thus, the issues facing Kerry's schools are different from those in Kildare and Dublin. The case studies will underscore how these demographic differences influence the realities that the Church must address in each type of area.

51 Figures provided to the authors by the Department of Education, 2020. The patronage of the schools opened were: 7 – ETBs; 10 An – Foras Pátrúnachta; 15 – Archdiocese of Dublin; 36 – Educate Together; 1 – Islamic Foundation of Ireland; and 1 – Scoil Sinead.

Table 10.3. Referenda results by county[a]

	National	Kerry	Kildare	Dublin
Same-Sex Marriage (2015)	62.07 %	55.38 %	67.92 %	71.06 %
Abortion (2018)	64.13 %	58.27 %	72.11 %	75.44 %

[a]Referendum Results, *The Irish Times.*

These rural, commuter and urban contexts also differ slightly in terms of their politics and votes in election and referenda. In these contexts, we see a similar continuum to the one that exists for key demographic factors. In general elections, the more urban the constituency, the more competitive it will tend to be. In other words, minor parties find greater levels of support among the urban electorate, whereas rural voters up until 2020 have generally and primarily supported candidates from Fianna Fáil, Fine Gael, and to a lesser extent Labour and an occasional Independent. Commuter regions lie somewhere in between; the three traditional parties remain strongest, but smaller parties experience episodic support.[52] Likewise in recent referenda on same-sex marriage and abortion, urban areas have been the most progressive and had the highest levels of support for change and the rural areas have been less supportive although still voted to pass both referenda (see Table 10.3).

71 % of Dublin residents voted in favour of passing the same-sex marriage referenda in 2015, compared to 68 % in Kildare, 62 % nationally and 55 % in Kerry. Similarly, 75 % of Dublin residents voted in favour of passing the abortion referenda in 2018, compared to 72 % in Kildare, 64 % nationally and 58 % in Kerry. These referenda figures reveal varied levels of attitudes towards the role of religion in Irish society and signal the potential support that may exist in these different regions for further secular policies to be enacted. Advocates of educational reform sought to build on the momentum of these referenda campaigns by mobilising increasing numbers of citizens to demand limits to the role of religion in Irish schools. The analysis in our cases studies examines to what extent the

52 McGraw, 2015.

Church responds differently across rural, commuter and urban contexts
based on these political trends in similar ways that Churches respond to
different demographic factors in these areas as well.

C. *Rural Ireland: Kerry's Response to Declining Population and
    Dwindling School Enrolments*

Kerry is a rural county in the southwest of Ireland known for its Irish-
speaking Gaeltacht communities, its attraction as a tourist destination
and a more traditional social outlook. The most significant challenge
Kerry faces is the declining population overall, which in turn poses a real
risk to the viability of its schools. As mentioned, most Kerry schools have
less than 100 pupils. These small schools are particularly vulnerable in
remote areas where a decrease in the child-bearing population, driven by
migration to urban centres for education and employment, has resulted
in student numbers falling to unsustainable levels, thus threatening their
ongoing survival.

    The threat of closing small, rural schools has elicited widespread fear
given the broader set of cutbacks rural Ireland has been experiencing in
recent years. Many small communities have seen local services reduced
significantly over the past decade with the closure of 160 local post offices
and nearly 140 rural Garda stations because of cost-cutting after the 2010
financial crisis.[53] While these services were, in the main, administrative
supports, the local post office is a highly valued social outlet for many in
rural Ireland. With their loss, many residents of rural Ireland now look
to the local GAA club, and school as the remaining pillars at the heart of
their communities. For small rural primary schools, the vast majority of
whom are Catholic, the challenge is clear – a declining student population
with many being attracted to larger schools in local towns. This was the

---

53   Garreth MacNamee, '"An Attack on Rural Ireland": Over 160 Post Offices to
     Close Nationwide', *theJournal.ie*, 2 August 2018 (<https://www.thejournal.ie/post-
     offices-closure-4161997-Aug2018/)>; Ralph Riegel, 'Flanagan rules out widespread
     re-opening of rural garda stations closed over past decade', *Irish Independent*, 16
     February 2019.

challenge that has faced several schools in Kerry in recent years. A brief view of how they have responded is illuminating in relation to the wider divestment debate.

Initial attempts to divest schools in Kerry were unsuccessful. There was national support for divestment from both the Department of Education and the Irish Catholic Bishops' Conference. However, the lack of clarity surrounding where the demand for change existed, how the process would be implemented and who would oversee the process doomed it from the outset. In 2010, the Department of Education identified ten areas nationally that might serve as pilots for the divestment of schools to a new multidenominational patron. For their part, the Irish bishops welcomed the pilot idea highlighting their long-held commitment to supporting a greater plurality of provision and stressing that 'the Catholic Church in Ireland does not see itself in the future as the sole or dominant provider of schools'.[54]

Killarney, a large tourist town at the gateway to the idyllic Ring of Kerry, seemed perfectly suited to be a pilot because it had twelve primary schools, all Catholic, within a 5-kilometre radius of the town. The pilot called for the local bishop, as patron, to cede the patronage of one of the twelve schools to a multi-denominational patron. The enthusiasm from the Department and the bishops was not mirrored on the ground in Killarney. One local priest, Fr Kevin McNamara, confirmed local frustration at the lack of consultation, an issue that would later become a feature of divestment efforts beyond Kerry. 'This has really just been thrown out there and there have been no meetings at all about it.'[55] His concerns were echoed by a local principal, who in the same local media drew attention to the failure to consult stakeholders in advance, 'We have received absolutely no information about how this would be carried out.'[56] No progress was made in the immediate aftermath of the announcement of the Killarney pilot. Part of the problem was that the local diocese lacked a cohesive approach. According to the Diocesan Secretary for Education, Fr George Hayes, the urgent often outweighs the important and developing a vision

---

54   'Church in Shift away from Schools Provision', *Irish Examiner*, 3 August 2010.
55   Kevin Hughes, 'Killarney School to Sever Ties with Catholic Church', *The Kerryman*, 11 August 2010.
56   Hughes, 2010.

for Catholic education in the region continually slips lower and lower on the agenda as more pressing issues predominate.[57]

Initial divestment was also undermined by the ongoing lack of clarity on parental demand. Additionally, there were significant difficulties purchasing land for non-Catholic schools. Three years after the initial floating of the pilot, a more comprehensive report on divestment was published by the Department of Education in 2013. The report, the result of surveys conducted with parents in thirty-eight towns and urban areas throughout Ireland, again highlighted Killarney as an area with clear 'viable demand' for greater choice of patronage. The report identified Educate Together as the patron favoured by parents surveyed and advised that 'the main patron (Catholic Bishop) should now be asked to consider re-configuration options that would provide accommodation for an Educate Together in the area.'[58] Educate Together was unable to procure a school facility over the proceeding four years despite much work with the community and Department of Education.[59]

Finally, in 2018, three of the eleven schools that have been divested in all of Ireland occurred in Kerry. Far from being inspired by deep ideological debates or as a response to provide greater variety of schools for a more diverse society, these cases of divestment were undertaken to save schools with low enrolments on the verge of closing. In each case, Bishop Ray Browne, the patron of these Catholic schools in Kerry, transferred the patronage to the local Kerry Education and Training Board (Kerry ETB). A significant appeal for local parents, communities and Bishop Browne was that the Community National School model would provide much needed resources to these deteriorating schools. The staff in Kerry ETB Head Office assumed control over finances, human resources and other administrative functions leading to a belief that 'this level of support enables

57   Fr George Hayes, Kerry Diocesan Secretary for Education, Personal Interview, October 2019.
58   *Report on the Surveys Regarding Parental Preferences*, 2013.
59   Educate Together, 'Educate Together on the Two Mile National School announcement: parents in Killarney Have Been Let Down', 12 June 2017. <https://www.educatetogether.ie/news/educate-together-on-the-two-mile-national-school-announcement-parents-in-killarney-have-been-let-down/>.

the schools and centres to focus their attention on the real work of teaching and learning.'[60] Unlike denominational primary schools with their private status, Community National Schools are State-operated and are therefore entitled to draw down a range of supports from the ETB not available to faith-based schools. This model of support to both school leaders and boards of management, coupled with the perceived increased access to State funding encouraged Bishop Browne and the local school communities to make this change in patronage.[61] Such supports, when matched with communities fearing the loss of a local school, offered a compelling proposition to help save schools with falling enrolment numbers according to Kerry ETB Director of Schools, Ann O'Dwyer.[62]

A brief review of the schools that divested underscores that the primary motivation for change was to keep these declining schools open. Two Mile School, also known as Cahooreigh National School, was located just outside Killarney. Student numbers had fallen to seventeen students in July 2016, which fuelled fears in the community that the school would not reopen in September for the start of the new school year. The school was one student shy of being allocated a second teacher and the concern was that as enrolment continued to contract, more parents would send their children elsewhere. Among those raising their concerns was the Cathaoirleach of the Killarney Area Municipal Authority, Brendan Cronin, who had formerly served as a board of management member of the school. Cllr. Cronin highlighted the deep tradition that small local schools have in communities like Cahooreigh,

> As someone with very strong links to the school, having been one of three generations of my own family to have attended as a pupil I am calling on the Department of Education not to take any drastic steps over its future.

60 Diocese of Kerry, 'Community National School in Killarney', June 2017, <https://www.dioceseofkerry.ie/2017/06/community-national-school-in-killarney/>.
61 Two years after reopening under the ETB Two Mile School had undergone a substantial refurbishment, which included the addition of a preschool on the site <https://www.radiokerry.ie/refurbishment-work-completed-two-mile-school/>.
62 'Kerry ETB to Open Third Community National School in Kerry', *radiokerry.ie*, 26 August 2019. <https://www.radiokerry.ie/kerry-education-training-board-open-third-community-national-school-kerry/>.

He cautioned the Department not to look solely at declining enrolment and encouraged the Department to recognise 'the impact of the decision on the broader community'.[63]

Councillor Cronin's fears were initially realised as Two Mile School did not reopen in September 2016. Nevertheless, Minister for Education Richard Bruton, TD, had recently initiated a new approach to increasing diversity of patrons called reconfiguration. This differed from the previous divestment approach in that the power to assign patronage of schools being handed over rested with the existing patron, namely the local bishop. It also sought 'live' handovers or schools that were currently operating, rather than merely a school building that most likely had been unused for some time. As part of this approach, the Department of Education approached the Bishop of Kerry in September 2016 with a request to transfer the school to another patron of his choosing under the reconfiguration process. Brendan Griffin, a local Fine Gael TD, organised a meeting in January 2017 between local citizens and officials from the Kerry ETB to explore the prospect of the school becoming a Community National School under the patronage of the Kerry ETB.[64] In March, seventy residents under the banner of Two Mile Community Group met to vote on their preferred future for the school. Their preference was for the school to become a Community National School and a request was made to Bishop Browne on foot of the vote. In June 2017, Minister Bruton announced that Two Mile School would open under a new patron, welcoming the decision by Bishop Browne to transfer patronage to Kerry ETB.[65]

Two Mile School reopened its doors in September 2017 to nine students as Kerry's first Community National School. Over the following two years, enrolment rose to twenty-six students, enough for the school to be staffed by two teachers, but well below the school's capacity of eighty

---

63   'Fears for Future of School over Dwindling Pupil Levels', *The Kerryman*, 2 July 2016.
64   'Kerry's First Community National School to Open in September', *Radio Kerry*, 13 June 2017. <https://www.radiokerry.ie/kerrys-first-community-national-school-open-september/>.
65   Dept. of Education, 'Two Mile National School to Open under New Patronage as Community National School in September', 12 June 2017. <https://www.education.ie/en/Press-Events/Press-Releases/2017-Press-Releases/PR17-06-12.html>.

students. While the reconfiguration process saved the school from complete closure, the level of interest in the option of a multi-denominational primary school in the Killarney area fell well short of that expressed in the 2013 survey. At that time, there were 110 first preferences expressed by parents for an English-language multi-denominational primary school.[66] Understanding this shortfall between expressed demand and actual demand for a multi-denominational school did not attract much media attention once the school was divested.

Unfortunately, even when surveys are conducted, this does not mean that it accurately reflects what parents want when given the actual choice. When new multi-denominational options become available, as the case studies demonstrate, parent choice for their school often goes well beyond selecting based on the religious ethos of the school. For some parents, they did not want to move their children out of their current schools. For other parents, uncertainty about the new patron's ethos or overall reputation caused them not to avail of the new option. According to the 2021 Genesis data discussed in Chapter 3, the top three reasons parents choose their child's school is driven by convenience of location, academic reputation and reputation for discipline.[67] Thus, ethos is often not the primary reason parents select a school for their child.

What was different this time around in the Two Mile School case given that there seemed to have been some demand for change years earlier? Bishop Browne emphasised that the outcome was fully in line with the wishes of the community, 'I welcome the reopening of the school under the patronage of Kerry ETB. I believe it offers a good prospect for its secure future, which is clearly the heartfelt desire of families in the local community.'[68] Educate Together disputed this claim, stating that this decision contradicted earlier 2013 surveys that had identified them as the favoured choice of parents in the Killarney area for a multi-denominational school. Educate Together criticised the State, claiming that 'the Government's reconfiguration plan lacked high standards of transparency and equality

66 *Report on the Surveys Regarding Parental Preferences*, 2013.
67 Genesis, *Articulating a new positioning for Catholic education in Ireland,* September 2021.
68 Diocese of Kerry, 2017.

in that all stakeholders were not fairly represented or consulted in the process'.[69] Despite Educate Together's claims, they were less successful in eliciting concrete plans to change. In contrast, what appears different when the Two Mile School finally divested is that concentrated efforts of one local community to save its school from closing helped mobilise politicians, church leaders and ultimately the State to act. Strong local interests appeared to predominate over national, ideological, or special interests once again, especially when they affected specific communities.

Two additional small schools in rural Kerry also faced growing fears about the ongoing viability of their local schools during the 2018/19 academic year. Situated in picturesque West Kerry in a more remote area than the Two Mile School, both schools had similarly low enrolments. Scoil an Ghleanna, a rural Irish-speaking school had fourteen students enrolled for August 2019, while Tahilla National School had only eight students enrolled for the upcoming school year.[70] The threat of closure encouraged both communities to explore options for increasing enrolment. Indeed, in the case of Scoil an Ghleanna, the idea of transferring patronage was first proposed in a suggestion box in the local church.[71] Public information meetings that included parents, local politicians and other interested individuals were conducted to explore alternative patronage options with the goal of helping the local community to make an informed decision.[72] Curiously, Kerry ETB was the only patron that was represented at these meetings, and its leaders emphasised that the Community National School model would provide a uniquely inclusive education that would be more representative of the community based on recent societal changes. This

69 Educate Together, 'Educate Together on the Two Mile National School Announcement: Parents in Killarney Have Been Let Down', 12 June 2017. <https://www.educatetogether.ie/news/educate-together-on-the-two-mile-national-school-announcement-parents-in-killarney-have-been-let-down/>.

70 O'Kelly, 27 August 2019.

71 'Four Primary Schools to Transfer to non-Denominational Model This Year', *RoscommonHerald.ie*, 27 August 2019. <https://roscommonherald.ie/2019/08/27/four-primary-schools-to-transfer-to-non-denominational-model-this-year/>.

72 'Meeting in Tahilla on Community School', *RadioKerry.ie*, 21 March 2019, (<https://www.radiokerry.ie/meeting-tahilla-community-school-march-21st-2019/>).

would involve some changes to curriculum, which the ETB continually highlighted to the community throughout the process.[73] Bishop Browne and Kerry ETB cited the community as the one driving the change.[74]

The short-term outcomes for both schools have been positive. Scoil an Ghleanna was able to retain its two-teacher status, thanks in no small part to the media coverage surrounding the transfer of patronage, and Tahilla National School saw its enrolment nearly double from eight to fifteen students for the start of the 2019/20 school year.[75] Given the novelty at the time of live schools transferring patronage, coupled with a fight for survival being at the heart of the endeavour, the schools garnered significant media attention both locally and nationally.

There is no doubt that staving off closure was a key motivating factor driving each of these divestment cases. Some local parents, however, did express interest in having their children gain a multi-denominational experience. In the case of Scoil an Ghleanna, one third of the students were non-Catholic before divestment and their parents were excited about changing to a multi-denominational ethos where their children would not be treated differently based on their faith. Even for Catholic parents, like Julianne McGillicuddy, it was important for her children to see people would not be excluded on religious grounds, 'We live in a multi-cultural society, it's really the way things should be going.'[76] Thus, even though saving their schools from closure was the dominant impetus for change, there was also some underlying desire for greater diversity that might also attract new families to join the school.

These practical concerns were central to the divestment process in these schools. They underscore the strength of local communities and their willingness to do whatever it takes to preserve their schools. This is especially relevant in small rural communities that are fighting for their survival on several fronts. These local interests have proven stronger than

---

73   'Meeting in Tahilla on Community School', 2019.
74   'Kerry ETB Takes over Two More Schools', 2019.
75   A new family to the area spotted coverage of the story on RTE News and enrolled their children in the school. <https://www.rte.ie/news/munster/2019/0901/1073201-kerry-school/>.
76   McCoy, 2019.

other ideological or national ideas about what is best in the educational sector. The bishops, not unlike elected politicians who often need to prioritise local concerns over national ones to ensure their ongoing support, can often be stifled by 'a fear of conflict at local level … and meeting resistance to divestment in communities'.[77] Such incentives undermine developing a strategic approach and lead to more reactive decision-making. Similar dynamics that unfolded in Kerry also occurred in other rural communities around Ireland during the same time. In most cases, Catholic schools were divested to the local Education and Training Board to prevent school closures.[78] Far from representing strategic and/or ideological choices, these examples highlight the driving force of local concerns at the heart of the divestment process.

One last factor that hinders greater numbers of schools from divesting is associated with the issue of property, which has hindered new patrons from assuming leadership in schools that otherwise may have transferred patronage. For example, there was one case in Kerry, where Educate Together worked for four years to assume patronage of Catholic school but it could not secure land or procure a school facility despite considerable work with the community and the Department of Education.[79] The lack of real change from divestment and the challenges facing new patrons in securing property and facilities may have been one of the reasons Richard Bruton, TD, Minister for Education and Skills (2016–18) transitioned from seeking divestment to instead pursuing reconfiguration. Whereas divestment refers to one patron handing over their land and facilities to a new patron, which became very legalistic and costly, reconfiguration refers to leasing land and facilities as an attempt to speed up the diversifying of primary school patrons. Additionally, in reconfiguration, a school could remain open and fully functioning with all the same staff and teachers while the patron and board of management is transferred, which is different from divestment where schools must close first before opening under a new patron.

---

77   Fr George Hayes, Personal Interview, October 2019.

78   At the same time as the three schools in Kerry were transferring patronage to become Community National Schools the same was happening in similar circumstances in counties Roscommon, Kildare, Louth, and Wexford.

79   Educate Together, 2017.

In this sense it was hoped reconfiguration, not divestment, would help the government achieve their goal of having 400 additional multi- and non-denominational primary schools by 2030. The Government, the argument goes, was not trying to assume ownership over property, but only trying to lease land and facilities from the Church on a twenty-four-year cycle to create more educational opportunities for students and families.[80] This shift in approach from divestment to reconfiguration may be the next big step for reformers to pursue to increase the speed of diversifying the primary school sector. Such an approach may also help reformers avoid having to challenge constitutional rights that can be difficult to alter.

D. Commuter Ireland: Kildare's Reflective and Consultative Process Lacks Scale and Impact

Kildare is a large county that encompasses both urban and rural elements, and it is among the most prominent new commuter regions bordering Dublin. Its population of just over 220,000 makes it a third larger than the more rural Kerry.[81] Between 2002 and 2007 alone, Kildare's population surged by 36 % and it has continued this expansionary trend, causing infrastructural shortages that stem from an inability to keep pace with economic growth. Commuter towns like Celbridge, Maynooth and Naas lie just over the border from Dublin and have experienced significant growth over the past twenty years with workers commuting daily for work, driven out of the city by either the spiralling housing prices that mark the capital, a desire to raise their families away from its busyness, or a mix of both. In 2016, Kildare had the highest percentage of young people 24 years old or younger in the country (37 %), and given that the county's population has not yet peaked, there is likely to be an increased demand for children and young people's services over the next decade.[82] In contrast to the declining rural population in Kerry, Kildare's

---

80   Seamus Conboy, Personal Interview, October 2019.
81   Central Statistics Office, 2016
82   *Kildare Local Economic and Community Plan 2016–2021*. <http://www.kildarelcdc. ie/wp-content/uploads/2016/01/Kildare-LECP-2016-2021.pdf>.

population has been radically transformed, with an influx of families with young children, many of whom did not grow up in Kildare.

The unusual combination of rural and urban characteristics creates different dynamics within the county. In the southern part of the county, the more rural landscape mirrors more closely the towns and villages of Kerry. This rural farmland dominates most of the county, standing in contrast to the urban sprawl and growing commuter belt on its eastern border. The more rural areas tend to have higher percentages identifying as Catholic and holding more conservative views on moral issues, whereas the newer, commuter areas have experienced an influx of families with evolving identities and interests. This mix has led to a more varied profile of primary school patrons than in Kerry, as 82 % of primary schools are Catholic, which is below the national average of 89 %. In recent years, many new schools have opened in the commuter belt region, built to serve the increasing school-going population there. These schools have largely been opened under the patronage of Educate Together, An Foras Patrúnachta (Irish-language schools) and Community National Schools.

Unlike Kerry, where greater diversity of provision has been driven by divestment of small rural schools at risk of closure, the changing patronage profile in Kildare has been facilitated mainly through the opening of new schools under multi-denominational patronage. In the nine years from 2011 and 2019, five new schools were opened and only one school was divested from its Catholic patronage to the local ETB.[83] The sole divested school, Brannoxtown National School, followed a trajectory to divestment like the three schools in Kerry. Falling numbers saw the small rural school reduced to one teacher and just one family enrolled for the 2017/18 school year.[84] After a concerted effort by locals to save the school, and with the agreement of the patron, the Archbishop of Dublin who serves as patron of schools on the Kildare/Dublin border, the school transferred patronage

---

83   Data provided to the authors by the Dept. of Education (2019)
84   Patrick Ward, 'Meeting to be Held over Future of Brannoxtown NS as They Receive Positive News', *KildareNow.com,* 13 April 2018. <https://www.kildarenow. com/news/news/405828/meeting-to-be-held-over-future-of-brannoxtown-ns-as-they-receive-positive-news.html>.

to Kildare and Meath Education and Training Board and reopened in August 2018 as a Community National School.

The lack of school divestments in Kildare with its higher number of schools appears driven by the lower percentage of small schools in the county. Additionally, many families have settled in rural areas to raise their families while commuting to urban centres like Dublin and the towns in the commuter belt, thus maintaining enrolment levels in small two- and three-teacher schools, the type that are less viable in more rural Kerry. Therefore, Bishop Denis Nulty of Kildare and Leighlin, the patron of most Catholic schools in the county, has not had to deal with a deteriorating enrolment landscape like in Kerry because his small schools remain viable.

The growth and shifts in population have placed considerable pressure on the State and local patrons to adapt to these rapidly evolving demographics by providing adequate numbers and types of school placements that parents are demanding. Curiously, however, the lack of sufficient planning and coordination among the various actors to meet these changing needs stunted any real progress on divestment. A survey conducted by the Department of Education in 2013 identified eight Catholic schools in the Diocese of Kildare and Leighlin that were good candidates for divestment. In 2018, local ETBs were asked by the Department of Education and Skills to conduct surveys as part of the 'Schools Reconfiguration for Diversity' process. One such survey in the Diocese of Kildare and Leighlin identified an area in which there were eight primary schools and where 24 % of responding parents of preschool children in the area reported that they would choose multi- or non-denominational education for their child if it were available. Despite this parental demand in the area, there was not much thought given to how their needs could be met. According to Maeve Mahon, Coordinator for Primary Education in the Diocese of Kildare and Leighlin, the selection of these schools in relation to the closest largest centre of population made little sense to local communities. It was unlikely that parents in one area would ever drive to schools in other areas of the diocese, thus undermining the feasibility of the proposed changes. Due to concerns over the shortcomings of both the process and the data, and following consultation with the key stakeholders in the area, the Diocese chose not to divest any of their schools.[85]

The Diocese of Kildare and Leighlin did, however, devise several solutions they believed would increase the diversity of primary school patrons in Kildare as well as enhance the ability of their Catholic schools to fulfil their ethos more authentically. Their first proposal was to amalgamate, or combine, two schools serving the same community to free up a newly vacated school building for a multi-denominational school. For example, two single-sex Catholic schools, one serving boys and one serving girls, could combine to form a new co-educational Catholic school. Again, this would provide an operational school building and site to a new multi-denominational school. This could greatly facilitate patrons seeking to open schools because it would be much easier and cost-effective to move into existing spaces rather than starting a school from scratch, which can be very costly in terms of securing land and erecting the buildings. According to Mahon, the Church could easily amalgamate more schools over the next five to ten years with the appropriate support being given to schools and local communities in preparation for this reality. Such proposals have not amounted to anything thus far. Frustrated local Church leaders have lamented the lack of structures or personnel within the Department of Education dedicated to this issue. There are dedicated personnel for class sizes, staffing, buildings, planning, etc., but there is no assistance for those areas seeking to increase provision through amalgamations or reconfigurations. Mahon believes that combining schools could be an important aspect of educational reform and the advancement of educational pluralism, but for it to be successful the Department of Education would need to incentivise and support Catholic patrons to pursue the process.[86]

The Diocese of Kildare and Leighlin has developed a highly intensive consultative process to help local communities and schools discern whether they wish to develop truly Catholic schools. Bishop Nulty is a firm believer that if divestment is ever going to work, each patron must develop

---

85   Maeve Mahon, Coordinator for Primary Education, Kildare & Leighlin, Personal
        Interview, October 2019.
86   Maeve Mahon, Personal Interview, October 2019.

their own unique ethos and have the freedom and autonomy to deliver it in their respective schools. Bishop Nulty lauds the existing pluralism in large towns in the county like Naas, 'where there is already a huge choice of patronage and that's to be welcomed'.[87] Yet, for real choice to be offered to parents, Bishop Nulty believes what is needed are real Catholic schools 'rather than simply a list of Catholic schools. Schools that are intentionally and culturally Catholic'. He points out that real pluralism does not currently exist because most the schools in the area are teaching in similar ways irrespective of their official ethos – which undermines real choice. The Bishop is 'amazed at how smoothly teachers move from one teaching sector to another, often seamlessly, one week in St. Mark's down the road, the next week in Educate Together a few kilometres away'.[88]

Bishop Nulty's team in Kildare and Leighlin developed a strategic process to help schools determine whether they wish to be truly Catholic or whether they could transition towards a different patronage model. Educational leaders, including Mahon and her colleague Bryan O'Reilly, the Patrons Secretary for Primary Schools in the Diocese, developed this thorough consultative process to engage the major stakeholders involved in Catholic schools in the diocese. The initial pilot programme was designed to include input from parishes and pastoral councils, boards of management, teachers and staffs of schools and broader groups of individuals from the local community. Each group was invited to share views on their values and preferences towards Catholic schools and other school models. To kickstart the process, the diocesan team first engaged parishes in areas where potential for change exists. If sufficient interest was expressed within a parish, the diocese facilitated various listening sessions with boards of management and then school staff, and then finally parents and the community. The educational leaders then helped the parish council and board

87   Bishop Denis Nulty, 'Bishop Denis Launches Catholic Schools Week', *Kildare & Leighlin Diocese*, 28 January 2019. <https://www.kandle.ie/bishop-denis-launches-catholic-schools-week/>.
88   Bishop Denis Nulty, 'Homily of Bishop Denis at Mass with Teachers and ACE Ireland', 11 September 2018. <https://www.kandle.ie/homily-of-bishop-denis-celebrates-mass-with-teachers-and-ace-ireland/>.

of management to review the feedback and findings and consider whether
to recommend divestment to the Bishop.

The short-term goal of these multiple rounds of meetings and focus
groups was to determine whether there was sufficient demand for intentionally Catholic schools. In the past, there was no need to articulate what a
'Catholic school' was because virtually all schools were Catholic, and their
identity was not in question. Given the scope and degree of change, what it
means to be Catholic is highly uncertain. The Kildare and Leighlin diocesan
educational leaders know what they hope an authentic school would look
like, but if there was no appetite for such a school in the local community,
they will seek to help local school communities find alternative patronage.
For O'Reilly, this process is also an important way to teach people that the
Church and its schools are not fundamentally concerned about power,
control and manipulation as they have often been characterised by critics
in recent years. Instead, O'Reilly argues that authentic Catholic schools
seek to introduce students to the person of Jesus and to a life of faith as they
develop holistically. The pilot programme provided diocesan leaders with
data and insights, which they, in turn, hope to employ to direct teachers,
students and families towards the schools that best match their values.[89]

The goal to help local communities and the overall educational system
by offering more authentic and diverse models for students, families and
teachers alike is certainly laudable. Yet, the scope and degree of mismatch
between demand for different models and what can realistically be offered
given limited resources is daunting. To figure out how to identify local
concerns and then be able to address and help the varied interests is difficult – and it is nearly impossible to please everyone. There are examples
in Kerry and in the Dublin Archdiocese where divestments occurred, the
staff supported the shift in patronage from being a Catholic school to becoming Community National Schools. Additionally, there was also considerable effort exerted to facilitate those teachers who preferred to remain in
a Catholic school by finding them another placement.[90] Yet, what should

---

89   Bryan O'Reilly, Patron's Secretary for Primary Schools, Kildare & Leighlin,
      Personal Interview, October 2019.
90   Bryan O'Reilly, Personal Interview, October 2019.

be done if a school community decided to remain Catholic, how would leaders find ways to allow teachers and staff who desire a more secular or multi-denominational school to find such a placement? An even greater challenge would arise if a mismatch developed between what teachers and staff desired and what many parents or members of a local community demanded. For example, in the case where many staff preferred to be a Catholic school and most parents do not want this, would the staff be given the choice to teach in a more secular and non-Catholic way because that is what the local community wants or move to a Catholic school.

There is no clear path for what to do in such cases, and it is also unclear how easily such shifts in ethos or placements could be made. There are endless possibilities because you could have different types and intensity of preferences at the various levels of parish and pastoral council, the staff and teachers, the board of management, parents and the local community – not to mention the desires of local priests or religious communities. In one local Kildare and Leighlin school, most of the staff expressed a significant measure of ambivalence about being an intentional Catholic school through the conversations in the consultation. Nevertheless, the school's founding religious community advocated for the school to remain Catholic.[91] This example underscores the almost infinite number of possibilities that emerged from the initial pilot programme. These consultations were designed to precisely reveal these types of scenarios and, in the process, to help local communities make informed decisions about their schools.

Unfortunately, this highly inclusive, consultative process drained already limited financial and personnel resources and has had limited impact to date. As of 2021, the process had only been completed in six schools, with none of the schools having been divested to date. The lack of a clear understanding of what change might look like was a hurdle to such progress. According to O'Reilly, until an alternative such as Educate Together or a Community National School is clearly explained in local areas, sufficient demand for change is unlikely.[92]

91 Bryan O'Reilly, Personal Interview, October 2019.
92 Bryan O'Reilly, Personal Interview, October 2019.

The Diocese of Kildare and Leighlin plans to apply lessons from this pilot experience and to identify additional parishes where the conditions are appropriate to initiate the process. However, diocesan leaders underscore the lack of resources and personnel to apply to conducting this process properly. Nevertheless, Kildare and Leighlin is one of the few, if not the only Catholic diocese, that has sought to approach the issue of divestment strategically by designating a person to examine the issue and developing a concrete plan and process to engage it. The lack of results in a place that has developed such a thoughtful and engaging process does not bode well for the broader divestment process.

Although it is easy to criticise the Church for its lack of action on implementing divestment – and divestment is something that all religious, political and civil society leaders want to see happen – to blame the Church appears overly simplistic. Unless greater coordination, planning and implementation occurs among the various patrons and the Department of Education, even the best plans and processes will not lead to significant change as the case of Kildare demonstrates. The lack of accountability and proper incentives to facilitate divestment on a greater scale mean that parents, local schools and communities and patrons will continue to operate independently of one another, and the prospects of large-scale change in the system are improbable.

E. Urban Ireland: Dublin's National Aspirations Give Way to Local Interests

Dublin, Ireland's capital city, has changed dramatically since the 1990s due to the Celtic Tiger economic boom. Physically, the city stretched upwards and outwards, with large apartment and office buildings appearing across Dublin to meet the demands of tech multinationals like Google, Facebook and Twitter that established European bases in an area that has been labelled the Silicon Docks. Whole new suburbs like Ongar, Citywest and Clongriffin, sprang up close to the M50 motorway, the radial route that snakes around the city from north to south. Along with this physical transformation, the demographic profile of the city was also transformed with an influx of migrants from Europe and further afield, attracted by well-paying job opportunities and an English-speaking population with a reputation for a warm welcome. The city has almost doubled from under 1 million residents in 1995 to Dublin and its suburbs passing 1.7 million residents in 2016.[93]

As Ireland's cosmopolitan hub, Dublin's inhabitants are religiously less active, politically more progressive and ethnically more diverse (see Tables 10.1, 10.2 and 10.3 in Section B). The dynamic growth of the Dublin population in recent decades, with its more diverse religious make-up, has had an impact on the patronage landscape in the county. Catholic primary schools, under the patronage of the Archbishop of Dublin Dermot Farrell, represent 77 % of all schools. This is well below the national average of 89 % and the lowest percentage of Catholic schools in any county in Ireland. Notwithstanding, the Archbishop is still patron of the largest number of primary schools nationwide, with 350 mainstream primary schools across Dublin (and an additional forty special primary schools).[94]

As mentioned previously, the growth of multi-denominational provision in Dublin has been driven almost exclusively by a surge in new schools, opened to meet the growing population in recent decades. Between 2000 and 2019, fifty-four of the seventy new schools (77 %) that opened in the county were multi-denominational schools.[95] Dublin also has very few small schools, and therefore there are few schools in the Archdiocese that have sought to divest their school patronage to prevent the school from closing.

As the divestment debates gained steam in the mid-2000s, Dublin was identified as the most probable place where divestment would happen so schools could keep pace with the rapid social changes and shifting parental demand for non-Catholic alternatives. It was Dublin where the highest percentage of minority and non-religious students resided, and it was also the place with the lowest percentage of those identifying as Catholic.

---

93   <https://population.un.org/wpp/>
94   Dept. of Education, 2019. <https://www.education.ie/en/Publications/Statistics/ Data-on-Individual-Schools/Data-on-Individual-Schools.html>.   Special schools are those that provide an education for children with a special educational need or disability.
95   Figures provided to the authors by the Department of Education, 2020.

Additionally, Dublin was the epicentre for ideological reformers and advocacy groups seeking change. As mentioned, former Catholic Archbishop Diarmuid Martin of Dublin was an early and ardent advocate of change, proclaiming his preference to reduce the Catholic Church's patronage of primary schools from 90 % to 50 %. Martin consistently talked about divestment as a useful means of rebalancing an untenable 'monopoly' that he called 'a historical hangover that doesn't reflect the realities of the times'. He also regularly echoed Bishop Denis Nulty's later view that the lack of diversity of provision 'was detrimental to the possibility of maintaining a true Catholic identity in Catholic schools'.[96] Despite these key demographic realities and combination of actors demanding increased divestment, little to no progress ensued. A brief analysis of recent developments in Dublin underscores how underlying social, political and cultural factors combined to help local interests overshadow and dominate these national and ideological calls for increased divestment of Catholic schools.

Although the Archdiocese was supportive of divestment, and even initiated early conversations with State officials, the then Minister for Education, Mary Coughlin, TD, confirmed in 2010 that the Department was assuming responsibility for identifying areas where demand would warrant divestment.[97] According to Monsignor Dan O'Connor, the Archdiocese of Dublin's Episcopal Vicar for Education, archdiocesan educational leaders have had, and continue to have, regular and constructive conversations with designated officials within the Department of Education about divestment since 2010.[98] Again, despite these conversations, little progress was made. One of the key challenges was determining true parental and community demand. There was no question that there were growing numbers of parents who desired a non-denominational school experience, but these parents were not always concentrated in the same areas, which made it hard for political and church leaders to make concrete changes

96   Genevieve Carberry, 'Catholic Control of Schooling not Tenable, Says Archbishop', *The Irish Times*, 17 June 2009.
97   <https://www.oireachtas.ie/en/debates/debate/dail/2010-05-20/9/>
98   Monsignor Dan O'Connor, Episcopal Vicar for Education, Archdiocese of Dublin, Personal Interview, July 2020.

that would honour parental demand but not disrupt local communities that were often opposed to any change.

By 2020, Departmental and Church officials had identified as many as twenty areas that were good candidates to divest schools from Catholic patronage to a multi-denominational patron. The glacial pace of gathering and processing information, let alone making any concrete proposals for change reveals the weakness in the overall process. The inability of the Department of Education, the Archdiocese, other patrons and local schools and communities to coordinate their efforts to produce a transparent, accountable and useful outcome was in high relief in the Portmarnock/Malahide area in north County Dublin. This area had been one of the first areas identified by the Department of Education through the 2013 survey process as a place that was ready to divest schools. Local developments in 2018 and 2019 exemplify the intense, contentious and highly disputed actions of the various stakeholders. These events also highlight the lack of a coherent process, presumably led by the State, to produce timely results.

In 2018, the local Education and Training Board conducted a survey in Portmarnock/Malahide to determine parental and community interest in divestment. Though the Department never published the results of the 2018 survey, they stated that there were 'indications of a movement for change'.[99] Over a quarter of the preschool parents in the area apparently expressed a preference for a multi-denominational school, while only 3% of the school places in the area were in a multi-denominational primary school.[100] Some disputed the numbers being batted around and argued that the original process for identifying the demand for more school choices was deeply flawed. Not only was there was a low response rate, but parents who did not send their children to preschools felt excluded.[101] Despite the uncertain, unpublished and disputed levels of parental demand for change,

---

99   Emma O'Kelly, 'Row over School Patronage after Claims Religious Holidays Will not be Marked', *RTE.ie,* 2 April 2019. <https://www.rte.ie/news/education/2019/0402/1040149-school-patronage/>.

100   Carl O'Brien, 'Removing School's Catholic Ethos Would Be "Brexit-type Disaster", Parents Told', *The Irish Times,* 2 April 2019.

101   Breda O'Brien, 'Divestment of Schools Requires More to Be Built', *The Irish Times,* 6 April 2019.

Department officials asked Archdiocesan educational leaders to conduct consultations in the area to help facilitate next steps and these leaders complied. Church educational leaders then met with local priests, boards of management, principals and parents to understand their concerns.[102] There are conflicting reports of how things unfolded from here, but there were intense propaganda wars among the different vested interests and affected individuals in the local community.

For many parents, the first information they heard of the divestment process was when they received letters from their schools informing them of an upcoming vote on the future patronage of their school. There was significant media buzz surrounding the content and tone of letters from four schools. Letters from Scoil Naomh Mearnóg (also known as St Marnock's), Scoil an Duinnínigh, St Oliver Plunkett's School and St Sylvester's School warned parents that if their schools were divested to a multi-denominational patron there would be no celebrations of St Patrick's Day and Easter, and Christmas standards like nativities and carol services would also be discontinued. Issues of a more secular nature were also raised as cause for concern by the schools. These included who would control parental fundraising, the lack of uniforms compromising student safety on school tours, grandparents no longer being permitted to be involved in the school and concerns that children from these schools might eventually have difficulty accessing the secondary schools in the area.[103] Additional, emotionally charged language called such moves a possible 'Brexit-type disaster'! St Sylvester's, the last school to send out letters, argued that the standard of education may drop at the school, that there would be unsafe practices for children, and that teacher contracts would be threatened.[104] The source of the letters varied from school to school, emanating from the principal, board of management, or the parent's association.

102   Monsignor Dan O'Connor, Personal Interview, July 2020.
103   Carl O'Brien, 'Pupils in Divested Schools "Will not Be Prevented" from Celebrating Christmas', *The Irish Times*, 2 April 2019.
104   Emma O'Kelly, 'Third Dublin School Sends Letter Warning of Consequences over Changing Patronage', *RTE.ie*, 3 April 2019. <https://www.rte.ie/news/2019/0403/1040323-school_patronage/>.

Minister of Education Joe McHugh, TD, posted a message on Facebook and Twitter directed at the parents, grandparents and school communities:

> A considerable amount of inaccurate information is being shared about what will happen if a school changes patron. These assertions have not been helpful. They are also creating fear and uncertainty. School authorities have a duty to share accurate and appropriate information as well as assuring them that celebrations such as Christmas, Easter and St. Patrick's would not be banned as had been asserted.[105]

Educate Together and the local Education and Training Board, the two patrons most likely to assume patronage of any divested school, also refuted these grossly unfounded claims by some local schools. They explained the importance of religious and cultural celebrations in multidenominational settings and underscored that all references to God would still be acceptable in schools because they 'don't deny God or religion, they embrace all faiths'.[106] Educate Together described all the claims made by the schools, especially accusations of unsafe practices, lower educational standards and concerns about teachers' rights, as incorrect, grossly misleading and categorically untrue, calling them 'nonsense' on Twitter.[107] In addition to the complaints by Educate Together and ETBs, some parents who were interested in increasing the diversity of schools in the area were also upset with the claims made by the schools. They felt it was a coordinated campaign to incite fear, uncertainty and doubt to halt divestment while drowning out their voices and wishes.[108] Despite

---

105   Joe McHugh, TD Delivering for Donegal. 'A Short Message for Parents, Grandparents and School Communities Where a Possible Change of Patron Is Being Assessed'. Facebook, 3 April 2019.

106   O'Kelly, 2 April 2019; 'Clarification on Educate Together's Equality-Based Ethos'. Educate Together, 7 November 2019. <https://www.educatetogether.ie/news/ethos-clarification/>; 'Another Day, Another Clarification Statement from Educate Together'. Educate Together, 3 May 2019. <https://www.educatetogether.ie/news/another-day-another-clarification/>; Sarah Caden, 'Christmas Is Safe … and so Is the Future of Our Schools'. *Irish Independent*. Independent.ie, 6 April 2019.

107   See Educate Together's 'Clarification' and 'Another Day' statements; Kelly, 6 April 2019.

108   O'Brien, 2 April 2019; O'Kelly, 3 April 2019.

these refutations, the school letters and subsequent media coverage raised fears and uncertainty amongst parents about the potential impact of divestment.[109]

Although many of the claims made by some local schools could be dismissed outright, the divestment process clearly had several problems that required further consideration. For one, many parents suggested that the need for change had not been explained or justified by the Department of Education. Additionally, parents suggested that neither they nor their schools had been able to get their questions answered by either the Department of Education or the Archdiocese.[110] Within days of the issue flaring up, Minister McHugh announced a review of the process for divesting schools in light of the concerns raised around the Portmarnock/Malahide process.[111] The following day the Archdiocese announced that it would postpone plans to hold a vote with parents in the area on divestment options following 'confusion and misinformation' over the implications for pupils.[112] The Archdiocese also publicly reminded the local communities that they were 'committed to working with the Minister for Education and his officials, along with other Patron bodies, in providing choice for parents and teachers in the education of our young people'.[113] The plan was to postpone the entire process until the Department of Education had officially published the results of the survey of the preschool families, which was set for the end of June 2019, but was never published.[114]

In hindsight, there were several additional weaknesses to the process. First, the survey conducted by the local ETB apparently was not circulated to large numbers. As part of local consultations, Monsignor Dan O'Connor,

109   Katherine Donnelly, 'Schools Should Not Be "Setting a Bad Example"', *Irish Independent,* 4 April 2019.
110   O'Kelly, 2019.
111   Carl O'Brien, 'McHugh to Review Process for Selecting Schools for Divestment', *The Irish Times*, 4 April 2019.
112   Carl O'Brien, 'Dublin School Patronage Vote Suspended over "Misinformation"', *The Irish Times,* 5 April 2019.
113   Monsignor Dan O'Connor, Personal Interview, August 2020.
114   Katherine Donnelly, 'Catholic Primary School Handover Put on Ice after Row over Wildly Inaccurate Claims', *Irish Independent*. Independent.ie, 5 April 2019.

Episcopal Vicar for Education for the Archdiocese of Dublin, reported that 'I found to my horror that nobody, no parent of the three hundred parents at that meeting, had been consulted by the Education Training Board'. In addition to the low sample size, O'Connor stated that several local school leaders in the Portmarnock/Malahide area reported that they had not been consulted either.[115] Second, local school leaders and parents reiterated concerns about the lack of communication from the Archdiocese and the Department of Education throughout the process. According to one local principal, Lorna Lavin of St Helen's Junior National School,

> I would say that we weren't given an upfront engagement, we weren't communicated with very clearly from our own Archdiocese or from the Department. So, it was very much hearing it, not in a very clear way, but hearing the rumours … so, I do think it was unfortunate that schools themselves, stakeholders, weren't informed more.[116]

For Lavin, divestment itself is already controversial, but the lack of transparency about the surveys and other aspects of the process exacerbated the situation. Lavin concluded that people were generally pleased with their schools and demand for change may have been overstated slightly. 'Whilst things have changed and there have been lots of changes in society over the last few years, I do feel that the majority are satisfied with the way that things are.'[117]

Unfortunately, the inadequate process allowed conversations to be dictated by scaremongering and rumours, rather than addressing legitimate concerns. For example, there was real concern among school leaders and teachers about their contracts and to whom they would ultimately report. According to Monsignor O'Connor, several teachers expressed the concern that 'I signed on to teach in a Catholic school under the Catholic Archbishop of Dublin and I don't want that to change'.[118]

As coverage of the issue receded, commentators questioned whether it was possible to divest larger schools that were assured of their future, unlike

---

115 Monsignor Dan O'Connor, Personal Interview, Personal Interview, July 2020.
116 Lorna Lavin, Principal of St Helen's Junior National School, Personal Interview, July 2020.
117 Lorna Lavin, Personal Interview, July 2020.
118 Monsignor Dan O'Connor, Personal Interview, July 2020.

the more rural schools, for whom their ongoing viability was in question.[119] Ultimately, all the schools in the Portmarnock/Malahide area have retained their patronage under the Archdiocese. Thus, despite a public willingness on the part of the Archdiocese and the Department of Education to advance the conversation at the community level, several factors conspired to derail the efforts in north Dublin. Issues around communication and timely consultation, transparency about the process guiding the identification of areas deemed suitable for divestment and the enduring fear of change and comfort with the status quo all exerted influence over the failure of the process.

Although public scrutiny and debate waned, several issues continued to be discussed. Archbishop Diarmuid Martin of Dublin warned that there was a danger of a new polarisation forming between religious and non-religious schools if they refused to learn what is good about each other.[120] Educate Together urged the Department to learn from this experience to prevent similar issues from arising when proceeding with the divestment process in more areas. They emphasised that 'parental demand should be paramount in driving the process for change' and called on the Department of Education to 'be aware of its responsibility to provide parents and the general public with accurate information about all school models'.[121] Additionally, commentators also questioned whether it was possible to use the reconfiguration, or 'live' model to divest schools that were so large and assured of their future, which were very different than many of the primary schools that were divested previously.[122]

119   Emma O'Kelly, 'The Year Students Marched for Their Future', *RTE.ie,* 24 December 2019. <https://www.rte.ie/news/2019-in-review/2019/1220/1102376-the-year-students-marched-for-their-future-2019/>.

120   Sarah MacDonald, 'Archbishop Warns against "New Polarisation" between Schools with Different Ethos', *Irish Independent*. Independent.ie, 15 April 2019.

121   'Educate Together Looks Forward to Delivering a National Network of Equality-Based Schools in Line with Proven Parental Demand', Educate Together, 2 July 2019. <https://www.educatetogether.ie/news/reconfiguration-surveys-2019/>.

122   Emma O'Kelly, 'Actions of Three Tiny Schools Will Interest Parents'. RTE. RTÉ, 27 August 2019. <https://www.rte.ie/news/ireland/2019/0827/1071113-school-patronage-change/>; O'Kelly, 24 December 2019.

In the end, the lack of clarity related to virtually every aspect of this process doomed it to failure and underscored the severe limitations of the divestment process. Establishing sufficient parental and community demand for different school patrons is essential, but it is unclear who should conduct these surveys, who all should be surveyed, and how the results should be shared. The lack of a clearly defined consultation process is also a critical weakness of the divestment process. Although the State would be an obvious candidate to lead the process, the Department has not taken the lead in the process or clarified its own perspective, let alone how other major actors should be included. Questions from among leaders of the Catholic Church and the multi-denominational patrons (Educate Together, Community National Schools and An Foras Pátrúnachta) about the State's leadership and goals further undermine the process. The process for conducting a 'vote' has also been woefully undetermined. Who gets a vote, how is a vote conducted, are non-school groups permitted to influence the views of those voting, what is the role of elected officials, etc., are merely a few of the unanswered questions that undermined the effectiveness of this divestment process in areas where there were significant differences of opinion on the best path of reform.

The lack of consensus and enkindling of further divisiveness underscore why divestment has been the least successful aspect of the overall reform of Ireland's primary school sector. There has not been a strong, consistent and explicit move to create large numbers of multi-denominational schools to cater to a new Ireland with diverse religious beliefs. This is not to say there is not demand for additional primary school patrons at the national or ideological level, but it is much more difficult to implement reform on the ground in local communities where such demand is dispersed and where any change from the status quo is difficult. Consequently, the few schools that did divest patronage changed hands for practical reasons, often related to declining enrolment numbers or bad school management. This may also explain why educational reformers moved on from divestment to seek change via admissions policies and curricular requirements.

Given Archbishop Martin's leading role in proposing the notion of divestment and the Archdiocese's status as the patron with the largest number of schools in the country, it is surprising perhaps that only one County

Dublin school has been divested to date. In that instance, the divestment was because of falling pupil numbers in the Greenhills area where a boy's school and a girl's school amalgamated, resulting in a building becoming available for Educate Together to open a school.[123] Since the Portmarnock/ Malahide experience, the Archdiocese does not appear to have actively pursued any further divestments of 'live' schools in Dublin.

Curiously, Archbishop Martin identified similar factors that undermined divestment – not all of them the Church's fault. First, he criticised local politicians for 'throwing spanners in the works' with calls for more consultation, which included more voices, but just stalled any practical steps towards divestment. Second, Martin also blamed leaders of religious communities, who he argued were 'fixated on questions of ownership and management', which was causing a 'stubborn reluctance' within the Church to let go of control of schools through the divestment process.[124] He was clearly frustrated by those within the Church who in his mind were more concerned about maintaining institutions for the sake of it rather than relinquishing schools. Again, he believed this dramatic reduction approach would create greater diversity and allow Catholic schools to be more authentically Catholic. Finally, ten years on from first raising the issue of divestment and with just one Catholic school divested in County Dublin, Archbishop Martin shared his view that there was not in fact demand for divestment on the ground. While acknowledging that the issue was a 'lively one', he shared his sense that people are not demanding divestment because they are happy with their local school, 'I'm not too sure on doorsteps that many people are asking for it, because if people are happy with their school, they are happy with their school'[125] Martin's experience and evolution of thought are quite indicative of broader realities within Irish society and the Church. In particular, the ability of local and vested

123   <https://www.education.ie/en/Press-Events/Press-Releases/2016-Press-Releases/ PR2016-27-06-1.html>
124   Christina Finn, 'Archbishop Says CHURCH Stubbornly Reluctant to Let Go of the Control of Schools', *TheJournal.ie*, 10 July 2017. <https://www.thejournal.ie/ archbishop-of-dublin-diarmuid-martin-3487927-Jul2017/>.
125   Patsy McGarry, 'Minister Accused of "spin" over School Places for Autistic Children', *The Irish Times*, 26 August 2019.

interests to defend their turf from strong ideas and calls for change continue to determine outcomes within Ireland.

VI. Concluding Thoughts on Divestment Cases and Geographic Variation

The desire to greatly expand the diversity of primary school patronage by reducing the number of Catholic schools and increasing the number of multi-denominational schools has not produced significant change. The mixture of opening new, multi-denominational schools in areas where population has either grown or shifted, and divesting schools in areas with stable or declining populations, has had limited impact on the overall numbers. In Dublin, one of the fastest growing populations, the predominant approach has been to open new multi-denominational schools. Since 2011, all thirty new schools were multi-denominational, which is a dramatic shift from the previous decade where nearly 40 % of new schools in Dublin were Catholic. In Kildare, all six of the new schools have also been multi-denominational schools. The five newly built schools were established in the growing commuter belt, whereas the one divested school was in an area of more stable population – a trend that is likely to continue.

Opening new multi-denominational schools in areas of stable or declining populations is untenable because there is not a need for additional school placements. Any new schools in these areas would be built to offer additional choice, versus meeting population needs, and therefore may not be politically or economically palatable. Therefore, increasing the provision of multi-denominational schools in areas of stable or declining population such as Kerry will depend heavily on the ability of the various actors to implement a meaningful programme of divestment. This may explain why three of the eleven divested schools nationally occurred in Kerry.

Recent data from the Department of Education indicates that the primary school-going population has peaked at an all-time high and is expected to drop by 24 % nationally over the next fifteen years.[126] It is projected that Dublin will experience a 28 % drop in enrolments, with the Cork–Kerry region projected to have a drop of 29 %. Such shifts in the projected school-going population points to a decreasing need for the establishment of new schools and may in fact call in to question the viability of existing smaller schools, the majority of which are Catholic. In this way, school closures, rather than divestment, may be the key driver in the rebalancing of the patronage landscape.

In the end, the fact that the few schools that have transferred their patronage are small, and often failing schools, underscores the significant limitations of the divestment process as a legitimate solution to the lack of diversity within the primary sector. Perhaps divestment is only possible when a school is in danger of closing. Even then, when schools with small enrolments are divested, it only provides further options for a small number of children, while real change will only happen if large Catholic schools in highly populated areas are divested.[127] The stark contrast between the process that occurred with successfully divested schools and the issues that arose in northern Dublin when there was an attempt to start the process of divesting a school at the same time, reinforces the idea that successful transfers may only be possible when the local community is motivated by a fear of losing their school. This raises doubt over whether it will be possible to achieve broader, more impactful changes that would affect the education of many children in highly populated areas through divestment.[128] Additionally, that most of the divested schools were more interested in using the multi-denominational model to attract more families rather than any focus on the values inherent in the multi-denominational model itself suggests that even when the schools change hands, dramatic change in terms of numbers or even the overall experience of the school

126   *Projections of Full-time Enrolment, Primary and Secondary 2020–2038*, Dept. of Education and Skills, November 2020. Available at: <www.education.ie>.

127   O'Kelly, 27 August 2019.

128   O'Kelly, 27 August 2019; 'Changing School Patronage: Pragmatism in Action Not Secularism'. *Irish Examiner*, 27 August 2019. <https://www.irishexaminer.com/breakingnews/views/ourview/changing-school-patronage-pragmatism-in-action-not-secularism-946569.html>; O'Kelly, 24 December 2019.

ethos often does not occur.[129] Nevertheless, the early divestment cases were still recorded as historic moments that successfully made 'live transfers' of patronage and were worthy of national attention.[130]

Much criticism for the slow pace of change has been laid at the feet of the Church. These case studies reveal that the Church's inaction may be indicative of broader trends in Irish society rather than merely the Church aimlessly resisting change of any kind. The incredibly strong gravitational pull of local interests and school communities appears to be the driving factor in shaping whether divestment is possible. When schools feared closure, virtually nothing could stop these parents and families from keeping their schools open even if it meant changing their patron and subsequent ethos. Likewise, when local school communities were largely satisfied with the status quo, virtually nothing could budge them to alter their school patronage. The prevalence of localism is striking.

The case of Dublin is a classic example of competing interests and a lack of incentives for any political, religious, or civic leader to take the required risks of time, resources and support to implement the necessary change. A quick look at the map reveals the overlapping political and religious boundaries within Dublin (Figure 10.1).

There are eleven parliamentary constituencies with forty-five elected officials. There are also four council areas consisting of thirty-one local electoral areas with a total of 183 councillors representing these various communities. These national and local elected officials represent different political parties and constituencies, so there are additional and competing visions for how best to serve national and local interests all the while maintaining their electoral appeal for upcoming elections. There are similar overlapping boundaries and relationships within the Church. As of 2020, there is one archbishop, two auxiliary bishops emeritus, and 515 priests serving in 198 parishes within the broader Dublin Archdiocese. As part of this, there are 350 primary schools in County Dublin. Although the Archbishop is patron of these schools, local principals and boards of management direct the schools. Many of these leaders are lay members of the Church, and they

129 McCoy, 2019.
130 O'Kelly, 24 December 2019.

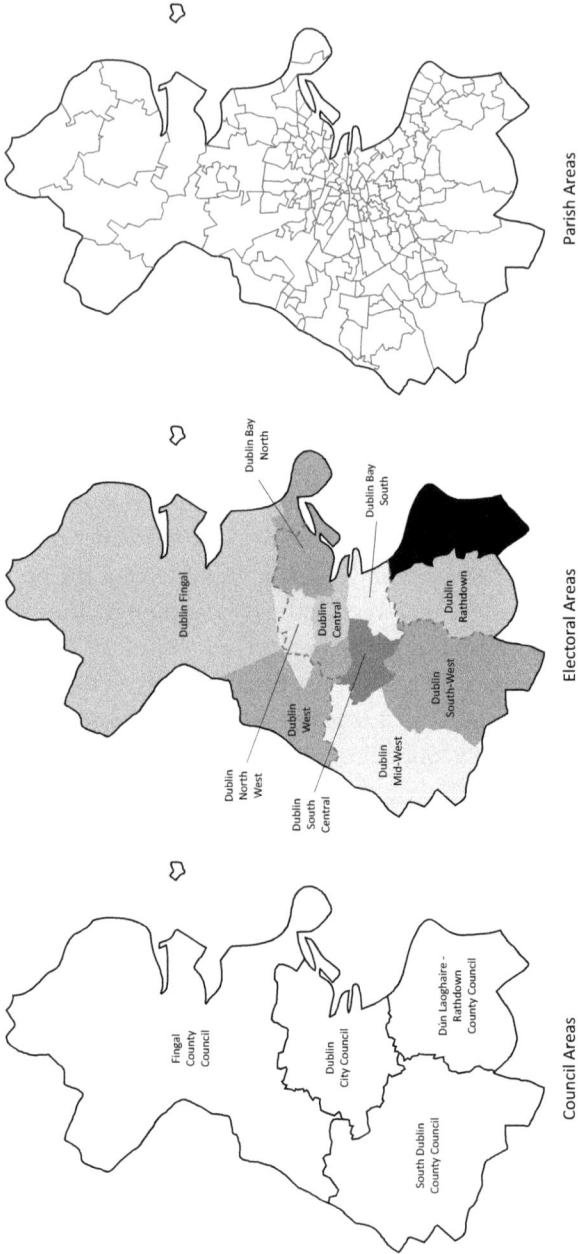

Figure 10.1. Political and Church jurisdictions in Dublin.

The authors are grateful for the work of Ian Huston on mapping the parish boundaries of the Archdiocese of Dublin. More information on this work can be found at <https://www.ianhuston.net/2017/04/mapping-dublin-parish-boundaries/>.

must work closely with their parish priests. It is difficult to measure the levels and quality of cooperation among these lay leaders and the priests charged with authority over local school communities, but there are certainly complex realities involved here too. It is not difficult to see how a disconnect emerges between national ideas, aspirations and strategies associated with divestment and how divestment – or any educational reform for that matter – is ultimately implemented on the ground in local communities. The case study of Dublin places this reality in high relief.

The lack of progress in the divestment process underscores the strength of local interests. It also helps explain why the other key primary school sector reforms, namely admissions and curriculum changes, have been framed much differently. For admissions, like the previous marriage equality and abortion campaigns, the issue is framed in terms of protecting individual rights and preventing discrimination. The emphasis on protecting children's rights also elevated support within an Irish society that was eager to overcome Ireland's historically bad track record for protecting children from abusive individuals and institutions. Curricular changes are also being framed in terms of protecting non-religious and minority religious students from discrimination and encouraging Catholic schools to find alternative ways to pass on their faith. These latter two issues take advantage of the mounting popular support for the cultural goals of diversity, pluralism, tolerance and inclusion to attract support without eliciting strong, concentrated and organised opposition at the local level. These latter two reform issues seek more bureaucratic solutions to their identified problems and therefore sidestep the challenges of amending the Constitution or adjudicating between competing constitutional rights inherent in divestment. The next two chapters underscore these different framings and reveal a potentially more successful reform strategy for those seeking to reduce or eliminate the role of Church in Irish primary schools.

CHAPTER II

Admissions

I. Introduction

In announcing the passing of the 2018 Education (Admission to Schools) Act, Minister Richard Bruton, TD, praised this 'historic' decision to balance the rights of non-denominational, Catholic and minority faith families. This legislation ended the ability of Catholic primary schools to select or deny enrolment to students based on their religious affiliation or identity. Mr Bruton said the changes were aimed at introducing a more 'parent-friendly, equitable and consistent' approach to how school admissions policies operate for the 4,000 State-recognised schools across the country.[1] This swift legislative act limited the once all-powerful Catholic Church's ability to shape and direct educational experiences in Ireland.

Of the three main educational reforms in Ireland's primary sector examined in detail in this book, the process leading up to the passing of the Admissions Bill is the most similar to what occurred in the marriage equality and abortion campaigns. As this chapter will highlight, civil society activists and academics slowly and gradually took advantage of social and demographic changes to attract support for reform. Similar to earlier campaigns, civil society activists and educational reformers highlighted international standards from the United Nations (UN) and the European Union (EU) to build support for an equality movement that framed salient issues in terms of human rights and anti-discrimination. In addition to bolstering legal, rights-based arguments, reformers appealed to the hearts of Irish citizens through personal stories of hardship and discrimination of

---

1   Carl O'Brien, ' "Baptism barrier" to Catholic schools to go next year', *The Irish Times*, 9 May 2018.

non-religious and minority religious students and families. Once sufficient public support and media attention was generated, civil society leaders motivated politicians to support narrow legislative change that could be passed without much public opposition. Reformers largely outmanoeuvred their opponents by framing issues in pithy ways such that irrespective of how real the 'baptismal barrier' really was, the nature of the debate cascaded towards support for change.

Despite the similarities with previous campaigns, there were some critical differences. First, the constitutional and legal issues are not as clear-cut in education as they were with marriage equality and abortion. In those campaigns, the issues were framed narrowly in terms of whether one particular action was constitutional or not, and voters and legislators chose between a simple yes or no decision. Educational issues are more complicated. Although the goal of expanding and protecting rights was similar, there are competing rights in the Constitution and there was considerable debate about how to balance differing views on the common good and individual rights. These competing rights include the patrons' right of selection and ability to ensure their schools' characteristic spirit, the parental right to choose a school that is consistent with their religious and/or philosophical beliefs (i.e. freedom of religion), and for the State's right to determine policies supporting social cohesion and fairness. Conflict over placements in schools deals with availability of places and balancing the rights of parents, patrons and the State.[2]

A second difference from previous campaigns, at least for civil society organisations, was the lack of financial resources available to support their mobilisation efforts. For example, Atlantic Philanthropies had provided four leading Irish civil society groups concerned with advancing LGBTQ+ rights with $8.8 million (approximately €6.8 million in 2011 rates) in grants between 2004 and 2011 to underwrite the organisational work in this area. 'The goal was to deliver legislative change on same-sex partnerships and transgender identity; encourage changes in mainstream services to incorporate the needs of LGBT people; ensure that the organisations that

---

2   David Tuohy, SJ, *Denominational Education and Politics: Ireland in a European Context*, Dublin: Veritas, 2013, 303 and 313.

served LGBT communities could be sustained over time; and increase cohesiveness within and across LGBT communities in Ireland.'[3] Atlantic Philanthropies was successful in that the four disparate groups they supported (Gay and Lesbian Equality Network (GLEN), Marriage Equality, Transgender Equality Network Ireland (TENI) and LGBT Diversity) overcame differing views and strategies about how to achieve change and worked closely together to help pass the Marriage Equality referendum in 2015. Interestingly, 'Atlantic did not identify as a goal achieving marriage equality, although it is clear that by identifying the preconditions for legally mandated equal treatment for LGBT people in Ireland such an outcome became possible. To achieve these goals, Atlantic understood the value of providing core support for organisations that were well-positioned to succeed.'[4]

In contrast to the well-funded marriage equality campaign, educational reforms have received scant financial resources. Equate was one of the leading reform-minded civil society organisations founded in 2015 by successful LGBTQ+ rights' activist Michael Barron to build on the momentum of the marriage equality referendum to facilitate educational reforms. High-profile advisory board members included former Education Minister Ruairí Quinn and Declan Ryan, the head of the philanthropic organisation One Foundation, which helped Equate gain initial and widespread attention.[5] The organisation received €200,000 per annum from the One Foundation but wound down its activities after only two years. There were conflicting stories about the organisation's demise, including some who believed that the Standards in Public Office (SIPO) had investigated Equate because of the laws that govern how organisations raise money during campaigns. Some believed that SIPO had given Equate an ultimatum to

---

3   Eric Brown, *Atlantic Insights: Advocacy for Impact*, Atlantic Philanthropies, 2016, <AP_Advocacy-Impact-Insights.pdf> (<atlanticphilanthropies.org>). In particular, see 'Yes: Marriage Equality's Path to Victory in Ireland', 66–88.

4   Brown, 2016.

5   Breda O'Brien, 'Move against Denominational Schools Not a Good Idea', *The Irish Times*, 21 January 2017; Greg Daly, 'Secular Education Campaign Shut down after Ethics Probe', *The Irish Catholic*, 31 January 2018. <https://www.irishcatholic.com/secular-education-campaign-shut-ethics-probe/>.

either close or return the money.[6] Others argued that disclosing the investigation to potential donors had limited Equate's fundraising capabilities, thus causing the organisation to close because it could no longer attract sufficient funds to be effective. Either way, the organisation ceased its activities, and other groups found themselves dramatically limited in their ability to raise funds because of ongoing questions about what constituted legal political campaigning. According to electoral law, organisations that receive more than €100 for the express purpose of political campaigning must register as third parties and they are then not allowed to receive more than €2,500 from any single donor during any one calendar year.[7]

Education Equality, another leading civil rights group promoting the removal of religion from Ireland's primary school at the same time, struggled to gain any significant financial support. They received an early gift of €10,000 from the Humanist Association of Ireland, but there was not much appetite among potential donors to give funds given the SIPO investigation into Equate's activities. Education Equality felt compelled to move away from its voluntary membership model to form a company limited by guarantee to protect its leaders from legal challenges in the wake of the SIPO treatment of Equate. This, then, limited financial support for its efforts and also made volunteers less willing to work on behalf of the organisation.[8] Whereas the marriage equality campaign had vast resources to support the organisational capacity of several civil society advocacy groups working together to bring about social and legislative change, the educational reform advocates lacked financial and personnel resources to catalyse their movement.

A third and final key difference between educational reforms and previous campaigns is that educational decisions do not just affect individuals and/or families as was the case in same-sex marriage and abortion. Instead, educational reforms affect other individuals and local communities because changes in school admissions or in the type of ethos in a school can

---

6   Daly, 2018.
7   Carl O'Brien, 'Group against Baptism Bar Derailed after Complaints', *The Irish Times,* 15 October 2018.
8   Paddy Monahan, Policy Officer for Education Equality, Personal Interview, October 2019.

influence the formation of all students and indirectly their families and the local community. Given the importance of schools to the vitality of local communities, small changes can trigger much larger consequences in the wider community and often elicit hostility towards proposed modifications.

The fact that most Irish parents are satisfied with their child's educational experience makes it harder to get these same parents to actively campaign to change the system. According to a 2021 Genesis survey commissioned by the Catholic Primary Schools Management Association (CPSMA), 79 % of parents reported being satisfied with the school their child was attending, with only 17 % of parents reporting feeling dissatisfied, and there was no major difference in satisfaction across regional or socio-economic lines.[9] A 2013 Department of Education survey found similar results although the question was asked slightly differently. In Killarney, for example, 32 % of respondents (694 preferences) stated that they would welcome a wider choice of patronage, while 19 % (135) of respondents stated that they would avail of that choice.[10] One could infer that 81 % of respondents in this area in Kerry that was being tested for its demand for change appeared satisfied with the status quo as it pertained directly to their children.

Another reason it is difficult to get parents to advocate for reform is that there are already large numbers of parents volunteering to support their schools via local boards of management in specific schools, parent associations and fundraising efforts, which also limits their willingness to spend more time working on these further reforms that may not impact their child's school. As we have seen in other chapters, the fact that many parents who are inclined to support educational reforms still prefer to have their children receive the sacraments in second and sixth class, also makes many parents less willing to actively campaign for broader, systemic change.[11] The 2021 Genesis survey results also indicated that 57 %

---

9   Genesis, *Articulating a new positioning for Catholic education in Ireland*, September 2021.

10 Department of Education and Skills, *Report on the Surveys Regarding Parental Preferences on Primary School Patronage*. <https://www.education.ie/en/publications/policy-reports/report-on-the-surveys-regarding-parental-preferences-on-primary-school-patronage.pdf> (Accessed: 29 January 2021).

11 Paddy Monahan, Personal Interview, October 2019.

of parents reported that their child's ability to 'make their sacraments' was a key factor influencing their choice of a school.[12] Later sections will discuss the challenges Education Equality encountered in convincing people that the 'baptismal barrier' issue mattered outside of Dublin and had more wide-reaching impact on the role of religion in all schools beyond just admissions.[13] Additionally, as children age of out each educational phase their parents often become less motivated to push for reform in that area. The high turnover rate of likely volunteers in education who are invested in change is different from other campaigns based more on identity, profession, or deep-seated values, where longer-term involvement is more likely. Each of these factors combine to undermine the mobilisation efforts of Education Equality and other groups seeking to activate citizens in ways that have previously led to referenda and legislative reform in other campaigns.

Despite these critical differences between the Admissions Bill and the previous campaigns on marriage equality and abortion, the Admissions Bill has been the most successful reform for those seeking to limit or remove the role of religion in Ireland's primary schools. Divestment has been stalled by a mix of intense local opposition and contentment with the status quo. Curricular change, as the next chapter on curriculum reforms will outline, has been bogged down in the complexity of creating consensus among a myriad of stakeholders during a period of rapid social and cultural change and therefore may take some time before real change occurs. However, admissions reform was passed and implemented because civil society leaders successfully framed the debate in ways that convinced politicians and broad sectors of society that supporting equality legislation in admissions would not undermine the role of religion in Ireland's primary schools altogether.

Educational reformers appeared to adopt the gradual, incrementalist approach that has proven successful in the decades-long campaign for achieving marriage equality. Civil partnerships were passed in 2010 almost under the radar and with cross-party support. Not only had twenty years of equality legislation shifted public opinion, but two years' experience of civil unions raised visibility and awareness that homosexual couples were

---

12   Genesis, 2021.
13   Paddy Monahan, Personal Interview, October 2019.

as loving and committed as heterosexual couples, and this paved the way in the lead-up to the referendum.[14] Likewise, it appears as though educational reformers considered admissions reform as the next step in the long arc of equality legislative achievements, and as soon as this legislation was passed, reformers immediately turned towards completely eliminating religion from Ireland's primary schools.

Recall that the Irish Constitution recognises the rights of parents as natural educators of their children and grants them the right to provide for the religious and moral education of their children (Article 42.1). As part of this right, the Constitution (Article 44.2.4) also creates the right for children to be exempted – or to opt-out – of religious education if they or their parents do not wish to receive any religious instruction in State-funded primary school. Reformers considered ways to undermine the adverse effects of the opt-out clause for students wishing to conscientiously avoid religious instruction and calls for an end to the integrated curriculum as the next steps towards this ultimate goal of eliminating religion from primary schools.

The remainder of this chapter will address the various aspects of how the Admissions Bill was passed, including a look at key social factors and arguments that led to its passing, the debates surrounding the actual legislation and the most likely consequences of the developments in this area. Special attention will be given to the critical role of civil society actors and academics in framing the debate, changing attitudes, mobilising citizens and ultimately encouraging politicians and political parties to enact this legislation.

II. Social Change and the Equality Movement

Advocates of admissions reform highlight the significant social and demographic changes as one of the main reasons changes in enrolment

---

14 Grainne Healy, Brian Sheehan, and Noel Whelan, *Ireland Says Yes: The Inside Story of How the Vote for Marriage Equality Was Won*. Kildare: Merrion Press, 2016, 5–6.

policies needed to occur. As the number of practicing Catholics continues to decline and the numbers of minority religious and those of no
religion persistently increases, reformers argue that schools needed to
alter how they enrol the diverse sets of students that now live in Ireland.
The overall Catholic population has decreased from its peak of 95 % in
1961 to 78 % in 2016.[15] Even fewer numbers of these Catholics are practicing their faith. Educate Equality regularly cites marriage data to underscore that when given the choice, even many Catholics are choosing not
to have a Church wedding. Since 1980, there has only been one year when
the proportion of Catholic weddings has not fallen. In 2018, only 51 %
of weddings were Catholic, and civil and humanist marriages reached
a new high of 37 % – and the trend is likely to continue in this direction. Advocates of reform suggest that these figures provide a more reliable indicator of religious practice than census data imply and signal the
more accurate religious practice of young Irish families.[16] Additionally,
the numbers of non-religious (including atheists and agnostics) has risen
from only 67,413 in 1991 to 481,388 in 2016 – a seven-fold increase and to
the point where 10 % of the overall Irish population identifies as having no
religion.[17] Finally, the number of Irish citizens of minority religions has
remained steady at 10 % of the population. Yet, the visibility of minority
religions has grown since declining numbers of Church of Ireland members have been replaced in the 2000s by immigrants, often non-White,
whose ethnicity and religion differed from mainstream Irish society. The
combination of these changing demographics indicates that 15 % to 20 %
of Irish primary students are either non-Catholic, non-religious, or children of immigrants and therefore may not be properly served by the predominantly Catholic primary school sector.[18]

15   <https://www.cso.ie/en/releasesandpublications/ep/p-cp8iter/p8iter/p8rrc/>.
16   David Graham, 'Opinion: Religious Instruction and Worship Should Take Place
      Outside of Core School Hours', 5 April 2018, journal.ie <https://www.thejournal.
      ie/readme/opinion-religious-instruction-and-worship-should-take-place-outside-
      core-school-hours-3937081-Apr2018/>.
17   <https://www.cso.ie/en/releasesandpublications/ep/p-cp8iter/p8iter/p8rnraa/>
18   Daniel Faas and Rachael Fionda, 'Ireland: A Shift Towards Religious Equality in
      Schools', in P. A. J. Stevens and A. G. Dworkin (eds), *The Palgrave Handbook of
      Race and Ethnic Inequalities in Education*, 2018, 605–31.

These social changes coincide with the gradual growth of the equality movement in Ireland, which emphasised the importance of human rights and non-discrimination. Recall that the Equal Status Acts, first passed in 2000 and subsequently updated several times through 2018, prohibit discrimination in the provision of goods and services, accommodation and education. The Acts cover the nine grounds of gender, marital status, family status, age, disability, sexual orientation, race, religion and membership of the Traveller community.[19] Key exemptions were granted to religious schools to either admit a student of a particular religious denomination in preference to other students or to refuse to admit a student who is not of that religion provided the school can prove that this refusal is essential to maintain the ethos of the school.[20] Objections to these exemptions grew as demographics shifted. The growing debates about religious discrimination first escalated when religion was combined with ethnicity and race to become a more high-profile social issue in the early 2000s.

Intercultural education and anti-racism had become a priority for the Department of Education since the 2000s. The National Action Plan Against Racism was initiated in 2002 and recommended that schools revise their policies to honour and reflect international conventions on human rights, equality and non-discrimination. Specifically, the plan called for equal treatment of children regardless of race, skin colour, gender, language, religion, political or other opinions, national, social or ethnic origin, potential special needs, or status at birth. At first, the focus was on being more inclusive of minority ethnic groups/immigrants and the Traveller community. Concrete lessons on interculturalism and anti-racism were proposed for all levels. Some critics thought that despite the recent momentum of the equality legislation in 1998 and 2000, the focus was narrowly kept on race and ethnicity. This narrow perspective, reformers argued, ignored the

---

19   <https://www.ihrec.ie/guides-and-tools/human-rights-and-equality-in-the-provision-of-good-and-services/what-does-the-law-say/equal-status-acts/#:~:text=They%20cover%20the%20nine%20grounds,membership%20of%20the%20Traveller%20community>.

20   Alison Mawhinney, 'A Discriminating Education System: Religious Admission Policies in Irish Schools and International Human Rights Law' *International Journal of Children's Rights*, 2012, Vol. 20, No. 4. DOI 10.1163/157181811X611054.

growing problems related to discrimination in enrolment and religious instruction curriculum for minority religious and non-religious students.[21]

The debates about religious discrimination escalated in 2007 when
over seventy immigrant families were denied placements in oversubscribed
schools in North County Dublin. For the first time, there was noticeable
and growing public concern that selecting pupils on the basis of religion
may also indirectly discriminate on racial grounds. The preferential treatment given to Catholic families in the 2007 Balbriggan crisis meant that
it was predominately children of African parents who were originally not
accepted into their local schools. These families had to be accommodated
in two new emergency schools that were built at the last minute.[22] The
public outcry was stoked as national television and print media shone a
spotlight on the treatment of these non-White immigrants. Several of these
families were Christian, but not Catholic, and they publicly lamented that
their children were denied access to their local school because they lacked a
baptismal certificate. This non-White immigrant experience was repeated
across several Dublin communities beyond Balbriggan, including Lucan and
Blanchardstown, areas with growing migrant populations.[23] In response,
the Catholic Archdiocese implemented a pilot scheme for two schools
in these communities with a high influx of immigrants. The pilot scheme
instituted a 'quota' whereby one-third of school places were reserved for
non-Catholics. The State also opened two 'emergency' primary schools in
Dublin which served predominantly non-Catholic children who had been
refused admission to existing schools.

Additional examples of immigrants not enrolling in schools across
Dublin where schools prioritised faith in their selection criteria led to
comparisons with apartheid regimes in South Africa. The necessary selection process employed in these oversubscribed schools was in line with
their schools' stated aim of providing a service to a particular faith group,
but it resulted in excluding ethnic groups, which was seen as racist and

21   Karin Fischer, *Schools and the Politics of Religion and Diversity in the Republic of
      Ireland: Separate but Equal*, Manchester: Manchester University Press, 2016, 70–5.
22   April Duff, 'Non-Catholics Need Not Apply: The Legal Status of Discrimination
      in Irish School Admissions Policies', *King's Inns Law Review*, 2017, Vol. 7, 20.
23   Fischer, 2016, 166–9.

inappropriate. Even though the State had ultimate responsibility for poor planning and lack of resources in providing sufficient school placements for a rapidly growing population, local Catholic schools absorbed the brunt of the criticism.[24] The then Minister of State for Children, Brian Lenihan, Fianna Fáil TD, commented on the inability of schools in meeting the needs of immigrants: 'All patrons are sincere, but there is still a problem. [...] Integration is impossible under our current system of patronage.'[25] These developments underscored the existence of religious discrimination for many Irish citizens who effectively have little choice but to seek access to denominational schools to avail of free public education.[26] For many, religious discrimination only became a reality when it was connected to race and ethnicity. The need for anti-racist programmes had already become widely accepted in Irish society. Such recognition paved the way for greater attention being given to religious discrimination against minority and non-religious students.

The outcry over treatment of immigrant children spurred civil society and educational reformers to increase their efforts to end what they considered religious discrimination in admissions policies. Educational reformers mimicked the strategies of previous LGBTQ+ and pro-choice activists by repeatedly employing international standards, institutions and reports to make their case for change. Activists highlighted several United Nations Committees that cited the need for Ireland to end discrimination of children in admissions policies and to increase the number of non- and/ or multi-denominational schools. These include the 2005 UN Committee on Elimination of Racial Discrimination, the 2006 UN Committee on the Rights of Children (charged with implementing 1989 International Convention on the Rights of the Child), and the 2015 UN Committee on Economic, Social and Cultural Rights.[27]

24 Tuohy, 2013.
25 Fischer, 2016, 70.
26 Eoin Daly and Tom Hickey, 'Religious freedom and the "right to discriminate" in the school admissions context: a neo-republican critique', *Legal Studies*, December 2011, Vol. 31, No. 4, 615–43, DOI: 10.1111/j.1748-121X.2011.00204.x.
27 Fischer, 2016.

In the wake of international pressure, as well as domestic calls to protect children following the Catholic Church's sexual abuse scandal, the
State created the Ombudsman for Children's Office (OCO) in 2004.
This autonomous body was created to be independent of Government and
other civil society actors and is accountable to the Oireachtas. Its charge
is to promote and safeguard the rights and welfare of children and young
people, to conduct investigations of complaints regarding actions by public
bodies, and to provide research and policy advice to Government and
other bodies. In a 2017 report on the Admissions Bill, the OCO also cited
several international standards as justification for change to admissions
policies and discriminatory practices in Irish primary schools. The report
references the following reports that it suggests Ireland was in breach of
compliance: the Convention on the Rights of the Child; the International
Covenant on Economic, Social and Cultural Rights (1999); the International
Covenant on Civil and Political Rights (2008); the UN Convention on
the Elimination of All Forms of Religious Discrimination (CERD); the
UN Human Rights Council (2012); the European Convention on Human
Rights (ratified by Ireland in 1953); and the European Commission Against
Racism and Intolerance (ECRI).[28] The fact that a semi-autonomous State
body was echoing civil society complaints and was reinforcing widely accepted international standards provided the air of legitimacy that further
challenged the State, Department of Education and all Government and
political leaders to take the calls for reform seriously.

At the same time issues of race were being associated with religious discrimination, there was also growing evidence that Ireland's denominational
system was also benefitting middle- and upper-income families who knew
how to take advantage of the system to gain admittance to schools of their
choice. By 2007, upward as many as 20 % of schools were oversubscribed
according to several studies, which heightened debates over the fairest
system of accepting students. When schools were oversubscribed, often in

28   Ombudsman for Children's Office, 'Observations, regarding the Department of
     Education and Skills' consultation paper on the role of denominational religion in
     the school admissions process and possible approaches for making changes', March
     2017.   <https://www.oco.ie/app/uploads/2018/04/OCO-observations-on-role-
     of-religion-in-school-admissions.pdf>.

more urban areas in Dublin, many non-religious and minority religious students failed to secure placement, had to travel significant distances, and often their parents needed to enrol them in preschool for an additional year to await placement. In area of high population growth, many parents of minority religions or no faith lived in fear that may not have a placement for their child when they come of age.[29]

Prior to admissions policy changes enacted in 2018, schools could base enrolment decisions on religion, the date at which a student applied (which benefitted long-standing residents), and previous connections to school (which also greatly advantaged many students, often from middle- and upper-class families).[30] Recent scholarship confirmed that higher income and better educated families were engaged in more active school choice. Darmody and Smyth from the Economic and Social Research Institute (ESRI) concluded that 'school choice in Ireland reflects the complex interplay of religion/beliefs and social characteristics, a pattern which has important implications for policy regarding school diversity'.[31] Therefore, the authors argue that even though the Irish Constitution protects parental choice, not all parents are able to access their preferred school. Those with stronger incomes and higher levels of education often have more choices available to them in school selection because they know that they have a higher probability of admittance if they apply early and have prior links to a school. Darmody and Smyth conclude that the concentration of more advantaged groups in certain schools may act as a further signal for middle-class parents seeking a school for 'children like mine', thus further reinforcing social differentiation. Though many reformers frame the school admissions debate in terms of religious and secular identities, key social factors such as income and parental levels of education also shape the equity of access to different schools.[32] As debates about creating more

29　Duff, 2017.
30　Merike Darmody, Emer Smyth, and Selina McCoy, 'School Sector Variation among Primary Schools in Ireland', *ESRI*, 2012, 30.
31　Merike Darmody and Emer Smyth, 'Religion and Primary School Choice in Ireland: School Institutional Identities and Student Profile', *Irish Educational Studies*, 2018, DOI: 10.1080/03323315.2017.1421091, 11.
32　Darmody and Smyth, 2018, 12–3.

diverse and inclusive schools gained tractions, it was clear that these practices could lead to schools becoming segregated in terms of students' ethnicity, socio-economic background and academic achievement.[33] These
arguments, like those around race and ethnicity, placed the calls for admissions policy reform into the context of a broader equality framework.
Many reformers believed that this broader argument about equality might
convince even those with strong religious beliefs that changes in admission
policies would help create a better, more diverse and inclusive Ireland. This
strategy had worked in the marriage equality and abortion campaigns and
might prove effective in the educational sector as well.

The results of the 2015 marriage equality referendum and the 2018
abortion referendum propelled and consolidated the human rights, equality
and non-discrimination agenda in Ireland. A new confidence was emerging
within Irish society that was less deferential to Church teachings and the
authority of institutional Church leaders. Rather than accepting the premise
that the Church, as patron of 90 % of primary schools, had certain rights
that needed to be preserved, reformers challenged church exemptions on
admissions policies. The slow pace of attempts to increase the number of
multi- and/or non-denominational school alternatives added fuel to the
reform fire. If more schools provided non-denominational education, the
issue of religious criteria would be less relevant. In this scenario, the State
would better honour both the right to an education and the freedom of
religion, and it would be legitimate for religious schools to select students
in ways that support their overall ethos. If sufficient placements in non-
denominational schools are not available, then using religion as a criterion
to select or deny admittance into a school would violate the freedom of
religion of non-religious and minority religious students. According to
Mawhinney, 'To uphold its human rights obligations the state would therefore be obliged to establish schools – either state schools or state-funded
schools – with an open-admissions policy or, alternatively, would be required to oblige existing religious schools to desist from discriminating in
favour of co-religionists.'[34]

33   Darmody, Smyth and McCoy, 2012, 20.
34   Mawhinney, 2012.

Legal scholars added their voices to those arguing that the State was discriminating against non-religious and minority religious students by allowing Catholic schools to admit students based on their faith.

> From the neo-republican perspective, we argue that legislative permission for dis-criminatory enrolment practices in state-funded religious schools entails the state licensing and facilitating the arbitrary 'intimidation' or 'invigilation', by private agents, of citizens' choice of religious affiliation. Far from preserving religious freedom by avoiding state interference in religions' autonomy, this stance facilitates the 'dom-ination' of religious choice and therefore invades freedom of religion, as conceived in the republican lens. Thus, we claim, religious discrimination underpins 'domin-ation', and 'domination' of religious choice is the antithesis of religious freedom.[35]

In real terms, this meant parents sometimes felt that to have their children admitted to a school of their choice they were forced either to feign a religious belief that they do not hold or to refrain from manifesting either another belief or their lack of belief.[36] Unlike some who argue that Catholic schools should be held to the equality standards because they are State-funded, the main issue is once again that there is little or no alternative for students with no religion or are of a minority religion, and therefore their religious freedom is being undermined.

The choice of language used by many reform advocates is highly indicative of the equality movement's arguments taking hold. For equality-based legal scholars like April Duff, it is hard to imagine how permission to discriminate in admissions policies is necessary to protect religious freedom. First, it is highly impractical that every person can have a school with their own distinctive religious ethos to give effect to their religious freedom. Second, Duff argues, it is unclear how it is necessary for religious schools to protect their ethos by accepting only students of their faith. It is not to suggest that religious schools do not have the right to teach and create a culture of their choosing, but there is little, if any, evidence according to Duff that a school's ethos has been undermined by admitting students of no or different faiths. A far greater sin for equality-based reformers, who consider one child being discriminated against because of their faith or

35   Daly and Hickey, 2011, 615–643, DOI: 10.1111/j.1748-121X.2011.00204.x. (35–6).
36   Daly and Hickey, 2011, 35–6.

lack thereof as one too many, is parents feeling compelled to baptise their child to get them into school. According to data from a survey conducted by Equate, the secular education advocates, 24 % of parents in the survey reported that they would not have baptised their child if baptism was not a requirement for admittance into their preferred school. Such data supports the notion that far too many parents are being penalised for their choice of religion, which is contrary to the principles of freedom of religion and freedom to express and practice one's religion.[37]

The issue of baptismal certificates serving as proof of a child having been baptised being required before for admittance into oversubscribed schools began gaining traction in 2010. Ruairí Quinn, a leading Labour TD and soon to become Minister for Education, observed that several schools in his Dublin Southeast constituency were requiring baptismal certificates as part of the admissions process. He suggested that 'as a result a new phenomenon is developing; the emergence of "compulsory Catholic"… [Parents] realise that a visit to the baptismal font is between them and access to a primary school place for their child… [They] are now required to make solemn vows, before a priest, to raise the child as a practising Catholic'.[38] Quinn became the leading proponent of radical reform as he assumed responsibility as Minister for Education in the new Fine Gael/Labour government after the 2011 election. As discussed in previous chapters, Quinn initiated the Forum on Patronage and Pluralism just after taking over the Department of Education and Skills. Perhaps not surprisingly, later that same year the Department issued a Discussion Paper which acknowledged that the 'enrolment policies and practices that served schools and parents well in the past may not now fully accommodate the needs and diversity of our modern society'.[39] Public discourse began regularly quoting data from various surveys that highlighted how growing numbers within Irish society wanted to reduce the ability of schools to rely on religious criteria for admissions. One such study conducted in 2012 suggested that 78 % of responding principals cited religion as a criterion in their admission

37 Duff, 2017, 1–22.
38 Ruairí Quinn, 'Time to Transfer Control of Primary Education.' *The Irish Times*, 26 January 2010.
39 Darmody and Smyth, 2018.

policies, and approximately one third required baptismal certificates for enrolment.[40] Even though this study only had responses from a small sample of thirty-seven principals, scholars and commentators used it as evidence for how widespread religion was being used in admissions decisions. The Report on the Forum called for legislation that would require all schools to publish their admissions policies and would also eliminate the ability of Catholic schools to make student selections based on their religious background. Quinn's promptings took the conversations about reform of admissions policies to the next level and ultimately led to the first draft of the Education (Admissions to Schools) Act in 2013 and the subsequent five years of debate before finally passing this key education legislation. The next section analyses the critical role civil society advocates assumed in delivering this reform.

III. Civil Society Activists Lead the Reform Movement

Civil society groups have been essential to reform movements in Ireland over the last forty years. In the abortion campaign, the Pro-Life Amendment Campaign (PLAC) initiated calls for the protection of life to be inserted into the Constitution starting in 1981 and helped pass the 8th Amendment in 1983. Decades later, Together for Yes, a co-alition of national civil society groups, combined forces to repeal the 8th Amendment in 2018. Additionally, several individuals and civil society groups championed LGBTQ+ rights since the late 1970s, culminating in the passing of the Marriage Equality Referendum in 2015. In that campaign, the leading civil society groups overcame their tactical differences and formed a united front in the Yes Equality campaign. GLEN, Marriage Equality and Irish Council for Civil Liberties (ICCL) worked together to lead a focused, positive-toned and methodical campaign that combined traditional and new methods. In both campaigns, the long-term goal of amending the Constitution was the culmination of years of

---

40   Mawhinney, 2012.

raising awareness, using courts and international standards to pressure risk-averse Irish politicians to legislate for change, and finally mobilising the media and citizens to demand change as well.

There have been similar dynamics brewing in the educational sector. A plethora of civil society groups have been raising awareness, highlighting international standards and mobilising demands for educational reform. As mentioned in Chapter 5, the voluntary group of parents who led the Dalkey School Project in 1978 initiated a project that would eventually become Educate Together, the leading network of multi-denominational schools in Ireland. The Educate Together movement has grown from a few parents to a professional organisation and network that has sought to provide diversity of provision one school at a time with the larger hope of changing the denominational system of education that Ireland inherited from the nineteenth century. In recent years as Irish society has dramatically transformed, a plethora of groups including Atheist Ireland and the Humanist Association of Ireland have repeated calls for reform and the end of religion's role in Irish schools.

The rise of education-specific groups has also been essential to the reform movement. Equate and Education Equality are two groups that stand out for their role in influencing the public discourse on admissions reform. A pattern of Irish politics is that when politicians would rather not engage in controversial issues that have the potential to alienate significant sectors and groups within Irish society, civil society groups often assume a greater role.

A. Equate

Equate was launched in December 2015 by Michael Barron, who had previously campaigned for LGBTQ+ rights. Equate described itself as 'a family and children's rights organisation that advocates for a substantial change in how primary and secondary school education is delivered in Ireland. We want all children to experience equality in their local school so that no child is isolated because of their identity, family background, religion or non-religion. Our education system should reflect the diversity of twenty-first century Ireland.'[41] The group sought to take advantage the equality movement's success in achieving marriage equality by keeping key politicians, donors and broader society mobilised around equality issues in education. As mentioned, its initial advisory board members included high-profile leaders such as former Education Minister Ruairí Quinn and Declan Ryan, head of the philanthropic organisation the One Foundation. These high-profile leaders provided legitimacy and media attention, which helped attract additional supporters among Ireland's political, social and economic classes. The One Foundation provided seed money to support the personnel and communication needs of the organisation.[42]

One of the primary goals of Equate was to raise public awareness of the need to reform admissions policies. Rather than trying to eliminate religion from education entirely, the strategy was to build momentum for tangible, concrete changes that could chip away at the Church's influence in education in ways that would not elicit too much negative pushback among conservative leaders and sectors of Irish society. To this end, and before the organisation was even officially launched, Equate commissioned a poll by Behaviour & Attitudes about Irish citizens' attitudes towards the educational system and the need for reform.

The 2016 data produced succinct soundbites on issues ranging from divestment, admissions and curriculum. In terms of divestment, 62 % of respondents agreed that reform of school patronage should be a key priority for the next government, and 46 % of parents in the survey reported that they would not choose a Christian school for their child if they had a choice locally. The data supporting change in admissions policies was overwhelming. 84 % of survey respondents agreed with the statement that the Irish education system should be reformed so that no child is excluded because of their religion or non-religion; and 77 % of respondents did not think a school should have the right to refuse admission to a child who has

---

41   <https://www.education.ie/en/The-Department/Action-Plan-for-Education-2016-2019/Submissions/EQUATE.pdf>.

42   Carl O'Brien, 'Campaign Seeks Equality for Children in Education System', *The Irish Times*, 9 December 2015.

a different religion to that of the school's patron. In terms of the baptismal issue, 23 % stated that they baptised their child because they believed they needed to for school admission, and one in five people reported that they were aware of someone who had baptised their child just to get them into the local school. In another part of the 2016 survey, 87 % of respondents agreed that the State has responsibility to ensure that children do not experience religious discrimination in the school curriculum. The impact of constantly citing international standards and Ireland's responsibilities also seemed to be bearing fruit, as 82 % of respondents agreed that Ireland should do all it can to honour its international human rights obligations to ensure equality in our education system.[43]

These results, although compelling and provocative, may be inflated because they deal with issues in the abstract or principle, without engaging the complex realities of how to implement such changes on the ground, let alone in the schools of their own children. It is tough not to support wanting to meet international standards on human rights. Recall that scholars of public opinion data often highlight the distinction between the 'easy' and the 'hard' facets of questions as a way of explaining how individuals may have complex beliefs on any one topic. Easy questions generally deal with a principle or an overall view, whereas hard questions focus on the implementation of such policies, forcing respondents to choose between solutions or policies.[44] The emphasis on these easy results was a strategic move on the part of Equate to generate further demand for change and to not lose momentum by detailing the complexities of how to achieve such change.

These data were widely used not only by the organisation in submissions made to the Department of Education and opinion pieces written to newspapers, but also in discussions of religious education issues by others in the media.[45] The survey results reinforced calls by academics, international

43   Equate, 'Religion and School: Parents' Voices', 2017, <https://media.wix.com/ugd/
      08f4c2_0655f34b38b049748cce39a75acc2bb7.pdf> (Accessed: 21 January 2021).
44   Pat Lyons, *Public Opinion, Politics and Society in Contemporary Ireland*. Dublin,
      Ireland and Portland, OR: Irish Academic Press, 2008.
45   John Walshe, 'Bruton Is Facing a Baptism of Parental Ire over the Catholic School
      Enrolment Policies'. *Irish Independent*. Independent.ie, 15 January 2017; Peter

organisations and other civil society groups to amend the Equal Status Act to ensure schools could not discriminate against children based on religion. The data were also used to bolster arguments for shifting religious instruction to the beginning or end of the school day to better honour the opt-out clause guaranteed in the Constitution and to remove religion from the school day altogether. Nevertheless, the immediate focus was on the Admissions Bill.

Even before the survey results had been officially published, Equate had been leveraging its ties to political parties from the marriage equality campaign to discuss the enrolment issue with political parties.[46] Equate began pushing for school admissions to be an election issue in 2016, believing that change could happen under the next government. The organisation's political connections were on full display when Minister Richard Bruton, TD, announced the formal consultation process associated with the Education (Admissions to Schools) Act at an Equate-sponsored event. Bruton discussed the four possibilities for admissions reform: 1) a catchment area approach, banning religious schools from giving preference to children of their own religion who live outside the catchment area ahead of non-religious children who live inside the catchment; 2) a 'nearest school rule', allowing religious schools to give preference to a religious child only where it is that child's nearest school; 3) a quota system, allowing a religious school to keep a certain number of places for children of that religion; and 4) an outright ban on schools using religion for admissions.

While announcing the four proposals for new admissions rules, Minister Bruton revealed his (and the Government's) preference when stating that 'it is unfair that preference is given by publicly funded religious schools to children of their own religion who might live some distance away, ahead of children of a different religion or of no religion who live close to the school'. The Minister also stated his belief that 'it is unfair that parents, who might otherwise not do so, feel pressure to baptise their

---

McGuire, 'We'd Be Hypocritical Standing in a Church Promising to Raise Our Kids as Catholics', *The Irish Times*, 7 April 2018.

46   O'Brien, 2015.

children in order to gain admission to the local school'.[47] It was not lost on observers that Bruton was announcing this Government-led consultation process sitting in front of an Equate banner alongside its leader Michael Barron. Equate had made no secret that it would not accept any change but a complete end to the baptism barrier.[48] For critics, the consultation process was muted from the start because the outcome appeared to be a foregone conclusion and there were only eight weeks permitted to accept submissions. The Association of Trustees of Catholic Schools (ATCS), which represents the interests of sixty-four Trustee bodies and patrons, raised its concern about the short process and the fact that Bruton had proposed issues of unfairness without explaining what was unfair in these processes. The ATCS also argued that the real issue was the lack of placements not the admissions policies.[49] Irrespective of these criticisms, Equate was deeply connected with political leaders and was positioning itself at the centre of the debate.

Equate took advantage of these close ties to consistently remind politicians and broader Irish society of their duty and responsibility to act now. Barron argued that 'we now have, for the first time, cross-party consensus on the need for this change to happen. Now is the time for the Government to deliver on its promises and get the job done. All political parties and Oireachtas members must continue to work together to enact this legislation without further delay.'[50] Although Equate's high-level access to politicians quickened the pace and nature of the debate, it also opened Equate and the Minister to questions of fairness and favouritism by Church leaders and media commentators. These questions, along with previously

---

47   Press Release, 'Minister Bruton Sets Out Plans to Reform the School Admissions System in Relation to Religion', 16 January 2017. <https://www.education.ie/en/Press-Events/Press-Releases/2017-Press-Releases/PR17-16-01.html>.

48   Carl O'Brien, 'Legal Questions over Plan to Remove School "Baptism Barrier"', *The Irish Times*, 29 June 2017; Carl O'Brien, 'Rights of Children Opting out of Religion Class "Must Be Respected"', *The Irish Times*, 11 July 2017.

49   Association of Trustees of Catholic Schools (ATCS), 'The Role of Religion in the Admissions Process in Primary Schools: Response to Consultation Paper', March 2017.

50   Michael Barron, 'It's Time to Stop Subcontracting Education to Religious Groups', *The Irish Times*, 2 January 2018.

discussed concerns raised by the Standards in Public Office about their funding sources, led Equate to shut down its operations just two years after it had started. In Barron's parting comments, he lauded the organisation's contribution through research, conferences, seminars, lobbying and support of parents to alter the role of religion in schools. Equate regularly provided practical solutions to legislators and increased public support through online communications and via regional community and parental forums. These tactics, Barron argued, helped Equate secure commitments in the programme for government to advance equality in education, a commitment by Community National Schools to stop preferencing one religion over others, and to shape the overall debate in the consultation on the 'baptismal barrier'. He concludes by passing the baton to Education Equality to build upon the achievements of Equate's two years of work.[51]

B. *Education Equality*

Education Equality is the other primary voluntary human rights organisation that was established to campaign for equality in the provision of education for all children regardless of religion. Education Equality had very targeted goals of ending religious discrimination in State-funded schools via changes to admissions, opting out of religious instruction and eliminating the integrated curriculum.[52] The first goal was to end discrimination in enrolment policies. They argued that growing numbers of students from minority religions or no religion always went to the bottom of waiting lists in oversubscribed schools. Therefore, they joined the chorus of civil society leaders demanding an end to using religious background as a criterion for admission to Irish schools.

The second goal was to underscore the segregating and stigmatising effects that they felt the opt-out of religious instruction had on minority religious and non-religious students. Paddy Monahan, one of the leaders

51 Barron, 2018.
52 Education Equality, 'Equality in Education: Your Questions Answered', <https://educationequalitydotblog.wordpress.com/education-equality-your-questions-answered/> (Accessed: 14 April 2021).

of Education Equality, described how the process works. During the daily thirty minutes of religious instruction, 'opted-out' children are typically moved to the back of the classroom and visibly segregated from their peers while absorbing the instruction regardless. Monahan claimed that many schools did not provide alternative lessons or activities during this time, which further undermined the experience for those seeking to opt-out of religious instruction. The lack of preparedness for many existing opt-out practices, as well as the stigmatising effects this segregation could have on children, combined to discourage many parents from exercising their human and constitutional rights to freedom of religion and conscience.[53] In shining a spotlight on the lack of State regulation in this area, Education Equality revealed the wide variation of practices in schools throughout Ireland, many of which are acceptable, but still many others that were not. Once again, these powerful descriptions and evocative stories moved people and stirred debate, but it was not always clear there was hard evidence to support the claims or to provide a sense for how widespread these experiences were. For change advocates, if it was happening to one student, that was sufficient for change, whereas defenders of the current practice argued that the vast majority of students were treated with sensitivity and care. The lack of much data complicated the debates on this issue.

To overcome these challenges, Education Equality believed that reformers should not focus on ending the denominational system of education altogether, which would be an extremely slow, costly and legally complex undertaking. Rather, Educate Equality argued that a more pragmatic approach was required, whereby the simplest solution would be to move religious instruction, including sacramental preparation, to the end of the school day under an 'opt-in' system. Some existing multi-denominational schools already offer optional religious instruction after hours, so it has been proven to work. Education Equality leaders reiterated that religious practice is a choice, not an obligation, and therefore this simple change could have a huge impact. It would, reformers argued, vindicate the rights

53   Paddy Monahan, Personal Interview, October 2019.

of all parents and end classroom segregation.[54] This would also help achieve Education Equality's third goal, which is to end the existing integrated curriculum. Although the 2017 removal of Rule 68 that had placed religious instruction at the heart of the primary school curriculum was a victory in this area, Education Equality wanted more. By moving all religion outside the school day, they believed that families could effectively choose whether their children receive faith formation.[55] Ironically, if this were achieved, this change would in essence end denominational education albeit in an indirect way.

Education Equality focused on admissions, opt-out and the integrated curriculum for practical and philosophical reasons. From a practical perspective, the incredible slow rate of divestment of Catholic schools and the insufficient rate of building or establishing multi- and non-denominational schools meant that real change was still decades away. A focus on more concrete, tangible changes that would undermine the ability of schools to segregate children based on religion or other socio-economic factors would have more immediate impact. From a philosophical perspective, leaders of Education Equality root their arguments in the broader equality movement and its emphasis on human rights and non-discrimination. So beyond not having the financial resources or land to build and establish new schools, leaders of Education Equality questioned whether the denominational system could foster the diverse, equal and inclusive society Irish citizens are increasingly demanding. 'We need to fundamentally examine whether our denominational schools, as currently run, are fit for purpose in a changing society – and whether the narrative of "school choice" is an appropriate response to diversity. The status quo is not sustainable, but neither is a response that would seek to segregate 5-year-olds along religious lines. We don't have the money, the land or the need to build a parallel school system for non-Christians.'[56] In another argument, Education Equality spokesman Paddy Monahan argues that 'the blindingly obvious effects of keeping the

54   David Graham, 'Opinion: Religion Is a Choice – Not an Obligation. Let's Make Religious Classes an Opt-In', 5 February 2020, journal.ie <https://www.thejournal.ie/readme/religious-education-ireland-4973515-Feb2020/>.

55   Education Equality, 'Equality in Education'.

56   Graham, 2018.

Equal Status Act and building more schools to create this idea of choice is segregation. We're going to have a Muslim school here, a Hindu school there. You're going to have kids growing up not meeting anyone from different backgrounds.'[57] For Monahan, this was incongruent with what most Irish citizens appeared to want.

C. Educate Together Raises Awareness and Frames the Debate

Education Equality employed a tried-and-tested, multi-pronged approach to achieving its reform agenda. They conducted political lobbying by interacting with courts and UN Treaty bodies, empowering parents and encouraging the public to demand change, all of which culminated in generating cross-party support for legislative change.[58] Learning from the success of the marriage equality movement's positive tone and highly personal approach, Education Equality helped frame all the debates in the values of the new Ireland, namely equality and fairness. It is not that they did not provide sophisticated arguments and concrete data to substantiate their claims, but their ability to come up with pithy slogans was key to their success. The catchy phrases were understandable and relatable and quickly became accepted, so much so that to argue against them made you look out of touch and insensitive. Winning the rhetoric game was a key aspect of Education Equality's successful campaigning.

The most successful example of this is the widespread use of 'baptismal barrier' to refer to the need to get baptised to gain admittance to Catholic schools when these schools were oversubscribed. Building on the data and arguments previously mentioned, reformers highlighted personal stories to give flesh to the numbers and arguments. For example, Education Equality leader Paddy Monahan described how his own 5-year-old, unbaptised son would not be able to attend the local primary school because it was oversubscribed. Under the Catholic school's enrolment criteria, priority is given

---

57   Áine McMahon, 'Parents Call for End to Religious Discrimination in Schools', *The Irish Times*, 3 July 2016.
58   Education Equality, 'Equality in Education'.

to children of Catholic parents, and therefore under the law at the time, his child absolutely would not be considered for enrolment in the school. If Monahan were to have his son baptised, however, he would automatically have jumped into the very top category on the list of enrolment criteria.[59]

Education Equality also played on the powerful image of discrimination when religion, race and ethnicity are combined. This combination is more difficult to ignore in the new Ireland that promotes itself as diverse, plural and inclusive. Monahan argues that 'the baptism barrier has prevented young children of the "wrong" religion from attending local taxpayer-funded schools while untold numbers of parents baptise their children, under State-imposed duress, to ensure the best educational opportunities. My friend Roopesh's young daughter, Eva, was rejected by primary schools on the basis of her Hindu religion. She did not ask for a new school, Hindu or otherwise, to be built – she asked her father, "Daddy, why can't I go to school with my friends from creche?"'[60]

Discrimination, Education Equality contends, does not just occur during admissions. These advocates argue that non-religious and minority students are regularly discriminated against in schools because of how opt-outs are implemented. Monahan employs the following thought-game to provoke his fellow Irish citizens to see how they would respond: a dark-skinned student sits at the back of the class for thirty minutes each day, and when the lesson was over, this student is invited to rejoin the rest of the class, which consisted of primarily White, native Irish students. There would be outrage at this explicit and State-permitted discrimination! And yet, Monahan argues, this is precisely what happens for students of no or minority religions from age 4 to 18 during religious education classes.[61]

Education Equality was adept at using these concrete and highly personal stories to capture peoples' imaginations and tug on the heart strings. Such charged images and stories help mobilise people to action as has been the case in previous reform campaigns. In addition to these highly evocative personal stories, Education Equality and other reformers peppered

59 Paddy Monahan, 'Equal Access to Education', *The Irish Times*, 19 October 2015.
60 Paddy Monahan, 'Community National Schools Are a Bad Idea', *The Irish Times*, 9 June 2016.
61 Paddy Monahan, Personal Interview, October 2019.

their arguments with phrases that make it difficult for the Church or other critics of reform to refute the claims. For example, the repeated use of 'non-discriminating schools' to refer to multi- or non-denominational schools implies that all Catholic schools are by their nature discriminatory. Likewise, reiterating 'publicly funded' schools implies that because Catholic schools receive money from the State, they should be required to follow all State guidelines. This glosses over the denominational structure of education whereby the State 'provides for' education while private patrons, including the Church, actually run the schools. By consistently talking about 'tax-payer' schools, these reformers underscore how the State financially supports Catholic schools and paints Catholic schools as not complying with State regulations. Such language calls to mind decades of Church sexual abuse and previous eras of the Church ignoring State guidelines. Again, the implication is that Catholic schools are more than welcome to maintain and preserve their ethos and provide a faith-based education, but they must then operate entirely as an independent, private school with no State support. Again, the idea is that once a school accepts State money, they have to follow equality legislation. These are subtle, but powerful terms that push people to accept the secular arguments for complete separation of Church and State in education. Like the baptismal barrier, if these terms of non-discriminating schools and publicly funded or tax-payer schools become more commonplace, it will be harder and harder for supporters of faith-based schools to counter these arguments.

Similar to what occurred in the same-sex marriage campaign, and to a lesser extent in the abortion campaign, the successful framing of the equality movement leaves the Church often appearing defensive and/or insensitive to the needs of others. Or worse, the Church appears to be looking out for its own interests, which was part of the underlying cause for the sexual abuse crisis in the eyes of many Irish citizens.

1. The Church's Response

The Church's official position had long been that its schools were inclusive and that they welcomed all children irrespective of religion, race, ethnicity, or socio-economic status. Nevertheless, several bishops, including then Bishop Michael Smith of Meath, argued in the early 2000s that parents who did not share the faith or who were not practicing their faith should not be allowed to take advantage of existing Catholic schools. Such views attracted widespread public attention and fuelled demands for reforms so that parents would not have to feign religious belief to get their children accepted into schools. The Catholic Information Office was quoted as saying: 'There was no change in its school enrolment policy, where Catholic schools were open to all children. However, many bishops would undoubtedly have some sympathy for Dr Smith's remarks when faced with a similar situation in which parents had lost contact with the Church were availing of Catholic schools.'[62]

In 2007, the Bishops Conference submitted a complaint to RTÉ when a teacher in an Educate Together school criticised Catholic school admissions policies. This teacher had previously been on the board of management of a Catholic school and reported that the enrolment policy in his former school gave priority to baptised children of Catholic parents – which did result in excluding some children from the school.[63] Although the Bishops Conference won this complaint, there was growing discontent on what was becoming known as the baptismal barrier. In response, growing numbers of bishops argued that the State (Department of Education) should take a more active role in providing non-denominational education for those who wanted it instead of expecting that the Catholic Church to provide and run schools in ways that were not consistent with their values and goals. This is one of the reasons why Archbishop Diarmuid Martin of Dublin had proposed the Church relinquishing as many as half of their schools in Dublin. At the same time the Church was supporting diversification, it consistently defended its ability to shape how its schools were operated.

As the proposed legislation on admissions reform surfaced after the Forum on Patronage and Pluralism in 2011–12, there were significant concerns from educational leaders within the Catholic Church. In particular, leaders were upset about the premise upon which the Admissions Bill was being propagated, and they were apprehensive about the negative impact

---

62   Fischer, 2016, 130.
63   Fischer, 2016, 132–3.

the proposed legislation would have on the Catholic ethos of its primary schools over the medium and longer term. The Catholic Primary Schools Management Association (CPSMA), which represents the boards of management of all Catholic primary schools, stated that the Admissions Bill was part of a 'secularisation agenda aimed mainly at the Catholic Church' and could lead to numerous legal cases by parents seeking to ensure a Catholic faith dimension for their children.[64]

The real issue, according to Catholic school proponents, was a lack of school placements due to poor Department of Education planning and lack of resources. Rather than the widely touted 'baptismal barrier', Catholic schools reiterated that there was no requirement for parents to have their children baptised to gain placement in a Catholic school.[65] Instead, CPSMA argued that 'the Admissions Bill will change only the names of those excluded from schools, not the fact that some pupils and their parents will be unhappy because they cannot get a place in their local school. Had the Minister focused on the evidence he would have realised that.'[66]

The first major criticism by Catholic school defenders was that the Admissions Bill was inspired largely by inconclusive and decade-old-data as the primary rationale for the new legislation. The Minister of Education and proponents of the Admissions Bill regularly cited data from a 2007/08 Economic and Social Research Institute (ESRI) study that reported that 20 % of Irish primary schools were oversubscribed. Even though a majority of primary schools were not oversubscribed, and therefore accepted all students who applied, the fact that one-fifth of schools had waiting lists was highlighted as a problem. In particular, reform advocates argued that religion was one of the key criteria for admissions in these oversubscribed

---

64   Carl O'Brien, 'Catholic Groups Warn of Legal Action over "Baptismal Barrier" Removal', *The Irish Times*, 3 January 2018.

65   Seamus Mulconry, 'CPSMA Responds to Minister Bruton's School Admission Policy Proposal', 16 January 2017. <https://www.catholicbishops.ie/2017/01/16/cpsma-responds-to-minister-brutons-school-admission-policy-proposal/> (Accessed: 18 January 2021).

66   Seamus Mulconry, 'Lack of School Places the Problem, not Baptism Barrier', *The Irish Times*, 14 May 2018.

schools, thereby resulting in discrimination against children of minority religions and no faith at all.

CPSMA criticised the over-reliance on this data, and it offered alternative figures to question the scale of the problem of oversubscribed schools and need for reforming admissions' policies. The Education Secretariat of the Catholic Archdiocese of Dublin conducted a survey in 2017 that found that waiting lists and the use of religion as the deciding factor in admissions was greatly overstated. This study indicated that only seventeen of the 384 schools that responded to the survey (456 schools received the survey) refused enrolment for a reason relating to baptismal certificates. This represents only 4 % of the total number of schools in Dublin. When looking at the total number of applicants and considering enrolment decisions, the survey results indicate that religion only affected 1 % of all school applications that did not result in enrolment in the school of their choice.[67] When asked in parliament to provide official data on the levels of oversubscription, Minister Bruton reported that 'schools are not required to report to my department on the number of applicants who are refused and the therefore the information requested by the Deputy is not available'.[68]

CPSMA once again concluded at the time that the real issue was a lack of buildings and school placements, which was compounded by parental behaviour regarding school choice. Specifically, CPSMA suggested that there was a growing trend by many parents to bypass their local school to seek enrolment in more socio-economically advantaged areas. This leads to over demand in certain areas, which also exacerbates the oversubscription problem. The day when most or all students walked or cycled to school is less prevalent as parents drive further distances to work and often drop their children off on the way. Even these trends are understudied according to CPSMA, which reinforced their demands for better data to justify making a key legislative change that will affect so few students.[69] CPSMA offered stark criticism of Minister Bruton, arguing that 'it is the responsibility of the Minister to Education to ensure there are sufficient school places in

67 Association of Trustees of Catholic Schools (ATCS), 2017.
68 Mulconry, 14 May 2018.
69 ATCS, March 2017.

local areas. Mr Bruton now admits he has failed to do so. Instead, he has accused local Catholic schools who cannot cope with demand in their area of discrimination (according to the Minister only Catholics discriminate, schools of other patron bodies prioritise). The phrase victim shaming springs to mind.'[70] For many, it was hard to hear the Church claiming that it was the victim when it had long been the dominant power in Irish society and still wielded or was perceived to wield considerable power in the educational sector. The fact that multi-denominational patrons had difficulty securing lands and buildings when the Church was perceived to have a surplus of land and buildings undermined the Church's victim argument. It did not matter that there was often a mismatch in terms of where surplus or empty Church property existed and where alternative patrons were seeking to establish schools, the Church's ownership of land and buildings was proof for opponents of its ongoing strength in the education sector. Add to this the long list of child victims of church leaders, which influenced why many of the Church's arguments were landing on deaf ears. In this sense, despite very valid arguments about the State's lack of resources and inadequate resources to keep up with changing demographics, the Church was losing the rhetoric game.

As legal counsel for CPSMA argued, there is no perfect way to ensure fairness in cases of oversubscription, especially because all parents will want to employ those criteria that will best ensure that their child gets place in the school.

> A good example of disagreement over fairness of criteria is to be seen in the affording priority to siblings of current students. Parents who succeed in getting their first child enrolled in a school of their choice will obviously be in favour of this criterion being applied in an application for a second child; parents of a child who has no siblings enrolled in the school, less so.[71]

---

70   Mulconry, 14 May 2018.
71   Liam Riordan, *CPSMA: Proposed Changes to Admissions in School*. Dublin: Mason, Hayes & Curran, 2015.

Given the complexities associated with admissions decisions in oversub-scribed schools, Church advocates view changes to religious exemptions as attacks on constitutionally protected rights of parents and patrons alike.

In addition to the extremely small numbers of children effected by admissions policies, Catholic school advocates suggest that the State has confirmed that Catholic schools are performing well. For example, the Department of Justice commented on the Admissions Bill by stating that 'at a general level the audit of school enrolment policies found no evidence of any system-wide enrolment practices that give rise to concern.'[72] Additionally, the Association of Trustees of Catholic Schools argues that Catholic schools are more inclusive than is often painted in the broader media. Based on evidence from school-wide evaluations conducted between 2010 and 2012, the Department of Education's Inspector's Report found that '96 % of schools were found to be managing their pupils effectively by, for example, fostering pupil-teacher interactions, by cultivating an inclusive, child-centred ethos and by using positive strategies to promote good behaviour. Incidental inspections similarly found that the management of pupils was effective in practically all (96 %) of the classrooms visited.'[73]

The other primary concern for most Catholic school advocates is their belief that the proposed legislation would infringe on parents' and children's right to freedom of religion and would also greatly limit the ability of patrons and boards of management to fulfil their duty to provide a faith-based education to those of the faith community they were established to serve. Several submissions underscored key precedents from the Irish Supreme Court that defend the freedom of religion and the exemptions of religious bodies to act in ways to support their ethos and values. The primary precedents that were then supported in the Education Act 1998 and the Equal Status Act 2000–11 include *Quinn's Supermarket Limited and Another v. The Attorney General and Others* (1972), *McGrath v. Maynooth College* (1979) and *Campaign to Separate Church and State Ltd v. Minister for Education* (1996). Despite these precedents, the Church fears that the State's increasing control and 'micro-managing' of every aspect of primary

---

72   ACTS, March 2017.
73   ACTS, March 2017.

education, including its 2016 unilateral removal of Rule 68, will continue to undermine the essence of Catholic education. The ATCS concludes that 'if the State removes the capacity of Faith schools to organise themselves, it will further encroach on religious freedom, undermine constitutional parental rights and breach the capacity of faith schools to carry out their statutory and legal obligations'.[74]

2. Media Attention

Despite strong evidence that the vast majority of all primary schools were actually diverse and inclusive, and the religious patrons had key rights within the Constitution, the Church's arguments seemed defensive or to miss the point about how individual children and parents were feeling marginalised or segregated. The fact that 'discrimination' language was taking root in most conversations undermined the effectiveness of the data provided by Church and other faith-based leaders. Additionally, there may not have been as much discrimination of non-religious or minority religious students once they enrolled in Catholic schools as was being regularly portrayed in the media and in public debates. However, the reform advocates and civil society leaders were winning the propaganda and framing battle such that change seemed necessary and inevitable. This competitive edge in how the issues were being framed helped explain how the issue gained traction among politicians and was beginning to cascade towards changing the admissions rules. Again, it appears as though the defenders of the Church position were making logical arguments that were not capturing the public imagination in ways that Education Equality and other reformers have so successfully done.

The communication and media strategies by reformers were effective, especially in focusing public attention on the admissions issue as a definite and meaningful change that could occur without disrupting the entire system. Salient issues within education tend to receive less attention within media than the hot-button issues of abortion or same-sex marriage. Nevertheless, what is similar is that key issues attract more

74   ATCS March 2017.

coverage when there is a specific political process and debate to focus the arguments and attention of media and readers alike. For example, there were only ten to twenty articles per year in the *Irish Independent* on abortion except for years when there was a referendum or key political debate. However, there were between 450 and 500 articles on abortion in the *Irish Independent* in 1983 and 1992 when there were referenda, and over 400 in 2013 when the Protection of Life during Pregnancy Act was passed after the tragic death of Savita Halappanavar. In education, the divestment/patronage issue was first mentioned in *The Irish Times* in 2007, and it peaked in 2015 with seventy articles. A combined total of nearly 120 articles over a two- to three-year period when the issue was being hotly contested during the Forum on Patronage and Pluralism in Irish Schools is significantly less than other contentious social and moral issues. School admissions and the 'baptismal barrier' gained attention beginning in 2015 and peaked with approximately 100 articles in 2017 and ninety articles in 2018 when the Education (Admissions to School) Act of 2018 was debated and ultimately passed. Thus, the existence of a clear-cut political process/debate focused the media's attention.

A more detailed analysis of the media coverage of admissions policies was provided in Chapter 7. Nevertheless, it is worth recalling a key finding. Not surprisingly, parents, school patrons and boards of management are key actors covered in the media during the admissions debates. However, the tightly framed political process meant that State/Government actors and institutions, political parties and civil society advocates were far more predominant in the media coverage. The consultative, open-ended nature of how divestment was engaged intentionally sought to include often under-heard voices within society and those most affected by proposed changes. Primary school admissions' policies were more narrowly framed within the context of a specific legislative act and addressed within a tighter period. This helps explain why political actors and reform advocates dominated the coverage. The strategic engagement of political actors in a process that could deliver immediate, but focused change made it easier for politicians and parties to support change at the national level. This was markedly different from the contentious and highly localised nature of divestment debates, where political actors were less keen to get drawn into the controversy or defended local interests that were contrary to nationally held positions.

Civil society and educational reformers successfully framed the debate to their advantage and increased media and public attention and support. The absence of easily recognisable civil society groups defending the role of religion in education, other than Catholic Bishops, and to a minor extent, Church of Ireland leaders, underscores that most actors discussing admissions policy sought change and they ultimately achieved it. Like trends during the same-sex marriage and abortion campaigns, civil society actors are visible, and can be successful, when they have political decision points such as referenda, deliberative bodies or specific legislation on which to focus their efforts. Such political focal points help keep the media's attention on critical issues, which outside these key political touchpoints tend to go unnoticed.

D. Education Equality Establishes a Ground Game and Mobilises Politicians

To ensure that the equality movement's efforts in education would not go unnoticed, Education Equality also sought to develop a stronger ground game. Despite the previously discussed financial and organisational realities that challenge mass mobilisation, Education Equality has implemented various organisational activities to advance its cause. First, it has conducted several online petitions. In 2015, they secured over 20,000 signatures in a petition to repeal the Equal Status Act.[75] Second, they have regularly facilitated public marches. In 2016, Educate Equality organised hundreds of people to march to Leinster House calling for an end to religious discrimination in State-funded schools.[76] Third, they also conducted a successful poster and video campaign that told the evocative stories of 100 parents and kids talking about classroom segregation.

---

75 Paddy Monahan, 'Segregation of Four-Year-Olds in Schools Has to Stop', *The Irish Times*, 15 December 2015.

76 McMahon, 2016.

Successive stories describing in provocative ways what it feels like to not truly opt-out of religious instruction or get a choice of the type of school they want were deeply moving. Curiously, many of the people telling the stories asked for anonymity because they feared backlash among the local community for demanding change.[77] The personal stories were gaining traction, but there was still an overall uneasiness about disrupting local community dynamics. This is another reason why Education Equality and other reformers have been focusing on tactics that can lead to legislative change without attracting too much attention from local communities who may not want to see change in their own school communities.

The final strategy employed by Education Equality was to take advantage of increased media attention and parental mobilisation to challenge politicians to pass admissions reform, which had been on the parliamentary docket since 2013. In previous campaigns, a popular threshold of nearly 60 % public support was usually needed before a majority of politicians were willing to actively support a controversial issue. Irish politicians, especially those from the historic Fianna Fáil and Fine Gael parties, were so dependent on generating broad electoral appeals that they tended to avoid alienating significant sectors within society by engaging controversial legislation before it was absolutely necessary. This sense of necessity, or impetus to act, usually occurs when challenger parties attract popular support for their clear, persistent and strong positions on emerging issues. Despite changing demographics and declining numbers of conservative and/or practicing Catholics, there were still significant portions of Irish society that supported the Church's role in education. Thus, major party politicians were hesitant to get too far in front of public opinion. Legal scholar April Duff argues that the unwillingness of past governments to repeal section 7(3)(c) of the *Equal Status Act of 2000* indicates that change on this issue is politically dangerous and may have to be achieved through other means such as the courts, international pressure, or mass mobilisation.[78]

According to Paddy Monahan, Education Equality's spokesperson, there was over 80 % public support for removing the 'baptismal barrier'

---

77   Paddy Monahan, Personal Interview, October 2019.
78   Duff, 2017, 21.

and legislating on admissions policies by the mid-2010s. As discussed in
Chapter 9 on political parties and their positions on education reform,
the 2016 *Which Candidate* Survey revealed that of the approximately
25,000 voter respondents, nearly 80 % (79.2 %) of respondents reported
that religion should not be a valid criterion for primary school admission.
An additional 13 % reported that religion could be factored into admission but only when other options were available to students. Only 8 %
testified that religious background should be utilised so that faith-based
schools could serve the students who belonged to their faith. Thus, two
years before the School Admissions Bill of 2018 was passed that forbade
Catholic schools from considering religious background as a valid criterion for admittance, there appeared to be overwhelming public support
to make this policy shift. This explains why Educate Equality maintained
their focus on this tangible and achievable reform and kept the pressure
on politicians to legislate on such a widely popular issue. Monahan added
that there was and continues to be considerably lower levels of public
support for removing the opt-out clause or having religion outside the
normal school day, which is why it has been difficult to sell politicians on
the need to act now.[79] According to the 2016 *Which Candidate* Survey,
only a third (33.6 %) of respondents agreed that religion should only be
taught outside of school; a majority (54.9 %) believed that students should
learn about multiple faiths not just one; and a small portion (11.6 %) reported that pupils should learn the religion of their school's ethos. Given
the evidence, the one-step-at-a-time approach undertaken by reform advocates appears to be consistent with successful strategies employed by
previous reform campaigns.

In addition to its primary efforts in raising public awareness and
establishing sufficient levels of public support to make legislative change
more likely, Education Equality also sought to make admissions an election issue in 2016. To this end, leaders from Education Equality met with
Minister for Education Richard Bruton, TD, several times during the
campaign to discuss the removal of the 'baptismal barrier'. Monahan described Bruton as highly pragmatic, and he applauded Bruton's desire to pass

---

79   Paddy Monahan, Personal Interview, October 2019.

feasible legislation. Education Equality wanted to avoid being too closely aligned with any one party, especially in light of the experience of Equate, and therefore they met with and educated each political party's education spokesperson in hopes that they could persuade these leaders to come to their side. The real goal was to secure support for passing the Admissions Bill and other educational reforms rooted in the equality movement by ensuring that these issues made it into party election manifestoes and, if possible, into the programme for government of the next governing coalition. For Monahan, the Labour Party has been the party most consistently advocating for educational reform and the gradual removal of religion from primary schools. He characterises the Green Party, People Before Profit and the Social Democrats as genuinely supportive of the proposed Admissions Bill, whereas he described Fianna Fáil and Fine Gael as more superficial in their support of the legislation.[80]

In an article from *The Irish Times* during the 2016 general election campaign, Monahan outlined the party positions on equal access to primary education. The extremely critical nature of his summary resembles a 'strike while the iron is hot' mentality. In other words, Education Equality wanted to put pressure on parties to define their positions while the media and voters were paying attention and interested in change. He suggested that the leading governing party, Fine Gael, included very little on education in their manifesto, with only a brief mention about divestment and creating new multi-denominational schools. This was too slow and did not address the real issues according to Monahan. Labour's manifesto mentioned access to schools being determined by proximity rather than focusing on religion. Despite Labour traditionally being the most reform-minded party, Monahan criticised Labour's Minister for Education Jan O'Sullivan, TD, for her proposed quota system that would ensure certain percentages of places in schools for children not of patron's religion. For Education Equality, this system was overly complicated, and it did not make enrolment blind to religion, which prioritised the rights of patrons over children. Next, Fianna Fáil was described as intentionally vague, with

---

80   Paddy Monahan, Personal Interview, October 2019.

some positive treatment of access for all children to local schools, but still giving some preference to children of the patron's religion within a locality even if co-religionists from outside the area would no longer receive preferential treatment. Sinn Féin, Greens, People Before Profit and the Social Democrats were highlighted for their support of ending religious discrimination in admissions to tax-payer funded schools.[81] Again, note the use of 'discrimination' and 'tax-payer funded schools', which are key rhetorical phrases from the equality movement. This rhetoric makes it difficult for proponents of faith-based schools to defend their practices because they are seen as harming the experience of children. Furthermore, the use of such accepted phrases signals to voters that they have an opportunity to pressure parties to act in ways consistent with what they had just done the previous year in passing marriage equality legislation.

IV. The Passing of the Education (Admissions to School) Act of 2018

The language employed by and popularised by Education Equality was not only being adopted by political parties and other civil groups such as Atheist Ireland and the Humanist Association of Ireland, but it was becoming widely accepted and used by such recognisable and respected organisations as the Irish Human Rights and Equality Commission (IHREC) and the Ombudsmen for Children Office (OCO). For example, the IHREC recommended that the Admissions Bill be passed to 'to give effect to the principle that no child should be given preferential access to a publicly funded school on the basis of religion.'[82] The OCO argued that of the four proposals for new admissions policies, the outright prohibition of religion as a criterion for admission should be adopted. For the Ombudsmen, the Catchment Area, Nearest School

81   Paddy Monahan, 'Where Do Parties Stand on Equal Access to Primary Education', *The Irish Times*, 18 February 2016.
82   Fischer, 2016, 157.

Rule and Quota System options do not provide for a non-discriminatory child rights-based approach to school admissions.[83]

The Ombudsmen's for Children proclaimed its ultimate preference for the complete removal of denominational religious classes from state-funded schools:

> While it is accepted that such a change will take time to be accepted and implemented, at both societal and legislative levels, it is considered that this is not a sufficient reason to continue the deferral of this issue. Therefore, as an interim measure, provisions should be made for the removal of religion from the integrated curriculum and the religious teaching of the school patron should be confined to a specific religion class. This would ensure that children who opt-out of these set religion classes would not be exposed to unwanted religious influence in other parts of the school day.[84]

This bold support by a highly reputable organisation among politicians and civil society provided considerable legitimacy to the reform advocates. Education Equality shared this view and believed that more work could be done in the short term to schedule religion classes at times sensitive to and convenient for parental needs. Such changes would, reformers argue, better respect the rights of freedom of thought, conscience, belief and religion for all children. Nevertheless, Education Equality and other reformers strategically chose to keep their focus on passing the Admissions Bill, before then shifting their public awareness campaigns and political lobbying efforts towards the opt-out and integrated curriculum issues.

The incremental, one small reform at a time approach that was so successful in the LGBTQ+ rights' movement was proving effective here as well. Education Equality leaders argued that their strategy was not to pursue larger constitutional change, but instead focus on the types of legislative changes they were able to achieve in the passing of the Education (Admissions to Schools) Act of 2018. This bill passed in July of 2018 with no formal vote in parliament. Similar to the civil unions legislation in 2010, the legislation had passed through the various stages of debate and had achieved essentially unanimous support from all parties that the final legislation was simply moved and approved by both houses of the Oireachtas. In

83 Ombudsman for Children's Office, March 2017.
84 Ombudsman for Children's Office, March 2017, 24–5.

addition to preventing Catholic schools from basing admissions decisions on the religious background of students (or their parents), the Admissions Bill banned waiting lists and fees relating to admissions in non-fee paying schools, set the limit on the numbers of school places that could be reserved for children of past pupils at 25 %, and required all schools that are not oversubscribed to admit all students that apply. According to Minister Bruton, these measures were enacted to provide more equitable access to children of all demographic groups, including religious, socio-economic status, race, ethnicity, etc.[85]

The language employed by various politicians during the final parliamentary debate before approving the legislation was representative of the key arguments that were dominant within civil society, public discourse and the media at the time. They confirm a sense that change was almost inevitable and this change in admissions was the next step in the longer arc of educational reform. For example, Minister Bruton acknowledged his pragmatic approach may not go far enough, but that it was the best that could have been achieved at the time, leaving action on the opt-out or the elimination of religion altogether for a later date. He stated in the Dáil, 'What we are really discussing is how to address the absolute constitutional right of a child to opt out of the religious activities within the school, if he or she chooses. This is what we are trying to do, and this is what my amendment provides for. Clearly, many people take the more radical view of taking religion out of schools altogether and not using schools for any form of religious instruction. These are legitimately held different points of view. I seek to develop the provision for children who want to opt out and to make sure it is a good provision.'[86] He added that lessons learned from the Forum on Patronage about good practices in this area would be implemented and enhanced, but that further consultation was required to iron out the best way to provide before or after school religious instruction.

Fianna Fáil's Education Spokesman, Thomas Byrne, TD, supported the Minister's call for further consultation to find the best way to move

---

85   O'Brien, 2018.
86   Dáil Debates, 30 May 2018. <https://www.kildarestreet.com/debates/ ?id=2018-05-30a.478>.

religious instruction to the end of the school day and offered his party's support for exploring this idea. Perhaps unsurprisingly given Fianna Fáil's historic tendency to want to create broad consensus on contentious issues, Byrne stated that 'it is important in our education system that we do not simply make laws and hand them down but that we bring the stakeholders along. That is the way the education system has worked in Ireland and the reason it has become the one it is today.'[87]

Several left-wing politicians used the final debate to underscore their desire for further reforms. Richard Boyd Barrett, a Solidarity-People Before Profit TD, employed language similar to that regularly promoted by Education Equality. He argued that in 'an education system which is publicly funded – even private schools receive some level of public funding – there should be a curriculum taught which is inclusive of everybody and does not have a bias in favour of or prefer a particular religious ethos or does not seek to impose a particular moral or religious view of the world'.[88] He adds that he defends freedom of religious expression and association, but he views this as separate from what should happen in State-funded schools. There is no question, Barrett added, that many denominational schools do not, nor would ever want to discriminate against any child, 'but the problem is that there is no protection against a situation where that is not the case'.[89]

Paul Murphy, also a Solidarity-People Before Profit TD, echoed Barrett's calls to eliminate religious education Ireland's primary schools. He first highlighted that the significant vote in favour of repealing the 8th Amendment to permit abortions in Ireland the previous week confirmed the power of the equality movement and a weakening of the once dominant Catholic Church in Irish society. He argued that Ireland is

[in] a struggle for equality and against oppression and a key part of that is the struggle for a secular society, where there is separation of church and State and where everybody's rights to practise religion are fully protected by the State, with no interference whatsoever. It is also, however, a society in which the State's resources

87 Dáil Debates, 2018.
88 Dáil Debates, 2018.
89 Dáil Debates, 2018.

are not used to promote any particular religion. The key battlegrounds for a secular society are in education and healthcare, where the lack of a secular society has a daily impact on people's lives.[90]

He reminded the Minister, who he says is more skilful and flexible than previous governments in passing the admissions legislation, that this issue will not go away. Confirming the gradualist approach promoted by Education Equality and other reformers, Murphy persuasively suggests that the movement afoot in Irish society will demand change on religious instruction, sex education and other issues. He concludes, 'People will increasingly demand that each of these issues be dealt with but, more generally, they will say we need a separation of church and State in this country. We will have a major movement around that. It is quite clear that movement will ultimately be successful. The question is how long and how far the Government and various establishment parties will resist that rising demand and how much resistance they will put up.'[91]

V. Post-Admissions Reform: The Next Steps

The success of the Admissions Bill, although not a complete win for reformers, marked a critical next step in the march towards reducing the role of religion in Ireland's primary schools. Similar to previous civil society movements, there is often overall agreement of the equality movement's ultimate goals in a sector, but there can be a wide array of competing strategies about the most effective means of achieving these goals. The classic example within the LGBTQ+ movement was whether supporting civil unions would be a necessary and sufficient steppingstone on the path towards complete marriage equality or whether such support would undermine the purer ideals of accepting nothing less legal recognition and associated rights and prevent advancement of the cause. Even

90   Dáil Debates, 2018.
91   Dáil Debates, 2018.

among those who agree that the incremental approach is the best strategy, there are differences about the best sequence of reforms to achieve the ultimate elimination of religion from Ireland's primary schools.

Education Equality's spokesperson Paddy Monahan contends that creating further equality within the current system requires relatively simple changes to legislation to remove exemptions for State-funded schools from equality legislation. Furthermore, he thinks that legislative enactments requiring all State-funded schools to teach faith formation during one distinct period of time after core school hours is achievable. In this scenario, those who wish to attend can do so and those who do not can be collected prior to the commencement of religious instruction.[92]

Education Equality, and Monahan more specifically, disagrees with some reformers who believe that a citizens' assembly specifically instituted to address educational reform is the most reasonable next step. Monahan believes this assembly would distract from the legislative reforms he considers likely to be passed in the next several years. The idea of a citizens' assembly for education had been floated in the immediate aftermath of the abortion referendum in May 2018. Former Labour Party Leader, Joan Burton, TD, highlighted Labour's proposal 'to use the Citizens' Assembly model to have a discussion based on a representative sample, as was done successfully in respect of marriage equality and repealing the eighth amendment. This is an important issue for communities, schools and institutions.'[93] Later in 2018, a diverse group of 100 citizens met at the Burren College of Art in Clare for a three-day conference on 'Towards a More Creative Education System'. The outcome from this symposium and the preceding consultations was a growing consensus calling for radical changes to Ireland's educational system. Former INTO Deputy General Secretary Catherine Byrne, who had worked extensively with Atlantic Philanthropies when it funded the

---

92 Education Equality, 'Equality in Education: Your Questions Answered', <https://educationequalitydotblog.wordpress.com/education-equality-your-questions-answered/> (Accessed: 14 April 2021).

93 Dáil Debates, 30 May 2018. <https://www.kildarestreet.com/debates/?id=2018-05-30a.478>.

original 'We the Citizens' assembly in 2011, proposed CAFE: the Citizens' Assembly for Education.[94]

Not unlike Education Equality, CAFE was a voluntary group that had a two-pronged approach to raising awareness and to ultimately achieve educational reform. First, they sought to secure cross-party backing for this new citizens' assembly on education. They initially motivated some parties to include reference to this citizens' assembly in their 2020 general election manifestos. The Green Party was even able to get Fianna Fáil and Fine Gael to agree to hold a citizens' assembly on education as part of their joint 2020 Programme for Government. This was seen as quite accomplishment by supporters of the recently created CAFE organisation. The Programme for Government stated: 'We will establish a Citizens' Assembly on the Future of Education ensuring that the voices of young people and those being educated are central.'[95] Thus, there appeared to be real momentum to use the citizens' assembly to increase public and political support engage educational reforms as had been done with previous citizens' assemblies and constitutional conventions in the marriage equality and abortion campaigns.[96]

The second strategy employed by the CAFE group was to mobilise and raise awareness at the grassroots level. In particular, the 'Bringing Education Alive for our Communities on a National Scale', or BEACONS, was created. This parallel process was overseen by the Teaching Council, which is the professional standards body for the teaching profession that was established in 2006 under the Teaching Council Act of 2001.[97] The goal was to engage students, teachers and parents in communal meetings throughout the country on a wide range of educational issues including the culture of control, a need for greater creativity and inclusion, and most importantly the need for greater student voice and agency within schools. Lessons

---

94   Martin Hawkes, 'Citizens' Assembly for Education Could Be a Game-Changer', 23 June 2020. <https://educationmatters.ie/citizens-assembly-on-education/>.

95   Hawkes, 23 June 2020.

96   Catherine Byrne, 'Education and a Citizens' Assembly', *The Irish Times*, 26 June 2020.

97   <https://www.teachingcouncil.ie/en/faqs/about-us/>.

learned from these listening sessions would eventually feed into the citizens' assembly.[98]

This early victory of earning official recognition to hold a citizens' assembly is not without challenges. In addition to education, the 2020 Programme for Government also proposed citizens' assemblies on gender equality, biodiversity, matters relating to drugs use, and one to consider the type of directly elected mayor and local government structures best suited for Dublin.[99] The increasing use of these assemblies to discuss a disparate set of topics may prove less effective than earlier assemblies. Although reform-minded campaigners certainly took advantage of these previous assemblies to hone their message and quicken the intensity of their public campaigns, there was already an appetite for change on many of these issues and politicians appeared more willing to act on specific proposals.

The initial scope of the educational assembly was framed in much broader terms than previous campaigns. For example, the topics that CAFE originally proposed for discussion were quite extensive and unlikely to lead to concrete, actionable outcomes that could achieve results in the short term. CAFE expressed the hope that the educational citizens' assembly would engage big questions about the values and purpose of education in line with CAFE's ideals: 'We are committed to supporting the development of a shared understanding of the value of education which addresses how education can prepare people of all ages to meet new societal, environmental, technological and economic challenges which face us all.'[100] Some of the original themes identified by CAFE as important to discuss include: Education for What?, Capacities for Thriving, Creativity and the Arts, Global Citizenship, Inclusion and Equity, Culture Shift, The Role of Parents and Life-long Learning.[101] These are unquestionably important

98 Hawkes, 23 June 2020.
99 *Programme for Government: Our Shared Future*, 2020, 40, 49, 77, 95 and 119; <https://www.gov.ie/en/publication/7e05d-programme-for-government-our-shared-future/>.
100 Hawkes, 23 June 2020.
101 Topics included in the original 'Proposal for Manifesto' of the Citizens' Assembly for Education (CAFE). Document shared with authors from Catherine Byrne in October 2019.

issues facing education; however, they are also complex, multifaceted and will take longer periods to adequately address, let alone create consensus on what actual change would entail.

The recommendations from previous citizens' assemblies that have attained successful outcomes have generally been more narrowly defined so that a legislative act or regulation could effect change. When citizens' assembly recommendations have led to constitutional referenda, they were framed in a binary proposal that allowed voters to vote yes or no to proposed amendments. This is one of the reasons Education Equality's Paddy Monahan argues that, if possible, it would be beneficial to avoid amending the Constitution. From his perspective, the Constitution already provides a solid rights-based framework that upholds and protects individual rights. There was an implicit hope that the acceptance of the equality movement's emphasis on human rights and non-discrimination would grow to the point where a majority of Irish citizens would view educational reforms through an equality lens. Eventually, reformers believed that a critical mass would be reached whereby a majority of Irish citizens would see the Constitution's protection of individual rights requiring the elimination of religion's role in primary education. By working with the Department of Education and ensuring quality legislation continues to be passed, Monahan argues that human rights will be protected without altering the Constitution.[102]

The combination of these various civil society groups each working towards similar ultimate goals but from different perspectives is reminiscent of the LGBTQ+ rights' movement. It was not until the Government announced in 2013 its plan to hold the marriage equality referendum in 2015 that the various civil society groups overcame their strategic and philosophical differences and were able to coordinate their efforts. As CAFE pursues its goals directed towards the educational citizens' assembly, Education Equality continues its efforts to incrementally pursue possible legislative reforms that further limit the role of religion in Irish primary schools.

The lack of popular support for the opt-out, the next step in the reform agenda, has reinforced the need for Education Equality to educate mainstream Irish citizens on the opt-out issue. This has become a focus of their

102   Paddy Monahan, Personal Interview, October 2019.

efforts in the 2020s. Education Equality views its next task as reminding the public and politicians alike that constitutional guarantees of students are not working in reality as considerable numbers of students are still experiencing exclusion, ignorance and a lack of understanding. From this perspective, the rights to withdraw from religious instruction and protection from being forced to attend a class that is contrary to their conscience are not effectively working in many Irish schools. Education Equality is also publicising existing research in Ireland that indicates that while most primary schools admit children from diverse religious backgrounds, the school ethos and curriculum do not adequately address the needs of children of minority faith backgrounds.[103] Paul Rowe, former leader of Educate Together, echoed these same arguments in his testimony to an Oireachtas Committee: 'Accommodating minority children is not the same as treating all children as equals and proposals to require schools to outline the alternative activities for these children do nothing to compensate for this inadequate arrangement.'[104] Education Equality made similar arguments about the religious education curriculum, underscoring that many non-religious and minority faith students are being forced to sit in the back of class as part of their opt-out. This, critics argue, is problematic because students may be exposed to conflicting sets of values at home and in school.[105] In making these types of arguments, Education Equality is connecting the 'ongoing discrimination' of students to the broader equality movement for which most Irish citizens have already accepted, and thus increasing support for the next legislative steps.

103   Daniel Faas, Merike Darmody and Beata Sokolowska, 'Religious Diversity in Primary Schools: Reflections from the Republic of Ireland', *British Journal of Religious Education*, 2016, Vol. 38, No. 1, 83–98, DOI: 10.1080/ 01416200.2015.1025700.

104   <https://www.educatetogether.ie/news/educate-together-raises-major-concerns-with-governments-education-admissions-to-school-bill-at-oireachtas-hearing/>.

105   Faas, Darmody and Sokolowska, 2016, 38:1, 83–98.

VI. Conclusion

This chapter examined how school admissions policies were swiftly changed in the 2018 Admissions Bill. Compared to divestment and curriculum, the process leading up to the passing of the Admissions Bill is the most like what occurred in the marriage equality and abortion campaigns. Civil society activists and academics took advantage of Ireland's social and demographic changes to redefine the problem as one of discrimination against non-religious, secular and minority religious students who had their rights to an education free of religion denied to them. Like earlier campaigns, civil society activists and educational reformers built support by highlighting international standards from the United Nations and European Union. These standards framed the issues in terms of human rights and anti-discrimination. Reformers also appealed to people through personal stories of hardship and discrimination of non-religious and minority religious students and families. Once reformers generated enough public support and media attention, they encouraged politicians to support narrow legislative changes that could be passed without much public opposition. Framing issues around equality and using phrases like 'baptismal barrier' moved the debate away the relatively small number of people affected towards support for change. The near unanimous support among politicians reflected the lack of any concerted opposition and is a testimony to how issue definition and solution identification won the day. The narrow focus limited those who opposed the measure and generated widespread support for this significant educational reform. Supporters of further reforms considered this one more necessary step in the gradual dismantling of the Church's role within Irish primary schools.

CHAPTER 12

Curriculum

I. Introduction

The role of religion within the Irish primary school curriculum is the third and final reform case study examined within this book. Religion has been integral to Irish primary schools since the nineteenth century. There was a brief period in the 1830s when Ireland explored establishing a truly national system of education whereby the State, not churches, owned and funded schools. In fact, the famous *Stanley Letter* (1831) sought to establish a national system wherein all schools would accept Catholic and Protestant children. The schools would teach the secular subjects to Catholic and Protestant children together and would separate them for classes on religious instruction, which were taught at specific times. Stanley underestimated the support by local Catholic clergy and the hierarchy to have denominational schools and the proposal to allow ownership by local patrons took on a momentum of its own.[1] What emerged at that time and has persisted since is a denominational/private system that the State funds and supports in various ways, but the individual patrons infuse with their characteristic spirit.

Ironically, it was precisely when Ireland started to undergo its initial period of modernisation and social change in the 1960s that the State consolidated the denominational nature of primary schools. First, the State issued the Rules for National Schools in 1965, which had within them guidelines on the primary school curriculum. Rule 68 is particularly prescient because it states, 'Of all the parts of a school curriculum

---

1   David Tuohy, SJ, *Denominational Education and Politics: Ireland in a European Context*, Dublin: Veritas, 2013, 210–17.

Religious Instruction is by far the most important .... Religious Instruction is, therefore, a fundamental part of the school course, and a religious spirit should inform and vivify the whole work of the school.'[2] The emergence of the 'integrated curriculum' in 1971 called for all teachers to imbue their teaching with a religious dimension, and civic and religious spirits were considered two sides of the same coin. For critics of the Church's role in education, these changes consolidated the denominational nature of primary schools where as the Constitution only acknowledged that denominational schools were an integral part of the system. Such a system, critics of religion argue, undermines the freedom of conscience and/or religion of many Irish citizens.[3]

Another key aspect of the 1971 Primary School Curriculum is that politicians and professional educators assumed a greater role in formulating the curriculum. According to a study of curricular changes over the last 100 years, the 1971 curriculum

> represented a seismic shift in state policy and attitude towards the education of children and set the tone for subsequent provision along the lines still delivered in the first decades of the twenty-first century. It was underpinned by the ideology of child-centred education, offering a wide range of subjects and encouraging discovery learning methods. While the core subjects of English, Irish, mathematics and religion remained, the relative focus on these subjects altered, with a greater emphasis placed on the English language. The inclusion of additional subjects such as music, art and craft, social and environmental studies and physical education allowed a greater focus on the aesthetic, physical, creative and emotional aspects of development.[4]

Although many of these changes took years to implement fully, the increase in numbers of subjects represents the State's attempt to respond to changes in society. The overloaded and ever-expanding primary curriculum of the twenty-first century has its roots in these earlier changes.

2   See Chapter IX of these rules for guidelines on Religious Instruction: <https://www.into.ie/media-centre/circulars/rules-for-national-schools-1965>.
3   Karin Fischer, *Schools and the Politics of Religion and Diversity in the Republic of Ireland: Separate but Equal*. Manchester: Manchester University Press, 2016, 11–27.
4   Thomas Walsh (2016): '100 Years of Primary Curriculum Development and Implementation in Ireland: A Tale of a Swinging Pendulum', *Irish Educational Studies*, DOI: 10.1080/03323315.2016.1147975; p. 8.

Ireland's current curriculum was implemented in 1999 after nearly a decade-long process of research, deliberation, consultation and review. This curriculum was implemented as Ireland's booming, Celtic Tiger economy was starting to roar. Some analysts suggest that a shift towards a commodification of education occurred at this time with an emphasis on the economy, and subsequent focus on consumers, management, evaluation, financial responsibility and performance indicators. As a result, the economy started to take precedence over cultural and religious dimensions. The place of God in schools was still prevalent, but changes in society had placed more emphasis on student-centred learning and preparing active citizens than creating good Catholics.[5] A key overall goal of this new 1999 curriculum was to 'nurture the child in all dimensions of his or her life – spiritual, moral, cognitive, emotional, imaginative, aesthetic, social and physical'. Given certain cracks in the Church's moral authority and declining beliefs and practices, it is not surprising that the focus on the spiritual was not grounded in any particular theological framework, but a more general social and cultural phenomenon independent of the Catholic Church.[6]

The dramatic changes in religious beliefs and practices occurring within Irish society more broadly were mirrored among younger generations of teachers. Thus, the very teachers being tasked to teach the Religious Education curriculum were themselves departing from practice and tenets of the faith. Questions emerged about how rich the teaching and faith formation could be if the teachers themselves do not believe. Further questions arose about whether faith formation should more appropriately be conducted in parishes and outside the classroom and the normal school day. By the late 2010s, these changes were catching up with teacher preparation and the need to prepare most teachers to work in Catholic schools irrespective of their own faith. By 2021, a majority of students earning their education degrees at the undergraduate or graduate levels in Ireland take courses in Catholic education. According to Dean Anne Looney at Dublin City University, on average, about 80 % of education students in each class choose to earn a Certificate in Catholic Education during

---

5   Fischer, 2016, 57–63.
6   Tuohy, 2013, 226.

their training. Her unofficial sense is that approximately a quarter take this course because they are sincerely interested. The other three-quarters of students, Looney contends based on informal and anecdotal evidence, take the course to hedge their bets so they are more qualified when seeking employment. Most of these students lack knowledge and depth about faith but realise that most teaching placements are in Catholic schools, so they need this qualification to get hired.[7] At some point, potentially soon, greater numbers of teachers-in-training may choose with their feet and decide not to take courses in religious education. In turn, more and more schools may, out of necessity and in contravention of the requirements set out by Irish Bishops, rely less on this qualification in hiring practices, which would undermine further need to offer such courses. In conversations with teachers, it is increasingly the case that principals and schools only ask about Catholic qualifications in interviews and never return to the theme or demand much proof of Catholic credentials once teaching.

Such realities, when combined with proposed changes in the content and time allotted to religion in the curriculum that are discussed below, reveal the subtle changes that are occurring. For all the division and uncertainty that exists now within political debates about primary school educational reform, these slow, imperceptible changes point to curriculum as the place where real change will occur. Change here could make reforms in the system a moot point!

In addition to the changes in religious practices and beliefs, Irish society more broadly has been transformed since 1999. The economic boom of the 1990s and the first decade of the twenty-first century utterly transformed Irish society. The boom altered incomes, the nature of the workforce, levels of educational attainment, the structure of family life, the percentage of immigrants and even where people lived. The social, cultural and racial homogeneity that once characterised Ireland has become less prevalent, hollowing out the consensus that facilitated a sense of national identity and made forging broad, cross-class policy appeals more feasible. Advances in technology and the unprecedented access to information available to all

---

7   Anne Looney, Executive Dean of the Institute of Education at DCU, Personal Interview, October 2019.

students have combined with dramatic social changes to totally alter the educational experience for children in Irish primary schools.

These extraordinary changes have increased demands for a new primary curriculum.[8] The challenge is how to keep and enhance those parts of the system that are working well, while responding to new needs based on cutting-edge educational research and demands from various sectors of society. Irish primary level students consistently achieve comparatively high results in reading, math and science. Enhancing the curriculum in these areas and adding additional subjects and themes to meet new needs is threatening to overload an already crowded curriculum. Educational leaders seeking to meet national priorities have already sought to increase time allotted to existing areas such as Social, Personal and Health Education (SPHE) and Physical Education (PE), while also exploring ways to add new subjects like Coding and Computational Thinking, Modern Foreign Languages and Education about Religions and Beliefs (ERB) and Ethics to the overall curriculum.

If making choices about all of these important educational trade-offs was not difficult enough, these curricular choices are being debated at a time when Ireland's overall denominational system of primary education is also being challenged. The relatively slow pace of increase in the numbers of non- and multi-denominational schools has increased calls for reform within the curriculum where change could happen sooner and have more systemic effect than waiting for divestment and new schools to alter the system. According to the National Council for Curriculum and Assessment (NCCA) Draft Primary Curriculum Framework, the process of creating greater diversity in the primary sector 'raises a question about the role of the state in ensuring education related to the religious and ethical aspects of human development is provided for and that respect for all members of society is promoted and nurtured in the process'.[9] Thus, there is even greater momentum to alter the role of Religious Education to make it part

8   National Council for Curriculum and Assessment (NCCA), 'Draft Primary Curriculum Framework: Primary Curriculum Review and Redevelopment', 2020, <https://ncca.ie/media/4456/ncca-primary-curriculum-framework-2020.pdf>.
9   NCCA, 2020, 2.

of a broader curriculum that engages religious, spiritual and ethical issues in a more plural approach.

II. Managing Curriculum Review: A State-led Consultative Process Seeking Consensus

The Irish State, as discussed in Chapter 2, has assumed greater overall control and regulation of education at all levels in recent decades. Despite the critical and ongoing role for patrons in Ireland's denominational primary school sector, the State is in charge. The Department of Education created the NCCA to be a representative body that advises the Minister for Education and Skills on key issues in education at primary and post-primary levels in Ireland. The NCCA was established on a statutory basis in 2001 to lead developments in curriculum and assessment and to support the implementation of changes resulting from this work. This was only two years after the 1999 curriculum was implemented, underscoring the educational sphere's constant evolution.

The NCCA is charged with the following:

- To work in a spirit of consensus and partnership by promoting an innovative and creative environment for all learners in schools and other educational settings.
- To advise the Minister for Education and Skills on the curriculum for Ireland's primary and post-primary schools.
- To determine the curriculum, which sets out what is to be taught and how learning in particular subject areas is to be assessed.[10]

10   <https://www.education.ie/en/The-Department/Agencies/National-Council-for-Curriculum-and-Assessment-NCCA-.html#:~:text=The%20role%20of%20the%20National,changes%20resulting%20from%20this%20work> (Accessed: 14 July 2020).

The NCCA's main body is the Council, which is a twenty-five-member body determined by the Minister for Education and Skills. The Council 'comprises nominees of the partners in education, industry and trade union interests, parents' organisations and one nominee each of the Minister for Education and Skills and the Minister for Children and Youth Affairs'.[11] The broad membership of the Council is designed to include a diverse set of voices within Irish society ranging from professional educators to parents to patrons to unions and those concerned with different types of children that are served in Irish schools. The NCCA's permanent staff coordinates research, public consultations and regular meetings with various stakeholders to support the Council's deliberations.

NCCA Director (Primary Schools), Patrick Sullivan, underscores the importance of this group and their deliberations in creating consensus. 'There is great weight given to the deliberations on the Council and the stakeholder input, and in the advice that's given then… In general, it's essentially agreed advice to the Minister.'[12] The Minister has significant latitude when considering the Council's recommendations. Although the Minister has other factors influencing their policy choices, including their personal views, as well as the demands of their constituents, political base, party and coalition partners, they have an incentive to listen to the Council. According to Sullivan, the vast majority of Council advice is accepted by the Minister. On occasions when the Minister ignores or disagrees with the Council's advice, the Council members feel undermined because their recommendations represent the culmination of a long process of research, consultation, deliberation and hard-fought consensus-building among key stakeholders in education and broader Irish society. Too much ignoring of the process and its results could undermine further contributions by these varied actors and could elicit greater public reaction against such decisions. A key reason for having such a detailed structure and consultative process is to engage as many voices as possible and to foster consensus, especially when confronted with controversial and difficult decisions.

11   <https://ncca.ie/en/about/council-2019-2022> (Accessed: 14 July 2020).
12   Patrick Sullivan, Director (Primary) of NCCA, Personal Interview, October 2019.

Building consensus by including key stakeholders in an ongoing consultative process that advises government has been successfully employed
in Irish politics and governance in recent decades. In particular, Ireland's
national system of wage bargaining, known as Social Partnership (SP),
was a key aspect of Irish governance from 1987 to 2010.[13] SP was initiated in 1987 and was widely recognised as one of the principal drivers of
Ireland's dramatic economic growth, which experienced an increase in real
GDP of 132 % from 1987 through 2005. The SP model in Ireland entailed
a process of consultation, negotiation and deliberation, with agreements
among the leaders of Irish government, trade unions (the Irish Congress
of Trade Unions), business leaders (the Irish Business and Employers'
Confederation), farmers and, eventually, members of the community and
voluntary sectors. Introduced during the economic crisis of the mid-1980s
(which featured 17 % to 20 % unemployment, 12 % to 16 % inflation, a 125 %
debt-to-GDP ratio and high levels of emigration), these three-year, renew-
able national agreements were expanded to encompass broad swathes of
economic policy: moderating wage increases, cutting taxes and improving
the effectiveness of public spending.

Social Partnership contributed powerfully to Ireland's economic revival and facilitated a consensus that persisted across periods of economic
austerity and prosperity. Precisely when the potential existed to shift electoral appeals away from long-standing Civil War political party loyalties
and towards programmatic differences on economic policy, SP fostered
consensus among political parties and civil society groups. As the Irish
economy rebounded in the 1990s, the number of groups represented within
the SP process also increased. Its policy domain was extended to include
potentially divisive issues such as social exclusion, inequality and poverty,
as well as issues that affected the tangible delivery of material benefits, such
as job training, ongoing professional development and costs of childcare.
A new model of economic policy-making resulted, a model characterised

---

13   For more on Social Partnership and its impact on the Irish political system,
      see Sean McGraw, *How Parties Win: Shaping the Irish Political Arena*. Ann
      Arbor: University of Michigan Press, 2015, 140–48.

by consultative and participatory relationships between government agencies and organised interests.

The increased uncertainty and competitiveness of Irish elections beginning in the early 1980s set the stage for the re-emergence and persistence of social pacts in Ireland from 1987 to 2010. The process strengthened ties to union members and working-class voters who had become disconnected from the political process. Social Partnership, at least initially, also provided Fianna Fáil with the vehicle (and cover) they needed to implement cuts in taxes and public spending, which were controversial and difficult to pass in parliament. The political uncertainty and lack of clear majorities had consistently made it more difficult to reach agreement on more complex and controversial economic and social policies. As comparative evidence suggests, social pacts can be more effective than legislation in securing meaningful reform in such contexts. They provide a vehicle to override internal coalition disagreements by shoring up support outside the legislative arena. This appears to have been the case in Ireland, as divisive and divergent coalition partners relied on SP to achieve consensus and to enact policy and avoid risking erosion of electoral support in the process.

This new, multi-layered framework of actors and networks altered the policy-making process. It was a more inclusive process, but it also underscored the technocratic, specialised and managerial dimensions of political decision-making. In large part because of SP, a broadly consensual approach to economic issues pervades the Irish political process, reducing the competitive space between the political parties on the very issues that define electoral competition and parliamentary contention in many advanced industrial democracies. Despite its shortcomings, the overall success attributed to Social Partnership has made consensus-making institutions an acceptable and useful way of making policy in Ireland. It is no surprise that a similar, broadly inclusive process was implemented to address complex and contentious issues within education.

The process of updating and reforming the national curriculum is a controversial undertaking during the best of times, and even more difficult when society is evolving at exponential rates. According to NCCA's

Patrick Sullivan, 'if society has an itch, it scratches education'.[14] Therefore, the shift from a homogeneous, White, Catholic Ireland to a plural, multi-cultural Ireland has called into question how Ireland's educational system is meeting the needs of its students. As Irish society's tectonic plates shift, views on what is acceptable or necessary to teach children also shift. Some defend the rights of the Catholic Church as the majority patron to preserve their ethos. Others call for secular education that is rooted in protecting human rights and providing an objective, neutral-free education. Still others are in the middle and are happy to have religious and secular views taught to their children.

The Council sits right in the middle of these debates. For Sullivan, the NCCA's key roles are to listen to these varied voices and to link them to cutting-edge educational research and pedagogy. 'In the work that we do, how we run our council and through all our structures and committees, subcommittees and development groups, and the way we go about consultation, we really do endeavour to collect the view of the many and the full spectrum of views – to consider those views and to take them on their merits – but also to set direction for curricula going wherever teaching and learning goes.'[15]

The NCCA is the expert, convener and referee. The staff consists of educational practitioners, leaders and scholars who bring their expertise to the process. The twenty-five member Council convenes various educational, political and societal interests into one body and deliberative process. The quality of deliberations depends in large part on how well each representative on the Council is in touch with the concerns of their groups and multivocal constituents. There is not enough time for the NCCA to meet with all patrons, managerial bodies, teachers, or parents – although they are always consulting these various stakeholders. The NCCA relies heavily on their Council members within this partnership model to share information with their respective organisations from the NCCA and to gather information and concerns from their groups to bring back to the Council. The extent to which the representatives speak more authoritatively

14   Patrick Sullivan, Personal Interview, October 2019.
15   Patrick Sullivan, Personal Interview, October 2019.

for their groups and less from their personal perspective, the greater the quality of the debate and the more likely whatever outcomes emerge will be respected by those outside the room where negotiations occur.[16]

For the purposes of the religious-secular debate, it is noteworthy that the Catholic Church (via Catholic Primary School Management Association, CPSMA) and the Church of Ireland (via Church of Ireland Board of Education, CIBE) have only one seat each. By contrast, nine members represent various unions, four seats represent various state and political interests, two seats are reserved for parent representatives and the others are spread among representatives from other patrons, joint managerial bodies and associations.[17] The sheer number of issues the Council must address further dilutes the 'religious' voice. For example, there is a need to include experts and stakeholders from primary, post-primary and third level education, as well as from very particular vested interests like special education. Thus, members representing explicitly religious interests are in the minority. The institutional Church has become only one voice among many within this process.

As referee, the NCCA listens to individual and group written submissions, as well as to bilateral conversations with key educational stakeholders. Certain voices are loud, and their organisational strength guarantees them a place at the table. This is especially true for teachers' unions and patrons. The NCCA pursues other voices too, intentionally seeking to move beyond hearing from teachers' perspectives to include student/children's perspectives. Sullivan reports that not all submissions are weighted equally. 'The social media aspect and online surveys are very easily, I suppose, venting opportunities for different sides of the debate. And then written submissions, for instance, where somebody sits down as an organisation and distils their view on a topic or an area. You know, there is a weight there. ... And while we report on the gamut of views that out there, it is essentially the Council who then sets the perspective of the NCCA.'[18]

16   Patrick Sullivan, Personal Interview, October 2019.
17   <https://ncca.ie/en/about/council-2019-2022> (Accessed: 14 July 2020).
18   Patrick Sullivan, Personal Interview, October 2019.

The make-up of the Council and the very structure of the decision-making process affects the results. The breadth and depth of conversations provide a certain air of legitimacy and endows institutional heft to the conclusions and recommendations proposed by the Council. It does not mean, however, that everyone agrees with the results. In fact, some Church leaders argue that the NCCA has underrepresented or underreported the large number of responses supporting Catholic education in their final proposals and reports.[19] Irrespective of whether this is true, it highlights the critical role the NCCA performs as gatekeeper and referee to the myriad of concerns raised when debating what makes it into the curriculum. Whatever comes out of these very structured processes carries more weight and drives change in the educational sphere. Similar to Social Partnership, this consultative process is inclusive of many groups and perspectives, but it also tends to make things more technical and can tend to depoliticise the debate.

Although the NCCA's consultative process contributes to depoliticising the debate, particular interests still robustly challenge State authorities when they feel their voices, or their rights, are being ignored or threatened. For example, the Church continues to raise concerns about the Education about Religions and Beliefs (ERB) and Ethics curriculum, the Relationships & Sexuality Education curriculum, and the proposed cut in time allocated to the patrons' time, etc. Ultimately, whether a group has their concerns fully addressed is somewhat negated by the consultative and inclusive nature of the Council and consultation processes.

III. The 2018–2021 Curriculum Review

The complexity and diversity of actors and views means that no one is ultimately happy, but the NCCA seeks to engage and lead the process of review. Specifically, the NCCA has undertaken a multi-year consultation process between 2018 and 2021 to review the entire primary school

19   Fr Paul Connell, Secretary of Education for the Irish Bishop's Conference, Personal Interview, October 2019.

curriculum. At its core, the NCCA emphasises diversity and pluralism as the new norm. The diversity of cultures, ethnicities, family structures and backgrounds, home languages, religions and religious practices, sexual identities, class and worldviews that now populate Irish classrooms calls for a curriculum that respects, values and engages these differences.

This is quite the shift from Rule 68 in the 1965 *Rules for National Schools* that secured religious instruction's place at the heart of the curriculum and school day. Now, religion appears fortunate to be even considered at all within an already crowded curriculum. One of academics influencing the NCCA's view, Jones Irwin from Dublin City University, underscores the complexity of adjudicating when there is a conflict between the national curriculum and the patrons' programme when trying to teach a consistent set of values across the primary system. That Irwin frames contrasting school approaches as religious versus ethical, philosophical, multi-belief and values education is striking. This framing suggests that (*the old*) religious approaches are not rooted in ethics, philosophy and values and only (*the new*) non- and multi-denominational approaches can ensure openness and diversity, and foster the common values that ensure cohesion and citizenship.[20]

There is a subtle, underlying tone supporting and recommending change in many NCCA documents. For example, an NCCA-funded report found that Ireland was unique in the fourteen jurisdictions investigated in which the religious education provided is learning from religion rather than education about religions and beliefs. Scholars of religious education suggest that 'learning about religion' provides an opportunity to understand a range of religious beliefs and rituals in a comparative and factual manner; whereas 'learning from religion' is more of a religious instruction approach that could lead to religious indoctrination through teaching a particular religion or faith.[21] The other thirteen jurisdictions either allow students to

---

20   Jones Irwin, 'Towards a Values-Led Redevelopment of the Primary Curriculum', Paper presented at the Institute of Education, Dublin City University, 3 December 2018, <https://ncca.ie/media/4427/towards-a-values-led-redevelopment-of-the-primary-curriculum.pdf>.

21   Daniel Faas, Merike Darmody and Beata Sokolowska, 'Religious Diversity in Primary Schools: Reflections from the Republic of Ireland', *British Journal of Religious Education*, 2016, Vol. 38, No. 1, 83–98, DOI: 10.1080/01416200.2015.1025700.

opt-in to religious instruction (usually by choosing a faith-based school / education system), teach a combination of religious instruction and education about religion and beliefs, or prohibit religious instruction. The report concludes that 'developing and implementing a programme which teaches students *about* other faiths and beliefs could be key to preventing such misunderstanding and to supporting pluralism and multi-culturalism' at a time when Ireland is changing so rapidly.[22] The use of international comparisons further bolsters the NCCA's implicit support for curriculum reform in Ireland.

The NCCA established a multi-year process of consultation and review with the ultimate goal of creating a new curriculum that is approved by the Minister for Education by 2024. The NCCA's process taps into contemporary research, a rich network of forty-three schools that meet regularly, deliberations with educational partners and stakeholders, and a public consultation that considers views from any interested parties within Ireland. The framework identifies eleven core principles and seven key competencies that guide the overall curriculum.

The proposed reforms are more relevant to the religious-secular debate when you dig into the time allotted to the five broad curriculum areas in the redeveloped curriculum because this is where real changes occur. The changes are subtle and, in many ways, are hard to argue against. Who does not support such things as a holistic education that respects diversity and inclusion? Who is not in favour of respecting human rights and eliminating discrimination? The heavy reliance on valence issues produces veiled consensus upon which everyone agrees even though it is unclear what must be cut to make room for such additions. Given the growing pluralism of religious experience, including a rising percentage of parents and students with no faith, these valence issues gain traction and calls for limiting the role of religion increase.

The five broad curriculum areas in the proposed new curriculum are Language; Mathematics, Science and Technology Education; Wellbeing;

---

22   Hilary Grayson, Sharon O'Donnell, and Claire Sargent, 'Key Findings Summary: Education about Religions and Beliefs and Ethics in Primary Education', National Foundation for Educational Research. <https://ncca.ie/media/1904/ key_findings_erbe_summary.pdf> (Accessed: 17 July 2020).

Arts Education; and Social and Environmental Education. Given the over-loaded nature of the existing curriculum, the question becomes which subjects must get curtailed. It is unlikely that core subjects will receive significantly less attention. Furthermore, many of the new subjects are tough to disagree with in principle. For example, who would not want their children to benefit from the new Wellbeing curriculum, which seeks to integrate children's social, emotional, and physical development? This subject aims to help students develop life skills so they can eventually become active citizens and connected members within their communities, who live physically and emotionally healthy lives, and understand human sexuality in balanced, relational and emotionally mature ways. It is difficult to question these goals. Likewise, the Social and Environmental Education also helps students 'appreciate and understand the world through learning about the rich diversity of peoples: their experiences, cultures, beliefs and environments in different times, places, and circumstances'.[23] In previous eras, when Ireland was more homogeneously White and Catholic, exposure to such diversity was less relevant or pressing. In the new Ireland, diversity is the new norm, and therefore these additions to the curriculum seem quintessentially reasonable and even necessary. The momentum for change is real and growing, but there is no guarantee how such reform will occur. All the more reason their successful implementation will hinge on how the reforms are framed and argued.

A. Education about Religions and Beliefs (ERB) and Ethics: A Challenge to Religious Education?

A prime example of a new curriculum challenging the ongoing prevalence of religious education was the proposed Education about Religions and Beliefs (ERB) and Ethics.[24] The Forum on Patronage and Diversity

---

23   NCCA, 2020, 14.
24   ERB and Ethics was first concretely explored in 2015 with the start of a consultation by the NCCA, after being proposed in 2012 by the Forum on Pluralism and Patronage. <https://www.irishtimes.com/news/education/religious-education-i-don-t-know-anybody-who-teaches-the-re-requirement-1.2418676>.

in Primary Schools tasked the National Council for Curriculum and Assessment to develop a new curriculum for ERB and Ethics and argued that all students in Irish schools must be exposed to this new subject. Although the Advisory Group commented that this new curriculum would not supplant Religious Education in denominational schools, it was clearly a 'win' for supporters of multi-denominational education that teach 'about' religion rather than 'from' or 'into' religion.[25] Ironically, the rights-based argument is questionable in this case. 'The actual right is that education will be in line with particular religious beliefs, not with some compromised approach to religious education. The appeal here cannot be to a right.'[26] So, the subtle shift to supporting teaching about religion lacks consensus, and it fails to protect a constitutional right for those who want to have religious education as part of their schooling and would leave many parents unsatisfied.

Nevertheless, the Forum on Patronage and Diversity in Primary Schools concluded that the State has a responsibility to ensure 'education about religion and beliefs (ERB) and ethics is available to all students. Any new programmes would be developed in consultation with the education partners and would be complementary to and not supplant existing religious education programmes, many of which already include some ERB.'[27] In effect, if the State was not sufficiently going to diversify school types, reformers, such as the Irish Human Rights and Equality Commission (IHREC), Atheist Ireland and proponents of non- and multi-denominational schools, sought to increase levels of diversity and inclusion within existing schools. Such reformers recognised the distinctions about how religion is taught, and they clearly preferred to teach and learn *about* religion as a subject, rather than learning *into* religion (i.e. faith formation) or learning *from* religion (which taps into the child's personal experience but may not be promoting a particular faith formation). This form of learning about religion, it is argued, enables children to learn about multiple faiths and other forms of belief systems in ways that can better balance personal

---

25   Forum Progress Report, 2014, 14.
26   Tuohy, 2013, 279.
27   'Forum on Patronage and Pluralism in the Primary Sector Progress to Date and Future Directions', July 2014, 12.

experience and religious beliefs while respecting those with different views and experiences.

Proponents of this approach to learning *about* religion argue that there is less explicit tension – or even discrimination – for those from minority faiths or who are non-religious. Their claims are rooted in existing research in Ireland which indicates that while most primary schools admit children from diverse religious backgrounds, the school ethos and curriculum do not adequately address the needs of children of minority faith backgrounds.[28] An additional survey of schools confirmed most students seeking to opt-out of religious education remained in the classroom and there were no clear alternatives to offer positive experiences for these students when others were learning religion. Given that current options available to those children who wish to opt-out of religious education classes can contribute to 'othering' and drawing negative attention towards these students, a shift to teaching about religion is a recommended alternative.[29]

The Forum recommendations called for greater efforts to protect the constitutional right of all students to opt out of religious education courses given these expressed concerns. There are several challenges associated with the opt-out clause.[30] First, the rights' perspective argues that any form of an opt-out insufficiently understands human rights and places a heavy burden on parents to anticipate what is being taught to request an exemption. There is also a tendency to succumb to the pressure to have their children learn with the majority. Many Catholic school leaders argue that they serve students from extremely diverse religious and ethnic backgrounds in sensitive and inclusive ways, but their 'good practices' are often overlooked by those seeking change. From this perspective, the conclusions of the Forum's Advisory Group implied that the denominational model

28   Faas, Darmody and Sokolowska, 2016, 38:1, 83–98.

29   Merike Darmody and Emer Smyth, 'Education about Religions and Beliefs (ERB) and Ethics: Views of Teachers, Parents and the General Public Regarding the Proposed Curriculum for Primary Schools', Consultation Paper, ESRI funded by NCCA, January 2017. <https://www.esri.ie/system/files/media/file-uploads/2017-01/BKMNEXT324.pdf> (Accessed: 14 July 2020). Also discussed with Emer Smyth in personal interview, October 2019.

30   See Tuohy, 2013, 281–9, for a more thorough treatment of these perspectives.

is incapable of dealing adequately with this issue. Second, a community perspective recommends overcoming the separation of children based on religions that may cause feelings of alienation by keeping all students together for a one-size-fits-all course on religious education. This ignores the differences among religions on how they want their faith taught. It also raises the issue of whether the State should even be involved in imposing a solution, which may in the end undermine the very concept of diversity by making everyone be the same. Third, there are logistical perspectives about rooms, supervision, timing and resources needed to protect the opt-out rights. Potential solutions included teaching religion at the beginning or end of the day or teaching religion only twice a week for longer periods so it would be easier to schedule for students opting out.[31] These various proposals underscore the Forum's inability or failure to underscore the complexity of rights in seeking to correct the mistakes of the past and reforming the system to meet changing needs. This corrective approach focused more on enhancing minority rights, which has challenged the perennially dominant Catholic Church, that rarely, if ever had to compromise in the past. Thus, for many Catholics, the feeling of compromise is one of loss and change because it is new to them.[32]

Like the conversations about divestment, there is widespread support for increasing diversity and inclusion in all Irish schools. There is even recognition that many schools, including Catholic schools, are inclusive and diverse, but there is considerable variation across the sector, which has elicited calls for reform to ensure this diverse and inclusive quality in all schools. According to a leading researcher from the ESRI, there is growing sensitivity towards ethnic and linguistic differences, but there is often less attention given to religious diversity. Symbolic representation, celebrations, holidays, festivals and other symbols are important and not always dealt with adequately in many schools, and teachers are often unprepared to address these differences.[33] Tensions rise when deciding on how inclusion should be done because those advocating for secular education have

---

31   Forum Progress Report, 2014, 22–5.
32   Tuohy, 2013, 287.
33   Emer Smyth, Research Professor at the Economic and Social Research Institute (ESRI) in Dublin, Personal Interview, October 2019.

different proposals than those who defend the rights of religious patrons to teach their religion and culture.

Results from an ESRI survey that was funded by the NCCA are indicative of these competing realities.[34] Keep in mind that the types of questions posed, and the quality of information possessed by respondents, can lead to respondents displaying contradictory beliefs. As we have discussed, scholars of public opinion data highlight the distinction between the 'easy' and the 'hard' facets of questions as a way of explaining how individuals may have complex beliefs on any one topic. Easy questions generally deal with a principle or an overall view, whereas hard questions focus on the implementation of such policies, forcing respondents to choose between solutions or policies.[35]

In the ESRI survey, when teachers, parents and the general public were asked about their attitudes towards this proposed curriculum on ERB and Ethics, there was overwhelming support for the broad aims and principles, i.e. the easy questions. For example, over 80 % of educators agreed with the proposed aims of the curriculum that emphasise values such as respecting, promoting and protecting human rights, diversity, inclusion, social justice and an overall sense of rights and responsibilities. Parents too were incredibly supportive of having their children learn about equality, diversity and tolerance. Even the general public recognised the positive goals of increasing tolerance and respect for diversity.

Nevertheless, there was much less certainty about what this looks like when you get into the details and explore options of how the new curriculum

34   See Darmody and Smyth, 2017, 21–32, for a fuller discussion of the survey results. The analysis is based on responses from 897 educators, 1,075 parents and 283 members of the general public. The datasets were checked to avoid multiple responses from the same person. This consultation process differed from traditional survey research in that respondents were not drawn from a nationally representative sample of the population. It is therefore not possible to estimate how many people were aware of the survey and, of this group, how many participated. Because participation was voluntary, those who completed the questionnaire were more likely to have held strong views on the subject.

35   Pat Lyons, *Public Opinion, Politics and Society in Contemporary Ireland*. Dublin, Ireland and Portland, OR: Irish Academic Press, 2008.

would alter current practice, that is, the hard questions. Among educators, there were strong, but split views on the role of religion in schools. While some teachers were critical about the inclusion of religious education in schools, others were supportive of it, and opinions seemed to be divided more or less in equal proportions. Advocating the removal of faith formation from schools was not surprisingly more evident in the responses from educators in the multi-denominational sector. For parents, responses to open-ended questions about how the curriculum would contribute to their child's learning demonstrated diverse views. Parents want their kids to learn about equality, diversity and tolerance (20 %); about social norms and morals (13 %), about different beliefs and critical thinking (nearly 25 %) and about a particular faith (11 %). About 13 % parents in open-ended questions explicitly and supportively mentioned keeping religious education in schools, and 20 % thought no changes were necessary.

In principle, most respondents supported the proposed curriculum as a positive way to enhance inclusivity in schools, which would in turn help students understand and contribute to social interactions in Ireland's new and diverse reality.[36] The main criticisms of the proposed ERB and Ethics curriculum were that the current primary curriculum was already overloaded; this curriculum might clash with the ethos of denominational schools; and that many of the aims and content were already covered by other subjects in the existing curriculum. Not surprisingly, the position of faith formation and sacraments within the curriculum proved to be the most divisive for each sector surveyed.

Given the Forum's recommendation to provide ERB and Ethics to all Irish primary school students, the NCCA sought to educate people about this proposed curriculum in principle and what it might look like practically. The NCCA reinforced that this new curriculum was an essential means by which Irish schools could achieve greater inclusivity and linguistic, ethnic, cultural and religious diversity. Additionally, the NCCA argued that it was not seeking to replace the patrons' programme or Religious Education in denominational schools, but it was embracing the teaching 'about' religion approach. For some, this approach was interpreted as the

36   Darmody and Smyth, 2017, 40.

next step towards eventually eliminating denominational education as growing course load demands will make having both approaches in the curriculum unsustainable.

The NCCA relied heavily on international standards set forth in the Toledo Principles, which promote an 'objective, critical, and pluralist' approach to education. In a consultation paper, the NCCA states: 'The introduction of ERB and Ethics as a central contributor to inclusive education and the development of respectful, pluralist environments further underlines the importance of being aware of the visible and hidden practices of a school community in the construction of inclusive school environments.'[37] For some opponents of change proposed by the NCCA, they feel as though denominational schools are being portrayed as having numerous 'hidden' practices that make them incapable of being inclusive and respecting diversity because they focus almost entirely on adhering to their own faith beliefs and forming students within this tradition. The fact that Religious Education (RE) was not even included in the final report of the consultation document was an additional sign to critics of reform that the NCCA was seeking to prioritise a secularising agenda. According to third level Religious Education Professor Dr Dan O'Connell from Mary Immaculate College in Limerick, 'It appears that the state is now trying to impose a subject/curriculum called ERB and Ethics while removing Religious Education from the curriculum.' By shifting RE to within the patrons' programme, the state would be removing the requirement for primary schools to teach any form of religious education to their students and exempting students from acquiring any religious literacy.[38]

The NCCA's reliance on the Toledo Guidelines became a big stumbling block, particularly among denominational schools and supporters of religious education, because they interpret these guidelines as secular and somewhat hostile towards including religious education within the

---

37 'Education about Religions and Beliefs (ERB) and Ethics in the Primary School: Consultation Paper', National Council for Curriculum and Assessment (NCCA), November 2015; <https://ncca.ie/media/1897/consultation_erbe.pdf> (Accessed: 1 July 2020).

38 Daniel O'Connell, 'Catholic Primary Schools – On Rapidly Thinning Ice', *The Furrow*, December 2018, 660–70 (664 in this case).

core curriculum. Eamonn Conway from Mary Immaculate College argued that the proposed ERB and Ethics curriculum was highly offensive to religious educators.[39] For Conway, he first argues that the Church welcomes greater alternatives in school types so that minority religions and those of no religion can have their rights respected and can attend a non- or multi-denominational school. This would preserve everyone's right to have the type of education they wished, including Catholics who could run their schools without fear that they would be forced to diminish or dilute their ethos and religious instruction to accommodate for those of other faiths or no faith. Importantly, the failure of the State to create sufficient alternatives of school types via divestment or establishing new schools is one of the chief reasons that reformers have looked to bring about change in other ways. Hence, attempts to update the curriculum. Seeking to achieve reform through the curriculum telescopes the conflict of parents' and students' rights versus patrons' rights. Ironically, these reforms create uniformity, rather than pluralism, by forcing all schools to teach in the same ways that reflect the teaching about religion rather than teaching from or into a particular religion.

Conway highlights what he considers are subtle shifts in the argument and its consequences. He argues that no education is neutral because the content and pedagogy are linked with values. Therefore, for Conway, even arguing that 'religious knowledge can be communicated neutrally is itself a secular belief. No education programme can bracket its formative dimension. Thus, the proposed ERB programme unavoidably forms students in a secularist understanding of religion.'[40] Conway also contends that Catholic schools are tolerant, inclusive and respectful of difference and otherness because the core value of seeing the human dignity of each students demands this respect and inclusion. The challenge for Conway and other defenders of Catholic schools is that there has been a gap between the Church's core values and how these values have been lived out in recent decades, especially in relation to the abuse scandal, which in turn

39   Eamonn Conway, 'Protecting Denominational Education', Paper to the Iona Institute, Monday, 21 January 2013.
40   Conway, 2013, 7.

colours perceptions of any Church activities, including schools. Therefore, Catholic school proponents need to provide more concrete examples of how Catholic schools behave in tolerant and respectful ways to overcome the perceptions operative within Irish society.

Defenders of Catholic schools were particularly concerned about proposals to delete Rule 68, which they argued would eliminate the statutory importance of Religious Education within the primary curriculum. For Conway, deleting Rule 68 would end integrating religion throughout the curriculum and would, in turn, require all primary school teachers to teach the secular values many reformers are highlighting. Rather than deleting Rule 68, which would dramatically alter religion's role within the curriculum, Conway suggested modifying it. Since the existing rules called for the inculcation of the practice of widely agreed upon values among religious and secular advocates such as charity, justice, truth, patience, temperance, obedience to lawful authority and all the other moral virtues, more modification rather than deletion may be warranted.[41] Tellingly, despite the concerns highlighted by Conway and with little public protest from the Church, the Minister for Education Jan O'Sullivan, TD, rescinded Rule 68 of National Schools in January 2016 calling it 'a symbol of our past, and not our future'.[42]

One last concern from defenders of the place for religion in Irish schools is that the proposed changes dilute real learning. The argument is that, if Catholic, or other denominational schools, are forced to present religious beliefs, rituals, images and artefacts 'objectively' and 'factually', they are disconnecting these from their community and lived experience in ways that lead to only superficial interpretation. Conway contends that students start to see religious beliefs and rituals, symbols and icons, as commodities that are part of a broader consumerist approach to education generally. Increasingly, Conway argues, students in all subjects are exposed to smatterings of knowledge rather than full academic disciplines to make education 'relevant'. This, he concludes, undermines learning in all areas,

---

41 Conway, 2013, 4.
42 Katherine Donnelly, 'Minister Scraps 51-Year-Old Religion Rule for Primary Schools', *Irish Independent,* 19 January 2016.

but it dilutes any real religious perspective, which over time, makes religion less relevant. In a competitive curriculum that is already overloaded, these subtle shifts point to religion's decline and the predominance of seeing education as objective, critical and pluralist, which is 'code' for many that the secular approach has won.

The NCCA's Patrick Sullivan acknowledged this stumbling block and even nodded to how 'objective' is often interpreted as secular. However, Sullivan also argues that what was intended when using the Toledo Guidelines was that a world view would not be discredited on the grounds that it was not the world view taught in a majority of classrooms. In other words, this approach acknowledges that differing world views exist, and they are neither right nor wrong, which could discredit them. Despite these stated intentions, in practice many still believe that the Toledo Guidelines require the whole curriculum to be viewed through a secular lens, which they believe would force teacher values, school culture, ethos, characteristics, spirit and so on to assume secular values.[43] The task of trying to balance or find a compromise between differing world views is a Herculean task especially when a previously dominant ideology must now interact as just one among many views and approaches within a national system.

The NCCA's consultation process offered four leading possibilities for how the ERB and Ethics curriculum would relate to the existing curriculum.[44] Although the NCCA repeatedly admits that these were mere proposals, they did not hesitate to signal their preferences. The first option was to include ERB and Ethics within the patron's programme. This, according to the NCCA, would not work because the teaching 'from' faith dominant within denominational schools would conflict with the more pluralist teaching about faith in the proposed curriculum. The NCCA feared that students will miss out on valuable learning and opposes this type of integration. Second, ERB and Ethics could be integrated across curriculum areas. Not to be confused with the integrated curriculum in place since 1971 that seeks to have religious education woven throughout the school day, this suggestion would have the new curriculum incorporated

43   Patrick Sullivan, Personal Interview, October 2019.
44   NCCA, 2015, 28–32.

into a number of other subjects, including Religious Education (RE), Social, Personal and Health Education (SPHE) and Social, Environmental and Scientific Education (SESE). The NCCA doubted whether this would significantly alter current teaching and learning practices. The third option proposed making ERB and Ethics a discrete curriculum and restates the Forum's recommendation that all children should be educated in this way. It justified this approach by arguing that good educational practice and the Toledo Guidelines confirm that religious literacy and learning about religion are superior to learning from religion when seeking to promote a diverse and inclusive society. And Fourth, ERB and Ethics could both be taught discretely and integrated across several subjects. This could, it was argued by the NCCA, help correct things that have been lacking in the Irish curriculum for decades. In the end, the NCCA offered these four different proposals to guide the multi-year consultative process. The initial attempt to introduce ERB and Ethics failed in 2016 owing to significant opposition from the Catholic Church that was 'underpinned by the legal rights enjoyed by denominational schools in protecting their religious ethos'.[45] However, the NCCA re-introduced the language of ERB and Ethics in the 2020 *Primary Curriculum Framework* by removing RE as a distinct subject and instead designating this part of the curriculum as 'Religious/ Ethical/ Multi-belief education- Patron's programme'.[46]

In an apparent attempt to bolster its preference to include ERB and Ethics in the new curriculum, the NCCA compared the content of the proposed curriculum to content of existing Religious Education programmes.[47]

---

45   Katherine Donnelly, 'Church's Backlash Blocks Change in Religion Classes', *Irish Independent*, 28 November 2016.

46   NCCA, 2020.

47   'An Overview of Education about Religions and Beliefs (ERB) and Ethics content in Patrons' Programmes', National Council for Curriculum and Assessment (NCCA), 2015.   <https://ncca.ie/media/4602/overview_of_patrons_programmes.pdf> (Accessed: 1 July 2020). The paper analyses in great detail the various patrons' programmes, including the Catholic Church's Programme *Grow in Love*; Church of Ireland's Programme *Follow Me*; the Jewish Religious Education Programme, the Muslim Religious Education Programme; Educate Together's Programme *Learn Together*; The Community National Schools' Programme *Goodness Me, Goodness You*; and John Scottus' Programme.

The report finds that the denominational programmes devote little time and limited range of content to educating students about religions. The new Catholic curriculum focuses on other religions for only 18 of 732 hours across the primary school curriculum. When they do study other religions, the report concludes that they tend to be about monotheistic religions and they generally do this in the later primary years.

Multi-denominational schools are different for obvious reasons. The Community National Schools Programme, *Goodness Me, Goodness You* (GMGY), seeks to nurture children of all faiths and none by creating a space where students can talk about their beliefs in a safe and respectful learning environment – which is an important aspect of ERB teaching. Educate Together's *Learn Together* curriculum, which was introduced in 2004 as a response to the State requirement to have some form of religious instruction during the school day, has a clear focus on ethical thinking and understanding various values and belief systems.[48] The study concludes that '*Learn Together* is an enquiry-based approach to learning "*about*" religions and beliefs, while the GMGY programme is closer to an exploration of personal beliefs which can be described as learning "*from*" religion and beliefs. Both programmes place an emphasis on the important learning ERB can have for children in primary schools both in terms of religion and beliefs as a cultural phenomenon (learning about religions) and as a personal exploration of belief (learning from religion).'[49] –

According to the NCCA report, the multi-denominational schools teach about religions and beliefs throughout the primary years and their students learn about many religions and beliefs, not just about monotheistic religions. The report also concludes that the multi-denominational sector has a greater variety of approaches to teaching about religions and beliefs. 'These range from a fact-based approach with discrete learning areas, to a multi-belief approach with a more integrated method of teaching about religions and beliefs.'[50] Not surprisingly, the report highlights that denominational schools teach ethics from a faith-based perspective and

---

48   Fischer, 2016, 98.
49   NCCA, 2015, 32–36.
50   NCCA, 2015, 50–1.

multi-denominational schools teach without promoting one faith perspective over another.

The clear implication is that the latter approach, where no faith or belief is considered better than others, is ideal if the ultimate goal is to be more inclusive and to truly reflect diversity. Too much focus on one faith is deemed inappropriate. The report subtly states early on that it does not address the 'hidden curriculum', which 'relates to the important messages that are conveyed to all those who enter the school by its physical and social environment'.[51] The mere mention of the 'hidden curriculum' is highly suggestive, indicating that most primary schools are unknowingly communicating mixed messages to their students and, therefore, are not being inclusive and fostering diversity.

These curricular debates are motivated by deeper normative and ideological underpinnings. The NCCA, for all its attempts to create an all-inclusive Council that listens to key stakeholders with competing interests and views, clearly favours including ERB and Ethics in the new curriculum. The NCCA's consultation papers and reports repeatedly highlight the distinctions about teaching from religion, into religion or about religion; and they favour the latter. This affirmation provides the plural, secular perspective with a certain degree of legitimacy. The fact that the main advisory agency within the State favours this approach signals to the broader educational sector that secular shifts are acceptable and perhaps even preferred. Additionally, as mentioned previously, some teachers appear to earn their certification to teach in Catholic schools primarily for practical professional purposes. It seems plausible that significant numbers of another key stakeholder, teachers, would alter their teacher formation and training if Catholic school requirements were dropped. Yet, despite this growing support for secular shifts, surveys continue to show deep divisions among teachers, parents and the broader public over the role of religion in primary schools. Thus, the attempts to move religious formation and instruction outside of school have gained momentum, but they have not reached a tipping point. Perhaps this lack of consensus on how the curriculum will work in a rapidly changing reality and absence of significant

51   NCCA, 2015, 12.

media attention helps explain why this new curriculum was 'kicked to touch' and laid dormant for a couple of years after considerable pushback from the Church.[52] Those who are concerned about the removal of religion from schools altogether worry about the fact that ERB and Ethics is still contained within the framework for the new curriculum. The fear is that despite the NCCA stating publicly that no decision has been made, the inclusion of ERB and Ethics suggests that it in practice, it will still be re-introduced, almost by stealth, when the new curriculum is enacted, albeit in what form it is still unclear. The 'waiting until a later day' approach seemingly at play in the ERB and Ethics debate is consistent with the long-term, incremental strategy adopted by proponents of secular reforms in primary education.

B. Time Allotment: The Politics of the Curriculum Timetable

Although the time allotted to the various subjects appears to be a minor, bureaucratic decision with minimal real impact, these decisions about time are highly contentious and do have significant potential to alter the primary education experience. The challenge of an already overloaded curriculum creates a zero-sum mentality whereby any increases in time for one subject is necessarily a loss for another subject. For many, subjects are not benign courses but windows into whole other worlds of values and outlooks on life. For those in the trenches, such as teachers, school leaders, patrons, civil society advocates, etc., issues about time allotment are proxies for other, more important issues, and thus this is where real battles occur.

The new, proposed curriculum divides subjects between Minimum Curriculum Time and Flexible Time. Minimum Curriculum Time provides a weekly time allocation for Language, Mathematics and Wellbeing, and a monthly time allocation for Science and Technology Education,

---

52   Emer Smyth, Personal Interview, October 2019. See also, <https://www.independent.ie/irish-news/education/churchs-backlash-blocks-change-in-religion-classes-35249798.html>

Social and Environmental Education and Arts Education. The goal is to provide teachers with flexibility in terms of how to cover material within these curricula, while preventing too much attention on any one subject. The second category, 'Flexible Time', is intended to better enable schools, at local level, to determine how best to use available resources to meet children's learning needs, interests and abilities and the needs of teachers and schools in terms of planning, teaching and assessing. Schools can focus on a theme or subject in more depth, or develop whole-school activities, or plan and carry out local projects. The Patron's Programme, which allows schools time to develop children holistically from the religious and/or ethical perspective to deepen the school's ethos, is part of this flexible time.[53]

The NCCA Framework offers three different options that seek to balance the various curricular needs. Each option provides possibilities for delineating time for each subject over a four-week period. For the purposes of our discussion, it is noteworthy that Religious Education is reduced from 2.5 hours to 2 hours per week in this proposed curriculum and would now receive less time as part of the Flexible Time curriculum than recreation would each week. For some religious leaders, this is perceived as a targeted attack on religious education. According to Seamus Mulconry, Secretary General of Catholic Primary Schools Management Association (CPSMA), the real danger is that the NCCA's proposed reduction in religious instruction time would further limit an already neglected subject. He argues that 'the reality is that there is no school in the country that's teaching (religion) half an hour a day. But if they get to limit that in de jure as well as de facto terms, then, it's an increase in their power.'[54]

A recent qualitative study of thirty Irish teachers who have experience teaching in Catholic schools in Ireland and the United States confirms that teaching religion is becoming less of a priority despite its guaranteed place in the current curriculum. Most of the teachers in this study reported that there was little importance placed on teaching religion and the quality of the curriculum was poor. For these limited numbers of teachers, religion has become just one subject among many and increasingly a non-essential

53   NCCA, 2020, 14–15.
54   Seamus Mulconry, Secretary General of CPSMA, Personal Interview, October 2019.

one that ends up getting sidelined in favour of other subjects. One teacher reported, 'Our religion curriculum isn't the best. And for me, I just ended up putting it to one side, because it's turning the kids off it. It's not activating the Catholic spirit in our classroom. So, I just ended up devising my own religion curriculum to teach in the classroom.' Others report that there is also a lot of pressure to teach other subjects in Ireland due to the demanding overall curriculum and, as a result, religion gets less attention. According to another teacher, 'You're teaching thirteen subjects and trying to fit time every single week to get everything done so it becomes tough to get half an hour of religion done every day... it's difficult with the amount of pressure that's put on you just to teach English, maths and Irish.' There can even be explicit pressure from the principal to limit the amount of time they spend on religion. One teacher reported that her principal said, 'You're doing too much religion time and that if an Inspector [from the Department of Education] came they would highlight this.' Another teacher said that her previous Irish school set aside time every day for every class to do religion, whereas her current school downplayed the need to teach religion. The teacher reported that in her current school only 'half the teachers [out of 13] are teaching religion on a weekly basis—that will be it—and our principal doesn't ever check whether we're actually doing any religion. There's zero follow-through on that. I know for a fact that some teachers in my school haven't opened the religion book once this year.'[55]

Unfortunately, there are no larger quantitative studies addressing this issue, but most practitioners would confirm this reality of less and less emphasis on teaching religion. In this context, it is unsurprising that strong proponents of religious education complain that that State should have no role in the Patrons' Programme. From this perspective, limiting the time allotted to Patrons is the next step in secularisation as the State finds a way in to shaping this previously protected curriculum.[56]

In defence of the proposed change in flexible time, Patrick Sullivan argues that the NCCA is trying to balance concerns about the overloaded

---

55   Monica J. Kowalski, Jonathan Tiernan and Sean D. McGraw, 'Catholic Education in Ireland and the United States: Teachers' Comparative Perspectives', *Research in Comparative and International Education*, 2020, Vol. 15, No. 2, 179.

56   Fr Paul Connell, Personal Interview, October 2019.

curriculum with advances in pedagogy that suggests more sustained and immersive learning experiences are essential for student growth. 'We're trying to put in more flexible time into the curriculum. Now, what that means is time has to come from somewhere. So, we've essentially taken time from everywhere to try and give more flexibility back to schools and to manage your time.' Sullivan acknowledges that some patrons can only see this as a reduction of their time and, therefore, a loss for them. The NCCA's view is that granting greater autonomy and flexibility and agency to schools and teachers is essential for providing better educational experiences for students and that this outweighs getting bogged down on specific time allotments. Their proposals seek to maximise this flexibility.[57]

Despite these arguments, these debates on curriculum and time allotment are where things get subtle and technical. Dr Anne Looney, Executive Dean of the Institute of Education at Dublin City University, former Chief Executive of NCCA from 2001 to 2016, highlights the subtle nature of changes that affect Religious Education in Irish primary schools. Looney reports that Religious Education was not included in the proofs of the 1999 primary school curriculum partly because some involved in the process did not believe the State had anything to do with religious instruction. According to Looney, she and Dermot Lane (President of Mater Dei Institute of Education at DCU) got language about religious instruction included in the final curriculum. The argument was that even though patrons determined content about religion, every child experienced some engagement with religious themes, and therefore, it needed to be recognised.[58] This inclusion in the curriculum reinforced religious instruction's legitimacy at that time.

Whereas Religious Education was nearly left out of the 1999 curriculum, whether intentionally or unintentionally, it is called something else in many current debates. Rather than referring to Religious Education, those proposing change often discuss the subject in terms of the Patrons' Programme. This helps define it by its source as opposed to what children are receiving, which is religious instruction or education about religion.

---

57 Patrick Sullivan, Personal Interview, October 2019.
58 Anne Looney, Personal Interview, October 2019.

This delineation started as an attempt to divide the day into what parts that the State should oversee, which would be considered the national curriculum, and the other parts of the school day, which would be determined by patrons and/or other local concerns. The original intent was to protect the interests of the patrons as they develop a curriculum that is aligned with their ethos. What took root was this distinction between required vs. flexible curriculum. Employing language like 'non-curriculum' time or 'flexible' time suggests that these aspects of the day are less essential and fundamental and, therefore, could be removed at some stage given the space limits already on the overall curriculum. Such subtle shifts in language fuels those people who are concerned that 'required' vs. 'flexible' language is being used as the next step of eliminating religion from the normal school day and shifting all faith and religious education outside the school day.[59] Religious education's overall legitimacy appears to be declining and its place within the proposed curriculum is under serious pressure.

Despite a widespread sentiment of 'the sky is falling' within religious education circles, many also point to these subtle changes in the curriculum – and the writing on the wall of religious education's ultimate removal from Irish primary schools – as an opportunity. Anne Looney, someone with a rich experience in curriculum design and the politics of reform, suggests that patrons could transform these losses or shifts in the curriculum to their advantage. Patrons could take ownership of religious instruction – and faith formation more broadly – and recognise the reality that the Church can no longer expect the State to do the work for it, let alone pay for it as well.[60] As the majority religion and patron, the Catholic Church has been lethargic and failed to act with much creativity or ingenuity in ways that minority religions have been doing for some time in offering life-giving and energetic religious education opportunities outside of school. Whereas minority religions were forced into this reality, the Catholic Church has relied on the State to pay its teachers to deliver its religious education programme including preparing children to receive their sacraments. By embracing change, Catholic schools could create a real

59   Anne Looney, Personal Interview, October 2019.
60   Anne Looney, Personal Interview, October 2019.

alternative for students, parents and teachers. The Church could increase the availability of Religious Education outside of the school day for greater numbers of students, and they might also then be able to teach religion in a much smaller number of schools that are more intentionally Catholic and allowed to be this by the State.

Despite such calls for optimism due to seeing these curricular changes as opportunities, there is much division within Catholic circles, including among bishops, priests, religious and lay people, about such shifts. Some catechists and Religious Education teachers believe that there is an opportunity here to enhance their offerings. There are also some allies within Irish National Teachers' Organisation (INTO) and other teachers' unions that feel such shifts in the curriculum might lead to real change, which would ultimately free up the overall curriculum and invite teachers to be part of schools whose ethos is more in line with their personal views on morality and social issues.[61] Again, still others believe a whole new system is possible where Catholic schools can be truly authentic Catholic schools, free from interference from the State. The sobering reality is that declining priestly and religious vocations and numbers regularly attending Church, combined with significant financial challenges, remind proponents of change that the costs of something new may be insurmountable.[62] Add to this, there is a minority of Catholics who see all reforms as part of a larger agenda. From this perspective, any change is merely the latest step in the process of removing the religion from primary schools, and eventually from all aspects of Irish society.

Is it merely a matter of time before these changes take root? Like what occurred in the areas of same-sex marriage and abortion, shifts in public opinion and what was acceptable by a majority of Irish citizens took several decades. At the end, change occurred more rapidly, but that was only when changes in attitude reached a tipping point and there were concrete proposals that focused political, civic and media attention on the issues in question.

61   Anne Looney, Personal Interview, October 2019.
62   Fr Paul Connell, Personal Interview, October 2019.

IV. Conclusion

This chapter reviewed how curriculum changes are being addressed within Ireland's primary school sector. The combination of the dramatic changes in religious beliefs and practices among Catholics and the growing numbers of non-religious or minority religious students and teachers has led reformers to demand changes to what Irish students learn. Divestment sought to address the problem of the lack of an adequate number of non-Catholic schools. Admissions reform addressed how to increase diversity within schools so the demographic background of the student body in all schools, even Catholic schools, was more diverse. Demands for curriculum reform seek to make the educational experience more diverse, equitable and inclusive once students are in school. The primary thrust of reformers is to reduce or eliminate the role of religion in the curriculum and school experience. Therefore, issues such as religious education, sacramental preparation, sex education and ethics are intensely debated. Advocates of reform argue that since Irish primary schools are State-funded schools, no child should be subjected to indoctrination in any of these subjects. This chapter described the nature of these debates and demonstrated how subtle, small and gradual changes are altering the role of religion within schools. Educational experts and practitioners have dominated these debates while politicians have largely remained silent, allowing the specialists, professionals and civil servants to figure it out. Although there are similar appeals to secularism, equality, diversity and inclusion, the more bureaucratic character of these policy changes means that whatever changes may occur will likely unfold without much fanfare, but could potentially have much more far-reaching impact, including the exclusion of religion from any aspect of the normal school day. Again, the issue definition and subsequent policy solutions being proposed greatly alter the politics of reform and leads to widely different outcomes. This helps explain how and why debates about curriculum reform have unfolded quite differently than both divestment and admissions.

CHAPTER 13

What's Next in Irish Primary Education Reform?

I. Introduction

There has been a powerful move in recent decades to reduce or eliminate the role of the Catholic Church in Irish society. The experience of the marriage equality and abortion referenda campaigns highlighted how such policy change was possible and also revealed that the institutional Church's influence in key aspects of Irish life was waning. The gradual and persistent campaigning among individuals, families and friends, celebrities, politicians, academics and civil society advocates paved the way for these outcomes. The culmination of decades of grassroots mobilisation combined with shifting religious and social attitudes within Irish society to convince politicians that change was possible without dividing their parties internally or undermining their electoral support.

The playbook for those seeking to reduce or eliminate the role of the Catholic Church within Irish primary education is similar, but more complicated than in these earlier campaigns. Change advocates likely need to reach the tipping point of 60 % support within Irish society for their reforms before the major parties offer their backing, thereby opening the path to policy change. There was over 80 % public support for changing school admission rules, which helps explain the smooth passing of this legislation. However, there is a lack of consensus on other educational reforms that would reduce the Catholic Church's influence in schools and increase diversity within the primary sector. As a result, politicians, especially major party elites, will likely proceed cautiously until clear-cut solutions present themselves or public support shifts. Any policy solutions must take account of the practical implications on communities that a changed system would entail. Although there continues to be broad support for many reforms in principle, parents and other affected individuals have, as was the case with divestment, forcefully rejected proposals that adversely and directly impact their child's educational experience and choices. The likelihood that reforms will succeed depends on how well advocates of reform generate support for rights-based arguments without eliciting strong local reactions against such changes.

As stated at the outset of this study, problems, policies and politics each have their own dynamic path, and real change occurs when the three streams join. This linkage of the three streams is the perfect storm for policy-making, bringing together problems, solutions and actors willing to engage and support particular outcomes. This perfect storm does not last forever as it requires multiple conditions to be in place simultaneously – changing social dynamics, rising awareness of a problem or new reality, changes in administration and shifts in the national mood. This same policy window can close quickly. As we mentioned in Chapter 1, some factors that can close a policy window include when a problem is fixed; or little progress is achieved, and the problem does not appear to be going anywhere; or the crisis that precipitated the elevated issue passes; or even when there is no single or easy solution and the difficulty to deal with an issue leads to in-action. Thus, policy change requires a lot of moving parts to work together at the same time, whereas the numerous obstacles and challenges to policy change can easily disrupt the process and close the window of opportunity.

The window of opportunity for policy change is different depending on which actor you are discussing. Politicians generally think in terms of the next election, civil servants in terms of careers, campaigners think in terms of generations and the Church commonly thinks in terms of centuries – or eternity! Children, who only get one childhood and one time to grow up in the Irish education system, depend on their parents and these other stakeholders to make decisions that shape their experience. Parents also have a critical role, but they often act to protect their own family's immediate interests without making choices with the broader common good in mind. These varied time horizons influence how leaders within these different sectors make strategic decisions to achieve their short-term, medium-term and long-term goals. As we have seen in the policy case studies, the different policy solutions create different sets of coalitions that either support or oppose such reforms. A review of the main concerns of the various actors helps us understand how the window for real policy change is perceived as a challenge or opportunity depending on one's perspective.

II. What's Next for the Catholic Church in Irish Primary Schools

The Catholic Church has been the dominant actor in Irish primary education for over a century, but this predominance has been waning with increasing speed in recent years. The scale of the Catholic Church's institutional, property and personnel resources in Irish primary schools suggests that the Church will remain, to some degree, involved in Irish primary schools in the years ahead. And yet, the Church's centuries-long time horizon for dealing with change may have lulled Church leaders into thinking their influence has no end date. For many Church leaders it may be stretching it too far to think that the Church could be stripped of its remaining influence in the education system. Yet, as with the issues of same-sex marriage and abortion, the proposed citizens' assembly on education could serve as a springboard to initiate this type of major change. At 64 years old, the average Irish Catholic bishop was born in 1957 at a time when nobody would have predicted that same-sex marriage or abortion would become a right protected by the Constitution. Given the dramatic shifts in recent years, these Church decision-makers must now realise that no change is impossible. Even the property rights enshrined in the Constitution are not a permanent bulwark against dramatic change.

The scope and pace of recent changes suggests that the window of opportunity for the Church to shape outcomes in Irish primary schools in any meaningful ways may be closing within years. The Church no longer holds a monopoly within education and must adapt to the ascendancy of the Department of Education and the growing pluralism of patrons and interests within the education sector. This new reality has eroded the Church's ability to promote and protect its vision, let alone control what happens in its own schools.

The institutional Church has become less successful in defending its positions in recent years and it had virtually no impact during the debates over the admissions legislation. The Church argued that the issue only affected a small number of schools and was related to the State's inability to keep up with society's demographic shifts rather than the Church discriminating against children based on religion. The Church's data-focused problem definition, which emphasised that few students were denied a placement in the school of their choice based on their religious identity, did not seem to matter to Irish citizens. For those steeped in equality and rights-based arguments, if one student was affected or discriminated against, change was needed. Furthermore, still others within Irish society ignored anything the Church said because they were scarred by the revelations about the child sexual abuse crisis since the 1990s. The heinous acts committed by religious individuals against children in religious institutions, and the institutional cover-up of this crisis, left many within Irish society unwilling to give the Church the benefit of the doubt on anything related to caring for children. Therefore, even arguments during the admissions debate that sought to bolster the Church's ability to offer a truly Catholic experience to its students could be construed by those with such anti-Church sentiments as the Church once again seeking to protect its own interests over and above those of children.

If Church leaders and Catholic school leaders fail to offer a coordinated and proactive set of strategies in the coming years, a de facto State primary school system may emerge where a changed society finds the Church irrelevant and the Church becomes just a landlord. The real issue is not the quality of the Church's lobbying efforts, but whether the Church can offer an authentic Catholic school experience in the future. As religious beliefs, attitudes and practices continue to shift, increasing numbers of Catholic schools are unable to staff their schools with teachers and leaders who care about the faith and want to pass it on to the students.

The effects of declining religious beliefs and practices among an ever-increasing proportion of Irish society are rippling and gaining momentum. Since virtually all primary schools are still Catholic, most students in teacher training programmes take courses on Religious Education because these are prerequisites for teaching in Catholic schools. The lack of non-Catholic school options forces many new teachers to accept a position in a Catholic school because it is the only place where they can get a job. Fewer Irish teachers are teaching in a Catholic school for any mission-related reasons than was the case decades earlier. Therefore, a less religiously minded and trained set of teachers are occupying greater numbers of positions within Catholic schools. The implications of this on the character and identity of Irish Catholic schools will need to be assessed and responded to by Catholic patrons as part of any reshaping of the system.

These teachers are on the front lines of teaching religion and preparing children for their sacraments when they themselves may no longer believe or practice their faith. In this context, it is not surprising that Religious Education is no longer the most important subject, as it once was in the 1971 national guidelines. Add to this the growing curricular demands within primary schools, and it is no wonder that Religious Education is increasingly perceived as a non-essential subject that ends up getting sidelined in favour of other subjects. A recent study asked teachers what subjects they most enjoyed teaching, with religion coming in second to last of eleven subjects.[1]

Most principals (80 %+) now believe that the time given to the teaching of religious instruction should be reduced and reallocated to subjects such as PE, SPHE and the sciences, which is in keeping with the proposal in the new Primary School Curriculum Framework from the NCCA.[2] There can even be explicit pressure from principals to limit the amount of time teachers spend on religion. According to a recent study

---

1   For more information see the *Children's School Lives* study (<www.cslstudy.ie>).

2   IPPN President and Minister for Education agree that the time is right to start a 'conversation' on the time given to religion in our Primary Schools, Irish Primary Principals Network, 15 February 2016. [<https://www.ippn.ie/index.php/advocacy/press-releases/6957-ippn-president-and-minister-for-education-agree-that-the-time-is-right-to-start-a-conversation-on-the-time-given-to-religion-in-our-primary-schools>]

mentioned in Chapter 12, a common teacher experience has been that principals will explicitly point out when teachers have been spending too much time on religion or alternatively school leaders fail to ever check whether religion was being taught.[3] Such trends are undermining the Church's professed opposition to changes in the curriculum at the national level since many of its own teachers, leaders and schools are not energetically teaching the faith at the local level. The current trajectory is pointing towards a primary school system more characteristic of a secular state system than a denominational one, notwithstanding the lingering hallmarks of a denominational past, such as the names of saints in the school's name.

If the Church chooses to be proactive in engaging with the new reality within Irish society, there is still an opportunity for it to retain its role as an important education stakeholder, albeit one of many. In this scenario, the Church could still influence policy if it finds a way to help craft an intentional Catholic school sector that stands as a strong pillar within a pluralist system where parents have real choice in the type of education they wish to access for their children. To this end, Catholic educational leaders will have to greatly enhance the quality, pace and scope of their efforts to revitalise Catholic schools. There are important renewal efforts within many sectors of Catholic education, including third level institutions and religious communities and trusts that are working hard to support teachers, leaders, boards of management and local communities so they can foster more authentic Catholic school experiences. In-service leadership programmes for those leading and aspiring to lead Catholic schools are now run by the trust bodies at 2nd level, while the CPSMA and the University of Notre Dame recently partnered on a similar offering at primary level.

These efforts may be too late if Church leaders do not also make the difficult decisions to let go of a considerable number of its schools so that real choice and diversity of alternatives of school types exists for students, families and teachers. This would require the Church to divest or amalgamate Catholic schools despite local opposition, and they have proven

3   Monica Kowalski, Jonathan Tiernan and Sean McGraw, 'Catholic Education in Ireland and the United States: Teachers' Comparative Perspectives', *Research in Comparative & International Education*, 2020, Vol. 15, No. 2, 171–85.

unwilling or unable to do this on any large scale to date. Again, if there is no diversity within the system, establishing or sustaining authentic Catholic schools will be nearly impossible, and the trends signal further decline in maintaining the characteristic spirit in many Catholic schools. The lack of any progress in divestment has led to other recent reforms that have whittled away at Church control within its own schools. 'In December 2015, Section 37.1 of the Employment Equality Act was passed into law, limiting the rights of a school board to give favourable treatment on religious grounds to employees or take action if employees are undermining ethos. In January 2016, the Department of Education rescinded Rule 68 of National Schools, which had mandated that "a religious spirit should inform and vivify the whole work of the school" and recognised Religious Instruction as the most important part of the school curriculum.'[4] The increasing pace of these reforms reinforces the challenge to the Church, which is used to operating on a different time horizon. Asking the multi-layered and multivocal Church to respond quickly and decisively when it is used to reforming over centuries is expecting a daunting shift in behaviour. Thus, there is a palpable tension within the Church that change is necessary, but this coexists with the fear that any change will further undermine the Church's future ability to shape the lives and institutions entrusted to its care. Such change, supporters advocate, can serve as the foundation for a process to renew the schools that will remain under Catholic patronage. The strength of Catholic schools, they argue should come not from their number, but from the quality of the authentic, faith-based education provided to children and families who desire it.[5] This shift from a focus on 'head-count' to 'heart-count' is a critical challenge that now confronts those responsible for Irish Catholic schools.

4   Teresa O'Doherty, 'Contextualising Catholic Education in Ireland', *Educatio Catholica,* Vol. 1–2, February 2020.
5   Jonathan Tiernan, 'Catholic schools must remain true to their foundations – status quo will not achieve this', *The Irish Times,* 30 July 2018.

III. What's Next for Civil Society and Educational Reformers in Irish Primary Schools

Whereas the Church has engaged policy change over centuries, campaigners have advocated and sought to usher in policy reforms within generations. Civil society groups, educational professionals and academics who support reducing or eliminating the role of the Catholic Church in Irish primary education have been working to achieve their goals since the mid-1970s. Initially, motivated parents sought a non-Catholic school experience, so they started their own schools. Over the years, the reform movement has grown from establishing additional schools and patronage types, including multi-denominational and Irish-language schools, to challenging every aspect of education policy. The growing popularity of the equality movement that started in Europe and has become widely accepted within Ireland in recent decades has bolstered the educational reformers' efforts.

The emphasis on human rights and non-discrimination in schools gained attention in the mid-2000s when growing numbers of non-White immigrants did not gain admittance to the schools of their choice. Over time, the equality movement also highlighted the impact of Ireland's educational system on the growing numbers of non-religious and minority religious Irish citizens. As these numbers continued to increase and the stories of their discrimination and mistreatment within Ireland's denominational system also became more widespread, the equality movement gained momentum. Therefore, the immediate aftermath of the abortion referendum witnessed heightened demands for eliminating the Church's role in education as the next domino to fall. These trends confirm the growing superiority of framing policy debates within the context of the cultural goals of diversity, pluralism, tolerance and inclusion. Within education debates, this elevates minority religions and non-religious/secular interests and challenges the once dominant Church to honour changes in society and these different sets of interests and values.

In terms of future policy reforms, civil society groups will likely remain central actors, committed to advocating for more equal provision at primary level from a rights-based perspective. If trends within Irish society concerning religious beliefs, practices and behaviours continue on the same trajectory, civil society advocates will likely achieve greater reforms in a matter of years. The very use of 'reform', let alone the frequency with which it is employed, implies that the current state of Irish education requires change, and it is a matter of finding those changes that will be most acceptable.[6] There may not be one triumphant moment for these educational reformers like there was in Dublin Castle in the wake of the marriage equality and abortion victories. Nevertheless, the march to reform continues. The change is likely to be gradual, with milestones along the way as occurred with Community National Schools removing all Religious Education and sacramental preparation from the school day and the passing of the 2018 Admissions Bill. The Irish Constitution's protection of property rights may prevent a wholesale takeover of Catholic schools by the State as some reformers advocate. This is one of the reasons why Richard Bruton, TD, then Minister of Education (2016–18) moved away from divestment and emphasised instead reconfiguration. This subtle, but important shift helped the Government overcome challenging legal and financial issues associated with property rights and ownership. By focusing on leasing land and facilities, civil servants helped the Government open a potential path to the realisation of increased choice at primary level for parents who desire a multi-denominational school for their children.

Similar small, but critical bureaucratic changes have the potential to lead to other important reforms. For example, the small, almost imperceptible changes in the curriculum may usher in greater change without much attention or opposition, which may be in the interests of reformers. Unlike divestment, which consistently generated intense local opposition, curricular changes such as the proposed shortening of the patrons' programme by thirty minutes a week by the National Council for Curriculum and Assessment (NCAA), coupled with the potential introduction of a programme of Education about Religions and Beliefs (ERB) and Ethics are important changes that have received little media or public attention.

6   David Tuohy, SJ, 'The Rhetoric of Reform and the Grammar of Economic Development', *Studies: An Irish Quarterly Review*, 2012, Vol. 101, No. 402, 139–52.

These incremental changes shift what is acceptable within society and soften the ground for additional reforms. Recall that civil partnerships were passed into law in 2010 with unanimous support in the Dáil and little public fanfare. Civil society advocates preferred this quieter approach because it helped TDs from more conservative constituencies support change without eliciting vocal and persistent local opposition. Many rural TDs wanted to support change but were weary of the potential for electoral backlash if the issue was more widely discussed. Tiernan Brady, a key lobbyist on civil partnership for GLEN (the Gay Lesbian Equality Network) noted:

> There was a real terror of dealing with LGBT stuff, I remember one very pro-LGBT left-wing TD, who had made great speeches in Dublin, and then very clearly said to me, 'there's no way I'm ever going to say anything at home, because gay rights is the third rail of rural politics, touch it and you die'![7]

The more silent approach proved successful. By the time the same-sex marriage referendum occurred five years later, society had become so accustomed to these changes that taking the next step seemed reasonable to many. Educational reformers hope that the boundary of what seems normal and acceptable will continue to expand with each reform like in these earlier campaigns so that further educational reforms will be achievable.

The next likely reforms are transferring the teaching of religion to the end of the school day and eventually outside the school day altogether. The argument is that non- and multi-denominational schools are already doing this effectively without undermining students' and parents' religious freedom and Catholic schools could do this too. For reformers, offering religious instruction and sacramental preparation outside of school would result in students and parents opting in rather than opting out. For many, the current practice of allowing non-Catholic students to opt-out of Religious Education has left many non-religious or minority students feeling isolated or discriminated against because of their religious identity.

---

7   Connor Hayes, 'Outing the Party: Irish Political Party Engagement in the 2015 Same Sex Marriage Referendum', Senior thesis, Department of Political Science, University of Notre Dame, 1 April 2016, 13.

This rights-based argument focuses on the individual and seeks to prevent any child from experiencing any form of discrimination based on their religious beliefs and practices. *The Irish Times* supported this view in a 2017 editorial: 'While religious schools have a right to express their characteristic spirit, faith-formation classes should not discriminate or exclude children... In an ideal world, religious instruction classes in State-funded schools should be held outside of normal school hours.'[8] Such arguments value individual rights over the constitutional right of private patrons to ensure their schools can fulfil their characteristic spirit. In multi- or non-denominational schools, removing religion from the school day is at the heart of their mission and creates space within a crowded curriculum and school day to teach subjects and incorporate community experiences that reinforce their patron's programme.

Yet, removing religion from the school day would restrict the ability of Catholic schools to offer an integrated curriculum whereby the Catholic ethos is sprinkled into every subject, lesson and school activity while finding greatest expression in Religious Education class. The 2016 abolishing of Rule 68, which declared religion as the most important subject in the school day and protected the time devoted to it, already diminished the ability of Catholic schools to express a key part of their ethos. This change 'contributes to the view that religion is a discrete subject which one learns about, rather than a religious spirit which informs the holistic formation of pupils in faith schools. This ministerial order is another example of how the secularisation of education is being affected by current government policies.'[9] Further changes that would remove religion from the school day altogether would undermine the very mission of what it means to be a Catholic school. Thus, this subtle shift in educational policy would essentially make all Irish primary schools non- or multi-denominational schools.

As Irish citizens become less religious and awareness of equality and non-discrimination issues within schools becomes the most common way of framing educational issues, the rights of Catholic patrons will continue

---

8   'Religion and schools: time for more radical reform', *The Irish Times*, 27 October 2017.

9   Eugene Duffy, 'Contextualising Catholic Education in Ireland', *Educatio Catholica*, Vol. 1–2, February 2020.

to lose support. Civil society advocates are winning the policy-framing aspect of these reforms, and this is paving the way for greater numbers of Irish citizens to support additional educational reforms. Like civil partnerships softening the ground for eventual support for same-sex marriage, the gradual educational reforms being pursued by civil society advocates and educational reformers is softening the ground for further limits on the influence of the Church in Irish primary education. The less direct attention that is generated on these types of issues, the more likely such reforms will pass as strong and vocal opposition never materialises. The slow, gradual and persistent march to reform points to it being only a matter of time before more radical reforms ending any meaningful role of the Church in primary education are enacted. Civil servants often play a key behind the scenes role in these gradual reforms. When there are insurmountable and highly visible costs, or when there are widespread divisions in society and within and among political parties, civil servants lack the political support to implement their medium and longer-term plans. When the costs are less visible or are not as publicly focused on, and when there is emerging consensus within society, civil servants are better able to coordinate and implement more lasting policy reforms often without much fanfare or attention.

Our analysis of the media's coverage of educational issues in Chapter 7 concluded that the media has played an important, but not leading role in the reform debates. The mainstream media generally present the critical issues and actors in neutral or positive light. However, like the case in the marriage equality and abortion campaigns, reformers often minimise or elevate reform issues in the media depending on how it will affect support for their goals. There tends to be greater media attention when there is a connection to the political process, because mainstream media likes to focus on elections, legislation and other political institutions like citizens' assemblies. Civil society advocates and reformers have been adept at mobilising mainstream media at key moments. Similarly, reform groups have become adept at using social media to change the hearts and minds of Irish citizens, which has also proven a key part of softening the ground to make further reform possible. In the marriage equality campaign, Yes Equality also mastered a modern social media campaign that won over the hearts and minds of new and old voters alike. As Chapter 8 discussed, the social media campaign was heavily skewed towards the Yes side, which cultivated a much stronger online presence than the Church.[10]

Similar trends are occurring within social media on educational issues as reformers are outmanoeuvring Catholic education leaders to shift the opinions of Irish citizens. A quick glance at social media activity suggests that there is a sophisticated approach by advocates of greater plurality of patronage and those advocating for a secularised education system. By contrast, there is little evidence of a strategic approach by the Church to address framing the problem, developing policy alternatives/solutions, or engaging the personal stories of its supporters in ways that could leverage social media channels to advance their agenda. As of 2021, these are the approximate combined followers on Facebook and Twitter for some of the key primary educational actors and institutions: 29,000+ for Educate Together; 12,000+ for Education and Training Board of Ireland (ETBI), who operates Community National Schools; 7,000 for Education Equality; 2,600 for the Catholic Primary Schools Management Association (CPSMA); and o for the Catholic Education Partnership. The Irish Catholic Bishops had nearly 22,000 followers, but most of these accounts are not dedicated to Catholic education and serve the Church more generally. The lack of content related to Catholic education in social media, especially compared to that of the key educational reformers, suggests that reformers are once again out-organising the Church to win over Irish citizens as they lay the groundwork for further changes that limit the role of the Church in Irish primary schools.

IV. What's Next for Political Parties and Irish Primary Schools

Politicians and party elites are always concerned about the next election, which means they have the shortest time frame of the major stakeholders

10   Hayes, 2016, 40.

in the educational debates. Major party candidates and leaders have little incentive to proactively engage further reforms given the potential for local opposition and the lack of consensus on many educational policy alternatives. The education of one's children and the role of faith in the life of a family are both deeply personal and Irish politicians have rarely interfered with these types of issues. Irish political parties have proven adept at assigning such salient issues to citizens' assemblies rather than jeopardising internal division and alienation of sections of the electorate. That said, the complexity and number of issues associated with further educational reforms and limits to the Church's involvement in primary schools do not easily translate into issues citizens' assemblies can engage and solve.

In the past, Ireland's two historically dominant political parties, Fianna Fáil and Fine Gael, often avoided controversial issues until a broader consensus within Irish society was achieved or an extra-parliamentary institution within the Irish State could address the issue so the parties would not have to engage it directly. When avoidance was not feasible, the major parties have regularly shifted their ideological programs to purposefully diminish voters' perceptions of policy differences between them and minor parties, particularly during general elections. These ideological shifts have muted the distinctive electoral appeal of minor parties on key issues, weakening their electoral support over a series of elections.[11]

This co-opting of minor party appeals by major parties when minor parties are tapping into issues with growing salience within Irish society is relevant for what has been occurring within the education debates. Major party leaders have recognised the difficulty in implementing divestment and other educational reforms that deeply affect local communities, so they have supported both sides of the debate and often focused on creating a consultative process that includes all the major stakeholders and leads to change only when most Irish citizens are ready. By contrast, Ireland's minor, and primarily left-leaning, parties have been stronger proponents of educational reforms that reduce or eliminate the role of religion in Ireland's primary schools. In 2021, the Social Democrats officially declared their goal

---

11   See Chapter 3 in McGraw, 2015.

of separating the Church from the State as they seek to establish a completely secular educational system in Ireland. Other minor parties support similar proposals. If social attitudes continue to evolve in the same direction, the major parties may have no choice but to increase their support for similar educational reforms or risk losing electoral support among key constituencies. The combination of growing support for equality, inclusion and non-discrimination; the relentless campaigning of civil society groups;, and the mounting support among political parties for a secular system could generate the type of consensus that major parties have traditionally relied on before supporting policy change.

As Chapter 2 outlined, the State has been assuming greater levels of control within the Irish primary sector despite the Church's ongoing areas of influence. In addition to funding salaries, programmes and other resources, the State also regulates the curriculum and admissions, and determines where new schools open. For many, the next logical step is total State control. Catholic educators and bishops might even be willing to support this if it meant that Church leaders could have greater autonomy to run their schools as they wish. This form of separation of Church and State, whereby the State still financially supports denominational schools, seems unlikely given the lack of resources facing the Irish State in the aftermath of the COVID-19 pandemic. Once again, if there were greater numbers of non- and multi-denominational schools available to those parents who sought such an educational experience for their children these debates would be irrelevant. Yet, as long as there are insufficient non-Catholic primary school placements and the State has other financial priorities, political parties will not support propping up the denominational system indefinitely. Here, too, reformers have won the framing debate as they continually argue that the State is using public funds to allow denominational schools to discriminate against non-religious and minority religious students under the current structure. The State's lack of resources and the growing acceptance of the equality movement's framing of educational issues combine to make an entirely secular educational system the more likely future reality as opposed to a state system that supports both secular and religious schools.

Key changes in the Irish party system may also hasten overall support for secular reforms in Irish primary education. First, the two-party dominance that marked Irish politics for nearly 100 years is over, and smaller parties are likely to play a critical, king-making role in government formation in the coming decades. The rising importance of small parties, and the fact that they can hold the balance of power in minority governments creates a situation whereby policy positions that seemed peripheral at one moment can gain an oversised influence through a change of government. Additionally, electoral volatility has more than doubled in the last three elections, leaving even Ireland's historically dominant parties, Fianna Fáil and Fine Gael, more vulnerable. According to an index of electoral volatility in Irish general elections, there was an average volatility index of 8.7 between 1930 and 1980, 12.4 between 1995 and 2000 and 23.8 since 2011.[12] As elections become more volatile and competitive in the contemporary period, even the larger parties will be seeking new ways to attract voters. This may lead them to act less cautiously and slowly about supporting secular reforms than during previous electoral periods if this will help them attract sufficient voters. The dramatic shifts in Irish party politics may combine with increased support within Irish society for secular reforms to make additional reforms more likely in the coming years especially if they can be framed in ways that do not generate opposition from active local communities.

The complexity of educational issues has created a different set of coalitions of those who support or oppose reforms than occurred in the previous marriage equality and abortion campaigns. The previous campaigns framed policy solutions in ways that focused on individual rights and creating a new Ireland that is inclusive and reflective of its growing diversity. The educational issues that have been framed in similar ways have proven more successful in generating broader public support that has in turn attracted additional political party support. The issue of divestment revealed how local schools, communities and institutions could still muster sufficient opposition to stall radical change at the local level. Major party elites and government officials seem content to patiently wait until support

12   R. Kenneth Carty, 'Into the Void: the Collapse of Irish Party Democracy', *Irish Political Studies*, 2022, forthcoming.

for additional educational reforms generates a large enough consensus to pass further legislation.

These trends also point in the direction of further reforms only being a matter of time. Smaller curricular reforms will likely continue to reduce the Church's control within its own schools. A proposed citizens' assembly may not be able to solve complex educational issues, especially given the constitutional and property issues entailed with some proposals. However, a citizens' assembly would generate focused and ongoing public attention on educational issues. The popular framing of educational issues within the context of helping Ireland embrace its diversity, equality and inclusion will likely continue to grow. As smaller parties align with civil society groups, educational reformers and growing numbers of individuals within Irish society, the major parties are likely to offer their support as well. In the end, the Church, still operating on a longer time horizon, may not be able to adapt quickly enough to counter these growing forces.

V. Concluding Thoughts

The book has provided a careful analysis of how the breath-taking social, economic and cultural changes occurring within Ireland in recent decades have impacted the Irish policy-making process. In drawing upon key lessons from the marriage equality and abortion campaigns, we have identified key aspects of the evolving nature of Church and State relationships in a secularising Ireland. The book has relied on several rich case studies to reveal the power of policy framing. The set of policy solutions that have been offered and engaged within the primary educational sector demonstrate how policy problems are addressed creates different coalitions of support and opposition. The choices about framing have affected whether policies increase in salience and are eventually passed into legislation. The interplay of civil society activists and organisations, the media, public opinion, political parties and civil servants determines how policy reforms live or die. As the window of opportunity for educational reform has opened further in recent years, the Church continues to struggle to determine a unified and effective response. The tide of reform continues to roll in and various actors have become more adept at increasing and broadening public support in ways that encourage political parties to endorse ongoing change, which provides civil servants the space and cover to initiate such change. The pace and degree of social, economic, cultural and political change experienced in Ireland in recent decades make it a telling case for anyone interested in how policy changes occur in changing societies, especially when a new consensus is not yet achieved.

Future policy studies will hopefully benefit from a careful reading of this book. This study has demonstrated that seemingly insurmountable policy changes can occur when a variety of factors coalesce. First, dramatic social change associated with changes in religious beliefs, practices and sense of belonging and identity have transformed the once homogeneous Irish society into a more diverse one. Next, dedicated campaigners defined the problem as Ireland's inadequate adapting to these evolving social realities and reframed solutions in the context of an ever-growing equality movement that embraces diversity, inclusion and equality as the core values of the new Ireland. As the media highlighted these values and greater numbers within Irish society gravitated towards these values, the reframing of policy problems in this light made major party elites more willing to support change. Rather than taking the once dominant Catholic Church head on, advocates of change have slowly and methodically reframed educational issues to focus on individual rights and the personal experiences of children and parents. Ironically, the Church had taken care of Irish families for centuries. Yet, as society evolved, advocates of change have surpassed the Church in their ability to determine who cares for children and how they do this through Irish schools. The deep ties to local communities and properties will sustain the Church's presence in Irish primary schools in the short-term, but the longer-term trends and momentum have eroded the Church's ability to hold on indefinitely. The dramatic changes that have occurred within Ireland on same-sex marriage and abortion, and are increasingly occurring within education, remind us that what once seemed inconceivable or unachievable decades ago is possible. Future studies will hopefully build on the analysis within this book to better measure and understand at what stage a policy issue is at within its broader life cycle to determine the likelihood of its passing. For students, academics, civil society leaders, policy-makers, civil servants and politicians alike, the answer to What's Next will be a perennial question and one hopefully this book has helped us think about in a more systematic way.

For the children of Ireland, What's Next will be, one hopes, fulfilled and productive lives that are shaped, in part, by their time in primary school classrooms. For most children, this time is a positive one with Irish primary schools delivering excellent educational and social outcomes for the students they serve. The patrons, principals, teachers and staff involved in running primary schools have much to be proud of in this regard. As all these stakeholders look to the future and continue to advocate for their preferred vision of what that looks like, it would serve everyone well to keep the interests of all children at the forefront of future policy-making.

Media Analysis Notes

To start this project, we began by determining the major categories of topics that were important for this research. Based on an initial meeting, the research team selected divestment, patronage, admissions and baptism barrier, religious instruction or education, curriculum (including Relationships and Sexuality Education (RSE), Education on Religious Beliefs (ERB) and Ethics and faith-based curriculum), Community National Schools and Education Training Boards, Educate Together, Gaeltacht schools or Gaelscoili, the Taoiseach and education and the Minister for Education and Skills and the Department of Education and Skills (including the various changes to the name over time). Two research assistants trialed different search terms in *The Irish Times* and the *Irish Independent* to become familiar with their databases to determine the best search terms that would produce results related to each of these categories.

When using *The Irish Times* website, both the section entitled 'the Newspaper' and the section entitled 'IrishTimes.com' were used to ensure a full search of all articles dating back to 1859 was possible. When looking for articles dated before 1996, 'the Newspaper' was used, while after 1996, 'the IrishTimes.com' was used. For each section, it was possible to search for an exact phrase by entering it as 'exact-phrase' or for the presence of a group of words generally in an article by entering 'exact phrase' in the search bar. The search terms first tried in *The Irish Times* database were 'patronage divestment', 'patronage', 'school patronage', 'baptism-barrier', 'school-admissions', 'sexuality-education', 'faith based curriculum', 'religious-education', 'denominational school', 'catholic-school', 'community-national-school', 'education-training-board', 'educate together', 'ethics-education', 'Education-About-Religions-and-Beliefs-and-Ethics' and 'Catholic-primary-school-management-association'.

When using the *Irish Independent* database, held on Irish Newspaper Archives, there are a number of possible search bars including 'ALL of these words', 'this EXACT word or phrase', 'ANY of these words' and 'EXCLUDE these words'. For every search, 'Irish Independent 1905-current' first had to be selected from the 'Filter by title' category. Results shown were always 'Articles', not 'Pictures' or 'Ads'. Search terms first trialed in this database, using 'this EXACT word or phrase' search, were 'patronage', 'baptism barrier', 'school admissions', 'relationships and sexuality education', 'sexuality education', 'relationships education', 'education on religious beliefs and ethics', 'religious beliefs education', 'ethics education', 'erbe', 'education about religious beliefs and ethics', 'faith based curriculum', 'religious curriculum', 'Catholic curriculum', 'integrated curriculum', 'religious teaching', 'religious instruction', 'multidenominational school', 'Catholic school', 'denominational school', 'Church of Ireland school', 'community national school', 'education training board', 'etbi', 'Catholic Primary School Management Association', 'cpsma' and 'Educate Together'.

There were several issues with many of these search terms. For example, 'school admissions' also included results such as articles about the admission price to events at schools and graduate schools. The following terms included job postings; 'patronage', 'sexuality education', 'religious teaching', 'religious instruction', 'multidenominational school', 'Catholic school' and 'denominational school' included job postings. Acronyms like 'rse' and 'erbe' always included results where those letters where in a longer word rather than being a stand-alone word. The term 'integrated curriculum' produced results for many kinds of education issues such as technology and punishment strategies. The terms 'multi-denominational school', 'Catholic school' and 'Church of Ireland school' all included results about any event involving a child who went to that kind of school, house listings that were in a specific catchment area for a kind of school and community events happening at these schools.

Therefore, several strategies were trialed to narrow down results to only relevant ones. The searches to try these strategies were: 'school' in 'ALL of these words' search and 'patronage' in 'this EXACT word or phrase' search; 'school' in 'ALL of these words' search, 'patronage' in 'this EXACT word or phrase' search and 'advertisement' in 'EXCLUDE these words' search;

'school' in 'ALL of these words' search and 'patronage' in 'this EXACT word or phrase' search; 'school' in 'ALL of these words' search, 'patronage' in 'this EXACT word or phrase' search and 'application' in 'EXCLUDE these words' search; 'school' in 'ALL of these words' search and 'patronage' in 'this EXACT word or phrase' search; 'school' in 'ALL of these words' search, 'patronage' in 'this EXACT word or phrase' search and 'required' in 'EXCLUDE these words' search; 'education' in 'ALL of these words' search and 'patronage' in 'this EXACT word or phrase' search; 'religious education' in 'this EXACT word or phrase' search and 'application' in 'EXCLUDE these words' search; 'religious teaching' in 'this EXACT word or phrase' search and 'application' in 'EXCLUDE these words' search; 'religious instruction' in 'this EXACT word or phrase' search and 'application' in 'EXCLUDE these words' search; 'patronage' in 'this EXACT word or phrase' search and 'school' in 'ALL of these words' search; 'patronage' in 'this EXACT word or phrase' search and 'teacher' in 'ALL of these words' search; 'patronage' in this 'EXACT word or phrase' search and 'education' in 'ALL of these words' search; 'divestment' in 'this EXACT word or phrase' search and 'school' in 'ALL of these words' search; 'divestment' in 'this EXACT word or phrase' search and 'education' in 'ALL of these words' search; and 'sexuality education' in 'this EXACT word or phrase' search and 'apply' in 'EXCLUDE these words' search. In order to test the usefulness and accuracy of these searches, each one was applied to a specific year by typing in January 1 of that year to the 'From date' category and December 31 of that year to the 'To date' category. First a search was done during the specified year using the original search term. Then a note was made on which articles were relevant to our topic and which were not, such as being job postings or related to other topics besides primary education. Then the new search was performed on the specified year, adding in search terms that might be able to limit the results, and the results were compared to ensure none of the relevant articles were lost and to determine what combination of search terms produced the fewest irrelevant results.

After data from both newspapers was compared, the research team decided that the most important categories from which to produce complete data and to discuss further were patronage and divestment, baptism barrier and school admissions, ethics education, Educate Together and Community National Schools and religious and sexuality education. Data on the number of articles written on these topics for each year from 1960–2019 was then gathered. The search terms used for *The Irish Times* were 'patronage-divestment', 'baptism-barrier', 'school-admissions', 'ethics-education', 'sexuality-education', 'religious-education' and 'educate-together'. The results from 'baptism-barrier' and 'school-admissions' were then added together to create the 'School Admissions and Baptism Barrier' category. Similarly, the results from 'sexuality-education' and 'religious-education' were combined to create the 'Religious Education and Sexuality Education' category. The need to ensure the identical search terms were used in both newspapers had to be balanced with the need to ensure only relevant results were included in these searches. Therefore, to match the searches completed in *The Irish Times* for the *Irish Independent*, the research team decided to use the following terms in the 'this EXACT word or phrase' search: 'divestment', 'ethics education', 'sexuality education', 'religious education' and 'Educate Together'. The results for 'religious education' and 'sexuality education' were then added together. For the 'School Admissions and Baptism Barrier' category 'school admission' in 'this EXACT word or phrase' was searched and 'baptism barrier' in 'this EXACT word or phrase' was searched; however, when recording the number of articles found in each year, each article was read to determine if it was relevant to primary education, and only then was it counted. These results were then combined into one category as with *The Irish Times*.

Later, it was realised that the results in the 'Religious Education and Sexuality Education' included many results related to other levels of education besides just primary, especially secondary when sexuality education is a much larger discussion. Therefore, this category was later amended. In *The Irish Times* the searches became "religious education primary" and 'sexuality education primary' for each year before the results were once again added together to create the final category. In the *Irish Independent*, the searches became 'religious education' in 'this EXACT word or phrase' and 'primary' in 'ALL of these words', which was added to 'sexuality education' in 'this EXACT word or phrase' and 'primary' in 'ALL of these words'. Primary curriculum as another important topic was also added later when it was realized that it provided the highest number of articles per year of any primary education issue. To produce these results, the search term 'primary curriculum' was used in *The Irish Times*, and 'primary curriculum' in 'ALL of these words' was searched in the *Irish Independent*. A single graph comparing the number of articles per year in each category (divestment, school admissions and baptism barrier, ethics education, sexuality education and religious education, Educate Together and primary curriculum) from 1960–2019 was then created for each newspaper.

The research team then determined that the topics that provided the most interesting and important as case studies were divestment, admissions and baptism barrier and curriculum. Therefore, all articles on these topics from 2010–19 were gathered. For each newspaper, the team created a spreadsheet with different pages for admissions and baptism barrier articles and divestment articles. On this spreadsheet each article was given an ID number and the newspaper it came from was recorded, as was the title of the article, the year it was published, and the full text of the article. From this, files were created to input all of the articles into Voyant Tools. We began with the divestment articles. For each year, we created a file with the year as a title name, so, for example, our files were titled simply 2019 or 2018, and they contained the full text of all of the articles in the divestment category which had been published in that year. We then put all of these files into Voyant and were able to see the most common words that appeared in all of those articles using both the 'trends' and 'terms' tools. We were also able to specify words for Voyant to ignore in order to see more interesting words that appear most frequently. Some of the stop words specified were education, children and school(s), which were added to Voyant's typical list of stop words that include articles, pronouns, prepositions and other generally accepted filler words in English. From this we were able to see more relevant common terms and ignore the ones that we expected to be present in articles about education and schools. We then completed our own hand analysis of the topics in all of these articles. This allowed us to specify broader ideas, such as the slow speed of divestment, which could not be encapsulated by any one word Voyant was able to find. We found we identified the same list of actors and single word issues as Voyant did, but we were able to add in more issues that were more complex. This entire process was repeated with the admissions and baptism barrier articles.

After determining the most common actors and issues across these articles, we turned our attention to a sentiment analysis. Based on the experience with Voyant that determined it was difficult for computer software to recognise the kinds of complex issues we had found common in the articles, we focused our attention on the actors. We created a dictionary in MeaningCloud of all the important actors we had seen throughout these articles, which included archbishop, bishop, board of management, Catholic, Community National School, Educate Together, Education Training Board, patron, community, parent, minister, Jan O'Sullivan, Ruairí Quinn, Mary Coughlan, Richard Bruton, Joe McHugh, Forum on Patronage and Pluralism, Labour Party, Sinn Féin, Fianna Fáil, Fine Gael, teacher, past pupil and Department of Education. Most of these entries included aliases as they can have multiple names in the articles, such as Jan O'Sullivan also being referred to as Minister O'Sullivan and Ms. O'Sullivan. We classified these terms under our own ontological classification in MeaningCloud (Top>Education>Actor) so they would be easy to separate from other entities in the sentiment analysis later. We then ran a topic level sentiment analysis of the articles in the divestment category using our 'user dictionary'. Once this analysis had been run, we filtered the results in the 'type' column to our ontological category. Thus, we were able to see the sentiment towards each of these actors in every article.

We then calculated the overall percentage of sentiment as either negative, positive, neutral, or none for each actor. We assumed that all negative and all positive polarities were the same (so we ignored the P+ or N+ rating and simply added them as one positive or negative rating respectively). We chose not to display the none polarity percentages as they are instances when MeaningCloud found the actor in an article but did not find any sign of sentiment expressed towards them. Often these are situations when the actor appears in a list or in an extremely brief sentence. We also counted the total number of times MeaningCloud had recognised the actor as being present within all of these articles. We grouped some actors together to create categories that more accurately reflected the way we had coded these articles earlier. We added together all results for bishop and archbishop; for Community National School and Education Training Board; and for minister, Jan O'Sullivan, Ruairi Quinn, Mary Coughlan, Richard Bruton and Joe McHugh. After creating these combined categories, we removed any actor that had fewer than ten mentions in MeaningCloud, as lower numbers than that made it possible for one article that expressed a sentiment towards an actor to drastically change the percentages and we wanted to ensure we only presented results that had enough data to be accurate. This was then repeated with the admissions and baptism barrier articles, using the same dictionary of actors and same process for combining categories and eliminating smaller ones.

Upon a quick review of the articles that were produced by searching for 'primary curriculum' in either database, it became clear that any analysis of these articles would be extensive and would produce many results irrelevant to the issue of secularisation in Ireland. We therefore decided to focus on comparing the general category of primary curriculum with the more specific actors and events involved in it. We collected data on the number of articles related to primary curriculum review and the National Council for Curriculum and Assessment (NCCA) that were published per year during the time 1990–2019 in each newspaper. The search term used in *The Irish Times* were 'primary curriculum review', 'National Council for Curriculum and Assessment' and 'NCCA'. The results from National Council for Curriculum and Assessment and NCCA were combined by taking whichever search produced the greatest number of articles for a given year. There was too much overlap between the results to add them together. In the *Irish Independent*, 'primary curriculum review' was searched in 'ALL of these words', 'NCCA' was searched in 'this EXACT word or phrase' and 'National Council for Curriculum and Assessment' was searched in 'this EXACT word or phrase'. The results were combined in the same way as *The Irish Times*. The results for both newspapers were then combined and a graph produced that compared the number of articles published per year on the issues of primary curriculum, primary curriculum review and the NCCA.

Bibliography

—— (2008) 'Educate Together Now Country's Fastest Growing Educational Movement', *Irish Independent,* 17 September.

—— (2010) 'Church in Shift Away from Schools Provision', *Irish Examiner,* 3 August. Available at: <https://www.irishexaminer.com/news/arid-30467859.html> (Accessed: 2 November 2021).

—— (2012) 'Red C Poll: Majority Demand X Case Legislation', *Business Post,* 1 December. Available at: <https://www.businesspost.ie/legacy/red-c-poll-majority-demand-x-case-legislation-7f275d21> (Accessed: 2 November 2021).

—— (2013) 'Poll Shows Strong Support For Abortion In Cases Of Rape, Fatal Foetal Abnormality', The Journal.ie, 20 January. Available at: <https://www.thejournal.ie/abortion-ireland-rape-fatal-foetal-abnormality-771180-Jan2013/> (Accessed: 2 November 2021).

—— (2016) 'Fears for Future of School over Dwindling Pupil Levels', *The Kerryman,* 2 July.

—— (2016) 'Majority Want to See Abortion in Certain Circumstances to Be Legal in Ireland', *Newstalk,* 21 January. Available at: <https://www.newstalk.com/the-pat-kenny-show/48-of-people-believe-the-8th-amendment-should-be-removed-according-to-poll-619566> (Accessed: 2 November 2021).

—— (2017) 'Archbishop Martin Urged to Intervene to Save Faughart NS', LMFM, 11 August. Available at: <https://www.lmfm.ie/news/lmfm-news/archbishop-martin-urged-to-intervene-to-save-faugh/> (Accessed: 2 November 2021).

—— (2017) 'Granting Patronage of Killarney School to Local ETB "Not What Parents Want or Deserve"', *Breaking News,* Breakingnews.ie, 13 June. Available at: <https://www.breakingnews.ie/ireland/granting-patronage-of-killarney-school-to-local-etb-not-what-parents-want-or-deserve-793416.html> (Accessed: 2 November 2021).

—— (2017) 'Kerry's First Community National School to Open in September', *Radio Kerry,* 13 June.

—— (2017) 'Parents Forced to Withdraw Pupils from Faughart NS', LMFM News, 9 August. Available at: <https://www.lmfm.ie/news/lmfm-news/parents-forced-to-withdraw-pupils-from-faughart-ns/> (Accessed: 2 November 2021).

—— (2017) 'People Were Polled with the Same Questions as the Citizens' Assembly. Here's What They Said', 1 November. Available at: <https://www.thejournal.ie/people-polled-citizen-assembly-3673017-Nov2017/> (Accessed: 2 November 2021).

—— (2017) 'Religion and Schools: Time for More Radical Reform', *The Irish Times*, 27 October.

—— (2017) 'Uncertain Future for School as Students Do Not Return', RTE.ie, 29 August. Available at: <https://www.rte.ie/news/education/2017/0829/900865-louth-school/> (Accessed: 2 November 2021).

—— (2018) 'Abortion Referendum: Yes Secures Landslide Victory', *The Irish Times*, 26 May.

—— (2018) 'Dáil Debates', KildareStreet, 30 May. Available at: <https://www.kildarestreet.com/debates/?id=2018-05-30a.478> (Accessed: 2 November 2021).

—— (2018) 'Ireland's Abortion Referendum: Don't Mention the Church', *Economist*, 24 March.

—— (2018) 'Irish Archbishops Say Abortion Vote Shows Church's Waning Influence', *The Guardian*, 27 May.

—— (2019) 'Changing School Patronage: Pragmatism in Action Not Secularism', *Irish Examiner*, 27 August. Available at: <https://www.irishexaminer.com/breakingnews/views/ourview/changing-school-patronage-pragmatism-in-action-not-secularism-946569.html> (Accessed: 2 November 2021).

—— (2019) 'Four Primary Schools to Transfer to Non-denominational Model This Year', *RoscommonHerald.ie*, 27 August. Available at: <https://roscommonherald.ie/2019/08/27/four-primary-schools-to-transfer-to-non-denominational-model-this-year/> (Accessed: 2 November 2021).

—— (2019) 'Kerry ETB Takes over Two More Schools', *RadioKerry.ie*, 26 August. Available at: <https://www.radiokerry.ie/kerry-etb-takes-two-schools-august-26th-2019/> (Accessed: 2 November 2021).

—— (2019) 'Kerry ETB to Open Third Community National School in Kerry', *radiokerry.ie,* 26 August.

—— (2019) 'Kiltoom/Cam: St John's National School, Lecarrow'. *Westmeath Independent*, 3 August.

—— (2019) 'Meeting in Tahilla on Community School', *RadioKerry.ie,* 21 March. Available at: <https://www.radiokerry.ie/meeting-tahilla-community-school-march-21st-2019/> (Accessed: 2 November 2021).

—— (2019) 'Our Schools Need the Freedom to be Truly Catholic', *The Irish Catholic*, 31 October. Available at: <https://www.irishcatholic.com/our-schools-need-the-freedom-to-be-truly-catholic/> (Accessed: 2 November 2021).

—— (2019) 'Religious Education Still Available for St. Joseph's NS Pupils Who Want It', *Shannonside News*, 25 July.

—— (2019) 'Roscommon's First Community National School to Open in Lecarrow'. Midwest Radio, 27 August. Available at: <https://www.midwestradio.ie/index.php/news/33226-roscommon-s-first-community-national-school-to-open-in-lecarrow> (Accessed: 2 November 2021).

—— (2019) 'South Roscommon School to Meet to Consider "Change of Ethos"', *Shannonside News*, 19 June.

—— (2020) 'Programme for Government: Our Shared Future', June. Available at: <https://www.documentcloud.org/documents/6944741-Programme-For-Government-June-2020.html> (Accessed: 2 November 2021).

Anderas, W. (2018) Twitter, 26 May. Available at: <https://twitter.com/Anneanswers> (Accessed: 12 March 2021).

Association of Trustees of Catholic Schools (2017) 'The Role of Religion in the Admissions Process in Primary Schools: Response to Consultation Paper', March.

Atlantic Philanthropies (2018) 'Marriage Equality: Lessons for Advocates'. Available at: <https://www.atlanticphilanthropies.org/insights/insights-books/advocacy-for-impact#marriage_equality> (Accessed: 2 November 2021)

BAI Code of Fairness, Objectivity & Impartiality, Rule 21, 2013.

Barron, M. (2018a) 'It's Time to Stop Subcontracting Education to Religious Groups', *The Irish Times*, 2 January.

Barron, M. (2018b) Twitter, 29 May. Available at: <https://twitter.com/michaelnbarron> (Accessed: 12 March 2021).

Bielenberg, K. (2018) 'Discussions to Start Soon on Transfer of Catholic Schools Transfer'. *Irish Independent*, 19 September.

Boland, R. (2007) 'Faith Before Fairness', *The Irish Times*, 8 September.

Breen, M., Courtney, M., McMenamin, I., O'Malley, E. and Rafter, K. (2019) *Resilient Reporting: Media Coverage of Irish Elections Since 1969*, Manchester: Manchester University Press.

Brinig, M. F. and Garnett, N. S. (2014) *Lost Classroom, Lost Community: Catholic Schools' Importance in Urban America*. United Kingdom: University of Chicago Press.

Brooks, D. (2012) 'Flood the Zone', *The New York Times*, 6 February.

Brown, E. (2016) *Atlantic Insights: Advocacy for Impact*, Atlantic Philanthropies. Available at: <https://www.atlanticphilanthropies.org/insights/insights-books/advocacy-for-impact> (Accessed: 1 November 2021).

Brown, E. (2021) *Yes: Marriage Equality's Path to Victory in Ireland*, 7 April. Available at: <https://www.comnetwork.org/insights/yes-marriage-equalitys-path-to-victory-in-ireland>.

Buck, M. (2020) *Renewing the Church-State Partnership for Catholic Education, Engaging with the Challenge of Academisation*. Oxford: Peter Lang.

Burns, S. (2019) 'Four Religious-Run Schools Switching to Multi-Denominational Model'. *The Irish Times*, 27 August. Available at: <https://www.irishtimes.com/news/ireland/irish-news/four-religious-run-schools-switching-to-multi-denominational-model-1.3998803>.

Byrne, C. (2020) 'Education and a Citizens' Assembly', *The Irish Times*, 26 June.

Caden, S. (2019) 'Christmas Is Safe … and so Is the Future of Our Schools', *Irish Independent*. 6 April.

Carberry, G. (2009) 'Catholic Control of Schooling not Tenable, Says Archbishop', *The Irish Times,* 17 June.

Casey, J. (2019) '80% of Educate Together Schools Opened in Last Decade Still in Temporary Accommodation', Breaking News, 27 August. Available at: <https://www.breakingnews.ie/ireland/80-of-educate-together-schools-opened-in-last-decade-still-in-temporary-accommodation-946592.html> (Accessed: 2 November 2021).

Catholic Primary Schools Management Association (2017a) 'CPSMA Responds to Minister Bruton's Decision to Remove Religious Criteria from Catholic School Admissions'. Available at: <https://www.cpsma.ie/cpsma-responds-to-minister-brutons-decision-to-remove-religious-criteria-from-catholic-school-admissions/> (Accessed: 2 November 2021).

Catholic Primary Schools Management Association (2017b) *CPSMA Responds to Minister Bruton's Decision to Remove Religious Criteria from Catholic School Admissions*, 29 July. Available at: <https://www.cpsma.ie/cpsma-responds-to-minister-brutons-decision-to-remove-religious-criteria-from-catholic-school-admissions/> (Accessed: 2 November 2021).

Catholic Primary Schools Management Association (2018) *Restoration of Capitation Grant Campaign Report*, 11 September. Available at: <https://www.cpsma.ie/restoration-of-capitation-grant-campaign-report/> (Accessed: 2 November 2021).

Catholic Primary Schools Management Association (2021a) 'About Us'. Available at: <https://www.cpsma.ie/about-cpsma/> (Accessed: 2 November 2021).

Catholic Primary Schools Management Association (2021b) 'Our Team'. Available at: <https://www.cpsma.ie/whos-who/> (Accessed: 2 November 2021).

Catholic Schools Partnership (2021) 'About Us'. Available at: <https://www.catholicschools.ie/csp/> (Accessed: 2 November 2021).

Catholic Schools Partnership (2014) *Catholic Education at Second Level in the Republic of Ireland: Looking to the Future*, Dublin: Veritas.

CEIST (2007) 'CEIST Charter'. Available at: <https://www.ceist.ie/wp-content/uploads/2019/04/Ceist-Charter-Latest.pdf> (Accessed: 2 November 2021).

Central Statistics Office (2016a) 'Census of Population 2016'. Available at: <https://www.cso.ie/en/releasesandpublications/ep/p-cp8iter/p8iter/p8rnraa/> (Accessed: 2 November 2021).

Central Statistics Office (2016b) 'The Proportion of Catholics in Ireland, 1881 to 2016'. Available at: <https://www.cso.ie/en/releasesandpublications/ep/p-cp8iter/p8iter/p8rrc/> (Accessed: 2 November 2021).

Central Statistics Office (2016c) 2016 Census. Available at: <https://www.cso.ie/en/ releasesandpublications/ep/p-cp8iter/p8iter/p8rrc/> (Accessed: 2 November 2021).

Central Statistics Office (2021) 'Mainstream National Schools and Pupils in Ordinary Classes', 1 June. Available at: <https://statbank.cso.ie/px/pxeirestat/ Statire/SelectVarVal/Define.asp?maintable=EDA51&PLanguage=0> (Accessed: 2 November 2021).

Children's School Lives (2020) Available at: www.cslstudy.ie> (Accessed: 2 November 2021).

Citizens Information (2021) 'Equality in the Workplace'. Available at: <https:// www.citizensinformation.ie/en/employment/equality_in_work/equality_in_ the_workplace.html> (Accessed: 2 November 2021).

Clegg, M. C., IBVM (2019) 'Policy and Partnership', *Studies, an Irish Quarterly*, Spring, Volume 108, No. 429.

Clow, B., Bernier, J., Haworth-Brockman, M. and Pederson, A. (2009) *Rising to the Challenge: Sex-and-Gender-Based Analysis for Health Planning, Policy and Research in Canada*. Nova Scotia: Atlantic Centre of Excellence for Women's Health.

Coen, S. (2018) 'Different Class: Families Opt for Steiner Path as an Alternative to Traditional Route Through Education', *Connacht Tribune*, 13 April. Available at: <https://archive-irishnewsarchive-com.proxy.bc.edu/Olive/APA/INA.Edu/ SharedView.Article.aspx?href=CTT%2F2018%2F04%2F13&id=Ar03400&sk= E2B53390>.

Coleman, J. S. (1994) *Foundations of Social Theory*. United Kingdom: Belknap Press of Harvard University Press.

Collins, S. (2013) 'Poll Suggests Strong Support for Proposed Legislation.' *The Irish Times,* 14 June. Available at: <https://www.irishtimes.com/news/poll-suggests-strong-support-for-proposed-legislation-1.1426365> (Accessed: 2 November 2021).

Collins, S. (2013a) 'Big Rise in Support for Legislation on Abortion', *The Irish Times,* 8 June.

Collins, S. (2013b) 'Over 70% Support X-Case Legislation On Abortion', *The Irish Times,* 8 June.

Collins, S. (2013c) 'Poll Shows Strong Support For Abortion In Cases Of Rape, Fatal Foetal Abnormality', *The Journal.ie.* 20 January.

Collins, S. (2016) ' "Irish Times" poll: Majority want repeal of Eighth Amendment', *The Irish Times,* 7 October.

Conboy, S. (2019). Primary Support Officer, Community National Schools, Personal Interview, October.

Connell, P. (2019) Executive Secretary for Education to the Irish Bishops' Conference, Personal Interview, October.

Conway, E. (2013) 'Protecting Denominational Education', Paper to the Iona Institute, 21 January.

Coolahan, J. (2003) *Attracting, Developing and Retaining Effective Teachers: Country Background report for Ireland,* Project Report, OECD Publishing.

Coolahan. J. (2014) 'Comment: We need to Pick up the Pace to Revitalise Our School System', *Irish Independent,* 2 July.

Crisis Pregnancy Agency (2006) *Irish Study of Sexual Health and Relationships.* Available at: <https://www.ucd.ie/issda/data/irishstudyofsexualhealthandrelationshipsisshr/> (Accessed: 2 November 2021).

Crowley and Others vs Ireland and Others (1980) Decision of the Supreme Court, Ireland.

Cruickhank, J. (2015) 'State and Church and School Patronage', Letter to the Editor, *The Irish Times,* 26 August.

Cullen, P. (2010) 'Complaints Upheld as Authority Rules "Prime Time" Report Lacked Balance', *The Irish Times*, 30 June.

Daly, E. and Hickey, T. (2011) 'Religious Freedom and the "Right to Discriminate" in the School Admissions Context: A Neo-republican Critique', *Legal Studies*, Vol. 31, No. 4, December.

Daly, G. (2018) 'Secular Education Campaign Shut Down after Ethics Probe', *The Irish Catholic*, 31 January, Available at: <https://www.irishcatholic.com/secular-education-campaign-shut-ethics-probe/>.

Darmody, M. and Smyth, E. (2017) 'Education about Religions and Beliefs (ERB) and Ethics: Views of Teachers, Parents and the General Public Regarding the Proposed Curriculum for Primary Schools', Consultation Paper, ESRI funded by NCCA, January. Available at: <https://www.esri.ie/system/files/media/file-uploads/2017-01/BKMNEXT324.pdf>.

Darmody, M. and Smyth, E. (2018) 'Religion and Primary School Choice in Ireland: School Institutional Identities and Student Profile', *Irish Educational Studies,* Vol. 37, No. 1, 1–17. DOI: 10.1080/03323315.2017.1421091.

Darmody, M. Smyth, E. and McCoy, S. (2012) *School Sector Variation Among Primary Schools in Ireland.* Dublin: Economic and Social Research Institute.

Department of Education (1995) *Charting Our Education Future.* Available at: <https://assets.gov.ie/24448/0f3bff53633440d99c32541f7f45cfeb.pdf>.

Department of Education (2007) '*Minister Hanafin Announces Intention to Pilot New Additional Model of Primary School Patronage*', Press Release, 17 February.

Department of Education (2012) 'Forum on Patronage and Pluralism in the Primary Sector Progress to Date and Future Directions', 12 July. Available at: <https://www.gov.ie/en/publication/99634e-the-forum-on-patronage-and-pluralism-in-the-primary-sector-report-of/>.

Department of Education (2013) *Report on the Surveys Regarding Parental Preferences on Primary School Patronage*. Available at: <https://www.gov.ie/en/publication/5d7e50-report-on-the-surveys-regarding-parental-preferences-on-primary-scho/>.

Department of Education (2014a) 'The Forum on Patronage and Pluralism in the Primary Sector', July. Available at: <https://www.education.ie/>.

Department of Education (2014b) *Forum on the Patronage and Pluralism in the Primary Sector: Progress to Date and Future Directions*, July. Available at: <https://www.gov.ie/en/publication/99634e-the-forum-on-patronage-and-pluralism-in-the-primary-sector-report-of/>.

Department of Education (2014c) *Primary Patronage New Schools 2014, Code of Conduct*. Available at: <https://assets.gov.ie/100059/f22a3138-9966-493f-b78d-f0c9e5dcc01f.pdf>.

Department of Education (2016) 'Action Plan for Education, 2016–2019', 29 September. Available at: <https://www.gov.ie/en/collection/action-plan-for-education-2016-2019/> (Accessed: 2 November 2021).

Department of Education (2017a) 'Minister Bruton sets out plans to reform the school admissions system in relation to religion', Press Release, 16 January.

Department of Education (2017b) 'Two Mile National School to Open under New Patronage as Community National School in September', 12 June.

Department of Education (2018), 'Minister Bruton commences plan to increase provision of multi- and non-denominational schools', Press Release, 28 May. Available at: <https://www.education.ie/en/Press-Events/Press-Releases/2018-press-releases/PR18-05-28.html> (Accessed: 2 November 2021).

Department of Education (2019) *Governance Manual for Primary Schools 2019–2023*. Available at: <https://www.gov.ie/en/press-release/df2a88-minister-mchugh-publishes-new-governance-manual-for-primary-schools-/?referrer=http://www.education.ie/en/Schools-Colleges/Information/Boards-of-Management/governance-manual-for-primary-schools-2019-2023.pdf>.

Department of Education (2020a) *Circular Letter 0038/2020*, 20 June.

Department of Education (2020b) *Projections of full-time enrolment, Primary and Secondary 2020–2038*, November. Available at: <www.education.ie>.

Department of Education (2021a) 'Bodies under the Aegis of the Department of Education and Skills'. Available at: <https://www.gov.ie/en/organisation-information/341d4e-bodies-under-the-aegis-of-the-department-of-education-and-skills/> (Accessed: 2 November 2021).

Department of Education (2021b) 'Patronage Assessment Report Primary Schools (2021)', February. Available at: <https://www.gov.ie/en/policy-information/866bf0-establishment-of-a-new-school/#patronage-of-new-primary-schools> (Accessed: 2 November 2021).

Department of the Taoiseach (2020) *Programme for Government: Our Shared Future*, 29 October. Available at: <https://www.gov.ie/en/publication/7e05d-programme-for-government-our-shared-future/> (Accessed: 2 November 2021).

Devine, D. (2013) 'Valuing Children Differently? Migrant Children in Education', *Children & Society*, July, Vol. 27(4), 282(13).

Diocese of Kerry (2017) 'Community National School in Killarney', June. Available at: <https://www.dioceseofkerry.ie/2017/06/community-national-school-in-killarney/> (Accessed: 2 November 2021).

Donnelly, K. (2016a) 'Church's Backlash Blocks Change in Religion Classes', *Irish Independent,* 28 November. Available at: <https://www.independent.ie/irish-news/education/churchs-backlash-blocks-change-in-religion-classes-35249798.html> (Accessed: 2 November 2021).

Donnelly, K. (2016b) 'Minister Scraps 51-Year-Old Religion Rule for Primary Schools', *Irish Independent*, 19 January.

Donnelly, K. (2019a) 'Catholic Primary School Handover Put on Ice after Row over Wildly Inaccurate Claims', *Irish Independent*, 5 April.

Donnelly, K. (2019b) 'Schools Should Not Be "Setting a Bad Example"', *Irish Independent,* 4 April.

Drumm, M. (2011) 'In My Opinion: Variety of Patronage Is Called for to Meet the Demands of Parents', *Irish Independent*, 12 October.

Dublin City University (2019) 'DCU's EQI Commissioned to Develop New Framework for Educate Together schools', 15 November. Available at: <https://www.dcu.ie/news/news/2019/Nov/DCU-EQI-commissioned-develop-new-framework-for-Educate-Together-schools.shtml> (Accessed: 2 November 2021).

Dublin City University (2021) 'Professional Diploma in Education'. Available at: <https://www.dcu.ie/courses/Postgraduate/institute_of_education/Professional-Diploma-Education-Ethical-Multidenominational> (Accessed: 2 November 2021).

Duff, A. (2017) 'Non-Catholics Need Not Apply: The Legal Status of Discrimination in Irish School Admissions Policies', *King's Inns Law Review*, Vol. 7.

Duffy, E. (2020) 'Contextualising Catholic Education in Ireland', *Educatio Catholica*, Vol. 1–2, February.

Economic and Social Research Institute (2012) *New Report on Diversity in Primary Schools in Ireland*, 23 October. Available at: <https://www.esri.ie/news/new-report-on-diversity-in-primary-schools-in-ireland> (Accessed: 2 November 2021).

Educate Together (2011a) 'Irish Human Rights and Education', 21 March. Available at: <https://www.educatetogether.ie/app/uploads/2019/01/Irish-Human-Rights-and-Education.pdf> (Accessed: 2 November 2021).

Educate Together (2011b) 'Submission to the Forum on Patronage and Pluralism', June. Available at: <https://www.educatetogether.ie/sites/default/files/patronage_forum_submission.pdf> (Accessed: 2 November 2021).

Educate Together (2011c) *Learn Together, an Ethical Education Curriculum for Educate Together Schools*. Available at: <https://www.educatetogether.ie/app/uploads/2019/02/Learn-Together.pdf>.

Educate Together (2015a) 'Patronage Manual, Primary', October. Available at: <https://www.educatetogether.ie/app/uploads/2019/01/Educate-Together-Patronage-Manual.pdf> (Accessed: 2 November 2021).

Educate Together (2015b), '"Lively Engagement" at Educate Together AGM 2015', 29 May. Available at: <https://www.educatetogether.ie/news/lively-engagement-at-educate-together-agm-2015/> (Accessed: 2 November 2021).

Educate Together (2016) 'Educate Together Raises Major Concerns with Government's Education (Admissions to School) Bill at Oireachtas Hearing', 15 December. Available at: <https://www.educatetogether.ie/news/educate-together-raises-major-concerns-with-governments-education-admissions-to-school-bill-at-oireachtas-hearing/> (Accessed: 2 November 2021).

Educate Together (2017) 'Educate Together on the Two Mile National School announcement: parents in Killarney have been let down', 12 June. Available at: <https://www.educatetogether.ie/news/educate-together-on-the-two-mile-national-school-announcement-parents-in-killarney-have-been-let-down/> (Accessed: 2 November 2021).

Educate Together (2019a) 'Another Day, Another Clarification Statement from Educate Together', April 3. Available at: <https://www.educatetogether.ie/news/another-day-another-clarification/> (Accessed: 2 November 2021).

Educate Together (2019b) 'Clarification on Educate Together's Equality-Based Ethos', 2 April. Available at: <https://www.educatetogether.ie/news/ethos-clarification/> (Accessed: 2 November 2021).

Educate Together (2019c) 'Educate Together Looks Forward to Delivering a National Network of Equality-Based Schools in Line with Proven Parental Demand', 2 July. Available at: <https://www.educatetogether.ie/news/reconfiguration-surveys-2019/> (Accessed: 2 November 2021).

Educate Together (2019d) 'Election Manifesto'. Available at: <https://www.educatetogether.ie/app/uploads/2019/01/General-Election-2016-Educate-> (Accessed: 2 November 2021).

Educate Together (2019e) *Find a Campaign Group,* Educate Together. Available at: <https://www.educatetogether.ie/schools/campaign-groups/> (Accessed: 2 November 2021).

Educate Together (2021a) 'Ethical Education at Primary Level'. Available at: <https://www.educatetogether.ie/about/ethical-education/primary/> (Accessed: 2 November 2021).

Educate Together (2021b) 'Ethical Education'. Available at: <https://www.educatetogether.ie/about/ethical-education/> (Accessed: 2 November 2021).

Educate Together (2021c) 'History'. Available at: <https://www.educatetogether.ie/about/history/> (Accessed: 2 November 2021).

Educate Together (2021d) 'Information for parents'. Available at: <https://www.educatetogether.ie/schools/parents/> (Accessed: 2 November 2021).

Educate Together (2021e) 'State Funding'. Available at: <https://www.educatetogether.ie/campaigns/state-funding/> (Accessed: 2 November 2021).

Educate Together (2021f) *Mission and Values.* Available at: <https://www.educatetogether.ie/about/values/> (Accessed: 2 November 2021).

Education Act, 1998.

Education and Training Boards Ireland (2021) 'ETBI Leadership Team'. Available at: <https://www.etbi.ie/about-etbi/etbi-team/> (Accessed: 2 November 2021).

Education Equality (2016) 'Equality in Education: Your Questions Answered', January. Available at: <https://educationequalitydotblog.wordpress.com/education-equality-your-questions-answered/ (Accessed: 2 November 2021).

Elkink, J. A., Farrell, D. M., Reidy, T. and Suiter, J. (2017) 'Understanding the 2015 Marriage Referendum in Ireland: Context, Campaign, and Conservative Ireland', *Irish Political Studies*, Vol. 32, No. 3.

Equate (2017) 'Religion and School: Parents' Voices', Available at: <https://media.wix.com/ugd/08f4c2_0655f34b38b049748cce39a75acc2bb7.pdf> (Accessed: 2 November 2021).

Faas, D. and Fionda, R. (2019) 'Ireland: A Shift Towards Religious Equality in Schools', in Stevens, P. A. J. and A. G. Dworkin (eds), *The Palgrave Handbook of Race and Ethnic Inequalities in Education*, Cham, Switzerland: Palgrave Macmillan, 605–31.

Faas, D., Darmody, M. and Sokolowska, B. (2016) 'Religious Diversity in Primary Schools: Reflections from the Republic of Ireland', *British Journal of Religious Education*, Vol. 38, No. 1.

Faas, D., Smith, A. and Darmody, M. (2018) 'Children's Agency in Multi-Belief Settings: The Case of Community National Schools in Ireland', *Journal of Research in Childhood Education*. doi: <https://doi.org/10.1080/02568543.2018.1494645>.

Faas, D., Smith, A. and Darmody, M. (2019) 'Between Ethos and Practice: Are Ireland's New Multi-denominational Primary Schools Equal and Inclusive', *Compare*, Vol. 49, No. 4.

Farrell, D. M. and Suiter, J. (2019) *Reimagining Democracy: Lessons in Deliberative Democracy from the Irish Front Lines*, Ithaca and London: Cornell Selects.

Field, L. (2018) 'The Abortion Referendum of 2018 and a Timeline of Abortion Politics in Ireland to Date', *Irish Political Studies*, Vol. 33, No. 4.

Finn, C. (2017) 'Archbishop Says Church Stubbornly Reluctant to Let Go of the Control of Schools', *TheJournal.ie*, 10 July. Available at: <https://www.thejournal.ie/archbishop-of-dublin-diarmuid-martin-3487927-Jul2017/>.

Fischer, K. (2016) *Schools and the Politics of Religion and Diversity in the Republic of Ireland – Separate but Equal?* Manchester: Manchester University Press.

Flynn, S. (2012) 'School Patronage Survey Queried', *The Irish Times*, 14 December.

Freytas-Tamura, D. (2018) 'Ireland Votes to End Abortion Ban, in Rebuke to Catholic Conservatism', *The New York Times,* May 26.

Galway & Roscommon Education & Training Board (2019) 'Galway Steiner National School to Become a Community National School under the Patronage of GRETB', 26 July.

Galway & Roscommon Education & Training Board (2019) 'Lecarrow Community National School to Open under the Patronage of GRETB', 26 July.

Gataveckaite, G. (2019) ' "It's Good for Them to Be Taught Inclusion" – Schools Drop Religious Ethos in Bid to Ensure Survival', *Irish Independent*, 27 August.

Genesis, *Articulating a new positioning for Catholic education in Ireland*, September 2021 [Provided to the authors for the purpose of this study].

Gerschenkron, A. (1962) *Economic Backwardness in Historical Perspective.* Cambridge: Harvard University Press.

Girvin, B. (1994) 'Moral Politics and the Irish Abortion Referendums', *Parliamentary Affairs*, Vol. 47, No. 2, 203–21.

Glendenning, D. (2010) *Education and the Law,* 2nd edn, London: Bloomsbury Professional.

Gov.UK (2021) *Set Up A New School.* Available at: <https://www.gov.uk/government/get-involved/take-part/set-up-a-new-school> (Accessed: 2 November 2021).

Government of Ireland (1999) *Primary School Curriculum.* Dublin: Stationary Office. Available at: <https://www.curriculumonline.ie/>.

Government of the Republic of Ireland (1937) *Bunreacht na hÉireann.* Dublin: Government Publications. Available at: <https://www.irishstatutebook.ie/eli/cons/en>.

Graham, D. (2018) 'Opinion: Religious Instruction and Worship Should Take Place Outside of Core School Hours', journal.ie, 5 April. Available at: <https://www.thejournal.ie/readme/opinion-religious-instruction-and-worship-should-take-place-outside-core-school-hours-3937081-Apr2018/> (Accessed: 2 November 2021).

Graham, D. (2020) 'Opinion: Religion Is a Choice – Not an Obligation. Let's Make Religious Classes an Opt-In', journal.ie, 5 February. Available at: <https://www.thejournal.ie/readme/religious-education-ireland-4973515-Feb2020/> (Accessed: 2 November 2021).

Grayson, H., O'Donnell, S. and Sargent, C. (2014) *Key Findings Summary: Education about Religions and Beliefs and Ethics in Primary Education*, National Foundation for Educational Research, December. Available at: <https://ncca.ie/media/1904/key_findings_erbe_summary.pdf> (Accessed: 2 November 2021).

Griffin, M. (2019) 'Catholic Schools in Ireland Today – A Changing Sector in a Time of Change', *Studies An Irish Quarterly Review*, Spring, Vol. 108, No. 429.

Griffin, M. (2020) Former Acting-CEO of County Dublin VEC, Personal Interview, September.

Harkin, S. and Hazelkorn, E. (2015) 'Restructuring Irish Higher Education Through Collaboration and Merger', in Curaj, A. et al. (eds), *Mergers and Alliances in Higher Education: International Practice and Emerging Opportunities*, New York: Springer Publishing.

Hawkes, M. (2020) 'Citizens' Assembly for Education Could Be a Game-Changer', Education Matters, 23 June. Available at: <https://educationmatters.ie/citizens-assembly-on-education/> (Accessed: 2 November 2021).

Hayes, C. (2016) 'Outing the Party: Irish Political Party Engagement in the 2015 Same Sex Marriage Referendum', Senior Thesis, Department of Political Science, University of Notre Dame, 1 April.

Hayes, G. (2019) Kerry Diocesan Secretary for Education, Personal Interview, October.

Healy, G., Sheehan, B. and Whelan, N. (2016) *Ireland Says Yes: The Inside Story of How the Vote for Marriage Equality was Won*. Kildare: Merrion Press.

Hesketh, T. (1990), *The Second Partitioning of Ireland?: The Abortion Referendum of 1983*. Laoghaire: Brandsma Books.

Holland, K. (2017) 'Removing the Baptism Barrier Is Largely Meaningless', *The Irish Times*, 20 January.

Horgan, J. (2001) *Irish Media: A Critical History Since 1922*. London: Routledge.

Horgan-Jones, J. (2019) 'Parents not Schools to Lead Communion Preparations, Says Archbishop of Dublin', *The Irish Times*, 3 December.

Houses of the Oireachtas (2010) 'Diversification of Primary School Provision: Statements', 20 May. Available at: <https://www.oireachtas.ie/en/debates/debate/dail/2010-05-20/9/> (Accessed: 2 November 2021).

Houses of the Oireachtas (2019) 'School Patronage', 30 January. Available at: <https://www.oireachtas.ie/en/debates/question/2019-01-30/114/> (Accessed: 2 November 2021).

Houston, I. (2017) 'Mapping Dublin Parish Boundaries', 3 April. Available at: <https://www.ianhuston.net/2017/04/mapping-dublin-parish-boundaries/> (Accessed: 2 November 2021).

Hughes, K. (2010) 'Killarney School to Sever Ties with Catholic Church', *The Kerryman,* 11 August.

Humphreys, J. (2014) 'Quinn Advises Teachers to Study RE to Boost Their Job Prospects', 21 June. Available at: <https://www.irishtimes.com/news/education/quinn-advises-teachers-to-study-re-to-boost-their-job-prospects-1.1840363> (Accessed: 2 November 2021).

Humphreys, J. (2015) 'Segregation Concerns Over Transfer of School Patronage', *Irish Times,* 1 January.

Humphreys, J. (2017) 'Christian Brothers Withdrawal Is not First Clash over Divestment', *The Irish Times*, March 10.

Hyland, Á. and Bocking, B. (2015) Religion, Education, and Religious Education in Irish Schools. *Teaching Theology and Religion*, Vol. 18, No. 3, 252–61, Available at doi.org: <https://doi.org/10.1111/teth.12292> (Accessed: 2 November 2021).

Hyland, Á. and Green, D. (2020) *A Brave New Vision for Education in Ireland: The Dalkey School Project 1974–1984*. Áine Hyland self-published, Dalkey.

Inglis, T. (1998) *Moral Monopoly: The Rise and Fall of the Catholic Church in Modern Irish Society*, 2nd edn, Dublin: UCD Press.

IPPN (2012) 'RedC Poll April 2012 – Patronage', April. Available at: <https://www.ippn.ie/index.php/component/mtree/the-news/press-releases/3899-redc-poll-april-2012-patronage> (Accessed: 2 November 2021).

IPPN (2016) 'President and Minister for Education Agree That the Time Is Right to Start a "Conversation" on the Time Given to Religion in Our Primary Schools, Irish Primary Principals Network', 15 February. Available at: <https://www.ippn.ie/index.php/advocacy/press-releases/6957-ippn-president-and-minister-for-education-agree-that-the-time-is-right-to-start-a-conversation-on-the-time-given-to-religion-in-our-primary-schools> (Accessed: 2 November 2021).

Irish Bishops' Conference (1978) 'Statement from the Irish Bishop's Conference on Proposed Legislation Dealing with Family Planning and Contraception'. Available at: <https://www.jstor.org/stable/27660602>.

Irish Catholic Bishops' Conference (2017) 'Delegation of Bishops Meet the Taoiseach and Government ministers', 31 August. Available at: <https://www.catholicbishops.ie/2017/08/31/delegation-of-bishops-meet-the-taoiseach-and-government-ministers/> (Accessed: 2 November 2021).

Irish Catholic Bishops' Conference (2021a) 'About Us'. Available at: <https://www.catholicbishops.ie/about/> (Accessed: 2 November 2021).

Irish Catholic Bishops' Conference (2021b) 'Education'. Available at: <https://www.catholicbishops.ie/education/> (Accessed: 2 November 2021).

Irish Catholics Bishops' Conference (2011) *Report on Catholic Primary Schools in the Republic of Ireland*, Catholic Schools Partnership. Available at: <https://www.catholicbishops.ie/2011/04/06/6-april-2011-catholic-schools-republic-ireland/> (Accessed: 2 November 2021).

Irish Episcopal Conference (2015) 'Catholic Preschool and Primary Religious Education Curriculum for Ireland', Dublin: Veritas.

Irish Human Rights and Equality Commission (2021) 'Equality Status Acts'. Available at: <https://www.ihrec.ie/guides-and-tools/human-rights-and-equality-in-the-provision-of-good-and-services/what-does-the-law-say/equal-status-acts/> (Accessed: 2 November 2021).

Irish National Schools Trust (1831) 'The Stanley Letter 1831'. Available at: <http://irishnationalschoolstrust.org/wp-content/uploads/2015/04/Stanley-letter-1831-Boards-Of-Management.pdf> (Accessed: 2 November 2021).

Irish National Teachers' Organisation (1965) 'Rule for National Schools'. Available at: <https://www.into.ie/media-centre/circulars/rules-for-national-schools-1965/> (Accessed: 2 November 2021).

Irish National Teachers' Organisation (2019) 'Primary Schools Remain Overcrowded and Underfunded', 10 September. Available at: <https://www.into.ie/2019/09/10/primary-schools-remain-overcrowded-and-underfunded/> (Accessed: 2 November 2021).

Irish Primary Principals Network (2010) *Primary School Governance, Challenges and Opportunities.* Available at: <https://issuu.com/ippn/docs/primary_school_governance-challenge>.

Irish Primary Principals Network (2017) *Irish Schools Face Shortage of Principals as Role's Managerial and Administrative Duties Deter Teachers from Stepping up to Leadership Role*, 8 March.

Irwin, J. (2018) 'Towards a Values-Led Redevelopment of the Primary Curriculum', Paper presented at the Institute of Education, Dublin City University, 3 December. Available at: <https://ncca.ie/media/4427/towards-a-values-led-redevelopment-of-the-primary-curriculum.pdf> (Accessed: 2 November 2021).

Jayaram K. and Moffat A. (2012) *Breaking the Habit of Ineffective Professional Development for Teachers*, McKinsey & Company, 1 January. Available at: <https://www.mckinsey.com/industries/public-and-social-sector/our-insights/breaking-the-habit-of-ineffective-professional-development-for-teachers> (Accessed: 2 November 2021).

John Paul II (1998) *Apostolos Suos.* Available at: <https://www.vatican.va/content/john-paul-ii/en/motu_proprio/documents/hf_jp-ii_motu-proprio_22071998_apostolos-suos.html>.

Joint Managerial Body (2021) 'About Us'. Available at: <https://www.jmb.ie/Who-we-are/About-Us> (Accessed: 2 November 2021).

Kelleghan, T., McGee, P., Millar, D. and Perkins, R. (2004) *Views of the Irish Public on Education: A Survey*. Dublin: Educational Research Centre.

Kelly, B. (2019) 'Galway Steiner NS Becomes GRETB Community School'. *Galway Daily*, 14 August. Available at: <https://www.galwaydaily.com/news/galway-steiner-school-becomes-gretb-community-school/> (Accessed: 1 November 2021).

Kennedy, F. (2002), 'Abortion Referendum 2002', *Irish Political Studies*, Vol. 17, No. 1, 114–28.

Kenneth Carty, R. K. (2022) 'Into the Void: The Collapse of Irish Party Democracy', *Irish Political Studies*, Forthcoming.

Kildare Local Community Development Committee (2016) *Kildare Local Economic and Community Plan 2016–2021*. Available at: <http://www.kildarelcdc.ie/wp-content/uploads/2016/01/Kildare-LECP-2016-2021.pdf> (Accessed: 2 November 2021).

Kingdon, J. W. (1984) *Agendas, Alternatives, and Public Policies*. Boston: Little, Brown.

Kissane, B. (2003) 'The Illusion of State Neutrality in a Secularising Ireland', *West European Politics*, Vol. 26, No. 1, 73–94.

Kowalski, M., Tiernan, J. and McGraw, S. (2020) 'Catholic Education in Ireland and the United States: Teachers' Comparative Perspectives', *Research in Comparative & International Education*, Vol. 15, No. 2, 171–85.

Lalor, J. P. (2013) *Educate Together: An Inclusive Response To The Needs Of A Pluralist Ireland?*, PhD thesis, Dublin City University, Dublin, January.

Larkin, E. (1984) *The Historical Dimensions of Irish Catholicism*, Washington, DC: Catholic University of America Press, and Dublin: Four Courts Press.

Lavin, L. (2020) Principal, St. Helen's Junior National School, Personal Interview, July.

Lavrakas, P. J. (2008) *Encyclopedia of Survey Research Methods* (Vols. 1–0). Thousand Oaks, CA: Sage Publications, Inc. Available at: doi.org: doi: <http://dx.doi.org/10.4135/9781412963947.n3>.

Lee, V. E., Bryk, A. S. and Holland, P. B. (2009) *Catholic Schools and the Common Good*. United Kingdom: Harvard University Press

Liffey, K. (2019) Former Director of Catechetics for the Irish Catholic Bishop's Conference, Personal Interview, October.

Limerick and Clare Education and Training Board (2019) 'Two County Clare Steiner National Schools to Become Community National Schools Under Patronage of the Authority', 26 July. Available at: <https://lcetb.ie/two-county-clare-steiner-national-schools-to-become-community-national-schools-under-patronage-of-the-authority/> (Accessed: 2 November 2021).

Looney, A. (2019) Executive Dean of the Institute of Education at DCU, Personal Interview, October.

Loughlin, E. (2018a) 'Church Hands over Just 11 Schools Despite Diversity Drive', *Irish Examiner*, 15 May.

Loughlin, E. (2018b) 'Labour Calls for Removal of Link between Church and State in Education', *Irish Examiner*, 29 May.

Lyons, P. (2008) *Public Opinion, Politics and Society in Contemporary Ireland.* Dublin, Ireland and Portland, OR: Irish Academic Press.

MacDonald, S. (2015) 'Archbishop Defends Right of Schools to Put Catholics First in Queue', *Irish Independent,* 5 August.

MacDonald, S. (2019) 'Archbishop Warns against "New Polarisation" between Schools with Different Ethos', *Irish Independent*, Independent.ie, 15 April.

MacNamee, G. (2018) ' "An Attack on Rural Ireland": Over 160 Post Offices to Close Nationwide', *theJournal.ie,* 2 August.

Madaus, G. F., Fontes, P. J., Kellaghan, T. and Airasian, P. W. (1979) 'Opinions of the Irish Public on Goals and Adequacy of Education', *Irish Journal of Education,* 13, 87–125.

Mahon, E. (2017) 'Investigating the Perceptions of Primary School Communities in the Republic of Ireland Regarding Their Catholic Identity', Dublin City University, January.

Mahon, M. (2019) Coordinator for Primary Education in Kildare and Leighlin Diocese, Personal Interview, October.

Mainwaring, B. and McGraw, S. (2019) 'How Catchall Parties Compete Ideologically: Beyond Party Typologies', *European Journal of Political Research*, Vol. 58, No. 2, 2 May, 676–96.

Maloney, C. (2016) 'Community National Schools and Faith', *The Irish Times,* 10 June.

Manning, H. (2018) ' "IRELAND IS DIFFERENT" Labour senator Aodhan O'Riordain Launches Petition to Remove Role of Religions in Irish Schools and Says Referendum Should Be Held', *The Irish Sun,* 9 July.

Martin, E. (2015) 'A Message on the Marriage Referendum', 1 May. Available at: <https://www.catholicbishops.ie/wp-content/uploads/2015/05/2015-May-02-Care-for-the-Covenant-of-Marriage.pdf> (Accessed: 2 November 2021).

Mawhinney, A. (2012) 'A Discriminating Education System: Religious Admission Policies in Irish Schools and International Human Rights Law', *International Journal of Children's Rights*, Vol. 20, No. 4.

McCárthaigh, S. (2019) 'One in Five Primary School Students in Classes of at least 30', *The Irish Times,* 2 August.

McCarthy, B. (2015) 'Despite a Lack of Faith, I Can Still Find a Place For Religion in My Life', *Irish Independent*, July 27.

McCormack, C. (2020) *Using Visible or Invisible Maps? A Case Study of the Role of the Diocesan Advisor in Voluntary Catholic Secondary Schools in the Republic of Ireland*, EdD thesis, Dublin City University.

McCoy, T. (2019) 'Three Irish Primary Schools to Convert from Catholic to Nondenominational', *IrishCentral.com*, 27 August. Available at: <https://www.irishcentral.com/news/ireland-primary-schools-non-denominational> (Accessed: 2 November 2021).

McDonagh, F. (2019) 'What Constitutes a Catholic School in 2019? A Legal Perspective', *Studies An Irish Quarterly Review*, Spring, Vol. 108, No. 429.

McGarry, P. (2017) 'Archbishop Martin Proved Right about School Patronage', *The Irish Times*, 12 July.

McGarry, P. (2018) 'The Faith of Ireland's Catholics Continues, Despite all', *The Irish Times*, 11 August.

McGarry, P. (2019) 'Minister Accused of "spin" over School Places for Autistic Children', *The Irish Times,* August 26.

McGraw, S. (2015) *How Parties Win: Shaping the Irish Political Arena*. Ann Arbor: University of Michigan Press.

McGraw, S. (2018) 'Data and Replication Files for "How Catchall Parties Compete Ideologically: Beyond Party Typologies" ', *European Journal of Political Research*. Available at: <https://github.com/mainwaringb/Ireland_EJPR_2018> (Accessed: 2 November 2021).

McGuire, P. (2018) 'We'd Be Hypocritical Standing in a Church Promising to Raise Our Kids as Catholics', *The Irish Times*, 7 April.

McHugh, J. (2019) 'A Short Message for Parents, Grandparents and School Communities Where a Possible Change of Patron Is Being Assessed', Facebook, 3 April.

McMahon, Á. (2016) 'Parents Call for End to Religious Discrimination in Schools', *The Irish Times*, 3 July.

MeaningCloud (2016) 'MeaningCloud Provides Entirely Customisable Sentiment Analysis to Get Maximum Accuracy', 19 April. Available at: <https://meaningcloud.pr.co/126379-meaningcloud-provides-entirely-customizable-sentiment-analysis-to-get-maximum-accuracy> (Accessed: 2 November 2021).

Meehan, A. and O'Connell, D. (2012) "The 'Deeper Magic of Life' – a Catholic response to the Forum on Patronage and Pluralism", *The Furrow*, June, Vol. 63, No. 6, 278–85.

Miller, G. (2003) "Financial Reporting in the Catholic Church", Harvard Business School, N9-104-057, 6 November, 1–4.

Monahan, P. (2015a) 'Do We Want to Discriminate against Children Based on Their Religious Status?', *Irish Times*, 21 August.

Monahan, P. (2015b) 'Equal Access to Education', *The Irish Times*, 19 October.

Monahan, P. (2015c) 'Patronage System and Education', *Irish Times,* 11 November.

Monahan, P. (2015d) 'Segregation of Four-Year-Olds in Schools Has to Stop', *The Irish Times*, 15 December.

Monahan, P. (2016a) 'Community National Schools Are a Bad Idea', *The Irish Times*, 9 June.

Monahan, P. (2016b) 'Where Do Parties Stand on Equal Access to Primary Education', *The Irish Times*, 18 February.

Monahan, P. (2019a) 'It's Self-serving for Church to Move Sacraments Out of School Hours', *Irish Times,* 11 December.

Monahan, P. (2019b) Policy Officer for Education Equality, Personal Interview, October.

Mulconry, S. (2017) 'CPSMA Responds to Minister Bruton's School Admission Policy Proposal', 16 January. Available at: <https://www.catholicbishops.ie/2017/01/16/cpsma-responds-to-minister-brutons-school-admission-policy-proposal/> (Accessed: 2 November 2021).

Mulconry, S. (2018) 'Lack of School Places the Problem, not Baptism barrier', *The Irish Times*, 14 May. Available at: <https://www.irishtimes.com/opinion/lack-of-school-places-the-problem-not-baptism-barrier-1.3493705> (Accessed: 2 November 2021).

Mulconry, S. (2019) General Secretary of the Catholic Primary Schools Management Association, Personal Interview, October.

Mullally, A. (2018) 'We are Inclusive but are we being Equal?' Challenges to Community National Schools Regarding Religious Diversity', PhD, Dublin City University.

Murray Tweet Index (2021). Available at: <https://www.murraytweetindex.ie/> (Accessed: 2 November 2021).

Murray, N. (2017) 'Schools Say Baptism Barrier Is Rare', *Irish Examiner,* January 23.

National Council for Curriculum and Assessment (2015a) 'An Overview of Education about Religions and Beliefs (ERB) and Ethics content in Patrons' Programmes'. Available at: <https://ncca.ie/media/4602/overview_of_patrons_programmes.pdf>.

National Council for Curriculum and Assessment (2015b) 'Education about Religions and Beliefs (ERB) and Ethics in the Primary School: Consultation Paper', November. Available at: <https://ncca.ie/media/1897/consultation_erbe.pdf> (Accessed: 2 November 2021).

National Council for Curriculum and Assessment (2015c) 'Education about Religions and Beliefs (ERB) and Ethics in the Primary School: Consultation

Paper', November. Available at: <https://ncca.ie/media/1897/consultation_erbe.pdf> (Accessed: 2 November 2021).

National Council for Curriculum and Assessment (2018a) *'Goodness Me, Goodness You! Programme for Junior Infants to Second Class Review Report: The Experiences of Stakeholders'*, May, Dublin: NCCA, 8.

National Council for Curriculum and Assessment (2018b) *Goodness Me, Goodness You, Curriculum for Community National Schools*. Available at <http://cns.ie/wp-content/uploads/2018/11/GMGY-Curriculum.pdf>.

National Council for Curriculum and Assessment (2018c) *Primary Developments: Consultation on Curriculum Structure and Time*, Final Report, January.

National Council for Curriculum and Assessment (2020) 'Draft Primary Curriculum Framework: Primary Curriculum Review and Redevelopment'. Available at: <https://ncca.ie/media/4456/ncca-primary-curriculum-framework-2020.pdf> (Accessed: 2 November 2021).

Nulty, D. (2018) 'Homily of Bishop Denis at Mass with Teachers and ACE Ireland,' Kildare and Leighlin Diocese, 11 September. Available at: <https://www.kandle.ie/homily-of-bishop-denis-celebrates-mass-with-teachers-and-ace-ireland/> (Accessed: 2 November 2021).

Nulty, D. (2019) 'Bishop Denis Launches Catholic Schools Week', Kildare and Leighlin Diocese, 28 January. Available at: <https://www.kandle.ie/bishop-denis-launches-catholic-schools-week/> (Accessed: 2 November 2021).

O'Brien, B. (2019) 'Divestment of SCHOOLS requires More to Be Built,' *The Irish Times*, 6 April

O'Brien, C. (2015) 'Campaign Seeks Equality for Children in Education System', *The Irish Times*, 9 December.

O'Brien, C. (2016) 'Keep 10% of Catholic School Places for Unbaptised, Says Group', *Irish Times*, 24 July.

O'Brien, C. (2017) 'Rights of Children Opting out of Religion Class "Must Be Respected"', *The Irish Times*, 11 July.

O'Brien, C. (2018a) ' "Baptism Barrier" to Catholic schools to go next year', *The Irish Times*, 9 May.

O'Brien, C. (2018b) 'Catholic Groups Warn of Legal Action over "Baptismal Barrier" Removal', *The Irish Times*, 3 January.

O'Brien, C. (2018c) 'Citizens' Assembly Should Debate Church Control of Education', *The Irish Times*, 29 May.

O'Brien, C. (2019a) 'Dublin School Patronage Vote Suspended over "Misinformation"', *The Irish Times*, 5 April.

O'Brien; C. (2019b) 'McHugh to Review Process for Selecting Schools for Divestment', *The Irish Times*, 4 April.

O'Brien, C. (2019c) 'Parents Leaving It to Schools to Prepare Children for Sacraments', *The Irish Times*, 15 May.

O'Brien, C. (2019d) 'Pupils in Divested Schools "Will Not Be Prevented" from Celebrating Christmas', *The Irish Times,* 2 April.

O'Brien, C. (2019e) 'Removing School's Catholic Ethos Would Be "Brexit-type Disaster", Parents Told,' *The Irish Times*, 2 April.

O'Connell, D. (2018) 'Catholic Primary Schools – On Rapidly Thinning Ice', *The Furrow*, December, 660–70.

O'Connell, J. (2013) 'I Became One of Those Parents I Used to Read about and Snigger', 10 April. Available at: <https://www.irishtimes.com/life-and-style/people/i-became-one-of-those-parents-i-used-to-read-about-and-snigger-1.1354270> (Accessed: 2 November 2021).

O'Connor, D. (2010) Monsignor, Episcopal Vicar for Education, Archdiocese of Dublin, Personal Interview, July.

O'Diomasaigh, S. (2015) 'Patronage System and Education', Letter to the Editor, *The Irish Times*, 11 November.

O'Kelly, E. (2015) 'State Gives Commitment to Catholic Church on Education', RTE.ie, 10 November. Available at: <https://www.rte.ie/news/special-reports/2012/0328/315388-educationfoi/> (Accessed: 2 November 2021).

O'Kelly, E. (2017) 'Documents Reveal Catholic Influence in State Schools', RTE.ie, 15 October. Available at: <https://www.rte.ie/news/analysis-and-comment/2017/1013/912199-schools-religion/> (Accessed: 2 November 2021).

O'Kelly, E. (2018) 'Louth School to Reopen after Forced Closure Last Year', RTE.ie, 20 July. Available at: <https://www.rte.ie/news/2018/0720/980054-scoil-naisiunta-bhrighde-louth/> (Accessed: 2 November 2021).

O'Kelly, E. (2019a) 'Co Kerry School to Keep Its Two Teachers after Appeal' RTE.ie, 2 September. Available at: <https://www.rte.ie/news/munster/2019/0901/1073201-kerry-school/> (Accessed: 2 November 2021).

O'Kelly, E. (2019b) 'Three Primary Schools Transfer from Catholic Patronage', RTE.ie, 27 August. Available at: <https://www.rte.ie/news/2019/0827/1071103-patronage/> (Accessed: 2 November 2021).

O'Kelly, E. (2019c) 'Actions of Three Tiny Schools Will Interest Parents', RTE.ie, 27 August. Available at: <https://www.rte.ie/news/ireland/2019/0827/1071113-school-patronage-change/> (Accessed: 2 November 2021).

O'Kelly, E. (2019d) 'Row over School Patronage after Claims Religious Holidays Will Not Be Marked', RTE.ie, 2 April. Available at: <https://www.rte.ie/news/education/2019/0402/1040149-school-patronage/> (Accessed: 2 November 2021).

O'Kelly, E. (2019e) 'The Year Students Marched for Their Future – 2019', RTE.ie, 24 December. Available at: <https://www.rte.ie/news/2019-in-review/2019/1220/1102376-the-year-students-marched-for-their-future-2019/> (Accessed: 2 November 2021).

O'Kelly, E. (2019f) 'Third Dublin School Sends Letter Warning of Consequences over Changing Patronage', RTE.ie, 3 April. Available at: <https://www.rte.ie/news/2019/0403/1040323-school_patronage/> (Accessed: 2 November 2021).

O'Mahony, C. (2016) 'In My Opinion: New Minister Must Act Quickly on Denominational Schools Issue', *Irish Independent*, 11 May.

O'Mahony, E. (2008) *Factors Determining School Choice*, Commission for Education of the Irish Bishops' Conference, April. Available at: <https://www.catholicbishops.ie/2008/04/01/factors-determining-school-choice/> (Accessed: 2 November 2021).

O'Mahony, E. (2011) *Parental Understanding of Patronage*, Irish Episcopal Conference, October. Available at: <https://www.catholicschools.ie/download/parental-understandings-of-patronage/> (Accessed: 2 November 2021)

O'Mahony, J. (1998) 'The Irish Referendum Experience', *Representation*, Vol. 35, No. 4, 225–36.

O'Reilly, B. (2019) Patron's Secretary for Primary Schools, Kildare & Leighlin, Personal Interview, October.

O'Sullivan, D. (2005) *Cultural Politics and Irish Education Since the 1950s: Policy Paradigms and Power*, Dublin: Institute for Public Administration.

O'Sullivan, D. (2013) *Religion and Ethos in Primary Schools*, Irish National Teachers Organisation.

O'Toole, F. (2009) 'Lessons in the Power of the Church', *The Irish Times,* 6 June.

O'Brien, B. (2017) 'Move against Denominational Schools Not a Good Idea', *The Irish Times*, 21 January.

O'Brien, C. (2017a) 'Legal Questions over Plan to Remove School "Baptism Barrier"', *The Irish Times*, June 29.

O'Brien, C. (2017b) 'Department of Education Intervenes to Help Improve Standards at Louth School'. *The Irish Times*, August 30.

O'Brien, C. (2018) 'Group against Baptism Bar Derailed after Complaints', *The Irish Times,* 15 October.

O'Connor, M. (2007) 'Sé Sí, Gender in Irish Education,' Department of Education. Available at: <http://www.sdpi.ie/other_des_publications/des_stats_SeSiGender_in_Irish_Ed_contents_overview.pdf> (Accessed: 2 November 2021).

O'Doherty, T. (2020) 'Contextualising Catholic Education in Ireland', *Educatio Catholica,* Vol. 1–2, February.

Ombudsman for Children's Office (2017) 'Observations, Regarding the Department of Education and Skills' Consultation Paper on the Role of Denominational Religion in the School Admissions Process and Possible Approaches for Making Changes', March. Available at: <https://www.oco.ie/app/uploads/2018/04/OCO-observations-on-role-of-religion-in-school-admissions.pdf> (Accessed: 2 November 2021).

Philanthropy Ireland (2017) 'One10, 2003–2014 Impact Report: The One Foundation'. Available at: <http://www.philanthropy.ie/backup/wp-content/uploads/2017/07/One10-2004-2013-Impact-Report-The-One-Foundation.pdf> (Accessed: 2 November 2021).

Pidgeon, M. (2020) 'Manifestos by Party', *Irish Manifestos Archive*, Fianna Fáil (2020), Green Party Manifestos (2007, 2016, 2020), Labour Party Manifestos (2011, 2016, 2020), Sinn Féin Party Manifestos (2007, 2011, 2016, 2020), Social Democrats Party Manifestos (2016, 2020), Michael Pidgeon – Dublin City Councilor, 21 February. Available at: www.michaelpidgeon.com/manifestos/index.html> (Accessed: 2 November 2021).

PRWeb (2018) 'MeaningCloud Cited in Independent AI-Based Text Analytics Platforms Report', 10 May. Available at: <https://www.prweb.com/releases/2018/05/prweb15471871.htm> (Accessed: 2 November 2021).

Putnam, R. (2000) *Bowling Alone: The Collapse and Revival of American Community*, New York: Simon and Schuster.

Putnam, R. (2007) '*E Pluribus Unum*: Diversity and Community in the Twenty-first Century', *Scandinavian Political Studies*, Vol. 30, No. 2, 150–1.

Putnam, R. and Campbell, D. E. (2012) *American Grace: How Religion Divides and Unites Us*. United Kingdom: Simon & Schuster.

Quinn, D. (2011) 'Letters: You'll All Miss Value of Catholic Ethos if it Goes', *Irish Independent,* 18 March.

Quinn, R. (2010) 'Time to Transfer Control of Primary Education', *The Irish Times*, January 26.

Quinn, R. (2019) Former Minister for Education (2011–14), Personal Interview, October.

Regan, A. (2018) Twitter, 27 May. Available at: <https://twitter.com/Aidan_Regan> (Accessed: 2 November 2021).

Renehan, C. and Williams, K. (2015) 'Religion, Education and Conflict in the Republic of Ireland', McKinney, S. and Zannoni, Z. (eds), in *Journal of Theories and Research in Education* Vol. 10, No. 1, 67–87, Special Issue, *Religion, Conflict and Education.*

Riegel, R. (2019) 'Flanagan Rules out Widespread Re-opening of Rural Garda Stations Closed over Past Decade', *Irish Independent,* February 16.

Riordan, L. (2015) *CPSMA: Proposed Changes to Admissions in School.* Dublin: Mason, Hayes & Curran.

Rowe, P. (2019) Former CEO of Educate Together, Personal Interview, October.

Sadlier, R. (2015) 'School Patronage', Letter to the Editor, *The Irish Times,* January 16.

Science Buddies (2006) 'Sample Size: How Many Survey Participants Do I Need?'. Available at: <https://www.sciencebuddies.org/science-fair-projects/references/sample-size-surveys> (Accessed: 2 November 2021).

Serhan, Y. (2018) 'Ireland's Very Secular Vote on Abortion', *The Atlantic*, 25 May.

Sheils McNamee, M. (2016) 'Here is how Ireland's Bishops Responded to Being Asked to Hand over Their Schools', *TheJournal.ie,* 1 August. Available at: <https://www.thejournal.ie/catholic-schools-divestment-ireland-religion-2876185-Aug2016/> (Accessed: 2 November 2021).

Shortall, R. (2018), Twitter, 29 May. Available at: <https://twitter.com/SocDems> (Accessed: 2 November 2021).

Sinnott, R. (2002) 'Cleavages, Parties, and Referendums: Relationships between Representative and Direct Democracy in the Republic of Ireland', *European Journal of Political Research*, 41: 811–26.

Smyth, E. (2019) Research Professor at the Economic and Social Research Institute (ESRI) in Dublin, Personal Interview, October.

Sturt, M. (1967) *The Education of the People*, London: Routledge and Kegan Paul.

Suiter, J. (2020) 'Ireland', Digital News Report. Available at: <http://www.digitalnewsreport.org/survey/2020/ireland-2020/> (Accessed: 2 November 2021).

Sullivan, P. (2019) Director (Primary) of NCCA, Personal Interview, October.

Teaching Council (2021) 'About Us'. Available at: <https://www.teachingcouncil.ie/en/faqs/about-us/> (Accessed: 2 November 2021).

The Canon Law Society Trust (1983) *Code of Canon Law* (English translation), London: Collins, 803–6.

Tiernan, J. (2018) 'Catholic Schools Must Remain True to Their Foundations – Status Quo Will not Achieve This', *The Irish Times,* 30 July.

Tiernan, J. (2020) 'Contextualising Catholic Education in Ireland', *Educatio Catholica Journal,* Vol. 1–2, February.

Torain, D. O. (1975) 'Letters to the Editor: Subversive Marxism', *Irish Press*, 18 July.

Traynor, C. (2015) 'Religious Education: 'I Don't Know Anybody Who Teaches the RE Requirement', 9 November. Available at: <https://www.irishtimes.com/news/education/religious-education-i-don-t-know-anybody-who-teaches-the-re-requirement-1.2418676> (Accessed: 2 November 2021).

Tuohy, D. (2012) 'The Rhetoric of Reform and the Grammar of Economic Development', *Studies: An Irish Quarterly Review*, Vol. 101, No. 402, 139–52.

Tuohy, D. (2013) *Denominational Education and Politics: Ireland in a European Context*, Dublin: Veritas.

United Nations (2019) 'World Population Prospects 2019'. Available at: <https://population.un.org/wpp/> (Accessed: 2 November 2021).

United Nations Human Rights Council (2021) 'Universal Periodic Review'. Available at: <https://www.ohchr.org/en/hrbodies/upr/pages/uprmain.aspx> (Accessed: 2 November 2021).

Veale, J. S. J. (1970) 'The Christian School', *Studies, An Irish Quarterly,* Winter, Vol. 59, No. 236.

Walsh, J., ed. (2007) *People and Place: A Census Atlas of the Republic of Ireland.* Maynooth: National University of Ireland, 329.

Walsh, T. (2016) '100 Years of Primary Curriculum Development and Implementation in Ireland: A Tale of a Swinging Pendulum', *Irish Educational Studies,* Vol. 35, No. 1, 1–16. DOI: 10.1080/03323315.2016.1147975.

Walshe, J. (1987), *Irish Independent,* August 5, in Farry, M. (1996) *Education and the Constitution.* Dublin: Round Hall Sweet & Maxwell.

Walshe, J. (2017) 'Bruton Is Facing a Baptism of Parental Ire over the Catholic School Enrolment Policies', *Irish Independent,* Independent.ie, January 15.

Walshe, J. (2019) Former Education Journalist/Aide to Minister Ruairí Quinn, Personal Interview, October.

Ward, P. (2018) 'Meeting to Be Held over Future of Brannoxtown NS as They Receive Positive News', KildareNow.com, 13 April. Available at: <https://www.kildarenow.com/news/news/405828/meeting-to-be-held-over-future-of-brannoxtown-ns-as-they-receive-positive-news.html> (Accessed: 2 November 2021).

Waterford & Wexford ETB (2019) 'First Community National School in Wexford: Waterford & Wexford Education & Training Board', 20 February. Available at: <http://waterfordwexford.etb.ie/latest-news/first-community-national-school-in-wexford/> (Accessed: 2 November 2021).

Welsh, M. (2014) 'Review of Voyant Tools', *Collaborative Librarianship,* Vol. 6, No. 2, 96–7.

Which Candidate (2021). Available at: <http://www.whichcandidate.ie/> (Accessed: 2 November 2021).

Whyte, M. (2019) Educational Policy and Development Officer, ETBI, Personal Interview, October.

Wolbrecht, C. and Hartney, M. T. (2014) 'Ideas about Interests: Explaining the Changing Partisan Politics of Education', *Perspectives on Politics,* American Political Science Association, September, Vol. 12, No. 3, 603–30.

About the Authors

SEAN MCGRAW is a Comparative Political Scientist specialising in Irish politics. He earned his BA and MDiv from the University of Notre Dame, MSc from the London School of Economics and Political Science, and PhD in Comparative Politics from Harvard University. He currently teaches Political Science at Boston College and is active as a mentor and philanthropic leader in the educational and mental health sectors. He has published *How Parties Win: Shaping the Irish Political Arena* (University of Michigan Press, 2015) and co-edited with Eoin O'Malley *One Party Dominance: Fianna Fáil and Irish Politics 1926-2016* (Routledge, 2017). His articles have been published in the *European Journal of Political Research, Parliamentary Affairs, Government and Opposition, Irish Political Studies, Research in Comparative and International Education,* and *Eire-Ireland: An Interdisciplinary Journal of Irish Studies.*

JONATHAN TIERNAN is the Education Delegate for the Irish Jesuits and their network of 5 secondary schools and 3 primary schools. He is a former primary school teacher having earned his BA from St. Patrick's College/ Dublin City University and his MEd from the University of Notre Dame. His writing has appeared in *The Irish Times, TheJournal.ie, Irish Catholic, Educatio Catholica Journal,* and *Research in Comparative and International Education.*

Index

Reimagining Ireland

Series Editor: Dr Eamon Maher, Technological
University Dublin

The concepts of Ireland and 'Irishness' are in constant flux in the wake of an ever-increasing reappraisal of the notion of cultural and national specificity in a world assailed from all angles by the forces of globalisation and uniformity. Reimagining Ireland interrogates Ireland's past and present and suggests possibilities for the future by looking at Ireland's literature, culture and history and subjecting them to the most up-to-date critical appraisals associated with sociology, literary theory, historiography, political science and theology.

Some of the pertinent issues include, but are not confined to, Irish writing in English and Irish, Nationalism, Unionism, the Northern 'Troubles', the Peace Process, economic development in Ireland, the impact and decline of the Celtic Tiger, Irish spirituality, the rise and fall of organised religion, the visual arts, popular cultures, sport, Irish music and dance, emigration and the Irish diaspora, immigration and multiculturalism, marginalisation, globalisation, modernity/postmodernity and postcolonialism. The series publishes monographs, comparative studies, interdisciplinary projects, conference proceedings and edited books. Proposals should be sent either to Dr Eamon Maher at eamon.maher@ittdublin.ie or to ireland@peterlang.com.

Lightning Source UK Ltd.
Milton Keynes UK
UKHW052025010522
R3051000001B/R30510PG402215UKX00001B/1